Guides students through a rich menu of Am   through food and eating

This book features a wide and diverse range of primary sources covering the cultivation, preparation, marketing, and consumption of food from the time before Europeans arrived in North America to the present-day United States. It is organized around what the authors label the "Four Ps"—production, politics, price, and preference—in order to show readers that food represents something more than nutrition and the daily meals that keep us alive. The documents in this book demonstrate that food we eat is a "highly condensed social fact" that both reflects and is shaped by politics, economics, culture, religion, region, race, class, and gender.

Food and Eating in America covers more than 500 years of American food and eating history with sections on: An Appetizer: What Food and Eating Tell Us About America; Hunting, Harvesting, Starving, and the Occasional Feast: Food in Early America; Fields and Foods in the Nineteenth Century; and Feeding a Modern World: Revolutions in Farming, Food, and Famine.

The book:

- presents primary sources from a wide variety of perspectives—Native Americans, explorers, public officials, generals, soldiers, slaves, slave-holders, clergy, businessmen, workers, immigrants, activists, African Americans, Hispanics, Asian Americans, artists, writers, investigative reporters, judges, the owners of food trucks, and prison inmates;
- illustrates the importance of eating and food through speeches, letters, diaries, memoirs, newspaper and magazine articles, illustrations, photographs, song lyrics, advertisements, legislative statutes, court rulings, interviews, manifestoes, government reports, and recipes;
- offers a new way of exploring how people lived in the past by looking closely and imaginatively at food.

Food and Eating in America: A Documentary Reader is an ideal book for students of United States history, food, and the social sciences. It will also appeal to foodies and those with a curiosity for documentary-style books of all kinds.

James C. Giesen is a history professor at Mississippi State University, and serves as the executive secretary of the Agricultural History Society and editor of the University of Georgia Press series, Environmental History and the American South.

Bryant Simon is a professor of history at Temple University and the author of four books and two edited collections, including most recently, *Food, Power, and Agency* (with Juergen Martschukat), and *The Hamlet Fire: A Tragic Story of Cheap Food, Cheap Government, and Cheap Lives.*

Uncovering the Past: Documentary Readers in American History
Series Editors: Steven Lawson and Nancy Hewitt

The books in this series introduce students in American history courses to two important dimensions of historical analysis. They enable students to engage actively in historical interpretation, and they further students' understanding of the interplay between social and political forces in historical developments.

Consisting of primary sources and an introductory essay, these readers are aimed at the major courses in the American history curriculum, as outlined further below. Each book in the series will be approximately 225–50 pages, including a 25–30 page introduction addressing key issues and questions about the subject under consideration, a discussion of sources and methodology, and a bibliography of suggested secondary readings.

Published

Paul G. E. Clemens
The Colonial Era: A Documentary Reader

Sean Patrick Adams
*The Early American Republic:
A Documentary Reader*

Stanley Harold
*The Civil War and Reconstruction:
A Documentary Reader*

Steven Mintz
*African American Voices: A
Documentary Reader, 1619–1877*

Robert P. Ingalls and David K. Johnson
*The United States Since 1945:
A Documentary Reader*

Camilla Townsend
*American Indian History:
A Documentary Reader*

Steven Mintz
*Mexican American Voices:
A Documentary Reader*

Brian Ward
The 1960s: A Documentary Reader

Nancy Rosenbloom
*Women in American History Since
1880: A Documentary Reader*

Jeremy Suri
*American Foreign Relations
Since 1898: A Documentary Reader*

Carol Faulkner
*Women in American History
to 1880: A Documentary Reader*

David Welky
*America Between the Wars, 1919–1941:
A Documentary Reader*

William A. Link and Susannah J. Link
*The Gilded Age and Progressive Era:
A Documentary Reader*

G. Kurt Piehler
*The United States in World War II:
A Documentary Reader*

Leslie Brown
*African American Voices: A
Documentary Reader,
1863–Present*

David Freund
*The Modern American Metropolis:
A Documentary Reader*

Edward Miller
*The Vietnam War: A Documentary
Reader*

James C. Giesen and Bryant Simon
*Food and Eating in America:
A Documentary Reader*

Food and Eating in America

A Documentary Reader

Edited by

James C. Giesen

Bryant Simon

WILEY Blackwell

This edition first published 2018
© 2018 John Wiley & Sons, Inc.

The right of James C. Giesen and Bryant Simon to be identified as the authors of the editorial material in this work has been asserted in accordance with law.

Editorial Office
350 Main Street, Malden, MA 02148-5020, USA

For details of our global editorial offices, customer services, and more information about Wiley products visit us at www.wiley.com.

Wiley also publishes its books in a variety of electronic formats and by print-on-demand. Some content that appears in standard print versions of this book may not be available in other formats.

Library of Congress Cataloging-in-Publication Data

Names: Giesen, James C., editor. | Simon, Bryant, editor.
Title: Food and eating in America : a documentary reader / by James C. Giesen, Bryant Simon.
Description: 1 edition. | Hoboken, NJ ; Malden, MA : John Wiley & Sons, 2018. |
 Series: Uncovering the past: documentary readers in American history | Includes index.
Identifiers: LCCN 2017041023 (print) | LCCN 2017046282 (ebook) | ISBN 9781118936412 (pdf) |
 ISBN 9781118936405 (epub) | ISBN 9781118936382 (cloth) | ISBN 9781118936399 (pbk.)
Subjects: LCSH: Food–United States–History–Sources. | Food habits–United
 States–History–Sources.
Classification: LCC TX353 (ebook) | LCC TX353 .F925 2018 (print) |
 DDC 641.300973–dc23
LC record available at https://lccn.loc.gov/2017041023

Cover Images: (Front cover foreground) © Everett Historical/Shutterstock; (Front cover background) © circlePS/Gettyimages; (Back cover) © OnstOn/iStockphoto
Cover Design: Wiley

Set in 10/12.5pt Sabon by SPi Global, Pondicherry, India
Printed and bound in Malaysia by Vivar Printing Sdn Bhd

10 9 8 7 6 5 4 3 2 1

Contents

Series Editors' Preface

Primary sources have become an essential component in the teaching of history to undergraduates. They engage students in the process of historical interpretation and analysis and help them understand that facts do not speak for themselves. Rather, students see how historians construct narratives that recreate the past. Most students assume that the pursuit of knowledge is a solitary endeavor; yet historians constantly interact with their peers, building upon previous research and arguing among themselves over the interpretation of documents and their larger meaning. The documentary readers in this series highlight the value of this collaborative creative process and encourage students to participate in it.

Each book in the series introduces students in American history courses to two important dimensions of historical analysis. They enable students to engage actively in historical interpretation, and they further students' understanding of the interplay among social, cultural, economic, and political forces in historical developments. In pursuit of these goals, the documents in each text embrace a broad range of written and oral sources, as well as photographs and illustrations.

Each volume in the series is edited by a specialist in the field who is concerned with undergraduate teaching. The goal is not to offer a comprehensive selection of material but to provide items that reflect major themes and debates; that illustrate significant social, cultural, political, and economic dimensions of an era or subject; and that inform, intrigue and inspire undergraduate students. The editor of each volume has written an introduction that discusses the central questions that have occupied historians in this field and the ways historians have used primary sources to answer them. In addition, each introductory essay contains an explanation of the kinds of materials available to investigate a particular subject, the methods by which scholars analyze them, and the considerations that go into interpreting them. Each source selection is introduced by a short head note that gives students key information and a context for understanding the document. Also, each section of the volume includes questions to guide student reading and stimulate classroom discussion.

"No matter who you are or what you do or where you live, food stands at the center of life." So begins James C. Giesen and Bryant Simon's tasty offering, *Food and Eating in America: A Documentary Reader*. The editors offer a smorgasbord of primary sources covering the history of the preparation and consumption of food from the time before Europeans arrived in America (the pre-Columbian era) to the present-day United States. Although their presentation unfolds chronologically, Giesen and Simon organize their source material around what they label the "Four Ps: production, politics, price, and preference." In doing so, they show readers that food represents something more than simple meals to consume and keep us alive. They demonstrate that the preparation and consumption of food by Americans has evolved over time and has been shaped by politics, economics, culture, religion, region, race, class, and gender. In fact, studying food and eating requires the kind of interdisciplinary approach that this documentary reader provides. Moreover, by looking closely and imaginatively at food, Giesen and Simon offer a new way of exploring how people lived in the past.

Food and Eating in America includes a broad range of primary sources that are bound to whet the appetite for consuming more than 500 years of American history. In this volume, Giesen and Simon present primary sources from a wide variety of perspectives. We hear from Native Americans, explorers, public officials, generals, soldiers, slaves, slaveholders, clergy, businessmen, workers, immigrants, activists, African Americans, Hispanics, Asian Americans, artists, writers, investigative reporters, judges, and prison inmates, all of whom participated in and influenced the production and consumption of food. We hear their diverse voices through speeches, letters, diaries, memoirs, newspaper and magazine articles, illustrations, photographs, song lyrics, advertisements, legislative statutes, court rulings, interviews, manifestos, government reports, and recipes. In introducing and presenting these documents, Giesen and Simon guide students through a rich menu that offers them a better understanding of American history through food and eating.

Steven F. Lawson and Nancy A. Hewitt
Series Editors

Part I An Appetizer: What Food and Eating Tell Us About America

No matter who you are or what you do or where you live, food stands at the center of life. Obviously, you cannot survive long without food, and neither can the people around you. Communities and nation states can't build forts or ships or railroads or bridges or airports or nuclear reactors if people don't have enough to eat. Wars can't be fought, and can't be won, without food, food for soldiers in the trenches and food for production workers and their families behind the lines. No matter what their faith, nationality, or background, people celebrate holidays and milestones with food. Think of the first, or the most recent, Thanksgiving. It is an American national holiday built around food, the bounty and promise of the United States, and the symbolism of a shared meal. When families and friends come together for births, marriages, confirmations, bar mitzvahs, and deaths, they typically eat. Religious celebrations like Ramadan and Yom Kippur involve fasting, followed by prayers that bless the wine and bread, then, and only then, lavishly scripted meals. In the United States, the second biggest day for eating (after Thanksgiving) is Super Bowl Sunday. Indeed, much of contemporary social life revolves around food, the focus of going out, and getting together. We post photos of our burritos and take selfies with our desserts. Eateries dot the landscapes of cities and suburbs, highways, and back roads from Maine to California. Cooking shows take up the endless time slots on cable television channels and recipes fill up pages of websites, newspapers, and magazines. Food apps glow on our phone screens.

Food and Eating in America: A Documentary Reader, First Edition.
Edited by James C. Giesen and Bryant Simon.
© 2018 John Wiley & Sons, Inc. Published 2018 by John Wiley & Sons, Inc.

As food stands at the center of daily life, it not only sustains life, it also kills. It can be contaminated or tainted. Run-off from the farms that produce our food contaminates our rivers and streams. Food waste—parts of the plants and animals that we don't cook or the scraps from our plates—clogs the nation's waterways and overflows its landfills. For farmers and workers, producing and processing food can be deadly as well, due to the often dangerous working conditions on farms and in processing plants. Not having enough food and the illnesses that result from having too little to eat still kill millions each year—more than 21,000 per day to be precise—in the world, while in the United States, having too much of foods laden with fat, salt, and sugar threatens the health of countless people.

Despite food's central role in the daily life and rituals of people now and in the past, studying food has for a long time remained at the margins of history writing. To be sure, scholars have researched famines, talked about feeding troops during wars, and remarked on changing diets and agricultural practices. But, foodways, meals, and the act of eating itself rarely made it into college textbooks or classroom lectures prior to the twenty-first century.

In recent years food's place on the margins of history has changed. Relying on new evidence and looking at old sources in news ways, historians of food and eating have written stacks of imaginative, wide-ranging, and influential histories of things like sugar, cod, and the hamburger. They have looked at the social, cultural, and architectural significance of fast-food joints and high-end French restaurants, and the inner-workings of animal factories in the fields and the gory efficiency of slaughterhouses in the cities. They have paid close attention to changes in understanding of biology, horticulture, nutrition, and ecology. They have discussed gender, dieting, and eating disorders, the appeal of Chinese food to Jews and Gentiles, and the growth of culinary tourism and foodie culture. They have talked about Native American cooking and the foodways immigrants from Europe, Asia, and Africa brought with them to the United States and took to other places in the diaspora. They have analyzed global protests against McDonald's and boycotts against local butchers in ethnic enclaves. They have traced the early stirrings of vegetarianism and the first whiffs of the countercultural cuisines of the 1960s. They have recounted strikes at processing plants and the organizing campaigns of cooks and waitresses. Collectively they have begun to imagine, conceive, and write about food, as the anthropologist Arjun Appadurai suggested (in an article in *American Ethnologist* in August, 1981) that they do, as a "highly condensed social fact."

This idea of food as a highly condensed social fact is the organizing framework for this book. What exactly does this concept mean? Essentially, it suggests that food represents more than just something to eat, calories to burn, or carbohydrates churning in our stomachs. Each meal, dish, and ingredient represents a crucial intersection of vital social forces that involve what we're going call the Four Ps: production, politics, price, and preference. The idea of food as a dense social fact means that every time we eat something we place ourselves within a complex mix of these four broad forces.

Think for a few minutes about what goes into a rather typical meal. Let's take as an example a Sunday dinner of roast chicken, mashed potatoes, and green beans. Perhaps the most obvious way to start thinking about this food is to ask how it arrived at our table. Each and every spice, ingredient, and item on the menu has a story, a process that brought it from the fields to our table, a process that throughout the majority of American history and for most Americans has meant many stops along the way. That process involves *production*, starting with who mined the salt, raised the chicken, picked the vegetables, and dug the potatoes. Who killed the chicken? Where did they do this killing? Where were the animals, for the meat and the milk, raised? What did they eat during their lives? What sorts of fertilizers or chemicals were sprayed on the beans or inserted into the soil? What role did the soil itself—or the rain, wind, and sunshine—play in the food's production? What networks were used to get these products to the stores and shops? In what form did they arrive? How did the feed get to farmers? Did it come from a local supplier or a big agribusiness? What role did science, research, and technology play in the process and in the development of new breeds of chickens, new potato plants, and new flavors? Who controls the parts of that process, from the growing to the science to the transportation?

As the documents that follow demonstrate, the answers to these questions changed over time. Before the American Revolution most Americans ate chicken rarely if at all, and the availability of green beans depended on the season and the location. Meals like this were unthinkable to most slaves, even into the mid-nineteenth century. As we'll read, potatoes had their own cultural place for Americans and the little tuber itself played a role in who became accepted as "American" and when.

Food involves domestic production as well. Who made the food for the Sunday dinner? A mother? A father? The whole family? A domestic worker? How was this work divided along gender lines? Did they make it from scratch? Where did they obtain and accumulate their culinary knowledge? How were the foods prepared and cooked? What devices or appliances were used to make the foods? Was it cooked on an open fire, or a gas or electric oven, or in a microwave? Were the potatoes produced with a hand masher or a Cuisinart or did they come as a powder in a box? Did some or all of the food come from the store? Was it prepared ahead of time? Who served it? Was the table set? Did everyone sit down to eat together? Did the house they live in have a separate space for eating? What did that space look like and where was it in relation to the kitchen? Did the family or group eat at a table or in front of a newspaper, a radio, a television, or iPhone screens?

This brings us to our second "P." Our food choices always involve *politics*. This might seem surprising. No one, of course, voted on that chicken dinner. It wasn't legislated somewhere that the family get together to eat Sunday supper together. But the dinner itself is the result of a political history that involves slavery, industrialism, imperialism, and nationalism. Those big historical processes often determined who ate what, where they ate, and how they ate. Each of these processes is rooted in politics. Throughout much of early American history, dinner was determined as much by natural constraints as by any other force—it was who had control over grazing land, the crop land, the wild animals, the seas and waterways. This control was just as political as a modern U.S. Department of Agriculture agent inspecting chicken carcasses at a packinghouse. Were the potatoes Yukon® Golds or the more generic "golden potato"? Why does that difference matter?

These are more than agricultural questions; they are political ones. As you'll see in the documents that fill this book, as the act of eating moves farther from the place of production, food becomes even more about politics. Think for a moment about where the green beans came from and how were they made it to the table. Did the farmer get a guaranteed price to grow them, or state-sponsored crop insurance? Were they produced by an American company on U.S. soil, or in another nation? Politicians have passed laws to encourage immigration so that landowners had access to cheaper labor, which in turn made the price of those beans, and our dinner, fall. Hopeful of winning votes in the Plains States, politicians give subsidies—basically a cash guarantee—for certain crops like corn, which pushes more farmers to grow the grain, a policy that, in turn, radically changes the price of food at the store and also our diets. Likewise, politicians and government agents insure that American farmers have access to foreign markets, and American eaters get "fresh" fruit from South Africa in the middle of winter. The United States government, like all modern governments, regularly gives advice on eating, pushing particular diets, and creating links between healthy people and good citizenship. In the documents that follow, food is at some times more politically important than at others. As you read the book, think about the eras when Americans' politics and food intersected. Why is food more politically important at some moments than others?

Third, what's the *price* of this chicken dinner? What a family spends on food is usually related to how much the individuals who make up the family earn and how much they value what they eat. Food is also, then, about economic class. The French gastronome, Jean Anthelme Brillat-Savarin commented in the early nineteenth-century, "Tell me what you eat and I can tell you who you are." Some might choose the chicken over beef, not because they prefer its taste, but because it is cheaper. For that same reason, they may have chosen a "regular" chicken over a free-range or organic bird. Yet sometimes Americans pick foods because they *are* more expensive. We want to treat ourselves or show off that we can afford them. Many of the documents in this book give us a look inside restaurant culture, where this is particularly true.

What, though, accounts for the price of a foodstuff at any given time and place? Certainly this involves supply and demand, but other factors are at work as well: natural disasters, land prices, machinery, fences, wages, energy costs, packaging, advertising, and research and development. Together these forces determine what a fast food chain or an individual grocer can charge for food. But what about the costs that aren't reflected on the menu or price sticker? How do we account for the environmental costs of some foods, the waste running off from animal farms, or the carbon emissions of trucks hauling vegetables from Florida to New York? What about the cost of injuries to workers in packing plants, or the health care bills for children who live on a steady diet of fast food? Who pays these costs? Are they incorporated into food price? What, in turn, are the *social* costs (or savings) of particular foods, menus, or diets?

The fourth question to ask about our Sunday dinner is why are we eating these things at all? This is essentially a question about our last "P," *preference*. What social and cultural factors lie behind our food choices? Why do we like the foods we like? People in some places and from some traditions eat things that others would never consider putting in their mouths. Where do we get our ideas about what food is, let alone what tastes good? Though genetics, biology, and chemistry certainly figure into our tastes, what we like and don't like is at the same time culturally informed. Just as we learn from those around us what to wear and what music to listen to, we learn what tastes good.

The first time someone cooks a Sunday dinner they may use a recipe, or have the help of a relative or friend working alongside. But where do the recipe come from? A family member? A television celebrity? How has it changed over time? What did a roast chicken look like in 1890 and then in

2010? What tastes complement the chicken, steamed green beans, or a casserole made from frozen beans and condensed mushroom soup topped with packaged fried onions? Did we pick this meal as a healthy alternative to meatloaf and gravy? How is "healthy" defined at a particular time and place? Where do we get our information from about what is healthy and what is not healthy? From people we know *and* from government agencies to be sure, and in the recent past from talking heads and food bloggers. How, by the way, does someone become an expert on food and healthy eating? Is science behind a given diet, or is it a TV celebrity? Do we choose to eat things that we think make us look good to others? Do we eat new things because we empathize with another culture, or because we want to show off our sophistication? Do we eat things that make us look more cosmopolitan or affluent, more manly or feminine? Food as performance has become more important in recent years as eating has become more public, especially through our Instagram and Facebook feeds.

In this book, students will learn how the highly condensed social fact of food reflects and shapes the America past, how our food choices reveal essential details about production, politics, price, and preference. But really the goal of this documentary reader is to show what food explains *to us about us* in the past and in the present.

As we'll see, the history of food and eating in America makes it clear that none of us is simply one thing or has one identity or set of preferences or politics; we have overlapping, sometimes even contradictory concerns, and affinities. We never just choose the foods we want, and we never have. When someone in the colonial world looked for something to eat, they were confronted with the natural limits of the seasons, constraints on productive capacities, and certainly the politics of the moment. The food of today entails the same overlap. One thing, then, that the readers of this book will learn as they grapple with the idea of food as a "highly condensed social fact" is that eating cuts across intellectual boundaries and rigid categories of analysis. Thinking about food pulls together a range of economic, social, and cultural forces, tying together ideas about race, class, and gender and merging economic history with labor, agricultural, and environmental history. To study food means to think like a sociologist, anthropologist, and historian all at once. In other words, it means thinking in critical and interdisciplinary ways.

Beyond learning how to use food as an interdisciplinary window into the past, this book stresses one other important skill set for students: the close analytical reading of and engagement with primary documents. In order to detect and identify the layers of meaning in a document, whether it is a bland government report, a tattered recipe, or a color-splashed advertisement, you need to become an active reader. That starts even before encountering the first word or image. As you approach each document, first ask yourself a set of key questions: When was the document produced? What was going on at the time, in that place? Does the document seem to reflect the times? Does the document have a geographically distinct origin and outlook? Perhaps most importantly, who produced the document and why? You cannot engage with the meaning of a document before understanding where it came from. Once you know who the producer of the document is, you can get to the ideas behind it. Is the author trying to "sell" a policy or an idea? A food or way of eating? An agricultural technique? How does the author or producer of the document make her/his case? What sorts of evidence does she/he use? Does the author produce statistics and tables of data to prove her/his claims? Do she/he use the testimonials of others? Does she/he suggest, as some advertisements do, that eating a certain food will make you happier, stronger, or sexier? Don't overlook chronology either. What does happier, stronger, or sexier look like at the moment the document was produced? That will tell us a great deal about a society's values. Posing the above questions will provide answers that help to better understand people, places and politics in the past.

This documentary reader has been organized to help students learn more about the history of food *and* about the history of the United States. At the same time, it will help you, the student, become a more active and engaged reader, a skill that is important not just for historical analysis but really any kind of complex thinking and reasoning. The chapters in the book have been organized in rough chronological order following the typical layout of a survey course in American history. The book starts before the Europeans arrived in North America and ends today inside a prison cafeteria. Each chapter features five to ten documents, and each document has an introduction that helps you to situate the source (and give you the crucial background information you need to become an active reader). The documents are followed by a list of discussion questions. These are rarely questions with a single easy answer; rather they are designed to help you better understand the document, think about its source, and reveal key aspects and tensions in the history of food and eating in the United States.

Part II   Hunting, Harvesting, Starving, and the Occasional Feast: Food in Early America

Chapter 1 Food in the New World: Pre-Columbian Era through the American Revolution

Document 1.1: The Cherokee Creation Story, "How the World Was Made, Wahnenauhi Version"

Since at least the seventeenth century, the Cherokee tribe of Native Americans lived in the southeastern United States. In the late-1800s, James Mooney, a self-taught ethnographer who worked for the government studying Native Americans, recorded the following story told by Cherokees about the beginning of the world. Prior to this passage, the myth tells of the earth being covered in water until land rose up out of it forming an island. This excerpt gives us many clues about how Cherokees' understanding of the process of turning animals and plants into food was central to their understanding of where life on earth itself came from.

After the world had been brought up from under the water, "They then made a man and a woman and led them around the edge of the island. On arriving at the starting place they planted some corn, and then told the man and woman to go around the way they had been led. This they did, and on returning they found the corn up and growing nicely. They were then told to continue the circuit. Each trip consumed more time. At last the corn was ripe and ready for use."

Another story is told of how sin came into the world. A man and a woman reared a large family of children in comfort and plenty, with very little

Food and Eating in America: A Documentary Reader, First Edition.
Edited by James C. Giesen and Bryant Simon.
© 2018 John Wiley & Sons, Inc. Published 2018 by John Wiley & Sons, Inc.

trouble about providing food for them. Every morning the father went forth and very soon returned bringing with him a deer, or a turkey, or some other animal or fowl. At the same time the mother went out and soon returned with a large basket filled with ears of corn which she shelled and pounded in a mortar, thus making meal for bread.

When the children grew up, seeing with what apparent ease food was provided for them, they talked to each other about it, wondering that they never saw such things as their parents brought in. At last one proposed to watch when their parents went out and to follow them.

Accordingly next morning the plan was carried out. Those who followed the father saw him stop at a short distance from the cabin and turn over a large stone that appeared to be carelessly leaned against another. On looking closely they saw an entrance to a large cave, and in it were many different kinds of animals and birds, such as their father had sometimes brought in for food. The man standing at the entrance called a deer, which was lying at some distance and back of some other animals. It rose immediately as it heard the call and came close up to him. He picked it up, closed the mouth of the cave, and returned, not once seeming to suspect what his sons had done.

When the old man was fairly out of sight, his sons, rejoicing how they had outwitted him, left their hiding place and went to the cave, saying they would show the old folks that they, too, could bring in something. They moved the stone away, though it was very heavy and they were obliged to use all their united strength. When the cave was opened, the animals, instead of waiting to be picked up, all made a rush for the entrance, and leaping past the frightened and bewildered boys, scattered in all directions and disappeared in the wilderness, while the guilty offenders could do nothing but gaze in stupefied amazement as they saw them escape. There were animals of all kinds, large and small—buffalo, deer, elk, antelope, raccoons, and squirrels; even catamounts and panthers, wolves and foxes, and many others, all fleeing together. At the same time birds of every kind were seen emerging from the opening, all in the same wild confusion as the quadrupeds—turkeys, geese, swans, ducks, quails, eagles, hawks, and owls.

Those who followed the mother saw her enter a small cabin, which they had never seen before, and close the door. The culprits found a small crack through which they could peer. They saw the woman place a basket on the ground and standing over it shake herself vigorously, jumping up and down, when lo and behold! large ears of corn began to fall into the basket. When it was well filled she took it up and, placing it on her head, came out, fastened the door, and prepared their breakfast as usual. When the meal had been finished in silence the man spoke to his children, telling them that he was aware of what they had done; that now he must die and they would be obliged to provide for themselves. He made bows and arrows for them, then sent them to hunt for the animals which they had turned loose.

Then the mother told them that as they had found out her secret she could do nothing more for them; that she would die, and they must drag her body around over the ground; that wherever her body was dragged corn would come up. Of this they were to make their bread. She told them that they must always save some for seed and plant every year.

Discussion questions

1. What factors make food easy or hard to attain in these stories? What role do the animals play in their transition from living organisms to food? What role does labor play?
2. Mooney tells us that the story explains the Cherokee understanding of "where sin came into this world." What part about the story is sinful? How would Cherokee have used this story to teach a lesson about sin? Does the story relate to other religions' ideas about sin?
3. How are the roles played by men and women different in these stories?
4. What do these stories tell us about the animals themselves? Are there differences between those used for food or not used for food? Do the myths suggest something about how Cherokees saw "wild" animals?

Document 1.2: John Smith's History of the Starving Times at Jamestown Colony (1609)

Two years into the English colonial experiment in the Virginia Colony at Jamestown, conditions were bleak. The colonists had come to the New World in 1607 with dreams of easy riches, but had found instead tensions and violence with Indians, and an environment that both fostered disease and made agriculture difficult. More than half of the colonists died during the first winter. By the fall of 1609, John Smith, the leader of the colony, had enacted some measures to stem the starvation, including creating a trading arrangement with a nearby Powhatan tribe and by telling colonists that "he who works not, eats not." In October, however, Smith was injured by an explosion of gunpowder and he left for England. At that point there were about 500 colonists in Jamestown. Seven months later only 60 colonists were alive. This period came to be known as "the starving time." With Smith gone, the Powhatans stopped trading with the English colonists, and murdered many who they found outside of the Jamestown fort. In addition, stores of saved corn were found to be infested with rats. Smith wrote this history of the time of his absence based on the recollections of those who survived.

...the Salvages no sooner understood Smith was gone, but they all revolted, and did spoile and murther all they incountered. Now wee were all constrained to live onely on that [food that] Smith had onely for his owne Companie, for the rest had consumed their proportions, and now they had twentie Presidents with all their appurtenances...

Now we all found the losse of Captaine Smith, yea his greatest maligners could now curse his losse: as for corne, provision and contribution from the Salvages, we had nothing but mortall wounds, with clubs and arrowes; as for our Hogs, Hens, Goats, Sheepe, Horse, or what lived, our commanders, officers & Salvages daily consumed them, some small proportions sometimes we tasted, till all was devoured; then swords, armes, pieces, or any thing, wee traded with the Salvages, whose cruell fingers were so oft imbrewed in our blouds, that what by their crueltie, our Governours indiscretion, and the losse of our ships, of five hundred within six moneths after Captaine Smiths departure, there remained not past sixtie men, women and children, most miserable and poore creatures; and those were preserved for the most part, by roots, herbes, acornes, walnuts, berries, now and then a little fish: they that had startch in these extremities, made no small use of it; yea, even the very skinnes of our horses. Nay, so great was our famine, that a Salvage we slew, and buried, the poorer sort tooke him up againe and eat him, and so did divers one another boyled and stewed with roots and herbs: And one amongst the rest did kill his wife, powdered her, and had eaten part of her before it was knowne, for which hee was executed, as hee well deserved; now whether shee was better roasted, boyled or carbonado'd, I know not, but of such a dish as powdered wife I never heard of. This was that time, which still to this day we called the starving time; it were too vile to say, and scarce to be beleeved, what we endured: but the occasion was our owne, for want of providence, industrie and government, and not the barrennesse and defect of the Countrie, as is generally supposed; for till then in three yeeres, for the numbers were landed us, we had never from England provision sufficient for six moneths, though it seemed by the bils of loading sufficient was sent us, such a glutton is the Sea, and such good fellowes the Mariners; we as little tasted of the great proportion sent us, as they of our want and miseries, yet notwithstanding they ever over-swayed and ruled the businesse, though we endured all that is said, and chiefly lived on what this good Countrie naturally afforded; yet had wee beene even in Paradice it selfe with these Governours, it would not have beene much better with us; yet there was amongst us, who had they had the government as Captaine Smith appointed, but that they could not maintain it, would surely have kept us from those extremities of miseries. This in ten daies more, would have supplanted us all with death.

But God that would not this Countrie should be unplanted, sent Sir Thomas Gates, and Sir George Sommers with one hundred and fiftie people most happily preserved by the Bermudas to preserve us: strange it is to say how miraculously they were preserved in a leaking ship, as at large you may reade in the insuing Historie of those Ilands.

Discussion questions

1. Many of the original colonists to Jamestown were gentry who believed they did not need to labor to provide their own food. What does this fact, along with the account of what happened as a result, tell us about social class and food production in the early colonial era?

2. Think about Smith's description of colonists resorting to eating "roots, herbes, acornes, walnuts, berries, now and then a little fish." What does that tell us about English expectations for what constitutes food?

3. Smith makes a point of saying that the starvation was caused not by the physical environment of Virginia ("not the barrennesse and defect of the Countrie, as is generally supposed"), but by the failure of "providence, industrie and government." What does he mean by this? Why might this be an important point to make to the readers of this history?

4. Historians and scientists have debated the legitimacy of Smith's claim that colonists resorted to cannibalism in his absence. Though for years many believed this to be only a story, recent scientific and archaeological evidence has confirmed at least one case of cannibalism. What does Americans' unwillingness to believe that cannibalism was possible tell us about the nation's relationship to its history? Does it tell us something about food taboos?

Document 1.3: English Artist John White's drawings of Native Americans fishing, cooking, and preparing corn (1580s)

In 1585, John White, an artist and illustrator from London, sailed with an English excursion to explore Roanoke Island, off the coast of present-day North Carolina. His sponsor, Sir Walter Raleigh, asked White to record in pictures the life of Native Americans that he encountered. Among his many maps and drawings of social and religious ceremonies are important records of Algonquin food production, preservation, and consumption.

The broyling of their fish ouer tḡ flame of fier.

113

The manner of their fishing

Discussion questions

1. Who was the audience for these images? How might people in England have understood these depictions of the Algonquin and their foodways? Are they depicted here as the savages that John Smith's history (Document 1.2) describes?
2. What does the fishing picture tell us about White's understanding of animal life underwater, on land, and in the air? What do we learn about the natural environment of the New World as it relates to food production?
3. The illustration of fish cooking over a fire can tell us about more than just how the Algonquins prepared fish. Think about what it reveals about preserving meat through smoking, about the amount of fish being cooked at once, and about where this fire might be.

Document 1.4: Edward Winslow on the "First" Thanksgiving, 1621

There are many stories about the origins of the day that Americans now celebrate as Thanksgiving. The most common story of the holiday's origin revolves around a feast celebrated by Plymouth colonists and the Wampanoag nation in 1621, although established days of thanks certainly predate colonial times and were not solely an English custom. Despite presidents Washington, Adams, and Monroe ordering national days of giving thanks during their presidencies, Thanksgiving did not become a permanent American holiday until Congress declared it so in 1941. Edward Winslow, a leader of the Pilgrim separatists, wrote the following excerpted letter to a friend in England about the colony's 1621 feast as well as the availability of wild and cultivated foods.

Loving, and old Friend,

…We set the last spring some twenty acres of Indian corn, and sowed some six acres of barley and peas, and according to the manner of the Indians, we manured our ground with herrings or rather shads, which we have in great abundance, and take with great ease at our doors. Our corn did prove well, and God be praised, we had a good increase of Indian corn, and our barley indifferent good, but our peas not worth the gathering, for we feared they were too late sown, they came up very well, and blossomed, but the sun parched them in the blossom.

Our harvest being gotten in, our governor sent four men on fowling, that so we might after have a special manner rejoice together after we had gathered the fruit of our labors; they four in one day killed as much fowl, as with a little help beside, served the company almost a week, at which time amongst other recreations, we exercised our arms, many of the Indians coming amongst us, and among the rest their greatest King Massasoit, with some ninety men, whom for three days we entertained and feasted, and they went out and killed five deer, which they brought to the plantation and bestowed on our governor, and upon the captain, and others. And although it be not always so plentiful as it was at this time with us, yet by the goodness of God, we are so far from want that we often wish you partakers of our plenty.

We have found the Indians very faithful in their covenant of peace with us; very loving and ready to pleasure us; we often go to them, and they come to us; some of us have been fifty miles by land in the country with them, the occasions and relations whereof you shall understand by our general and more full declaration of such things as are worth the noting, yea, it has pleased God so to possess the Indians with a fear of us, and love unto us, that not only the greatest king amongst them, called Massasoit, but also all the princes and peoples round about us, have either made suit unto us, or been glad of any occasion to make peace with us, so that seven of them at once have sent their messengers to us to that end. Yea, an Isle at sea, which we never saw, hath also, together with the former, yielded willingly to be under the protection, and subjects to our sovereign lord King James, so that there is now great peace amongst the Indians themselves, which was not formerly, neither would have been but for us; and we for our parts walk as peaceably and safely in the wood as in the highways in England. We entertain them familiarly in our houses, and they as friendly bestowing their venison on us. They are a people without any religion or knowledge of God, yet very trusty, quick of apprehension, ripe-witted, just. The men and women go naked, only a skin about their middles.

...For fish and fowl, we have great abundance; fresh cod in the summer is but coarse meat with us; our bay is full of lobsters all the summer and affordeth variety of other fish; in September we can take a hogshead of eels in a night, with small labor, and can dig them out of their beds all the winter; we have mussels and othus at our doors: oysters we have none near, but we can have them brought by the Indians when we will; all the spring-time the earth sendeth forth naturally very good sallet herbs: here are grapes, white and red, and very sweet and strong also. Strawberries, gooseberries, raspas, etc. Plums of three sorts, with black and red, being almost as good as a damson: abundance of roses, white, red, and damask; single, but very sweet indeed. The country wanteth only industrious men to employ, for it would grieve your hearts (if as I) you had seen so many miles together by goodly rivers uninhabited, and withal, to consider those parts of the world wherein you live to be even greatly burdened with abundance of people. These things I thought good to let you understand, being the truth of things as near as I could experimentally take knowledge of, and that you might on our behalf give God thanks who hath dealt so favorably with us.

...When it pleaseth God, we are settled and fitted for the fishing business, and other trading; I doubt not but by the blessing of God the gain will give content to all; in the mean time, that we have gotten we have sent by this ship, and though it be not much, yet it will witness for us that we have not been idle, considering the smallness of our number all this summer. We hope the merchants will accept of it, and be encouraged to furnish us with things needful for further employment, which will also encourage us to put forth ourselves to the uttermost.

Now because I expect your coming unto us with other of our friends, whose company we much desire, I thought good to advertise you of a few things needful; be careful to have a very good bread-room to put your biscuits in, let your cask for beer and water be iron-bound for the first tire if not more; let not your meat be dry-salted, none can better do it than the sailors; let your meal be so hard trod in your cask that you shall need an adz or hatchet to work it out with: trust not too much on us for corn at this time, for by reason of this last company that came, depending wholly upon us, we shall have little enough till harvest; be careful to come by some of your meal to spend by the way, it will much refresh you. Build your cabins as open as you can, and bring good store of clothes and bedding with you; bring every man a musket or fowling-piece, let your piece be long in the barrel, and fear not the weight of it, for most of our shooting is from stands; bring juice of lemons, and take it fasting; it is of good use; for hot waters, aniseed water is the best, but use it sparingly; if you bring any thing for comfort in the country, butter or sallet oil, or both is very good; our Indian corn, even the coarsest, maketh pleasant meat as rice, therefore spare that unless to spend by the way; bring paper and linseed oil for your windows, with cotton yarn for your lamps; let your shot be most for big fowls, and bring store of powder and shot: I forbear further to write for the present, hoping to see you by the next return, so I take my leave, commending you to the Lord for a safe conduct unto us. Resting in Him,

Your loving friend,
E.W.
Plymouth in New England this 11th of December, 1621.

Discussion questions

1. Why would this particular story of the First Thanksgiving become the most popular among Americans in the nineteenth and twentieth centuries? What is it about this description of food, eating, and social relations that Americans find so compelling?
2. How does Winslow weave Christianity through this description of foodways in the Plymouth Colony? What does it tell us about his understanding of food itself? Of religion itself?
3. What does this letter tell us about the differences between hunting, gathering, and growing of food in the colonial era?
4. Winlsow ends his letter with some instructions for English people who might be thinking about moving to the New World. What does this passage tell us about the importance of food preservation and importation to the colonial experiment?
5. Think about Winslow's descriptions of Wampanoags. What role are they playing in the production and processing of foods for the colony?

Document 1.5: A Micmac Perspective on Europeans' Way of Life, near Quebec (c. 1677)

Europeans in the New World encountered Native American culture with a profound sense of superiority. In this passage we see that the reverse also could be true. In the speech below, translated by a French traveler, an elder in the Micmac tribe near present-day Quebec responds to the questions of a French missionary about Native Americans' devotion to the traditions of tribal life. As you'll read, food is central to the Micmac critique of French life.

I am greatly astonished that the French have so little cleverness, as they seem to exhibit in the matter of which thou hast just told me on their behalf, in the effort to persuade us to convert our poles, our barks, and our wigwams into those houses of stone and of wood which are tall and lofty, according to their account, as these trees. Very well! But why now, do men of five to six feet in height need houses which are sixty to eighty? For, in fact, as thou knowest very well thyself, Patriarch—do we not find in our own all the conveniences and the advantages that you have with yours, such as reposing, drinking, sleeping, eating, and amusing ourselves with our friends when we wish? This is not all, my brother, hast thou as much ingenuity and cleverness as the Indians, who carry their houses and their wigwams with them so that they may lodge wheresoever they please, independently of any seignior whatsoever? Thou art not as bold nor as stout as we, because when thou goest on a voyage thou canst not carry upon thy shoulders thy buildings and thy edifices. Therefore it is necessary that thou prepares as many lodgings as thou makest changes of residence, or else thou lodgest in a hired house which does not belong to thee. As for us, we find ourselves secure from all these inconveniences, and we can always say, more truly than thou, that we are at home everywhere, because we set up our wigwams with ease wheresoever we go, and without asking permission of anybody. Thou reproachest us, very inappropriately, that our country is a little hell in contrast with France, which thou comparest to a terrestrial paradise, inasmuch as it yields thee, so thou safest, every kind of provision in abundance. Thou sayest of us also that we are the most miserable and most unhappy of all men, living without religion, without manners, without honour, without social order, and, in a word, without any rules, like the beasts in our woods and our forests, lacking bread, wine, and a thousand other comforts which thou hast in superfluity in Europe. Well, my brother, if thou dost not yet know the real feelings which our Indians have towards thy country and towards all thy nation, it is proper that I inform thee at once. I beg thee now to believe that, all miserable as we seem in thine eyes, we consider ourselves nevertheless much happier than thou in this, that we are very content with the little that we have; and believe also once for all, I pray, that thou deceivest thyself greatly if thou thinkest to persuade us that thy country is better than ours. For if France, as thou sayest, is a little terrestrial paradise, art thou sensible to leave it? And why abandon wives, children, relatives, and friends? Why risk thy life and thy property every year, and why venture thyself with such risk, in any season whatsoever, to the storms and tempests of the sea in order to come to a strange and barbarous country which thou considerest the poorest and least fortunate of the world? Besides, since we are wholly convinced of the contrary, we scarcely take the trouble to go to France, because we fear, with good reason, lest we find little satisfaction there, seeing, in our own experience, that those who are natives thereof leave it every year in order to enrich themselves on our shores. We believe, further, that you are also incomparably poorer than we, and that you are only simple journeymen, valets, servants, and slaves, all masters and grand captains though you may appear, seeing that you glory in our old rags and in our miserable suits of beaver which can no longer be of use to us, and that you find among us, in the fishery for cod which you make in these parts, the wherewithal to comfort your misery and the poverty which oppresses you. As to us, we find all our riches and all our conveniences among ourselves, without trouble and without exposing our lives to the dangers in which you find yourselves constantly through your long voyages. And, whilst feeling compassion for you in the sweetness of our repose, we wonder at the anxieties and cares which you give yourselves night and day in order to load your ship. We see also that all your people live, as a rule, only upon cod which you catch among us. It is everlastingly nothing but cod—cod in the morning, cod at midday, cod at evening, and always cod, until things come to such a pass that if you wish some good morsels, it is at our expense; and you are obliged to have recourse to the Indians, whom you despise so much, and to beg them to go a-hunting that you may be regaled. Now tell me this one little thing, if thou hast any sense: Which of these two is the wisest and happiest—he who labours without ceasing and only obtains, and that with great trouble, enough to live on, or he who rests in comfort and finds all that he needs in the pleasure of hunting and fishing? It is true, that we have not always had the use of bread and of wine which your France produces; but, in fact, before the arrival of the French in these parts, did not the Gaspesians live much longer than now? And if we have not any longer among us any of those old men of a hundred and thirty to forty years, it is only because we are gradually adopting your manner of living, for experience is making it very plain that those of us live longest who, despising your bread, your wine, and your brandy, are content with their natural food of beaver, of moose, of waterfowl, and fish, in accord with the custom of our ancestors and of all the Gaspesian nation. Learn now, my brother, once for all, because I must open to thee my heart: there is no Indian who does not consider himself infinitely more happy and more powerful than the French.

Discussion questions

1. How does food fit into this critique of French life?
2. What do we learn about the different ways that the act of eating interacts with other aspects of society—from social relations to architecture—in seventeenth-century French and Micmac society?
3. What does food choice say about "poverty"?
4. Is there a critique of market capitalism embedded in this speech?

Document 1.6: John Winthrop, Jr., Report to the Royal Society of London on Indian Corn (1662)

John Winthrop, Jr. (also known as John Winthrop the Younger) was the son of a founder of the Plymouth Colony and became a Fellow of the Royal Society of England, a group founded in 1660 to advance research and understanding of science. This is his report to the society's science journal, Philosophical Transactions.

The corn used in New England, before the English planted there, is called by the natives, Weachin, known by the name of Maize, in some southern parts of America; where, and even in the northern parts, amongst the English and Dutch, who have plenty of wheat and grain, this sort of corn is still much in use both for bread and other kind of food. The ear is for the most part about a span[1] long, composed of several rows of grains, 8 or more, according to the goodness of the ground; and in each row, usually above 30 grains, of various colours, as red, white, yellow, blue, olive, greenish, black, speckled, striped, &c. sometimes in the same field, and the same ear. But the white and yellow are the most common. The ear is cloathed and armed with several strong thick husks. Not only defending it from the cold of the night, and from unseasonable rains, but also from the birds. The stalk grows to the

---

[1] About 9 inches (23 centimetres)

height of 6 or 8 feet; more or less, according to the condition of the ground, or kind of seed. The Virginian grows taller than that of New England. And there is another sort used by the Northern Indians far up in the country, that grows much shorter than that of New England. It is jointed like a cane, and is full of sweet juice, like the sugar-cane. And a syrup as sweet as sugar may be made of it. Also meats sweetened with it, have not been distinguished from the like sweetened with sugar…

The manner of planting is in rows, at equal distance every way, about 5 or 6 feet. They open the earth with a hoe, taking away the surface 3 or 4 inches deep, and the breadth of the hoe; and so throw in 4 or 5 grains, a little distant one from another, and cover them with earth. If two or three grow, it is well; for some of them are usually destroyed by birds, or mouse-squirrels. The corn grown up a hand's length, they cut up the weeds, and loosen the earth about it, with a broad hoe: repeating this labour, as the weeds grow. When the stalk begins to grow high, they draw a little earth about it: and upon the putting forth of the ear, so much as to make a little hill, like a hop-hill; after this, they have no other business about it, till harvest. After it is gathered, it must, except laid very thin, be presently stripped from the husks; otherwise it will heat, grow mouldy, and sometimes sprout. The common way is is to weave the ears together in long traces by some parts of the husk left thereon. These traces they hang upon stages or other bearers withindoors, or without; for, hung in that manner, they will keep good and sweet all the winter after, though exposed to all weathers. The natives commonly thresh it as they gather it, and dry it well on mats in the sun; then bestow it in holes in the ground, well lined with withered grass and mats, and then covered with the like, and overall with earth: and thus it is kept very well till they use it.

…Where the ground is bad or worn out, the Indians used to put two or three of the fishes called aloofes under or adjacent to each corn-hill; whereby they had many times a crop double to what the ground would otherwise have produced. The English have learned the like husbandry, where these aloofes come up in great plenty, or where they are near the fishing-stages; having there the heads and garbage of cod-fish, at no charge but the fetching. The fields thus ploughed for this corn, after the crop is off, are almost as well fitted for English corn, especially summer grain, as pease, or summer wheat, as if lying fallow, they had had a very good summer tilth. The Indians and some English, at every corn-hill, plant with the corn, a kind of French or Turkey beans: the stalks of the corn serving instead of poles for the beans to climb up with. And in the vacant places between the hills they plant squashes and pompions; loading the ground with as much as it will bear. And many, after the last weeding, sprinkle turnep-seed between the hills, and so after harvest have a good crop of turneps.

Discussion questions

1. Winthrop devotes much of this description of maize to the specific details of farming it. Why would the English scientists in the Royal Society be interested in the agricultural side of corn farming? In what way is this science?
2. To what extent does Winthrop discuss the Native Americans who developed the way of planting and processing corn that Winthrop describes? Is he looking down on, or praising, Native American agricultural methods here?
3. In the final section Winthrop describes the advantages of co-planting beans and other crops with corn. How might this have effected diet and recipes?
4. Does Winthrop's description of corn—its taste, its physiology, its protection from the weather and pests—give us a hint as to why it is the most prevalent crop in the United States still to this day?

Document 1.7: Observations on American Vegetables Versus English Vegetables, from John Josselyn, *New-England's Rarities Discovered* (1672), and Francis Higginson, *New-England's Plantation* (1630)

Josselyn, an educated son of the Engish gentry, and Higginson, a minister and early colonist in Massachusetts, sent back to England observations on the plants of the New World and how Native Americans and English colonists were using them.

From John Josselyn, New-England's Rarities Discovered *(1672)*

Indian Wheat, of which there is three sorts yellow, red, and blew; the blew is commonly Ripe before the other a Month.... It is hotter than our Wheat and clammy; excellent in *Cataplasms* to ripen any Swelling or impostume. The decoration of the blew Corn, is good the wash fore Mouths with. It is light of digestion, and the *English* make a kind of Loblolly of it to eat with Milk, which they call *Sampe*; they beat it in a Morter, and lift the flower out of it; the remainer they call *Homminey* so boiled, and mix their Flower with it, cast it into a deed Bason in which they form the Loaf, and then turn it out upon the Peel, and presenty put it into the Oven before it spreads abroad; the Flower makes excellent Puddens.

Wild-Leekes, which the *Indians* use much to eat with their fish.

Indian Beans, falsely called *French beans*, are better for Physick and Chyrurgery than our Garden Beans.

Squashes, … a kind of Mellon, or rather Gourd, for they oftentimes degenerate into Gourds; some of these are green, some yellow, some longish like a Gourd, others round like a Apple, all of them pleasant food boyled and buttered, and season'd with Spice; but the yellow *Squash* called an Apple *Squash*, because like an Apple, and about the bigness of a Pome-water, is the best kind; they are much eaten by the *Indians* and the *English*, yet they breed the small white Worms … in the long Gut that vex the Fundament with a perpetual itching and a desire to go to stool.

From Francis Higginson, New-England's Plantation *(1630)*

In our plantation we have already a quart of milk for a penny, but the abundant increase of corn proves this country to be a wonderment. Thirty, forty, fifty, sixty are ordinary here. Yea, Joseph's increase in Egypt is here outstripped with us. Our planters hope to have more than a hundred fold this year, and all this while I am within compass—what will you say of two-hundred fold and upward? It is almost incredible what great gain some of our English planters have had by our Indian corn. Credible persons have assured me, and the party of it himself announced the truth of it to me, that from the setting of 13 gallons of corn, he hath had an increase of 52 hogsheads,[2] every hogshead holding seven bushels of London measure, and every bushel was by him sold and trusted to the Indians for so much beaver as was worth 18 shillings, and so of this 13 gallons of corn which was worth 6 shillings 8 pence, he made about £327 of it the year following, as by reckoning it will appear; wherefore you may see how God blesseth industry in this land. There are not such beautiful and great ears of corn I suppose anywhere else but in this country, being also of variety of colors as red, blue and yellow, etc. And of one corn there springeth four or five hundred. I have sent you many ears of divers colors that you may see the truth of it. Little children here by plant-ing of corn may earn much more than their own maintenance.

They have tried our English corn at new Plymouth plantation, so that all our several grains grow here very well, and have a fitting soil for their nature.

Our governor hath store of green peas growing in his garden as good as ever I ate in England. This country aboundeth naturally with store of roots of great variety and good to eat. Our turnips, parsnips and carrots are here

[2] A large container like a cask or barrel; unrelated to the head of an actual pig.

bigger and sweeter than is ordinarily found in England. Here are also store of pumpkins, cucumbers, and other things of that nature which I know not. Also, divers excellent pot-herbs grow abundantly among the grass, as strawberry leaves in all parts of the country and plenty of strawberries in their time, and pennyroyal, wintersavory, sorrel, brooklime, liverwort, carvel and watercresses, also leeks and onions are ordinary, and divers medicinal herbs. Here are also abundance of other sweet herbs delightful to the smell, whose names we know not, etc., and plenty of single damask roses very sweet and two kinds of herbs that bear two kinds of flowers very sweet, which they say, are as good to make cordage or cloth as any hemp or flax we have.

Excellent vines are here up and down in the woods. Our governor hath already planted a vineyard with great hope of increase. Also, mulberries, plums, raspberries, corrance, chestnuts, filberts, walnuts, smalnuts, hurtleberries and haws of whitethorn near as good as our cherries in England, they grow in plenty here.

Discussion questions

1. Josselyn's observations of New England plants speak to food, medicine, and health all at the same time. What does this suggest about the English colonies and his audience back in Europe?
2. Higginson's observations focus on both the region's ability to produce one crop in great quantity, and on its diversity of plants for food. Are these two ideas in tension with one another in the colonies? How might that change over time?
3. Josselyn describes some cooking practices of Indians and the English. Does he compare the two? How so? Can you see any foods emerging here that we eat today? What are they and why have they lasted?
4. Why does Higginson focus on the governor's success in farming and procuring food?

Document 1.8: A Soldier's Perspective on the Revolutionary War, Selections from the Memoir of Private Joseph Plumb Martin (1777)

The French military leader and emperor Napoleon Bonaparte is famous for saying that "an army marches on its stomach." Indeed, war brings shortages of all kinds of materials, food foremost among them. With soldiers enlisting to fight, there are fewer people at home to tend to crops and raise animals. Supply lines delivering food from the homefront to the battlefront are constantly broken by the enemy or by nature. The Revolutionary War was no exception to this rule. Food shortages were a concern for soldiers on both sides of the lines. Here we read excerpts from the memoir of an American soldier who first enlisted at the age of 15 and experienced some of the most famous and violent battles of the war. We join his memoir in the winter of 1779–80, which he called "the hard winter."

The period of the revolution has repeatedly been styled, "the times that tried men's souls." I often found that those times not only tried men's souls, but their bodies too; I know they did mine and that effectually…. We arrived at camp after a tedious and cold march of many hours, some with frozen toes, some with frozen fingers and ears, and half starved into the bargain. Thus ended our Staten Island expedition.

Soon after this there came on several severe snowstorms. At one time it snowed the greater part of four days successively, and there fell nearly as many feet deep of snow, and here was the keystone of the arch of starvation. We were absolutely, literally starved;—I do solemnly declare that I did not put a single morsel of victuals into my mouth for four days and as many nights, except a little black birch bark which I gnawed off a stick of wood, if that can be called victuals. I saw several of the men roast their old shoes and eat them, and I was afterwards informed by one of the officer's waiters, that some of the officers killed and ate a favourite little dog that belonged to one of them.—If this was not "suffering" I request to be informed what can pass under that name … The fourth day, just at dark, we obtained a half pound of lean fresh beef and a gill of wheat for each man, whether we had any salt to season so delicious a morsel, I have forgotten, but I am sure we had no bread, (except the wheat,) but I will assure the reader that we had the best of sauce; that is, we had keen appetites. When the wheat was so swelled by boiling as to be beyond the danger of swelling in the stomach, it was deposited there without ceremony.

After this we sometimes got a little beef, but no bread; we, however, once in a while got a little rice, but as to flour or bread, I do not recollect that I saw a morsel of either (I mean wheaten) during the winter, all the bread kind we had was Indian meal. We continued here, starving and freezing, until, I think some time in the month of February…

This day we arrived at Woodbury, New-Jersey, which was the end of our present journey. We encamped near the village, planted our artillery in the road at each end of it, placed our guards and prepared to go into fort Mifflin, on Mud-Island. The reason of my referring to the above-mentioned battle, was, that we found several barrels of salted herrings, which the enemy had left in the flight, and as we had but a very small quantity of provisions we were glad to get these. I endeavored to eat some of them but found them miserable food. They appeared to have been caught soon after the flood, and could neither be broiled nor boiled so as to be made eatable.

I found nothing more here for bellytimber than I had in the line, and got nothing to eat till the second day after I had joined the corps. I have heard it remarked by the old farmers, that when beasts are first transferred from one place to another, that if they keep them without food for two or three days, it will go far towards wonting them to their new situation. Perhaps it might be so thought by our commanders. Be that is it would, I got nothing, as I have said, till the second day I had been with them; we then drew, if I remember right, two days rations of our good old diet, salt shad, and as we had not, as yet, associated ourselves into regular messes, as is usual in the army, each man had his fish divided out by himself. We were on the green before the meetinghouse, and there were several cows feeding about the place, I went into the house to get something to put my fish into, or some other business, and staid longer than I intended, or rather ought to have done, for when I came out again, one of the cows was just finishing her meal on my shad, the last I saw of it was the tail of a fish sticking out of the side of her mouth. I was vexed enough to have eaten the weight of it off her carcass, but she took care of that, and I had another opportunity (if well improved) of mortifying my body by fasting two days longer, but I got something among the men, as poorly as they were off, to sustain nature till I could get more by some means or other. Such shifts were nothing strainge to us.

While lying here, I one day rambled into the woods and fields, in order if possible, to procure something to satisfy the craving of nature. I found and ate a considerable quantity of chestnuts ... I returned to camp just at sunset, and met our orderly sergeant, who immediately warned me to prepare for a two day's command.—What is termed going on command, is what is generally called going on a scouting party, or something similar ... I told him I would go ... I had much rather go on such an expedition than stay in camp; as I stood some chance while in the country to get something to eat....

We marched from Valentine's hill for the White Plains, in the night. There were but three of our men present. We had our cooking utensils, (at the time the most useless things in the army,) to carry in our hands. They were made of cast iron and consequently heavy. I was so beat out before morning, with hunger and fatigue, that I could hardly move one foot before the other. I told my messmates that I *could not* carry our kettle any further; they said they *would* not carry it any further; of what use was it? they had nothing to cook and did not want any thing to cook with.

Discussion questions

1. Martin's comments about the lack of food are also criticisms of other aspects of a soldier's life. In what way was he using the lack of food to say something about war and the army?
2. What role does the natural environment play in these memories? Does nature have actual power in shaping the outcomes of wars?
3. What advantages did the colonists have over the British in the battle to feed their troops? Did the British have any advantages over the colonists?
4. These excerpts from Martin's memoir, taken together, give us a window into how the very category of food—the question of what is food—changes. When, where, and why does this category change?

Document 1.9: A General's Perspective: A Letter from General Horatio Gates to Major General Caswell (August 3, 1780)

Horatio Gates was one of the most powerful military leaders of the Revolutionary War, though he had a mixed record of success on the battle field. When he writes the following letter to Major General Richard Caswell, Gates is in charge of the Continental army in the South. At the time, Caswell was the major general of the North Carolina troops, though he had served as that state's first governor from 1777 to 1780. At the time of the letter, Gates is preparing his men for a battle against the British in Camden, South Carolina. The battle, which would occur less than two weeks after he sent this letter, was a major defeat for the Americans and marked the end of Gates's military career.

To Major General Caswell
West Side of Peedee near Masque's Ferry 3ᵈ August 1780

Sir
I had the honor to address [your] Excellency from Hillsborough the 19ᵗʰ ultimo by General Huger. The Distress this Army has suffered, and still Continues to suffer, for Want of Provisions has perhaps destroyed the finest Opportunity that could be presented of driving the Enemy's Advanced Posts, in all likelihood even unto Charles Town. Lord Cornwallis is believed to be gone to Savannah. — has weakened his Main Body at Camden, where Lord Rawdon commands, and withdrawn the Troops from Augusta, Cheraw and Anson Court House. I am astonished that I have no Intelligence of any Flour coming to me from the Interior part of the State. Your Exʸ cannot believe this miserable Country (already Ravaged by the Enemy, & gleaned by the Militia under the Generals Caswell and Rutherford) can afford an Handful to me. — I must believe from your Excellency's Letter, in answer to mine from Richmond, that

you had thus done all you thought necessary to provide us. — I am anxious that this Letter should find your Excell^y and the Executive Council at Hillsborough, exerting all your Authority and Influence to supply your almost famish^d Troops—Flour and Rum are the Articles most in request in this Climate, which bad water contributes to render more unwholesome—Rum is as necessary to the Health of a Soldier as good Food—Without these, full Hospitals and a thin Army will be all that your State or the Congress can depend upon in the Southern Depart—for my own part, I have never lost one Moment in pressing the Army forward from the Instant I join^d it to this Moment; and when I can do more, more shall be done—Depend not, Sir, upon Commissaries, they will deceive you—depend only upon honest men of sound Whig Principles—and whose Souls are superior to sordid Gain—General Stevens, with the Virginia Militia, is halted at Buffalo Ford, Fifty Miles in my Rear, and cannot proceed for Want of Provisions—I march To-morrow at Daybreak.

I am &c,
HG

Discussion questions

1. What do you think Gates means by "Rum is as necessary to the Health of a Soldier as good Food"? What are the environmental issues that make rum so important? What about morale?
2. Why does Gates suggest that Caswell should not trust the commissaries, which were the part of an army unit in charge of efficiently distributing food and supplies?
3. Does this document shed any light on why Gates's men faced such a resounding defeat two weeks later in Camden?
4. What does Gates suggest about the natural landscape where he has camped with his men? How does he suggest it has changed since the beginning of the war?

Document 1.10: Selections from *The Autobiography of Benjamin Franklin* (1791) on Communal Eating and Vegetarianism

Benjamin Franklin's autobiography is a treasure of historical information on the attitudes of early Americans on a variety of subjects from politics to science to food. Here we read excerpts that deal with his thoughts on the benefits of eating together as a family, no matter the food served, and his thoughts on eating meat.

At [my father's] table he liked to have, as often as he could, some sensible friend or neighbor to converse with, and always took care to start some ingenious or useful topic for discourse, which might tend to improve the minds of his children. By this means he turned our attention to what was good, just, and prudent in the conduct of life; and little or no notice was ever taken of what related to the victuals on the table, whether it was well or ill dressed, in or out of season, of good or bad flavor, preferable or inferior to this or that other thing of the kind, so that I was bro't up in such a perfect inattention to those matters as to be quite indifferent what kind of food was set before me, and so unobservant of it, that to this day if I am asked I can scarce tell a few hours after dinner what I dined upon. This has been a convenience to me in traveling, where my companions have been sometimes very unhappy for want of a suitable gratification of their more delicate, because better instructed, tastes and appetites.

...I believe I have omitted mentioning that, in my first voyage from Boston, being becalm'd off Block Island, our people set about catching cod, and hauled up a great many. Hitherto I had stuck to my resolution of not eating animal food, and on this occasion I consider'd, with my master Tryon, the taking every fish as a kind of unprovoked murder, since none of them had, or ever could do us any injury that might justify the slaughter. All this seemed very reasonable. But I had formerly been a great lover of fish, and, when this came hot out of the frying-pan, it smelt admirably well. I balanc'd some time between principle and inclination, till I recollected that, when the fish were opened, I saw smaller fish taken out of their stomachs; then thought I, "If you eat one another, I don't see why we mayn't eat you." So I din'd upon cod very heartily, and continued to eat with other people, returning only now and then occasionally to a vegetable diet. So convenient a thing is it to be a *reasonable creature*, since it enables one to find or make a reason for everything one has a mind to do.

... Keimer[3] wore his beard at full length, because somewhere in the Mosaic law it is said, "*Thou shalt not mar the corners of thy beard.*" He likewise kept the Seventh day, Sabbath; and these two points were essentials with him. I dislik'd both; but agreed to admit them upon condition of his adopting the doctrine of using no animal food. "I doubt," said he, "my constitution will not bear that." I assur'd him it would, and that he would be the better for it. He was usually a great glutton, and I promised myself some diversion in half starving him. He agreed to try the practice, if I would keep him company. I did so, and we held it for three months. We had our victuals

---

[3] Samuel Keimer was Franklin's boss in a printing business in Philadelphia.

dress'd, and brought to us regularly by a woman in the neighborhood, who had from me a list of forty dishes, to be prepar'd for us at different times, in all which there was neither fish, flesh, nor fowl, and the whim suited me the better at this time from the cheapness of it, not costing us above eighteen-pence sterling each per week. I have since kept several Lents most strictly, leaving the common diet for that, and that for the common, abruptly, without the least inconvenience, so that I think there is little in the advice of making those changes by easy gradations. I went on pleasantly, but poor Keimer suffered grievously, tired of the project, long'd for the flesh-pots of Egypt, and order'd a roast pig. He invited me and two women friends to dine with him; but, it being brought too soon upon table, he could not resist the temptation, and ate the whole before we came.

Discussion questions

1. On what did Franklin base his ideas about what to eat, specifically on whether or not eating fish was ethical?
2. How do we reconcile the many contradictions about food that are contained in these three excerpts? Why can't he remain consistent in his approach to food? Is this common among Americans? Humans?
3. What does Franklin think are the benefits of eating together as a family? How does this way of eating relate to Franklin's socioeconomic class? Do we see different kinds of eating in other times and places in history?

Chapter 2   Food, Foodways, and Conflict in the Early Republic

Document 2.1: Amelia Simmons, *American Cookery* (1796), "Preface," and Selected Recipes

American Cookery was not the first cookbook in America, but it was the first American cookbook. We know little about Simmons other than that she was probably a laborer in a kitchen. The book became very popular and was reprinted several times throughout the eastern United States.

PREFACE.

As this treatise is calculated for the improvement of the rising generation of *Females* in America, the Lady of fashion and fortune will not be displeased, if many hints are suggested for the more general and universal knowledge of those females in this country, who by the loss of their parents, or other unfortunate circumstances, are reduced to the necessity of going into families in the line of domestics, or taking refuge with their friends or relations, and doing those things which are really essential to the perfecting them as good wives, and useful members of society. The orphan, tho' left to the care of virtuous guardians, will find it essentially necessary to have an opinion and determination of her own. The world, and the fashion thereof, is so variable, that old people cannot accommodate themselves to the various changes and fashions which daily occur; *they* will adhere to the fashion of *their* day, and

Food and Eating in America: A Documentary Reader, First Edition.
Edited by James C. Giesen and Bryant Simon.
© 2018 John Wiley & Sons, Inc. Published 2018 by John Wiley & Sons, Inc.

will not surrender their attachments to the *good old way*—while the young and the gay, bend and conform readily to the taste of the times, and fancy of the hour. By having an opinion and determination, I would not be understood to mean an obstinate perseverance in trifles, which borders on obstinacy— by no means, but only an adherence to those rules and maxims which have flood the test of ages, and will forever establish the *female character*, a virtuous character—altho' they conform to the ruling taste of the age in cookery, dress, language, manners, &c.

It must ever remain a check upon the poor solitary orphan, that while those females who have parents, or brothers, or riches, to defend their indiscretions, that the orphan must depend solely upon *character*. How immensely important, therefore, that every action, every word, every thought, be regulated by the strictest purity, and that every movement meet the approbation of the good and wise.

To pickle Cucumbers.

Let your cucumbers be small, fresh gathered, and free from spots; then make a pickle of salt and water, strong enough to bear an egg; boil the pickle and skim it well, and then pour it upon your cucumbers, and stive them down for twenty four hours; then strain them out into a cullender, and dry them well with a cloth, and take the best white wine vinegar, with cloves, diced mace, nutmeg, white pepper corns, long pepper, and races of ginger, (as much as you please) boil them up together, and then clap the cucumbers in, with a few vine leaves, and a little salt, and as soon as they begin to turn their colour, put them into jars, stive them down close, and when cold, tie on a bladder and leather.

To Roast Beef.

The general rules are, to have a brisk hot fire, to hang down rather than to spit, to baste with salt and water, and one quarter of an hour to every pound of beef, tho' tender beef will require less, while old tough beef will require more roasting; pricking with a fork will determine you whether done or not; rare done is the healthiest and the taste of this age.

Roast Mutton.

If a breast let it be cauled, if a leg, stuffed or not, let be done more gently than beef, and done more; the chine, saddle or leg require more fire and longer time than the breast, &c. Garnish with scraped horse radish, and serve with potatoes, beans, colliflowers, water-cresses, or boiled onion, caper sauce, mashed turnip, or lettuce.

Discussion questions

1. The very long subtitle of this book ends with the claim that these recipes were "adapted to this country. And all grades of life." In the passages above, what evidence do we see that her claim was true?
2. Much of the preface discusses food as "fashion." What does Simmons mean by this? Is this true today?
3. How does the format of the recipes differ from cookbooks today and what does that tell us about ingredients, kitchens, and methods of the eighteenth century?
4. What do the recipes reveal about the way that early Americans were eating? Think about the size of the dishes prepared and the timing of their completion.

Document 2.2: The Preface, Introduction, and Assorted Recipes from Mary Randolph, *The Virginia House-Wife* (1824)

> *Mary Randoph was born in 1762 into a well-connected Virginia family. She married a planter, and lived in both their Chesterfield County plantation house and a mansion in Richmond. Eventually the family lost its fortune and was forced to run a boarding house.*

PREFACE.

The difficulties I encountered when I first entered on the duties of a house-keeping life, from the want of books sufficiently clear and concise to impart knowledge to a Tyro, compelled me to study the subject, and by actual experiment to reduce every thing in the culinary line, to proper weights and measures. The method I found not only to diminish the necessary attention and labour, but to be also economical: for, when the ingredients employed were given just proportions, the article made was always equally good. The government of a family, bears a Lilliputian resemblance to the government of a nation. The contents of the Treasury must be known, and great care taken to keep the expenditures from being equal to the receipts. A regular system must be introduced into each department, which may be modified until matured, and should then pass into an inviolable law. The grand arcanum of management lies in three simples rules:—"Let everything be done at a proper time, keep every thing in its proper place, and put every thing to its proper use." If the mistress of a family, will every morning examine minutely the different departments of her household, she must detect errors in their infant state, when they can be corrected with ease; but a few days' growth gives them gigantic strength: and disorder, with all her attendant evils, are introduced. Early rising is also essential to the good government of a family. A late breakfast deranges the whole business of the day, and throws a portion of it on the next, which opens the door for confusion to enter. The greater part of the following receipts have been written from memory, where they were impressed by long continued practice. Should they prove serviceable to the young inexperienced housekeeper, it will add greatly to the gratification which an extensive circulation of the work will be likely to confer.

INTRODUCTION.

Management is an art that may be acquired by every woman of good sense and tolerable memory. If, unfortunately, she has been bred in a family where domestic business is the work of chance, she will have many difficulties to encounter; but a determined resolution to obtain this valuable knowledge, will enable her to surmount all obstacles. She must begin the day with an early breakfast, requiring each person to be in readiness to take their seats when the muffins, buckwheat cakes, &c. are placed on the table. This looks social and comfortable. When the family breakfast by detachments, the table remains a tedious time; the servants are kept from the morning's meal, and a complete derangement takes place in the whole business of the day. No work can be done until breakfast is finished. The Virginia ladies, who are proverbially good managers, employ themselves, while their servants are eating, in washing the cups, glasses, &c; arranging the cruets, the mustard, salt-sellers, pickle vases, and all the apparatus for the dinner table. This occupies but a short time, and the lady has the satisfaction of knowing that they are in much better order than they would be if left to the servants. It also relieves her from the trouble of seeing the dinner table prepared, which should be done every day with the same scrupulous regard to exact neatness and method, as if a grand company was expected. When the servant is required to do this daily, he soon gets into the habit of doing it well; and his mistress having made arrangements for him in the morning, there is no fear of bustle and confusion in running after things that may be called for during the hour of dinner. When the kitchen breakfast is over, and the cook has put all things in their proper places, the mistress should go in to give her orders. Let all the articles intended for the dinner, pass in review before her: have the butter, sugar, flour, meal, lard, given out in proper quantities; the catsup, spice, wine, whatever may be wanted for each dish, measured to the cook. The mistress must tax her own memory with all this: we have no right to expect slaves or hired servants to be more attentive to our interest than we ourselves are: they will never recollect these little articles until they are going to use them; the mistress must then be called out, and thus have the horrible drudgery of keeping house all day, when one hour devoted to it in the morning, would release her trouble until the next day. There is economy as well as comfort in a regular mode of doing business. When the mistress gives out every thing, there is no waste; but if temptation be thrown in the way of subordinates, not many will have power to resist it; besides, it is an immoral act to place them in a situation which we pray to be exempt from ourselves.

The prosperity and happiness of a family depend greatly on the order and regularity established in it. The husband, who can ask a friend to partake of his dinner in full confidence of finding his wife unruffled by the petty vexations attendant on the neglect of household duties—who can usher his guest in the dining-room assured of seeing that methodical nicety which is the essence of true elegance,—will feel pride and exultation in the possession of a companion, who gives to his home charms that gratify every wish of his soul, and render the haunts of dissipation hateful to him. The sons bred in such a family will be moral men, of steady habits; and the daughters, if the mother shall have performed the duties of a parent in the superintendence of their education, as faithfully as she has done those of a wife, will each be a treasure to her husband; and being formed on the model of an exemplary mother, will use the same means for securing the happiness of her own family, which she has seen successfully practised under the paternal roof.

Assorted Recipes

TO DRESS TURTLE.

Kill it at night in winter, and in the morning in summer. Hang it up by the hind fins, cut off the head and let it bleed well. Separate the bottom shell from the top, with great care, lest the gall bladder be broken, which must be cautiously taken out and thrown away. Put the liver in a bowl of water. Empty the guts and lay them in water; if there be eggs, put them also in water. It is proper to have a separate bowl of water for each article. Cut all the flesh from the bottom shell, and lay it in water; then break the shell in two, put it in a pot after having washed it clean; pour on as much water as will cover it entirely, add one pound of middling, or flitch of bacon, with four onions chopped, and set it on the fire to boil. Open the guts, cleanse them perfectly; take off the inside skin, and put them in the pot with the shell; let them boil steadily for three hours, and if the water boils away too much, add more. Wash the top shell nicely after taking out the flesh, cover it, and set it by. Parboil the fins, clean them nicely—taking off all the black skin, and put them in water; cut the flesh taken from the bottom and top shell, in small pieces; cut the fins in two, lay them with the flesh in a dish; sprinkle some salt over, and cover them up. When the shell, &c. is done, take out the bacon, scrape the shell clean, and strain the liquor; about one quart of which must be put back in the pot; reserve the rest for soup; pick out the guts, and cut them in small pieces; take all the nice bits that were strained out, put them with the guts into the gravy; lay in the fins cut in pieces with them, and as much of the flesh as will be sufficient to fill the upper shell; add to it, (if a large turtle,) one bottle of white wine; cayenne pepper, and salt, to your taste, one gill of mushroom catsup, one gill of lemon pickle, mace, nutmegs and cloves, pounded, to season it high. Mix two large spoonsful of flour in one pound and a quarter of butter; put it in with thyme, parsley, marjoram and savory, tied in bunches; stew all these together, till the flesh and fins are tender; wash out the top shell, put a puff paste around the brim; sprinkle over the shell pepper and salt, then take the herbs out of the stew; if the gravy is not thick enough, add a little more flour, and fill the shell; should there be no eggs in the turtle, boil six new laid ones for ten minutes, put them in cold water a short time, peel them, cut them in two, and place them on the turtle; make a rich forcemeat, (see receipt for forcemeat,) fry the balls nicely, and put them also in the shell; set it in a dripping pan, with something under the sides to keep it steady; have the oven heated as for bread, and let it remain in it till nicely browned. Fry the liver and send it in hot.

ASPARAGUS.

Set a stew-pan with plenty of water on the fire, sprinkle a handful of salt in it, let it boil, and skim it; then put in the asparagus prepared thus: scrape all the stalks till they are perfectly clean; throw them into a pan of cold water as you scrape them; when they are all done, tie them in little bundles, of a quarter of a hundred each, with bass, if you can get it, or tape; cut off the stalks at the bottom, that they may be all of a length; when they are tender at the stalk, which will be in from twenty to thirty minutes, they are done enough. Great care must be taken to watch the exact time of their becoming tender; take them just at that instant, and they will have their true flavour and colour; a minute or two more boiling destroys both. While the asparagus is boiling, toast a slice of a loaf of bread, about a half an inch thick;

brown it delicately on both sides; dip it lightly in the liquor the asparagus was boiled in, and lay it in the middle of a dish; pour some melted butter on the toast, and lay the asparagus upon it; let it project beyond the asparagus, that the company may see there is a toast. Do not pour butter over them, but send some in a boat.

CARROTS.
Let them be well washed and scraped—an hour is enough for young spring carrots; grown carrots will take from an hour and a half to two hours and a half. The best way to try if they are done enough, is to pierce them with a fork.

PICKLING.
LEMON PICKLE.
Grate the yellow rind from two dozen fine fresh lemons, quarter them but leave them whole at the bottom; sprinkle salt on them, and put them in the sun every day until dry; then brush off the salt, put them in a pot with one ounce of nutmegs, and one of mace pounded; a large handful of horse radish scraped and dried, two dozen cloves of garlic, and a pint of mustard seed; pour on one gallon of strong vinegar, tie the pot close, put a board on, and let it stand three months--strain it, and when perfectly clear, bottle it.

TOMATO CATSUP.
Gather a peck of tomatos, pick out the stems, and wash them; put them on the fire without water, sprinkle on a few spoonsful of salt, let them boil steadily an hour, stirring them frequently; strain them through a colander, and then through a sieve; put the liquid on the fire with half a pint of chopped onions, half a quarter of an ounce of mace broke into small pieces; and if not sufficiently salt, add a little more—one table-spoonful of whole black pepper; boil all together until just enough to fill two bottles; cork it tight. Make it in August, in dry weather.

TO MAKE A CURRY OF CATFISH.
Take the white channel catfish, cut off their heads, skin and clean them, cut them in pieces four inches long, put as many as will be sufficient for a dish into a stew pan with a quart of water, two onions, and chopped parsley; let them stew gently till the water is reduced to half a pint, take the fish out and lay them on a dish, cover them to keep them hot, rub a spoonful of butter into one of flour, add a large tea-spoonful of curry powder, thicken the gravy with it, shake it over the fire a few minutes, and pour it over the fish; be careful to have the gravy smooth.

Discussion questions

1. Much of what Randolph writes in the Preface and Introduction are her thoughts on management of the kitchen. What do these documents tell us about her expectations of who should do what kind of labor? She mentions both servants and slaves who help in the kitchen. What role do they play? What is the ultimate role of the housewife?
2. Think about the cooking and serving process that Randolph has outlined from the perspective of a Virginia slave. What does Randolph's oversight of slave labor tell us about slave behavior? Does this document tell us why working in the house was seen by most slaves as an advantage over working in the field?
3. Randolph uses the word "economical" in the Preface. Do these documents, including the recipes, tell us something about the waste of food, labor, or money?
4. Curries are a dish generally thought to have arrived in the United States in the twentieth century, brought by Indian immigrants, but here is a recipe from the early nineteenth century that seems true to its modern form. How might we explain the presence of this dish and of curry powder's presence in the United States?
5. Think about the ingredients that Randolph calls for in her recipes. Do they tell us something about trade networks and the increasing reach of American consumers?

Document 2.3: Unidentified artist, *Benjamin Hawkins and the Creek Indians* (Painting, c. 1805)

The central figure in this painting is Benjamin Hawkins, who was a Revolutionary War soldier, aide to George Washington, delegate to the Constitutional Convention, U.S. Senator, and, from 1785 to his death in 1816, an official representative of the government in Native American affairs. In this position he negotiated treaties with several tribes, learned the Creek language, and is said to have been adopted by the tribe. In the early 1800s he began teaching agriculture to Creeks at his Georgia plantation. In 1805 he reported to Congress that "Our Indian neighbors are advancing, many of them with spirit, and others beginning to engage, in the pursuits of agriculture and house hold manufacture. They are becoming sensible that the earth yields subsistence with less labor and more certainty than the forest, and find it in their interest from time to time to dispose parts of their surplus and waste lands for the means of improving those they occupy, and of subsisting their families while they are preparing their farms." The painting depicts a scene at Hawkins's plantation with Creek Native Americans.

Discussion questions

1. What is happening in the painting? What do you think Hawkins is telling the Indian men in the center of the painting? The men are holding a plow—what does that tell us?
2. How do the figures on the left and right sides of the painting contrast? What do they represent? How are crops and food represented here?
3. What is the significance of the breastfeeding woman on the left?
4. Study the background. What is the artist telling us about Hawkins's plantation? Do we think Hawkins was a major cotton planter? Why are the buildings and animals prominent in the background?

Document 2.4: John Lewis Krimmel, *The Quilting Frolic* (Painting, 1813)

Painter John Lewis Krimmel was born in 1786 in Germany and arrived in the United States in 1809. Though he probably had no formal training before arriving in the country, he quickly took to painting humorous, lively portraits of life in Philadelphia. The first work that gained public attention was his

Pepper-Pot: A Scene in the Philadelphia Market *(1811), which shows an African American in a market serving bowls of soup to women, men, and children of various social classes. Krimmel became known for such scenes that show the rich details of bustling city life. The painting below also hints about class, race, and food in the early republic. The scene depicts the inside of a Pennsylvania middle-class household during a quilting party.*

Discussion questions

1. What can we learn about middle-class foodways from this scene?
2. The woman who is serving bread—is that a look of trepidation on her face as she looks toward the visitors near the door? Who is serving the food? Who is stealing a bite to eat?
3. What do the furnishings and crockery, especially the plates and cups, tell us about this family? What do you make of the gun over the door?
4. What does the popularity of paintings like these tell us about views of middle-class life? Did middle-class Americans in this period learn something about themselves in these paintings? Might it change their expectations for food and materialism?

Document 2.5: Excerpt from Joseph Doddridge, *Notes on the Settlement and Indian Wars of the Western Parts of Pennsylvania and Virginia* (1824), Chapter 5, "Beasts and Birds"

The term "Columbian Exchange" refers to the massive swapping of biological material (plants, animals, diseases) between the western and eastern hemispheres that was launched by Columbus's voyages at the end of the fifteenth century. To say that the nature of each of these places was radically transformed is no overstatement. The process had a major impact on what and how humans ate food on both sides of the Atlantic. In the following passage Joseph Doddridge, a man who grew up in the Pennsylvania and Virginia frontiers in the late 1700s, recalls just how much had changed in the native plant and animal life by 1824. Note the influence of hunting for food and of farming on these alterations to the "wilderness."

The reader need not expect that this chapter will contain a list of all the beasts and birds which were tenants of the western wilderness at the time of its first settlement. I shall only briefly notice a few of those classes which have already totally or partially disappeared from the country, together with those which have emigrated here with our population. This enumeration, as far as it goes, will serve to show the natural historian a distinction between those beasts and birds which are naturally tenants of the wilderness and refuse the society of man, and those which follow his footsteps from one region to another, and although partially wild yet subsist in part upon his labors.

The buffalo and elk have entirely disappeared from this section of the country. Of the bear and deer but very few remain. The wolves, formerly so numerous, and so destructive to the cattle, are now seldom heard of in our older settlements …

The wild turkeys, which used to be so abundant as to supply no inconsiderable portion of provision for the first settlers, are now rarely seen …

The black and grey squirrels still remain in the country. These beautiful but destructive little animals gave great annoyance to the first settlers of our country, by devouring large quantities of their corn in the fields before it was fit for gathering. There is something singular in the history of the squirrels. Sometimes in the course of a few years they become so numerous as to threaten the destruction of whole crops; when, as if by common consent, they commence in emigration from west to east, crossing the river and countless numbers. At the commencement of their march they are very fat, and furnish an agreeable article of diet; but towards its conclusion they become sickly and poor, with large worms attached to their skins … the cause of this phenomenon is, I believe, unknown. It cannot be the want of food; for the districts of countries which they leave are often as fruitful or more so than those to which they direct their course ...

In return for the beasts and birds which have left us, we have gained an equal number from the Atlantic side of the mountains, and which were unknown at the first settlement of the country ...

Our mornings and evenings are now enlivened with the matins and vespers of a great variety of singing birds, which have slowly followed the immigration from the other side of the mountain.

The honeybees are not natives of this country; but they always keep a little advance of the white population.... Rats, which were not known here for several years after the settlement of the country, took possession of it, in its whole extent and one winter season....

Thus our country has exchanged its thinly scattered population of savages for a dense population of civilized inhabitants, and its wild beasts and large, carnivorous fowls, for domesticated animals and fowls, and others which although wild are inoffensive in their habits, and live at least partially on the labors of man. This has been affected here perhaps in less time than such important changes were ever affected in any other region of the earth.

Discussion questions

1. What do we mean by "wilderness"? Using Doddridge's text as a guide, how would you say wilderness changes or does not change over time? Is there a wilderness without people?
2. Though Doddridge speaks very little here about hunting and farming, how are both of these implicated in the changes that he's describing?
3. Do we get a sense of how foodways themselves are changing by the early nineteenth century on the Virginia frontier? Can we see here a change in what constituted food?
4. What might explain the introduction of the animals and insects that Doddridge describes?

Document 2.6: Selections from English Phrenologist George Combe, *Notes on the United States During a Phrenological Visit in 1838–9–40, vol. II.* (1841)

George Combe was a Scottish phrenologist—phrenology was a "science," popular in the nineteenth century, that suggested connections between head size and human personality and aptitude. In other words, Combe believed that head shape determined intelligence. Phrenology had thousands of followers all over the globe. In the 1830s, Combe traveled to the United States to lecture on phrenology and conduct research. He visited several prisons and other institutions and made many other observations about American life. His observations on foodways both inside and outside these intuitions are revealing.

The Asylum for Colored Orphans.—To-day we visited the asylum in Twelfth Street for colored orphan children. It was open in July 1837, and is managed by ladies. It contains between 50 and 60 Negro children, both sexes, from five or six to twelve or thirteen years of age. They are clothed, fed, boarded, and taught; and although the building is too small for so great a number, it is kept in excellent order.... In the course of my inquiries, I learned that a considerable number of deaths have occurred within the first two years. The disease in the majority of cases was scrofula[1] in one or other of its varied forms. It was ascribed to the scanty and improper diet of the children before admission, and to the insufficiency of nutriment contained in the regular but light food supplied in the asylum. For sometime no animal food was allowed, and Indian corn, meal, and brown bread made of rye and unbolted wheaten flour, were among other things largely used. One of the consequences of this kind of diet was inordinate irritation of the mucous membrane of the bowels, and almost constant diarrhoea. The orphans were so enfeebled, that many sunk under the acute and epidemic or contagious diseases peculiar to childhood, which more robust children were passed through in safety. Both the managers and physician became convinced of the necessity of improving the diet of the establishment. A change was accordingly made in this respect, as well as in others of equal importance, and was followed by a remarkable improvement in health of the children. Animal food is now used four times a week in a solid form, and twice in soup. White bread, rice and milk, vegetables of the season, &c. are abundantly supplied. It is now a year since there has been a death in the asylum, where no less than 15 deaths occurred during the preceding 18 months. This extraordinary exemption from mortality is not ascribed to change of diet only, but to this and other ameliorations of perhaps greater importance, introduced by the enlightened and benevolent managers of the asylum. The experiment, however, has been repeatedly made of going back from the better to the poorer kinds of food, and uniformly with injurious consequences.

American Hotels.—The hotels in the western region of New York State are on a large scale and very good.... The meals are served with amazing dispatch. We were generally first and last at table, yet only 15 minutes, by

---

[1] A disease similar to tuberculosis that causes swellings in one's glands.

my watch, elapsed between our sitting down and rising up. Within that time 150 persons had crammed down a breakfast. "You Europeans," said an American, "eat as if you actually enjoyed your food!" "Assuredly we do,— and you Americans will never escape from dyspepsia and headaches until you also learn to enjoy your meals."

The Bad Health of American Women.—...The American ladies generally ascribe their maladies to the very variable climate of their country. This may have some influence; but their own habits appear to me to contribute much more to their sufferings. They rarely walk abroad for the sake of fresh air and exercise.... They do not properly regulate their diet; pies, pastry, and animal food, are consumed in quantities too abundant for a sedentary life....

Discussion questions

1. Taking all of these passages in mind, how does food fit into Combe's observations about American life? Are the food problems he's describing symptoms of a larger American culture?
2. Is Combe painting Americans as ignorant of the effects of food on health? Or is it that Americans misunderstand the connection?
3. Why were upper class, educated people like Combe so seemingly concerned about the plight of institutionalized people at this time? What was going on in the cities of the world to create this interest?
4. What do the conditions of the orphanage tell us about race and class in the northern United States in the mid-nineteenth century.

Document 2.7: A Variation of the Lyrics of "Home Sweet Home," a Popular Song of the Early Republic (c. 1830)

Many moral reformers of the first-half of the nineteenth century were convinced that the United States was becoming a nation of drunkards. Historian W. J. Rorabaugh has found that from about 1800 to the Civil War, Americans drank more alcohol per capita than nearly any other nation on earth, reaching a peak of nearly six gallons per person per year of distilled spirits like whiskey, rum, and gin in 1830. Some of this consumption was directly linked to food. Since fresh produce was not refrigerated, it spoiled quickly unless cured by salt, acid, or liquor. In addition, fried meats, which were very popular because the cooking method was fast, paired well with whiskey. That beverage was especially prevalent on the frontier where surplus supplies of corn were more efficiently shipped to markets on the east coast in the form of liquor than as whole grain. The following song, popular in the 1830s, hints at several ways that liquor consumption was related to food and eating habits.

Mid plenty of bacon and bread tho' we jog,
Be it ever so strong, there's nothing like grog.
A shot from the jug sends such joy to the heart,
No eating on earth could such pleasure impart.
Grog, grog, sweet, sweet grog.
There's nothing like grog, there's nothing like grog.

Discussion questions

1. In what way does this song suggest that for some Americans, drinking and food were competing against each other? Does the singer choose grog over bacon and bread?
2. What does the use of "jog" tell us about the act of eating?
3. What does the popularity of this song tell us about food and drink in the early republic?

Reference

Rorabaugh, W.J., *The Alcoholic Republic: An American Tradition* (New York: Oxford University Press, 1979), 8.

Part III Fields and Foods in the Nineteenth Century

Chapter 3   Slavery and Food in the Old South

Document 3.1: Selections from Frederick Douglass, *Memoirs* on Food and Slavery (1845)

It is important to recognize that there was no singular slave experience. The institution existed in the American colonies and the United States for 246 years. It found its home in a large and diverse geographic region, in bustling cities and remote rural outposts. American slavery was not just a labor system for farm work; it was an entire industry of its own, one that was supported by banks and companies all over the United States and the world. Therefore it is impossible to talk about "slave food" as a single subject. Food differed greatly, for instance, for a slave working as an artisan in Baltimore in 1650 and one laboring in a Louisiana cotton field in 1860. The following documents offer windows into how and what slaves ate, but by no means give us a complete view.

Frederick Douglass was born a slave in 1818 on a plantation on Maryland's Eastern Shore. He escaped from his slave master in 1838, eventually settled in Massachusetts and became the most famous black abolitionist of the nineteenth century. In the following passage Douglass is describing the plantation in Talbot County, Maryland where he lived as a slave. The plantation raised tobacco, corn, and wheat, which was taken to market in Baltimore. Douglass's master worked for Colonel Lloyd, a wealthy planter.

Food and Eating in America: A Documentary Reader, First Edition.
Edited by James C. Giesen and Bryant Simon.
© 2018 John Wiley & Sons, Inc. Published 2018 by John Wiley & Sons, Inc.

Colonel Lloyd kept from three to four hundred slaves on his home plantation, and owned a large number more on the neighboring farms belonging to him....The overseers of these, and all the rest of the farms, numbering over twenty, received advice and direction from the managers of the home plantation. This was the great business place. It was the seat of government for the whole twenty farms. All disputes among the overseers were settled here. If a slave was convicted of any high misdemeanor, became unmanageable, or evinced a determination to run away, he was brought immediately here, severely whipped, put on board the sloop, carried to Baltimore, and sold to Austin Woolfolk, or some other slave-trader, as a warning to the slaves remaining.

Here, too, the slaves of all the other farms received their monthly allowance of food, and their yearly clothing. The men and women slaves received, as their monthly allowance of food, eight pounds of pork, or its equivalent in fish, and one bushel of corn meal.

...We were not regularly allowanced. Our food was coarse corn meal boiled. This was called *mush*. It was put into a large wooden tray or trough, and set down upon the ground. The children were then called, like so many pigs, and like so many pigs they would come and devour the mush; some with oyster-shells, others with pieces of shingle, some with naked hands, and none with spoons. He that ate fastest got most; he that was strongest secured the best place; and few left the trough satisfied.

When Douglass was ten, his master sent him to work in the house of Hugh Auld in Baltimore. He found life in the city much different than what he had known on the rural plantation.

I had resided but a short time in Baltimore before I observed a marked difference, in the treatment of slaves, from that which I had witnessed in the country. A city slave is almost a freeman, compared with a slave on the plantation. He is much better fed and clothed, and enjoys privileges altogether unknown to the slave on the plantation. There is a vestige of decency, a sense of shame, that does much to curb and check those out-breaks of atrocious cruelty so commonly enacted upon the plantation. He is a desperate slaveholder, who will shock the humanity of his non-slave-holding neighbors with the cries of his lacerated slave. Few are willing to incur the odium attaching to the reputation of being a cruel master; and above all things, they would not be known as not giving a slave enough to eat. Every city slaveholder is anxious to have it known of him, that he feeds his slaves well; and it is due to them to say, that most of them do give their slaves enough to eat. There are, however, some painful exceptions to this rule. Directly opposite to us, on Philpot Street, lived Mr. Thomas Hamilton. He owned two slaves. Their names were Henrietta and Mary. Henrietta was about twenty-two years of age, Mary was about fourteen; and of all the mangled and emaciated creatures I ever looked upon, these two were the most so. His heart must be harder than stone, that could look upon these unmoved. The head, neck, and shoulders of Mary were literally cut to pieces. I have frequently felt her head, and found it nearly covered with festering sores, caused by the lash of her cruel mistress. I do not know that her master ever whipped her, but I have been an eye-witness to the cruelty of Mrs. Hamilton. I used to be in Mr. Hamilton's house nearly every day. Mrs. Hamilton used to sit in a large chair in the middle of the room, with a heavy cowskin always by her side, and scarce an hour passed during the day but was marked by the blood of one of these slaves. The girls seldom passed her without her saying, "Move faster, you *black gip!*" at the same time giving them a blow with the cowskin over the head or shoulders, often drawing the blood. She would then say, "Take that, you *black gip!*" continuing, "If you don't move faster, I'll move you!" Added to the cruel lashings to which these slaves were subjected, they were kept nearly half-starved. They seldom knew what it was to eat a full meal. I have seen Mary contending with the pigs for the offal thrown into the street. So much was Mary kicked and cut to pieces, that she was oftener called "*pecked*" than by her name.

Seven years later Douglass was taken by his owner from Baltimore to a house in Talbot County, Maryland.

I have now reached a period of my life when I can give dates. I left Baltimore, and went to live with Master Thomas Auld, at St. Michael's, in March, 1832. It was now more than seven years since I lived with him in the family of my old master, on Colonel Lloyd's plantation. ... It was tenfold harder after living in Master Hugh's family, where I had always had enough to eat, and of that which was good. I have said Master Thomas was a mean man. He was so. Not to give a slave enough to eat, is regarded as the most aggravated development of meanness even among slaveholders. The rule is, no matter how coarse the food, only let there be enough of it. This is the theory; and in the part of Maryland from which I came, it is the general practice,—though there are many exceptions. Master Thomas gave us enough of neither coarse nor fine food. There were four slaves of us in the kitchen—my sister Eliza, my aunt Priscilla, Henny, and myself; and we were allowed less than a half of a bushel of corn-meal per week, and very little else, either in the shape of meat or vegetables. It was not enough for us to subsist upon. We were therefore reduced to the wretched necessity of living at the expense of our neighbors. This we did by begging and stealing, whichever came handy in the time of need, the one being considered as legitimate as the other. A great many times have we poor creatures been nearly perishing with hunger, when food in abundance lay mouldering in the safe and smoke-house, and our pious mistress was aware of the fact; and yet that mistress and her husband would kneel every morning, and pray that God would bless them in basket and store!

In 1833, Douglass was hired out to a local farmer named Edward Covey, who was known as a cruel master. Covey regularly whipped Douglass.

I have said that this mode of treatment is a part of the whole system of fraud and inhumanity of slavery. It is so. The mode here adopted to disgust the slave with freedom, by allowing him to see only the abuse of it, is carried out in other things. For instance, a slave loves molasses; he steals some. His master, in many cases, goes off to town, and buys a large quantity; he returns, takes his whip, and commands the slave to eat the molasses, until the poor fellow is made sick at the very mention of it. The same mode is sometimes adopted to make the slaves refrain from asking for more food than their regular allowance. A slave runs through his allowance, and applies for more. His master is enraged at him; but, not willing to send him off without food, gives him more than is necessary, and compels him to eat it within a given time. Then, if he complains that he cannot eat it, he is said to be satisfied neither full nor fasting, and is whipped for being hard to please! I have an abundance of such illustrations of the same principle, drawn from my own observation, but think the cases I have cited sufficient. The practice is a very common one.

Discussion questions

1. Why would a city slave receive more food than one working on a rural plantation? Would there be more food available on a farm or in the city?
2. Why would a master want to be known as someone who fed his slaves well?
3. What do we learn about the power of food here? Douglass juxtaposes physical abuse with starvation in several of these passages. What can we

learn about how slaves viewed food? Consider, too, the instance where Covey uses excess molasses as a punishment.

4. Douglass makes two powerful comparisons between slaves eating and pigs eating. What do these tell us about both slaves and animals?

Document 3.2: Excerpts from Harriet Jacobs, *Incidents in the Life of a Slave Girl* (1861) on Slaves' Weekly Rations, Punishments for Slaves' Stealing Food from Master, and Slave Taste Testers for Master

Like the Diary of Frederick Douglass, Incidents in the Life of a Slave Girl *is the narrative of a person born into slavery but who eventually escaped. Harriet Jacobs was born on the coast of North Carolina in 1813. By the time she was a teenager Jacobs was already evading the sexual advances of her master, Dr. James Norcrom (who Jacobs calls "Dr. Flint" in the book). Like Douglass, Jacobs writes a good deal about food shortages and the ways in which finding access to extra nourishment was a punishable offense.*

Little attention was paid to the slaves' meals in Dr. Flint's house. If they could catch a bit of food while it was going, well and good. I gave myself no trouble on that score, for on my various errands I passed my grandmother's house, where there was always something to spare for me. I was frequently threatened with punishment if I stopped there; and my grandmother, to avoid detaining me, often stood at the gate with something for my breakfast or dinner. I was indebted to *her* for all my comforts, spiritual or temporal. It was *her* labor that supplied my scanty wardrobe. I have a vivid recollection of the linsey-woolsey dress given me every winter by Mrs. Flint. How I hated it! It was one of the badges of slavery.

Jacobs eventually had a consensual relationship with a white neighbor in the hopes that this would protect her from her owner's sexual advances. She gave birth to two children. Flint responds by sending Jacobs and one of her children to his plantation.

The next day my new mistress began her housekeeping. I was not exactly appointed maid of all work; but I was to do whatever I was told. Monday evening came. It was always a busy time. On that night the slaves received their weekly allowance of food. Three pounds of meat, a peck of corn, and perhaps a dozen herring were allowed to each man. Women received a pound and a half of meat, a peck of corn, and the same number of herring.

Children over twelve years old had half the allowance of the women. The meat was cut and weighed by the foreman of the field hands, and piled on planks before the meat house. Then the second foreman went behind the building, and when the first foreman called out, "Who takes this piece of meat?" he answered by calling somebody's name. This method was resorted to as a means of preventing partiality in distributing the meat. The young mistress came out to see how things were done on her plantation, and she soon gave a specimen of her character. Among those in waiting for their allowance was a very old slave, who had faithfully served the Flint family through three generations. When he hobbled up to get his bit of meat, the mistress said he was too old to have any allowance; that when niggers were too old to work, they ought to be fed on grass. Poor old man! He suffered much before he found rest in the grave.

Discussion questions

1. Do some simple calculations on the calories of the weekly rations that Jacobs describes and compare that to an average American intake in a week today. How did slaves get by on this food?
2. What kinds of foods were not provided to slaves? What might be the short- and long-term consequences of a diet that relied heavily on meat and grain?
3. How was access to food a form of resistance for Jacobs?
4. Overall, what was Jacobs trying to teach her white northern readers about the way that food worked in the slave system?

Document 3.3: Images of the Antebellum South

Much of how and what southerners, white and black, ate during the century before the Civil War was determined by where they were. Slavery and white supremacy were factors in how food was prepared and put on the table. The following images give us some clues about these social rules and their material manifestations. Kitchens, for instance, were seldom part of the main house, whether in a rural or urban setting, since the risk of fire was too great. African Americans served as cooks for nearly every white family that owned any slaves. This history of cooking profoundly influenced regional foodways.

Whitsett-Hurt-Hanna House, Perry County, Alabama, view from rear with slave kitchen on right.

Slave kitchen and laundry building, Hugh Foster House, Bullock County, Alabama.

Slave woman in kitchen, Refuge Plantation, Camden County, Georgia.

Dining room, Melrose Plantation, Natchez, Mississippi.

Discussion questions

1. The Whitsett-Hurt-Hanna House was a mansion in an urban setting. Many cotton planters built palatial estates in towns or cities, rather than having their families live on the plantations themselves. Why might they do that? What advantages did the town location provide in terms of food and eating?

2. What does the dining room of the Melrose mansion in Natchez tell us about the eating habits of wealthy slave owners? Who would have been in the room when the family was eating? What about when they had company?

3. Slaves like the woman pictured at the Georgia plantation built skills that were prized by slaveholders. What does this photograph tell us about the variety of techniques and tools that she would have had to master to serve a multicourse dinner in a dining room like that at Melrose?

4. Note the large fan-like contraption, called a punkah, above the table in the Melrose photograph. The long cable ran from its top to a corner of the room where a slave child would stand during meals and pull it gently. The movement would make the air move slowly around the food and the diners. However, the function was not to cool the people. What do you think it was? What does it tell us about the environment of these houses and the cleanliness of the food?

Document 3.4: Excerpts from Daniel R. A. C. Hundley, *Social Relations in Our Southern States* (1860)

Hundley wrote this book as an answer to the growing northern abolitionist sentiment of the 1850s, sentiment in part fostered by memoirs like those quoted above. Hundley was an Alabama native who earned a law degree at Harvard University and then ran a real estate company in Chicago. As a southerner working in a bustling northern city, he became irritated by the portrayal of the South as a region with only rich whites, slaves, and poor whites. Thus he wrote Social Relations in Our Southern States *as a way to explain the social class system of the region. Hundley is here speaking of the southern white middle class, of which he believed northerners were mostly unaware.*

They belong to many different callings, professions, and trades; and we propose to speak of them according to their several pursuits. There are among them farmers, planters, traders, store-keepers, artisans, mechanics, a few manufacturers, a goodly number of country school-teachers, and a host of half-fledged country lawyers and doctors, parsons, and the like. Since the South is mainly agricultural, however, perhaps the larger proportion of her middle classes are to be found among the tillers of the soil; of these, therefore, we shall endeavor to speak first.... He is usually a slaveholder, owning from five to fifty negroes, (sometimes more,) and generally looks after their management himself. If he does employ an overseer, the latter habitually eats at the table of his employer, and in many cases it is difficult to distinguish employer from employé, so similar are they in every respect—dress, manners, speech, and *tout* ensemble.

...But he will persist in eating hog and hominy; believes bacon to be better than any other kind of meat, or a corn hoe-cake or well-cooked ash-cake superior to the finest flour bread that ever was baked. Our Yankee readers, however, need not blame him so much for this predilection; for we have never eaten any good bacon yet out of the South, unless it came from there originally; and corn, hoe, and johnny cakes, are very different in Kentucky or Virginia from what they are in Massachusetts or Illinois—which is partly owing to the better quality of the Southern corn, and partly to the difference between the old-fashioned cuisine of the South and the modern cooking-stove of the Free States. In the Southern States, generally, the kitchen is disconnected wholly with the dwelling-house—is a house apart to itself, indeed, and is appropriated to nothing beside. At one end rises a magnificent (in proportions, we mean) chimney of brick or stone, with a fire-place about ten feet across, more or less, well supplied with pot-hangers, cranks, ovens, pots, skillets, griddles, pans, and the like. Every thing is cooked in the old-fashioned way, and, to our liking, is much more palatable than food cooked in smothering stoves or furnaces ranges or any thing of the kind. Perhaps we could not give the reader a better idea of the real corn bread of the South, than by quoting the following practical remarks on the subject from Dr. Hall's Journal of Health to which they were contributed by a gentleman of Kentucky:

"A corn-dodger is not now what it used to be. Originally it was a corn-meal dumpling. In very early Kentucky times, the universal dinner, winter and spring, at every farm-house in the State, was a piece of middling bacon, boiled with cabbage, turnips, greens, collards or sprouts—cabbage-sprouts—according to the season. The pot, if the family was a large one, contained about ten gallons, and was nearly filled with clean pure water: the middling and the greens were put in at the proper time, to give them a sufficient cooking. Almost always the cook would make with water and corn-meal and a little salt, dough-balls, throw them into the pot, and boil them thoroughly with the rest. These were called *dodgers* from the motion giving them by the boiling water in the pot. They eat very well, and give a considerable variety to a dinner of bacon and collards. A dodger in modern times is corn-bread baked in a roll about the size of your hand, and about three times as thick, and in my judgment is not a veritable first-rate dodger, unless when on the table it bears the impress of the cook's fingers on it, in placing it in the oven to bake.

"A pone of bread is corn-bread baked in a skillet or small oven. The skillet or oven when at the proper heat is filled with corn dough, which when baked and turned out, is a pone of bread. A hoe-cake is not now what it used to be. I do not believe there will ever be any more good hoe-cakes baked. I have an unextinguishable longing for hoe-cake—real hoe-cake, such as the black woman Jinny, my mother's cook, always baked. It gets its name from the mode of baking. It was originally baked upon a hoe. An old hoe, which had been worn right, was placed upon live coals of fire, with the eye down, and on it the cake was baked. Now, hoe-cake is baked upon a griddle, or was before cooking-stoves came into use. It just occurs to me, may not the cooking-stove militate against the griddle?

"Corn-dodger, corn-pone, and hoe-cake are different only in the baking. The meal is prepared for each precisely in the same way. Take as much meal as you want, some salt, and enough pure water to knead the mass. Mix it well, let it stand some fifteen or twenty minutes, not longer, as this will be long enough to saturate perfectly every particle of meal; bake on the griddle for hoe-cake, and in the skillet or oven for dodger or pone. The griddle or oven must be made hot enough to bake, but not to burn but with a quick heat. The lid must be heated also before putting it on the skillet or oven, and that heat must be kept up with coals of fire placed on it, as there must be around and under the oven. The griddle must be well supplied with live coals under it. The hoe-cake must be put on thin, not more than or quite as thick as your forefinger; when brown, it must be turned and both sides baked to a richbrown color. There must be no burning—baking is the idea. Yet the baking must be done with a quick lively heat, the quicker the better."

Discussion questions

1. Why would Hundley spend so much time describing simple cornmeal cakes in a book that is supposed to be a defense of the South against abolitionist slander?
2. What is Hundley's point about social classes as they relate to food and eating?
3. How is the description of the southern kitchen a statement about slave conditions?
4. Hundley clearly identifies the "right" kind of hoe-cake as being like that cooked by his mother's slave cook, Jinny. Think about Hundley as a child. How would food have affected his understanding of race and labor as he grew older?

Document 3.5: Selections from Planter James Battle Avirett, *The Old Plantation: How We Lived in Great House and Cabin Before the War* (1901)

James Battle Avirett was born on a plantation in eastern North Carolina to a wealthy and well-connected family. After college he became an Episcopal priest, served as a Confederate chaplain during the Civil War, and wrote several books in his later life. The memoir excerpted here is Avirett's attempt to record what life was like in the Old South before the war, a time that he believed was "wretchedly misunderstood." In this passage Avirett is walking the reader around the plantation, giving a tour of a typical scene on a typical day.

"Wait until breakfast to-morrow," said my brother John, "and when you have eaten our rice bird, fat as butter, bones and all, you will [recognize] that this bird of the Carolinas, fatted on rice in the milky state, is the most delicate, toothsome food I ever tasted."

… As these two young gentlemen, mounted on horseback, turned the heads of their horses away from the river they came up with an old negro, "Uncle Daniel," riding in a cart drawn by a mule, well laden with corn in the ear. The old man is on his way to one of the feeding stations to give some twenty-five or thirty bullocks their evening meal. These are being fatted for the early winter markets, and had you time, reader, to inspect them closely you would find fine specimens of the Durham breed of cattle, of the large size and of admirable fattening properties, of which the proprietor was very proud.

… There are some other things before us and we must hurry on. Let us go back to the old mansion, and in the description which we would leave of it let us insert two or three features of the outhouses, and just one on the interior of the house. Let us go upstairs and on the back piazza, which you observe is without roof, and see what Edith and Kate, the maid servants of the writer's sisters, are doing. They are helping Handy, the dining room servant, to bring up large trays of fruit—peaches, pears and apples—to be dried up there, where nothing will disturb them in the hot rays of the sun. What fruit is that of deep blood color? That is the wild plum of the plantation and those trays over there are full of whortleberries and wild currants. All of this wild or uncultivated fruit has been purchased from the young servants of the estate, gathered by them in the adjoining woodland stretching far away to the south. The storeroom was thus well supplied with delicious dried fruit, and in the winter pies, tarts and dumplings came in as a part of the dessert.

... On the line of the fence dividing the poultry yard from the dog kennel, on the slope of the hill, do you observe that brick house partly embedded in the hillside? That is the most complete dairy or springhouse in this section of the State. Take down that calabash or gourd and dip down into that deep basin of crystal water which wells up in the center. No limestone there. Pure freestone or soft water and deliciously cool and very potable. Those troughs all around the sides of the dark, cool room are for the pans of milk. Let us count them. One, two, three and so on to twenty-four pans of milk. How yellow and rich it looks while the cream is coming to the top. Here come the milkmaids now. Do you observe, as they come through the side gate *en route* to the dairy, with what ease and apparently with what security they balance those large milkpails filled with milk, on their heads and without touching them with their hands? What is the secret of their ability to do this? Perfect health and strength, with long training from childhood up, running through generations, it may be from the jungles of Africa.

> "How many cows are you now milking, Aunt Abby?"
> " 'Bout twenty-five, suh."
> "What do your cows eat now?"
> "Dey's on the secon' crap of rice now, suh."

Thus with twenty-five cows to milk and those fed on the second growth of the rice field, after the crop has been harvested, you will quite understand both the quantity and quality of the milk and butter which graced the old planter's table.

The object of the proprietor of this estate was to produce, as nearly as possible, everything consumed, as well on the plantation proper, as in the turpentine orchards....Aside from the large number of beeves butchered on the estate, there were annually a large number sent to the market, while five hundred hogs every winter went to the shambles, providing the meat rations of the whole plantation. These furnished a supply of hams for the planter's table, in number so great that they went over from year to year, so that on a highday or a holiday it was not an unusual thing to have a ham on the table seven years old. The writer is entitled to an opinion on the subject of hams, and he here ventures to say that not even the Smithfield ham of Virginia nor that of Westphalia in Europe surpasses those which found their deep russet color in the green hickory and corncob smoke of the old plantation smokehouse. The flocks of sheep, both those on the plantation proper and those under the care of the white tenants in the turpentine orchards, yielded a fine supply of lambs in the spring of the year to go with the green peas of the early garden, with plenty of mutton throughout the year; while in the wool, both for home use and the markets, there was no little profit. Just here let it be observed that among those ill informed upon subjects upon which they do no little talking, and but little well informed thinking, the idea is common that there was little or no care taken in the selection of the breeds of farm animals on the Southern estates. It is true that the "razor-backed" hog was seen running at large and sometimes as wild as the country in which they were found. At the same time, on this estate and many others there were several improved breeds of swine, the Essex, the Poland China, the Jersey Reds, the Little Guinea, the Chester Whites, and that perfection of a farm animal of its kind, the Berkshire. The proprietor gave particular attention to the breeding of the Merino and Southdown sheep, while among his herds of cattle could be found as fine specimens of Durham and Devon breeds as one might care to see. This you must remember was before the introduction of the Alderney, Jersey or Guernsey from those small islands of England.

Among other products of this estate were large crops of the black-eyed pea, that Southern substitute for clover and with this advantage to the pea, in that it was both grain and forage; some eighty or a hundred bags of cotton, with rice, tobacco and sorghum for home use. One can quite understand that when all the crops of this estate had been carefully harvested and the hog-killing or butchering season was over, with the era of "hog and hominy" fairly ushered in, there was a reign of such an abundance of good things as demanded with full warrant the observance of Christmas, that blessed queen of all the plantation highdays and holidays, to which justice in nowise could be done until at least a full week had been allowed for this high tide of enjoyment, in both great house and cabin, to expend its force, finding its ebb on January second, when all entered on the duties of the new year.

... On the plantation in the old South no sooner was the harvest well over than slow yet methodical preparation for Christmas was entered upon. The fruits of the earth gathered in, the large stores of animal food well looked after, the planter bent his energy to the fattening of his bullocks and hogs. The butchering season, or the hog killing time, was a joyous event to the servants on the estate. On this plantation it was no child's play to provide the meat rations for so many servants, and there were no vegetarians among them. The truth is, among men the rule seems to be that the lower the form of civilization the more meat consumed. Be this as it may, about the twentieth of November the hogs and bullocks were as fat as they could roll, and "de hog killin'" began. The salt employed in curing the meat in those days was the large grain Turk's Island article which was well pounded or ground by being beaten in long wooden troughs with heavy wooden pestles. This to the young servants was a great frolic, and one could always tell when the neighbors were butchering by the noise of the salt pestles which could be heard for miles on a clear, cold morning. In order that there should be no loss or waste, and that plenty of time should be allowed for consuming the "chines and the chitterlings," the hogs were not all butchered at once, but with an interval of ten days or two weeks between each killing. In this way the sausage, so deliciously seasoned with pot herbs, the juicy tenderloins, the tempting spareribs, the delicious sweetbreads, and perhaps the most delicate of all, the brains of the animals—in fine, everything coming to the old planter's table at this season of the year—made up a breakfast good enough for a king. The young servants were careful to save every bladder from the several hundred hogs, which they blew up with their own hot breath, introduced through a joint of reed inserted in the neck, and which after being securely tied with bits of cotton string, were hung up over the fireplaces in their cabins. They thus supplied themselves abundantly with Christmas guns, exploding them in place of the modern firecracker, during this high festival.

Discussion questions

1. What kinds of food were available to Avirett's family, according to this description, and where did they come from?
2. What do these memories tell us about food and seasonality?
3. Note the publication date of this book. How might the hindsight of the post-Civil War perspective alter white and black recollections of food and farming in the antebellum period? What might time and distance change memories of master-slave relationships during slavery? Would white southerners have painted the institution in a more or less positive light? How do you think these ideas effected these discussions of food?
4. What exactly are the "Christmas guns" described in the final passage? What do they tell us about slave life? What do they tell us about hogs?

Document 3.6: Excerpts from William H. Robinson, *From Log Cabin to the Pulpit, or Fifteen Years in Slavery* (1913)

William Robinson was born a slave in Wilmington, North Carolina in 1848. He fled from his master several times, but as this excerpt from his memoir, published when he was 65 years old, details escaped slaves could live on the run for months at a time. Here he details an escape brought on when his mother, the house cook, made biscuits that their owner deemed poor tasting.

One morning a few days later, [my master] found fault with the biscuits and asked me what was the matter with them. I told him I didn't know. He then jumped up from the table and called mother. We, from the least to the largest, were taught when called by our mistress, or master to answer and go toward that voice. So mother was coming to him and he met her on the porch, between the kitchen and the dining room. He asked mother why she was crying—I had told her about his throwing the water in my face—and before she could answer him he knocked her from the porch to the ground. This was more than I could endure. An ax handle was on the opposite side from which mother fell. He stood over her, cursing and kicking her, and I knocked him down with the ax handle.

I knew my only hope of escape was to run away, so I started at once....I went to the three mile farm, arriving there about the time they were going to dinner. I went to an old mother...[and] I told her what I had done. She gave me a chunk of fat meat and half of a corn dodger and directed me the way to a hiding place....Quite late that night I got opposite the hiding place....There was no boat around and I was afraid to go into the water, but the same impulse that drove me into the cane brake caused me to go into the water. With a long reed for a staff I waded into the water until I heard the voice of a man, in the real coarse negro dialect, "who is dat?"... I finally succeeded in convincing him that I was not a spy but an actual runaway. Then he allowed me to advance, and as I sat on the top of the rocky mound with him he prayed long and earnestly for the time to come when God would raise up a deliverer to lead us in some way out of bondage....In a few minutes I looked across the field and saw two men coming with poles on their backs, and I got excited again, and called his attention to the fact. He assured me that they were men who had been off seeking food. They were stealing.

Our people in those days were naturally good hunters, but never shot anything larger than a coon nor smaller than a chicken, always good on the wing with the latter. They threw their game down. It consisted of some fat hens and meat they had returned to their homes and secured.

There was always an understanding between the slaves, that if one ran away they would put something to eat at a certain place; also a mowing scythe, with the crooked handle replaced with a straight stick with which to fight the bloodhounds.

The cook came out, made a hot fire of hickory bark, thoroughly wet the chickens and wrapped them in cabbage leaves and put them in the bed of ashes; then he proceeded to make his bread by mixing the corn meal in an old wooden tray and forming it into dodgers, rolling them in cabbage leaves and baking in the ashes. These are known as ash cakes, the most nutritious bread ever eaten. Of course the chickens retained all their nutriment because the intestines had not been taken out of them. But now he returned to them and catching them by both feet he stripped the skin and feathers off, then took the intestines out and put red pepper and salt in them and then returned them to the oven to brown. Parched some corn meal for coffee. Breakfast being ready, the guests came from the sleeping place, fifteen in number, the two huntsmen made seventeen, the old man and myself making nineteen in all, all runaways.

Discussion questions

1. Why did the runaways kill only animals in size between a chicken and raccoon?
2. How did they procure the meat that they brought back to the runaway's camp?
3. Why does Robinson note that the intestines were not taken out of the chickens?
4. What do you think it means to "parch some corn meal for coffee"?

Document 3.7: Excerpts from Allen Parker, *Recollections of Slavery Times* (1895)

Little is known about Allen Parker beyond what he wrote in this book, published 30 years after the end of the slavery. Born around 1835, he lived as a slave in Chowan County, North Carolina. Like many former slaves who wrote following emancipation about their experiences in bondage, Parker goes into great detail to describe how and what slaves ate. For Parker, food was not only something doled out at the master's command.

Men and women who were not married lived in the common quarters as I have said, but the men and women lived in separate cabins. On some plantations each slave had to do his or her own cooking, but on the others there was a cookhouse called the kitchen where not only the food for the master's family was cooked, but also the food of such slaves as did not live in families.

The kitchen was generally under the control of female slaves who did the cooking with the help of one or two more slaves and perhaps a boy to run errands. The woman in charge would most likely be called Aunt Dina, or Aunt somebody else, and was quite a personage upon the plantation, as she not only did the cooking but also looked out for the laundry work, and had the general charge of such of the slave children as did not live with their mothers, in separate cabins.

These children did not have any regular allowances but went to the kitchen for their meals.

The food being most commonly thick sour milk and hoe cake.

The milk would be poured into a trough something like a pig's trough. Then each child would be given a piece of hoe cake and an iron spoon and allowed to go to the trough and eat as much as they wanted.

Meat was sometimes given them, but not very often, and then it was only what would be called waste in most families. Good masters sometimes gave the children meat, generally pork, three times in a week.

Fat pork was thought to improve the looks of the children, by giving the skin an oily look.

Sometimes when the master had company, he would have the children all sent up to the mansion house so that he might show them off.

When this was to be done he would send word to Aunt Dina to have the children washed and put into clean shirts. When this was done Aunt Dina would take each child separately and grease its mouth so that the child would look as if they had been eating meat.

When they were all fixed according to Aunt Dina's idea of smartness they would be sent to the house, and told to stand in a row before the master, who would point to them with about the same kind of pride that he would have in showing a flock of good sheep, or a lot of good hogs...

COON HUNTING.

Although the slave's life was very far from being pleasant it was not without its pleasures and enjoyments, for our masters were willing we should enjoy ourselves after they had got all the work they thought they could out of us.

One of the diversions we had was coon hunting.

The coon is an animal a little larger than a large house cat, His fur is gray mixed with bluish white and brown. His full name is raccoon, but as the colored people of the south were pretty well acquainted with him they generally called him "Coon."...

Two or three men or boys generally go together on a coon hunt, taking with them one or more dogs who are trained for this purpose, and are known as coon dogs...As soon as the dogs got upon the track of the coon they set up a peculiar cry well known to the hunters, who then follow on as fast as they can....As soon as the dogs come up to him a fight ensues, in which the dogs always are the victors. In a few minutes the coon is dead, and the sport is over for the night.

The game is carried home dressed, the skin being carefully saved and dried in the sun, while the coon himself furnishes a good meal or two to his captors and their friends.

There is another animal known as the opossum, called by the colored people 'possum. This animal is also used as food, and is hunted in about the same manner as the coon....When the opossum is killed his skin is not taken off, but he is put into a kettle of hot water and scalded till the hair comes off, as do the butchers of the hog, where he is treated in like manner. The opossum is generally cooked by being roasted in his skin, and when served with roasted sweet potatoes makes a fine dish that is much admired by the colored people.

The slaves believed that the wild game was intended for them, for while the master was enjoying his roast beef or lamb, he did not think that his slaves needed anything of the sort, but he had no objection to the slaves' having anything they could get to eat, provided they got it without any expense to their master.

Black bears were to be found in the woods, and though bear meat was considered good eating, the slaves gave the bears a very wide berth, for in order to hunt him a gun was needed, and the slaves were not allowed to have any such weapons.

Once in a while wild turkeys would be caught in the woods. Panthers, wild cats, and foxes were somewhat common, but these were not meddled with by the slaves. There were several kinds of poisonous snakes in the woods and swamps, but it was not often that the slaves were bitten by them.

Discussion questions

1. Parker discusses the aesthetic effects of a good diet on slave children. Why was it important to slaveholders that slave children appeared to have been eating meat when it was not actually important to them that they ate meat?
2. How would the post-emancipation life of a slave like Parker affect his memories of eating at a trough, or hunting for food?
3. Parker opens his hunting section by saying that this was a form of fun that was allowed by the owner. How was it more than recreation?
4. What do you think Parker means when he writes that slaves thought "wild game was intended for them"? What does that say about other kinds of food or other animals? What kind of long-term effect might this have on poeple's understanding of nature as they experience freedom?

Chapter 4   Agriculture and Food in the Age of Reform

Document 4.1: Advice on Farm Management, from *The New England Farmer and Horticultural Journal* (1828)

The following articles are from a single issue of a farm newspaper from September 1828. The paper was produced by an agricultural society in Massachusetts. As you will read, the editors were mainly concerned about improving the efficiency and profitability of New England farms, but to do that meant to change not only methods of food production, but also storage, transportation, and consumption. Many of the articles were culled from other papers, both in the United States and abroad, and from other circulars and bulletins published from other societies.

FARMER'S GARDENS

A garden, under a proper system, is the most valuable acquisition to a farmer, with a view both to comfort and economy. Many culinary articles may be obtained from a well cultivated and sheltered garden, which cannot be raised in the field, or will not grow in exposed situations, with equal luxuriance and perfection. Attention, likewise, should be paid to the selling of different articles and various seasons, by which an earlier and a more equal, as well as more regular supply for the table, may be obtained. It is also of use to employ a piece of ground in a garden, for raising cabbages,

Food and Eating in America: A Documentary Reader, First Edition.
Edited by James C. Giesen and Bryant Simon.
© 2018 John Wiley & Sons, Inc. Published 2018 by John Wiley & Sons, Inc.

Swedish turnips, and other plants to be afterwards transplanted into the fields. The refuse of the garden may be given with advantage to pigs and cows. At the same time working in the garden should always be considered as of inferior consideration to the business of the farm; and on no account ought the farmer's attention to be materially drawn off from his crops of grain and grass.

BANKING UP HOUSES

The best mode of banking up houses, so as to keep frost from cellars, and render the lower rooms warmer that they would be otherwise, is to set single boards on edge, parallel with, and about a foot and a half from the sills or sleepers of the house....Fill in a layer of dirt between the boards and sills, and over that place a layer of straw or other litter...The straw of litter will effectually prevent the frost from penetrating your cellar to spoil your vegetables. Next to a smoky house, and a scolding wife, a freezing cellar is earnestly to be deprecated, and if possible, avoided.

TO PURIFY RANCID BUTTER

Melt it with a slow fire, and a well glazed earthen vessel, to which put soft water, working them well together, and when it is cold, take away the curd and the whey at the bottom; do it a second and a third time in rose water, always working then well together. The butter thus clarified will be of the sweetest delicious taste. The preceding recipe (taken, we believe, originally from an English paper,) is of some consequence if correct. Try and let us know how it succeeds.

BLACKSTONE CANAL

We learn that the canal is now rendered navigable to Oxbridge in this county, and that it is expected, unless delayed by unfavorable weather, that the whole work will be so far completed by the first week of October next, that boats may pass...

Discussion questions

1. What can we tell about the readers of *The New England Farmer* from the breadth of subjects of these articles? What can we tell about the publishers of the newspaper?
2. What does the garden article tell us about food production? Who was to eat the produce of the garden?

3. Note the mention of the selling of goods from the garden. What does this tell us about markets for vegetables? Who would be buying these? How would the farmer get these goods to market?
4. Why was a canal being built a newsworthy item for a farmer in rural Massachusetts? What does it tell us about food and mobility in the nineteenth century? Can we speculate as to how the diet of residents in Boston might change as the result of this and other canals?
5. The joke at the end of the "banking up" selection offers an interesting window into gender expectations around farmhouses, and it implies something about the paper's readers. Given the advice offered in all of these pieces, what can we determine about where the dividing line was between food production, storage, and preparation in terms of gender?

Document 4.2: Selections from Medicus, *The Oracle of Health and Long Life Containing Plain and Practical Instructions for the Preservation of Sound Health...*(1837)

Though published in London, this book, written by a medical doctor using the pseudonym Medicus, was certainly read and considered by many Americans. Its popularity came from its purported expertise; the public's interest in science in general and medicine in particular was gaining throughout the first half of the nineteenth century.

INTRODUCTION

Though a certain period of existence is, by the laws of Nature, prescribed to the life of man, yet daily experience proves, that that period may be either shortened or prolonged in a considerable degree, according as the truths relating to health and disease, and the principles of life and death, or understood and called into action. This knowledge, it has been well said, "should form an important part of general education; for no axiom is of more indisputable authority than this—that ignorance abridges life, and knowledge extends its duration."... The rules for the attainment and the preservation of health, include also the science or the knowledge of the means of extending life to the longest period allowed to mortals...Health and long life will be the reward of those who will be at the pains to obtain the knowledge of the causes upon which both depends...Notwithstanding all the high sounding pretensions of "the progressive knowledge of the age," and "the rapid March of intellect," it is not yet generally known, that a short life is not being an inevitable consequence of a weak constitution; for delicate and nervous people afford daily examples, that by minute and unremitting attention to food, regimen, exercise, etc. they have an equal chance of long life with those gifted with the best and strongest constitutions.

A knowledge of the proper kinds of food for the support of the human body in the best health, should, if possible, be acquired by every human being, since individual health is necessarily an important object, and without which every other earthly good soon ceases to be a blessing. Errors in diet, it has been sententiously and truly said, are the great source of disease...

It is not eating, but digestion, that gives strength and nutriment to the body, and repairs its daily losses. Neither does the quantity of nourishment depends on the quantity of food; for superfluous food becomes excrement instead of elements; and if it be not speedily evacuated, oppresses the system, and occasions disease.

1. The Number and Periods of Meals.
    Regularity and the number of meals, and the periods at which they are taken, as of the first important; on it much of the equable and pleasant enjoyment of health depends...in general, three frugal meals in the course of the day seem the most desirable, and the best adapted to the wants and Constitution of the human frame, while at the same time they are the best suited to the digestive organs.

2. The Periods and Intervals of Meals.
    The periods at which meals should be taken, and the intervals that should elapse between them, deserve attention. The practice which leaves the great bulk of the day without a meal, and then crowds two or three together, is manifestly bad, as it leaves the body in the state of exhaustion and fatigue, which strongly tend to enfeeble the powers of digestion. To confirm and preserve health, whatever maybe the number of meals taken, they should be taken at regular times and stated periods; and they should be regulated by the strength or debility of the stomach, any quantity and quality of the food taken, or to be taken, at the preceding or following meal....

3. The Proportional Quantity of Animal and Vegetable Food.
    Such diversity of opinion has subsisted among physiologists, respecting the proportional quantity of animal and vegetable matter necessary to the healthful sustenation of the human frame....It may be broadly said, that the best and the only sure guide in obtaining the desired knowledge of the subject, must be the circumstances of climate, season of the year,

exercise, previous habits, age, and individual peculiarity of constitution. In hot climates, a vegetable diet may be carried to a great extent without injury; while in cold climates, an almost entire subsistence on animal food will not produce any very pernicious effects; as from the want of heat, a greater stimulus is required for the system, and also from the smaller degree of perspiration, and a little tendency to putrefaction which the fluids discover in such climates...

4. The Quantity of Food to be taken at Meals.
    ... The appetite and the feelings are generally the best indicators of the necessary quantity of food which we require; and the safest guide to depend on in this respect, is the particular state of health of the individual, and the bodily exhaustion or repletion do which is subject to the time of each repast. Let him partake of those things which he finds best agree with his feelings, and which do not during his general health, and as soon as he feels himself satisfied and refreshed, desist, for nature has established that sympathy between the taste in the stomach, that what disagrees with the one is seldom agreeable to the other. Besides, the more food is relished, the better it is masticated, and the gastric juice attacks it at a great number of points, and dissolves it more speedily and effectually, which is the source of all the digestion and nourishment. But in consulting your appetite, never be induced to partake of more than one kind of food, for a variety of dishes creates an artificial appetite, inducing want to eat more than is necessary; and as variety of food does not harmonize in the stomach, but requires different exertions of its muscular powers, it is not digested at the same time, and a greater labor is imposed on it then it possibly may be capable of bearing with impunity.

Discussion questions

1. How does the author use his medical training to bolster his authority in doling out this advice?
2. What factors other than food determine physical health, according to Medicus?
3. How different from modern day advice are the author's four points of eating advice?
4. For a document that gives advice on eating, there's very little here about actual food. Why might that be?

Document 4.3: Selections from Lydia Maria Child, *The American Frugal Housewife* (1829)

Lydia Maria Childs was a popular writer of fiction and advice books in the first half of the nineteenth century. The book was so popular with American female readers that it was reprinted 33 times in 25 years.

The true economy of housekeeping is simply the art of gathering up all the fragments, so that nothing be lost. I mean fragments of time, as well as materials. Nothing should be thrown away so long as it is possible to make any use of it, however trifling that use may be; and whatever be the size of a family, every member should be employed either in earning or saving money.

Look frequently to the pails, to see that nothing is thrown to the pigs which should have been in the grease-pot. Look to the grease-pot, and see that nothing is there which might have served to nourish your own family, or a poorer one.

See that the beef and pork are always under brine; and that the brine is sweet and clean.

See that the vegetables are neither sprouting nor decaying: if they are so, remove them to a drier place, and spread them.

Examine preserves, to see that they are not contracting mould; and your pickles, to see that they are not growing soft and tasteless.

As far as it is possible, have bits of bread eaten up before they become hard. Spread those that are not eaten, and let them dry, to be pounded for puddings, or soaked for brewis. Brewis is made of crusts and dry pieces of bread, soaked a good while in hot milk, mashed up, and salted, and buttered like toast. Above all, do not let crusts accumulate in such quantities that they cannot be used.

With proper care, there is no need of losing a particle of bread, even in the hottest weather.

Make your own bread and cake. Some people think it is just as cheap to buy of the baker and confectioner; but it is not half as cheap. True, it is more convenient; and therefore the rich are justifiable in employing them; but those who are under the necessity of being economical, should make convenience a secondary object. In the first place, confectioners make their cake richer than people of moderate income can afford to make it; in the next place, your domestic, or yourself, may just as well employ your own time, as to pay them for theirs.

Eggs will keep almost any length of time in lime-water properly prepared. One pint of coarse salt, and one pint of unslacked lime, to a pailful of water.

If there be too much lime, it will eat the shells from the eggs; and if there be a single egg cracked, it will spoil the whole. They should be covered with lime-water, and kept in a cold place. The yolk becomes slightly red; but I have seen eggs, thus kept, perfectly sweet and fresh at the end of three years. The cheapest time to lay down eggs, is early in spring, and the middle and last of September. It is bad economy to buy eggs by the dozen, as you want them.

If you have a greater quantity of cheeses in the house than is likely to be soon used, cover them carefully with paper, fastened on with flour paste, so as to exclude the air. In this way they may be kept free from insects for years. They should be kept in a dry, cool place.

If it be practicable, get a friend in the country to procure you a quantity of lard, butter, and eggs, at the time they are cheapest, to be put down for winter use. You will be likely to get them cheaper and better than in the city market; but by all means put down your winter's stock. Lard requires no other care than to be kept in a dry, cool place. Butter is sweetest in September and June; because food is then plenty, and not rendered bitter by frost. Pack your butter in a clean, scalded firkin, cover it with strong brine, and spread a cloth all over the top, and it will keep good until the Jews get into Grand Isle. If you happen to have a bit of salt-petre, dissolve it with the brine. Dairy-women say that butter comes more easily, and has a peculiar hardness and sweetness, if the cream is scalded and strained before it is used. The cream should stand down cellar over night, after being scalded, that it may get perfectly cold.

Suet and lard keep better in tin than in earthen. Suet keeps good all the year round, if chopped and packed down in a stone jar, covered with molasses. Pick suet free from veins and skin, melt it in water before a moderate fire, let it cool till it forms into a hard cake, then wipe it dry, and put it in clean paper in linen bags.

Have all the good bits of vegetables and meat collected after dinner, and minced before they are set away; that they may be in readiness to make a little savoury mince meat for supper or breakfast. Take the skins off your potatoes before they grow cold.

If you live in the city, where it is always easy to procure provisions, be careful and not buy too much for your daily wants, while the weather is warm.

Have a bottle full of brandy, with as large a mouth as any bottle you have, into which cut your lemon and orange peel when they are fresh and sweet. This brandy gives a delicious flavor to all sorts of pies, puddings, and cakes. Lemon is the pleasantest spice of the two; therefore they should be kept in separate bottles. It is a good plan to preserve rose-leaves in brandy.

The flavor is pleasanter than rose-water; and there are few people who have the utensils for distilling. Peach leaves steeped in brandy make excellent spice for custards and puddings.

It is thought to be a preventive to the unhealthy influence of cucumbers to cut the slices very thin, and drop each one into cold water as you cut it. A few minutes in the water takes out a large portion of the slimy matter, so injurious to health. They should be eaten with high seasoning.

Discussion questions

1. Based on the advice above, for whom is this book written? What all can we determine about the typical reader? What does this say about class, geography, education, and gender in the period?
2. We learn a lot from this document about what one defined as "frugal" in the 1800s. Is there anything here that seems extravagant? What social groups can be frugal?
3. What does this advice suggest about rural versus urban living? What does it suggest about seasonality?
4. Use this as a chance to think forward in time. What would American housewives be doing differently or the same 50 and 100 years later? What advice still applies today?

Document 4.4: Excerpts from Sylvester Graham, "A Defence of the Graham System of Living" (1837)

Graham is perhaps best known today as the inventor of the Graham cracker, but in the early nineteenth century he was a well known and influential social reformer who preached temperance and moderation. Graham was fundamentally conservative in the sense that he believed the bustling, high-paced world of the 1800s was bad for one's health. He bemoaned how "luxury reigns triumphant." He therefore preached restraint from consuming alcohol, tea, coffee, or meat, as well as sexual activity. He offered the book quoted below as an antidote against sensuality, "the prevailing vice of the age." But it is a mistake to understand Graham's intentions—and his great number of followers—as cynical or ill-informed. He believed his recommendations were based in the latest science of the human body. Much of this book is a description of the body, sometimes with long quotations from medical books about the skeletal system, the muscles, and nervous system. Indeed, Graham's diet recommendations were based on what he understood—and what we can say for the time was a very accurate—physiological understanding of the human body. To bolster his recommendations on diet, medicine, and fitness, the book begins with several testimonies of medical doctors, like those in the Portland

Medical Association, who claimed that, if readers followed Graham's advice, a
"physician's services [would be] rarely needed."

EFFECTS OF LUXURY

When Luxury, soft enervating Luxury, had once gained admission among the societies of men, she waved her vampyre wing, and killed her victims into a fatal security, while she employed herself in the accomplishment of their destruction....

When we revert to the primitive ages, we find a hardy race, blessed with an almost incredible length of years, compared with those of modern longevity—a race of beings unused to superfluities who asked no other food than nature presented, and quenched not their thirst with a beverage prepared by art. How sadly changed ! now we are *born* diseased; the very air that first expands our lungs is loaded with corruption; the unnatural nourishment of our earliest periods proves often a prolific source of suffering; swathed in bandages, and oppressed with clothing, our bodies become enfeebled and deformed; and, as we advance in years, irrational restraint subdues our physical strength, and more irrational education the energies of our minds; new luxuries are sought after; the appetite begins to fail and those miserable palliatives, foreign spices and stimulating food, through ignorance of their ultimate effects, are employed as restoratives. These excite unnatural thirst; inebriating drinks succeed, and when intoxication supervenes, our powerless limbs are laid upon a couch of down, where broken slumber, horrid dreams, or nightmare's close embrace, conspire to rob us of repose. Day after day we madly persevere in our destructive course, while languor, restlessness, and irritability, with a long train of nervous diseases, characterize our condition, through years of suffering and of pain, until the almost welcome moment of our dissolution arrives.

Whatever we may once have been, at a period more or less remote, it is certain, that as a nation, luxury has now destroyed our health, perverted our morals, debased our intellects, and, in its prevalence and increase, the philosopher may foresee the downfall of a people, once famed for their intelligence, their virtue, and their freedom....

OF ALIMENT

All food is either of animal or vegetable origin, the different varieties of which may be arranged as follows:

1. *Animal food,* such as the flesh of quadrupeds, of birds, and fishes; sometimes the *germs* of animals, as eggs; and the *animal secretion* called milk, subsequently converted into butter and cheese.

2. *The germs or seeds of vegetables*, such as wheat, rye, barley, oats, beans, peas, chesnuts, walnuts, &c.

3. *The seed-vessels of vegetables*, such as apples, pears, peaches, grapes, strawberries, blackberries, &c.

4. *The roots of vegetables*, such as potatoes, parsnips, beets, carrots, turnips, radishes, &c.

5. *The leaves of vegetables*, such as cabbage, lettuce, spinnage, &c.

6. *Infusions*, of animal and vegetable substances, as soup; of vegetable substances, as tea, coffee, &c.

7. *Fermented liquors*, such as the various descriptions of wine, ale, beer, porter, cider, &c.

8. *Distilled liquors*, as brandy, gin, and spirits.

9. *Water*.

10. *Narcotic substances*, as tobacco and opium.

11. *Condiments*, as pepper, mustard, &c.

By studying the habits of man, with regard to diet, we are unable to arrive at any definite knowledge of the natural food of his species. His present mode of living is altogether artificial. Dr. Paris says, that "there is scarcely a vegetable which we at present employ, that can be found growing naturally. Buffon states that our wheat is a factitious production, raised to its present condition by the art of agriculture. Rye, barley, and even oats, are not to be found wild ; that is to say growing naturally in any part of the earth, but have been altered, by the industry of mankind, from plants not now resembling them even in such a degree as to enable us to recognize their relations. The acrid and disagreeable *apium graveolens* has been thus transformed into delicious celery; and the colewort, a plant of scanty leaves, not weighing altogether half an ounce, has been improved into cabbage, whose leaves alone weigh many pounds, or into a cauliflower of considerable dimensions, being only the embryo of a few buds, which, in their natural state, would not weigh many grains. The potato, again, derives its origin from a small and bitter root, which grows wild in Chili, and at Monte Video. If there be any who feel skeptical on the subject of such metamorphoses, let him visit the fairy bowers of horticulture, and he will there perceive that her magic wand has not only converted the tough, coriaceous covering of the almond into the soft and melting flesh of the peach, but that, by her spells, the sour sloe has ripened into the delicious plum, and the austere crab of our woods into the golden pippin; that this again has been made to sport in endless variety, emulating in beauty of form and color, in exuberance of fertility and in richness of flavor, the rarer productions of warmer regions and more propitious climates."

Cultivation alters the whole aspect of nature. Plants, in a wild state, when removed and cultivated in our gardens, become what naturalists call monsters....Our domestic animals are also unlike the wild ones of the same species. The deviation has become at last so great, that the original stock from which the animals descended is doubtful. In the hog, the sheep, the cow, and the dog, we can no longer recognize the form and color of the wild ones from which they are descended....Since both vegetables and animals are altered by cultivation, it is scarcely possible to decide upon the natural food of man, except by comparing his structure with that of wild animals. That he was not intended to subsist on animal food, we infer from his organization; the form of his teeth, and the structure of his alimentary canal, clearly indicate that he is not adapted to the devouring of flesh.

... A general objection to abstinence from animal food arises from the fear expressed, that animals would increase too rapidly; but we know that in India the law forbids the destruction of animal life, yet neither the ox nor the sheep increase in such a ratio as to excite alarm. Horses, which are not destroyed either in Europe or in America, are not likely to become so numerous as to overrun those countries.

The ground employed to fatten and nourish animals sufficient for the consumption of one family, would, if properly cultivated, yield enough to support five families; and hence, if population should ever increase to the extent that has been apprehended, the rearing of animals would be a serious evil.

Animal food is a powerful stimulus to the whole system; it increases the circulation, excites a temporary fever, and facilitates perspiration. The constant repetition of such unnatural stimuli, at length wears out the system, and those who have been much addicted to their use, either die prematurely, or linger through a miserable existence, afflicted with the most distressing chronic disorders.

The effects of animal food on the moral character is one of the most deplorable evils arising from its use. It communicates to some minds a coarseness and ferocity of disposition, and renders the temper irritable and petulent; the passion of anger is either induced or strengthened by its use. We all know that those animals which feed on flesh, are savage, cruel, and ferocious; on the contrary, those which feed on vegetables are mild and inoffensive. What a contrast between the tiger, renowned for his cruel, savage, and treacherous disposition, and the inoffensive lamb, which we have adopted as the emblem of innocence! So universal was this belief among the ancients, that they have ascribed the origin of wars to the destruction of animal life. Indeed, if a people religiously abhorred the idea of shedding the blood of an innocent animal, can we believe that their voices would ever rise in shouts of exultation over the smoking ruins of a city, whose streets were deluged by the blood of its inhabitants? Thousands who now use animal food, would abandon it for ever, if they were obliged to slaughter the innocent victims themselves; and even when they are slaughtered, every process and art of cookery, and the addition of stimulating spices, must be employed, to overcome the disgust which naturally arises from the idea of devouring the dead flesh of animals.

... Reason and experience emphatically exclaim, "eat no animal food;" but if it is used at all, let it be eaten as seldom as possible, avoiding high-seasoned meat, and abstaining from animal food during the warm months of summer. Dinner is the only meal at which it is at all admissible to eat flesh. Not more than one kind, however, at a meal, should be indulged in, and that either roasted, broiled, or boiled—boiling is the most proper method, rendering the meat less stimulating, although depriving it of a portion of its nutritive properties; but frying, a very common mode of cooking, is highly censurable.... Meat should never be served with made gravies, nor with seasonings of any kind, unless it be a very small quantity of salt. The flesh of young animals, such as veal, lamb, and young pork, should not be eaten. As a general rule, all substances, whether fruits, vegetables, or animals, are not so wholesome nor so digestible when young, as after they have arrived at maturity.

Beef is the most wholesome, and the most nourishing kind of animal food; it should be but slightly cooked. Mutton is the most digestible of all flesh-meat, and is highly nutritious. Next to beef, it deserves a preference. The fat, however, should be avoided; it is more difficult of digestion than that of any other animal. Pork is the most indigestible of animal aliments... All species of game, as venison, rabbits, and hares, are very heating or stimulating, and not so well adapted to the stomach as the flesh of domestic animals.... Poultry is preferable to many kinds of animal food....Fish are less nutritious than flesh, although not so stimulating. From their strong tendency to putrefaction, it is not safe to use them, except in moderate quantities....All shellfish should be avoided; they are extremely indigestible, particularly crabs and lobsters. Eggs also contain much nutriment in a small space, a great objection, as will be shown hereafter, to any kind of food: when they are boiled hard, they are almost as indigestible as bullets.

Those who choose to eat animal food may make a judicious selection, from the various kinds, with considerable advantage to their bodily health. But, once more, I repeat my advice, and sincerely, too—eat no animal food, whether it be fish, flesh, or fowl.

Discussion questions

1. Graham begins with an indictment of luxury. What does he mean by this term and how does it relate to food and diet?
2. One of the core ideas in the selection above is that food is not what it used to be. How does Graham explain the idea of altered food? What is his larger point when he says that crops grown by American farmers are

not found in nature? How is science wading into understandings of food? Is the line between "natural" and "unnatural" food moving? Is he suggesting that unnatural things were not food at all?

3. How is Graham's menu of diet recommendations an antidote against sensuality itself?

4. Why might his moral message about vegetarianism have reached a wide audience in this time period?

Document 4.5: The Mormon "Word of Wisdom" (1833)

In 1833 in Kirtland, Ohio, Mormon leader Joseph Smith received a "revelation from God" detailing what Church of Latter Day Saints members (known as Mormons) could eat, drink, and smoke. The revelation came several weeks after Smith had begun a training school for recent converts. The school met above a store in a small room where, each day, the men present would light pipes, filling the room with smoke, then begin spitting tobacco juice on the floor. Smith's wife Emma complained to him that it was difficult to keep the floors of the room clean. Several weeks later Smith received his revelation. As you will read, it did not stop at tobacco. The "Word" also bans consumption of "hot drinks," which was to mean specifically tea and coffee.

---

1. A Word of Wisdom, for the benefit of the council of high priests, assembled in Kirtland, and the church, and also the saints in Zion—

2. To be sent greeting; not by commandment or constraint, but by revelation and the word of wisdom, showing forth the order and will of God in the temporal salvation of all saints in the last days—

3. Given for a principle with promise, adapted to the capacity of the weak and the weakest of all saints, who are or can be called saints.

4. Behold, verily, thus saith the Lord unto you: In consequence of evils and designs which do and will exist in the hearts of conspiring men in the last days, I have warned you, and forewarn you, by giving unto you this word of wisdom by revelation—

5. That inasmuch as any man drinketh wine or strong drink among you, behold it is not good, neither meet in the sight of your Father, only in assembling yourselves together to offer up your sacraments before him.

6. And, behold, this should be wine, yea, pure wine of the grape of the vine, of your own make.

7. And, again, strong drinks are not for the belly, but for the washing of your bodies.

8. And again, tobacco is not for the body, neither for the belly, and is not good for man, but is an herb for bruises and all sick cattle, to be used with judgment and skill.

9. And again, hot drinks are not for the body or belly.
10. And again, verily I say unto you, all wholesome herbs God hath ordained for the constitution, nature, and use of man—
11. Every herb in the season thereof, and every fruit in the season thereof; all these to be used with prudence and thanksgiving.
12. Yea, flesh also of beasts and of the fowls of the air, I, the Lord, have ordained for the use of man with thanksgiving; nevertheless they are to be used sparingly;
13. And it is pleasing unto me that they should not be used, only in times of winter, or of cold, or famine.
14. All grain is ordained for the use of man and of beasts, to be the staff of life, not only for man but for the beasts of the field, and the fowls of heaven, and all wild animals that run or creep on the earth;
15. And these hath God made for the use of man only in times of famine and excess of hunger.
16. All grain is good for the food of man; as also the fruit of the vine; that which yieldeth fruit, whether in the ground or above the ground—
17. Nevertheless, wheat for man, and corn for the ox, and oats for the horse, and rye for the fowls and for swine, and for all beasts of the field, and barley for all useful animals, and for mild drinks, as also other grain.
18. And all saints who remember to keep and do these sayings, walking in obedience to the commandments, shall receive health in their navel and marrow to their bones;
19. And shall find wisdom and great treasures of knowledge, even hidden treasures;
20. And shall run and not be weary, and shall walk and not faint.
21. And I, the Lord, give unto them a promise, that the destroying angel shall pass by them, as the children of Israel, and not slay them. Amen.

Discussion questions

1. What is the rationale that drinking alcohol is bad? Compare this to that given by Graham and others in this chapter.
2. Think about the implications not just for consumption of food and drink outlined here, but for production and economics. How did this rule effect what Mormons could do other than in terms of eating and drinking?
3. Why the exception for wine that people have made for themselves?
4 How do these rules about food and alcohol also touch on ideas about cleanliness and health?

Document 4.6: Political Cartoon: "A Member of the Temperance Society" (c. 1833)

Little is known about the origins of the following cartoon, housed today in the American Antiquarian Society collection, except that it was produced during the 1830s when the first great temperance movement was underway in the United States. The movement was aimed at curbing consumption of alcoholic beverages.

Discussion questions

1. The literal message of the cartoonist is that this man is not exercising temperance—there is a bottle of wine on the table and others on the cart next to him—but also that he is not showing restraint where food is concerned. Explain how the artist sees this connection.
2. What does the artist imply with the man's body, dress, and posture? Any guesses as to what the cord hanging down near his head was for? What is the author's point by drawing that as part of the scene?
3. Look carefully at the food in the image. What does the cartoonist imply not just by the amount, but by the type?

Document 4.7: Family Dietary Advice from William Andrus Alcott, *The Young Wife* (1837)

Alcott was a medical doctor, teacher, and reformer who wrote more than 100 books during the first half of the nineteenth century. He is best known for his advice books on diet and relationships, books that sometimes linked the two things. Like Graham, he advised against intense courtship between young men and women and was a staunch advocate of vegetarianism. Alcott penned this book, The Young Wife, *as a "reference to the appropriate sphere and duties of woman in matrimonial life." To give a sense of the topics covered in the book, there are chapters titled "Submission," "Love," "Delicacy and Modesty," "Domestic Economy," "Dress," and "Moral Influence on the Husband."*

PUNCTUALITY

...Do you know how much is the value of the time of ten men, who are compelled by your tardiness to wait ten minutes each for their dinner? Here are a hundred minutes of valuable time lost to them; how much is that a month?— How much a year? I say nothing of the vexation, but only the pecuniary loss.

DOMESTIC ECONOMY

... Nor is it to be forgotten, that servants educate, in a greater or less degree, the older members of our families. It is impossible not to be influenced more or less by them, be our age or circumstances what they may. Our food, our drink, the air we breathe, the clothes we wear, depend more or less for their excellence or want of excellence, on those who prepare them for our use. How much is the human character, at any period of life, though much more in early youth, affected by the quality and condition of the food we eat, the purity or impurity of the water we drink, and the proper ventilation and cleanliness of our rooms ! So long as all these, and a thousand other things of daily occurrence, continue to modify our feelings, and ultimately to form or change our character, and so long as these matters are entrusted to the management of servants, just so long will it be true that they educate us.

... Much time is spent by housewives in mashing, chopping, and bruising food. Every kind of food should be so left by cookery as to task, to their fullest reasonable extent, the masticatory organs—the teeth. And yet, is it not correct to say that three fourths of the effort spent in what is called cookery, has a tendency to encourage the teeth in indolence, or at least a waste of time? Let us take a brief survey. Here is milk, a food comparatively wholesome, at least for children. Yet how much time is spent in making butter, cheese, porridge, custards, ice creams, &c., which, to say the least, are no better food, for children or adults, than milk.

Here is wheat. From this, instead of simple coarse bread, we make fine flour bread, cakes of every kind—some sweet, others only shortened—pie-crust, puddings, dumplings, toast, &c. instead of plain dishes from Indian meal, we torture it in various ways, and mix it with sundry other articles, and add to it butter, molasses, &c. Instead of eating the simple boiled or roasted potato, we mash it, and add butter, pepper, mustard, vinegar, sauces, gravies or horseradish, and make it into bread, pies, and soups, or mix it with turnips or fish. Even the simple rice cannot be eaten, so we think, without butter, molasses, cream, milk, sugar or honey; nor beans and peas without butter, pork, pepper or vinegar. Nay, even the apple must be changed by baking, roasting, grating, and making into pies, dumplings and birds' nests. Instead of eating simple meat, boiled, roasted or dried, it must be smoked, and covered with vinegar, pepper, mustard, horseradish, sauce or gravy, or made into pies, hash or sausages.

Then in regard to drinks, instead of simple water, we have an array of instruments and vessels, and herbs, foreign and domestic, for manufacturing, at considerable expense, tea, coffee, shells, chocolate, and so on; and we have pitchers, tumblers, and the like, for beer, cider, wine, and other more offensive mixtures. In short—for this is only a mere specimen—there are scarcely any limits to this department of human folly, nor to the waste of time which it involves, without adding one iota to the sum total—to the aggregate—of that pleasure or happiness to which man's nature is originally entitled. On the contrary, it greatly diminishes both.

Useful cookery, though a curious and important art, is not, by any means, complicated. It consists simply in preparing those substances which God has given us for food, such as the farinaceous vegetables and the fruits, in such a way as is best adapted to the most healthy condition of the human stomach and general system.

There is a great deal of female time taken up in useless, hollow morning calls, and in idle, unmeaning ceremonies. A great deal of waste is involved in dressing in a manner which is as far removed from nature's simplicity, as is our modern system of cookery. The material, as well as the fashion, not only of every kind of dress, but of all sorts of furniture, is such as to involve, first and last, a great waste of precious and invaluable time.

There is no need of all this. It is pitiable—it is wicked. Woman was never made to be thus trifled with. Her influence is too pervading and too powerful to be expended—three fourths of it at least, and probably nine tenths—in a manner which is not merely useless, but rather quite injurious. We say again, therefore, still more distinctly, that the waste of such a vast amount of female energy and time is not only bad economy, but an offence in the sight of Heaven itself.

In the language of another work, whole years, in the aggregate, of every house-keeper's life, might be saved for the benefit of her race. If the best food now known were in general use, and no other—and if cookery, whenever it could not improve it, were wholly dispensed with, more than half of the female labor now expended might be saved, to be devoted to the more glorious purpose of assisting in elevating and improving the hearts and minds of husbands, brothers, sisters and children, and the world around us. We admit, most cheerfully, that as a means of producing vigorous minds and good hearts, a due attention to food, drink, clothing, &c. is indispensable. It is nothing less than the carrying on of one department of the labor assigned to woman by the Creator—the physical education of herself and of those around her. But to see a patient and laborious female spending nearly her whole time in ministering to the mere physical wants of man, in the various stages of his existence—infancy, childhood, youth, manhood and age—and doing all this with the utmost cheerfulness, and without appearing to realize that God has given her a higher and nobler office, or at the least, without finding any time to perform its duties, is indeed most lamentable. It was observed that woman plods on in the narrow, unworthy track assigned her, with the utmost cheerfulness. She does so; and I have never been more forcibly reminded of the power of habit, than when attempts have sometimes been made to emancipate her.

Discussion questions

1. Does the idea of people as products of their environment—the water they drink and food they eat—tell us something about the tensions rising between environment and labor in the American middle class in the nineteenth century?
2. Alcott makes an interesting point about the act of eating itself when he says that "Much time is spent by housewives in mashing, chopping, and bruising food. Every kind of food should be so left by cookery as to task, to their fullest reasonable extent, the masticatory organs—the teeth." What does he mean by this? What is his reasoning for advising that cooks leave more of the food preparation to the teeth than to the kitchen counter?
3. Alcott is opposed to cooking that combines many ingredients or attempts to make the food more flavorful, though he says that cooking is a "curious and important art." Why is he opposed to preparing tastier food? Is it simply about the labor involved? The cost? What might be going on in nineteenth century culture that would prompt Alcott to look at something like rice with butter, rather than simply boiled rice on its own, as an unnecessary trifle?
4. What is the connection between food and pleasure?
5. If all American women had suddenly taken Alcott's advice, would they, as he suggests, be "emancipated"?

Chapter 5   Food on the Frontier

Document 5.1: Thomas Jefferson's Agrarian Ideal, from *Notes on the State of Virginia* (1785)

Seen most often as a document about the political effects of a rural, farm-based economy versus an urban, manufacturing-based economy, Notes on the State of Virginia *is also a wonderful document on food production in the early United States. Often overlooked is Jefferson's writing on how cash crops effect food availability in town and country. But clearly the larger message of the passages below is one about the effect of farming and farmers on a nation's morality. In many ways this document is the origin of the intoxicating and seemingly permanent ideal of romantic agrarianism in the United States. Here we read the young nation's most prominent intellectual's thoughts about how the act of farming raised the morals of those who did it, in stark contrast to the effect of factory work. Farmers—not to mention politicians and marketers— would long cling to this portrayal, which has an impact on food production and habits of eating to this day.*

QUERY XIX [Manufactures]
The present state of manufactures, commerce, interior and exterior trade?…

The political economists of Europe have established it as a principle that every state should endeavour to manufacture for itself; and this principle,

Food and Eating in America: A Documentary Reader, First Edition.
Edited by James C. Giesen and Bryant Simon.
© 2018 John Wiley & Sons, Inc. Published 2018 by John Wiley & Sons, Inc.

like many others, we transfer to America, without calculating the difference of circumstance which should often produce a difference of result. In Europe the lands are either cultivated, or locked up against the cultivator. Manufacture must therefore be resorted to of necessity not of choice, to support the surplus of their people. But we have an immensity of land courting the industry of the husbandman. Is it best then that all our citizens should be employed in its improvement, or that one half should be called off from that to exercise manufacturers and handicraft arts for the other? Those who labour in the earth are the chosen people of God, if ever he had a chosen people, whose breasts he has made his peculiar deposit for substantial and genuine virtue. It is the focus in which he keeps alive that sacred fire, which otherwise might escape from the face of the earth. Corruption of morals in the mass of cultivators is a phenomenon of which no age nor nation has furnished an example. It is the mark set on those, who not looking up to heaven, to their own soil and industry, as does the husbandman, for their subsistence, depend for it on the casualties and caprice of customers. Dependence begets subservience and venality, suffocates the germ of virtue, and prepares fit tools for the designs of ambition. This, the natural progress and consequence of the arts, has sometimes perhaps been retarded by accidental circumstances: but, generally speaking, the proportion which the aggregate of the other classes of citizens bears in any state to that of its husbandman, is the proportion of its unfound to its healthy parts, and is a good-enough barometer whereby to measure its degree of corruption. While we have a land to labour then, let us never wish to see our citizens occupied at a work-bench, or twirling a distaff....The loss by the transportation of commodities across the Atlantic will be made up in happiness and permanence of government. The mobs of great cities add just so much to the support of pure government, as sores do to the strength of the human body. It is the manners and spirit of a people which preserve a republic in vigour. A degeneracy in these is a canker which soon eats to the heart of his laws and constitution.

QUERY XX [Commercial productions]
A notice of the commercial productions particular to the state, and of those objects which the inhabitants are obliged to get from Europe and from other parts of the world?

In the year 1758 we exported 70,000 hogsheads of tobacco, which was the greatest quantity ever produced in this country in one year. But its culture was fast declining at the commencement of this war and that of wheat taking its place: and it must continue to decline on the return of peace. I suspect that the change in the temperature of our climate has become sensible to that plant, which, to be good, requires an extraordinary degree of heat. But it requires still more indispensably an uncommon fertility of soil: and the price which it commands at market will not enable the planter produce to produce this by manure. Was the supply still to depend on Virginia and Maryland alone, as its culture becomes more difficult, the price would rise, so as to enable the planter to surmount those difficulties and to live. But the western country on the Mississippi, and the midlands of Georgia, having fresh and fertile lands in abundance, and hotter sun, will be able to undersell these two states, and will oblige them to abandon the raising tobacco altogether. And a happy obligation for them it will be. It is a culture productive of infinite wretchedness. Those employed in it are in a continued state of exertion beyond the powers of nature to support. Little food of any kind is raised by them; so that the men and animals on these farms are badly fed, and the earth is rapidly impoverished. The cultivation of wheat is the reverse in every circumstance. Besides clothing the earth with herbage, and preserving its fertility, it feeds the labourers plentifully, requires from them only a moderate toil, except in the season of harvest, raises great numbers of animals for food and service, and diffuses plenty and happiness among the whole. We find it easier to make an hundred bushels of wheat than a thousand weight of tobacco, and they are worth more when made.

... it is not easy to say what are the articles either of necessity, comfort, or luxury, which we cannot raise, and which we therefore shall be under a necessity of importing from abroad, as everything hardier than the Olive, and as Hardy as the fig, maybe raised here in the open air. Sugar, coffee and tea, indeed, are not between these limits; And habit having placed them among the necessities of life with the wealthy part of our citizens, as long as these habits remain, we must go for them to those countries which are able to furnish them.

Discussion questions

1. Jefferson's "those who labour in the earth are the chosen people of God," comment has often been repeated by farmers and politicians in the two centuries since he wrote it. Given the larger context of his writings here, what exactly did he mean by this? What was he arguing against? Think about the political repercussions of his statement.
2. Much of Jefferson's arguments in both of these excerpts rely on the logic that there is a frontier to the West, beyond which lie great and fertile lands, that will constantly change the economy of states back east like

Virginia. How does the frontier shape Jefferson's arguments here? How might his logic change as the frontier disappears?

3. Farmers, Jefferson argues, are universally moral people whose work is determined by themselves and the earth, not the "casualties and caprice of customers." To what degree could this have been true for Virginia farmers? What about farmers on the frontier? How would this change as cities grew and more urbanites depended on food supplied by farmers?

4. How does tobacco growth change food habits? How does it affect social classes differently? What about for slaves versus free workers?

Document 5.2: Excerpt from Judge William Cooper, *A Guide in the Wilderness* (1810)

In many ways William Cooper's book is a response to Jefferson's Notes on the State of Virginia. Cooper was born outside of Philadelphia, but made his name and wealth as a politician, judge, storekeeper, and land speculator in New Jersey and New York. He was intent on establishing well-ordered, compact towns in the "wilderness" of New York and founded two such places. He believed strongly that these towns would only flourish if they were densely populated and built on a diversified local economy.

It is the same of Cooperstown and of all the others where industry, art, and capital are condensed; and all those originally distributed in large lots have ceased after a few years to increase, insomuch that wherever you will mention a town in which each man has his cow, his team, his wagon, and his barn, you will find it to be a place of little trade, consequently of little wealth; but wherever the artist, the merchant, or man of profession, has neither bread, butter, milk, cheese, flesh meat, nor garden-stuff, but what he purchases with the earnings of his calling, there, I engage, you will find trade, comfort, and plenty; there each living by the art in which he is versed, there will be no awkward waste of time, no slovenly or loitering habits; the baker will live by baking, the butcher by his trade, the flour merchant by buying and by selling; schools, churches, and professional merit will advance; all useful skill will increase. And however strange it has appeared to you that I should, where land is so abundant, propose to restrict the settler in the occupation of it, yet certain it is, that if they would prosper they must choose one of two things: either to have so much land as will employ all their industry and support them by its produce, or to leave its cultivation entirely to others, and betake themselves exclusively to the exercise of their trade.

You seem to be prepossessed with the idea of pleasure and advantage, in mixing rural labours with the exercise of professions, and of the mechanic arts. Such a picture of human life may gratify the imagination, but it is romantic; and both contentment and wealth lie in the road I have traced, if an extensive field of observation and many years' experience can be trusted.

Discussion questions

1. How does Cooper's vision for settlement differ from Jefferson's? Are there differences in region that make each the appropriate prescription for their respective subjects?
2. The production of food—and the question of where grain comes from and who makes it into bread—is central to Cooper's vision. If you were a potential émigré to Cooperstown, would you feel confident that there would be a stable food supply?
3. What kinds of infrastructure did frontier towns rely upon to make sure food was readily available?
4. Does the extremely limited existence of slavery in New York play a role in how Cooper may see an ideal frontier place?

Document 5.3: Food in the West with Lewis and Clark (From their Journals, 1804)

Following the Louisiana Purchase of 1803, President Thomas Jefferson commissioned an exploratory expedition to investigate what precisely the United States had bought with its 828,000 square-mile acquisition. Jefferson selected Meriwether Lewis and William Clark to command the exploration party, which was joined as well by several volunteers from the army. Their goal was to explore a water route from the west coast to the east, to make contact with Indian tribes, and to document the land, water, and animals they encountered. Their diaries document not only the food they took with them for their journey, and how and what they ate along the way, but also the farm and food possibility of the West itself.

Keep in mind as you read of how he ate in the West that, before the journey, Lewis lived in the White House, where he was a frequent guest at multicourse meals of foods considered both fine and exotic and that included the best wines shipped from Europe. At one White House meal where Lewis was present, the menu was "Rice soup, round of beef, turkey, mutton, ham, loin of veal, cutlets of mutton or veal, fried eggs, fried beef, [and] a pie called macaroni."

Clark, September 11, 1804

here the man who left us with the horses 22 days ago and has been a head ever
Since joined, us nearly Starved to Death, he had been 12 days without any
thing to eate but Grapes & one Rabit, which he Killed by shooting a piece of
hard Stick in place of a ball-. This man Supposeing the boat to be a head
pushed on as long as he Could, when he became weak and fiable deturmined
to lay by and waite for a tradeing boat, which is expected Keeping one horse
for the last resorse,—thus a man had like to have Starved to death in a land of
Plenty for the want of Bulletes or Something to kill his meat we Camped on
the L. S. above the mouth of a run a hard rain all the after noon, & most of
the night, with hard wind from the N W. I walked on Shore the fore part
of this day over Some broken Country which Continus about 3 miles back &
then is leavel & rich all Plains, I saw Several foxes & Killed a Elk & 2 Deer. &
Squirels the men with me killed an Elk, 2 Deer & a Pelican

> Some rain all day to day & Cold
> I walked on Shore Saw Several foxes Several Villages of Prarie dogs,
> and a number of Grouse

Lewis, May 9, 1805

Capt C. killed 2 bucks and 2 buffaloe, I also killed one buffaloe which
proved to be the best meat, it was in tolerable order; we saved the best of the
meat, and from the cow I killed we saved the necessary materials for making
what our wrighthand cook Charbono calls the boudin blanc, and immediately set him about preparing them for supper; this white pudding we all
esteem one of the greatest delacies of the forrest, it may not be amiss therefore to give it a place. About 6 feet of the lower extremity of the large gut of
the Buffaloe is the first mosel that the cook makes love to, this he holds fast
at one end with the right hand, while with the forefinger and thumb of the
left he gently compresses it, and discharges what he says is not good to eat,
but of which in the squel we get a moderate portion; the mustle lying underneath the shoulder blade next to the back, and fillets are next saught, these
are needed up very fine with a good portion of kidney suit; to this composition is then added a just proportion of pepper and salt and a small quantity
of flour; thus far advanced, our skilfull opporater C-o seizes his recepticle,
which has never once touched the water, for that would intirely distroy the
regular order of the whole procedure; you will not forget that the side you
now see is that covered with a good coat of fat provided the anamal be in

good order; the operator sceizes the recepticle I say, and tying it fast at one end turns it inwards and begins now with repeated evolutions of the hand and arm, and a brisk motion of the finger and thumb to put in what he says is bon pour manger; thus by stuffing and compressing he soon distends the recepticle to the utmost limmits of it's power of expansion, and in the course of it's longtudinal progress it drives from the other end of the recepticle a much larger portion of the ____ than was prevously discharged by the finger and thumb of the left hand in a former part of the operation; thus when the sides of the recepticle are skilfully exchanged the outer for the iner, and all is compleatly filled with something good to eat, it is tyed at the other end, but not any cut off, for that would make the pattern too scant; it is then baptised in the missouri with two dips and a flirt, and bobbed into the kettle; from whence after it be well boiled it is taken and fryed with bears oil untill it becomes brown, when it is ready to esswage the pangs of a keen appetite or such as travelers in the wilderness are seldom at a loss for.

Lewis, July 13, 1805

...I saw a number of turtledoves and some pigeons today. of the latter I shot one; they are the same common to the United States, or the wild pigeon as they are called. nothing remarkable in the appearance of the country; the timber entirely confined to the river and the country back on either side as far as the eye can reach entirely destitute of trees or brush. the timber is larger and more abundant in the bottom in which we now are than I have seen it on the Missouri for many hundred miles. the current of the river is still extreemly gentle. The hunters killed three buffaloe today which were in good order. the flesh was brought in dryed the skins wer also streached for covering our baggage. we eat an emensity of meat; it requires 4 deer, an Elk and a deer, or one buffaloe, to supply us plentifully 24 hours. meat now forms our food prinsipally as we reserve our flour parched meal and corn as much as possible for the rocky mountains which we are shortly to enter, and where from the indhan account game is not very abundant. I preserved specemines of several small plants to day which I have never before seen. The Musquetoes and knats are more trouble-some here if possible than they were at the White bear Islands. I sent a man to the canoes for my musquetoe bier which I had neglected to bring with me, as it is impossible to sleep a moment without being defended against the attacks of these most tormenting of all insects; the man returned with it a little after dark.

Lewis, August 16, 1805

I sent Drewyer and Shields before this morning in order to kill some meat as neither the Indians nor ourselves had any thing to eat. I informed the

Ceif of my view in this measure, and requested that he would keep his young men with us lest by their hooping and noise they should allarm the game and we should get nothing to eat, but so strongly were there suspicions exited by this measure that two parties of discovery immediately set out one on ech side of the valley to watch the hunters as I beleive to see whether they had not been sent to give information of their approach to an enemy that they still preswaided themselves were lying in wait for them. I saw that any further effort to prevent their going would only add strength to their suspicions and therefore said no more. after the hunters had been gone about an hour we set out. we had just passed through the narrows when we saw one of the spies comeing up the level plain under whip, the chief pawsed a little and seemed somewhat concerned. I felt a good deel so myself and began to suspect that by some unfortunate accedent that perhaps some of there enimies had straggled hither at this unlucky moment; but we were all agreeably disappointed on the arrival of the young man to learn that he had come to inform us that one of the whitemen had killed a deer. in an instant they all gave their horses the whip and I was taken nearly a mile before I could learn what were the tidings; as I was without stirrups and an Indian behind me the jostling was disagreeable I therefore reined up my horse and forbid the indian to whip him who had given him the lash at every jum for a mile fearing he should loose a part of the feast. the fellow was so uneasy that he left me the horse dismounted and ran on foot at full speed, I am confident a mile. when they arrived where the deer was which was in view of me they dismounted and ran in tumbling over each other like a parcel of famished dogs each seizing and tearing away a part of the intestens which had been previously thrown out by Drewyer who killed it; the seen was such when I arrived that had I not have had a pretty keen appetite myself I am confident I should not have taisted any part of the venison shortly. each one had a peice of some discription and all eating most ravenously. some were eating the kidnies the melt and liver and the blood runing from the corners of their mouths, others were in a similar situation with the paunch and guts but the exuding substance in this case from their lips was of a different discription. one of the last who attacted my attention particularly had been fortunate in his allotment or reather active in the division, he had provided himself with about nine feet of the small guts one end of which he was chewing on while with his hands he was squezzing the contents out at the other. I really did not untill now think that human nature ever presented itself in a shape so nearly allyed to the brute creation. I viewed these poor starved divils with pity and compassion I directed McNeal to skin the deer and reserved a quarter, the ballance I gave the Chief to be divided among his people; they devoured the whole of it nearly without cooking...

Discussion questions

1. What does Lewis's August 16, 1805 entry tell us about his understanding of food and civilization? How does he interpret the starving Indians' behavior and how does Lewis himself use the food to indicate his rank?
2. Even in the remote wilderness of the West, Lewis and Clark relied not just on simple foods eaten in their natural state, but ate prepared foods as well. How did they do this? Why?
3. Think about the amount of calories that the members of the expedition must have burned in an average day and contrast that with the "emensity of meat" that Lewis describes. Why the reliance on meat? What were the limitations of their diet?

Document 5.4: Selections from *The Diary of Patrick Breen* (1846)

Americans were drawn to the frontier for a variety of reasons. For many, the cities of the East were getting too busy or good farmland too scarce. The West promised adventure and opportunity. By the 1840s thousands of Americans were making the trip over the Rockies every year in search of a better life in California or Oregon. The trip usually took five months by wagon train. One group of families, known as the Donner Party, became separated from the regular Oregon Trail and a larger group of traveling families, and 87 members of the party became trapped by snow just west of the present-day border between California and Nevada, north of Lake Tahoe. For four months over the winter of 1846–1847, the families were trapped. Only 48 members of the party survived. Most starved to death.

"came to this place on the 31st of last month that it snowed we went on to the pass the snow so deep we were unable to find the road, when within 3 miles of the summit then turned back to this shanty on the Lake, Stanton came one day after we arriveed here we again took our teams & waggons & made another unsuccessful attempt to cross in company with Stanton we returned to the shanty it contiuneing to snow all the time we were here we now have killed most part of our cattle having to stay here untill next spring & live on poor beef without bread or salt"
— November 20, 1846

"still snowing now about 3 feet deep...killed my last oxen today will skin them tomorrow gave another yoke to Fosters hard to get wood"
— November 29, 1846

"... snow about 5 ½ feet or 6 deep difficult to get wood no gong from the house completely housed up looks as likely for snow as when it commenced, our cattle all killed but three or four them, the horses & Stantons mules gone & cattle suppose lost in the Snow no hopes of finding them alive"
  — December 1, 1846

"... Keyburg sent bill to get hides off his shanty & carry them home this morning, provisions scarce hides are the only article we depend on, we have a little meat yet, may God send us help"
  — January 17, 1847

"... those that went to Suitors not yet returned provisions getting very scant people getting weak liveing on short allowance of hides"
  — January 26, 1847

"... Peggy very uneasy for fear we shall all perish with hunger we have but a little meat left & only part of 3 hides has to support Mrs. Reid she has nothing left but one hide..."
  — February 5, 1847

"... J Denton trying to borrow meat for Graves had none to give they have nothing but hides all are entirely out of meat but a little we have our hides are nearly all eat up but with Gods help spring will soon smile upon us"
  — February 10, 1847

"... Mrs Graves refused to give Mrs Reid any hides put Suitors pack hides on her shanty would not let her have them says if I say it will thaw it then will not, she is a case"
  — February 15, 1847

"... shot Towser today & dressed his flesh Mrs Graves came here this morning to borrow meat dog or ox they think I have meat to spare but I know to the Contrary they have plenty hides I live principally on the same"
  — February 23, 1847

"... The Donnos told the California folks that they commence to eat the dead people 4 days ago, if they did not succeed that day or the next in finding their cattle then under ten or twelve feet of snow..."
  — February 26, 1847

"... there has 10 men arrived this morning from bear valley with provisions we are to start in two or three days & Cash our goods here there is amongst them some old they say the snow will be here untill June"
— March 1, 1847

Discussion questions

1. Newspaper accounts of the Donner Party differed greatly between west and east. Why would papers in places like New York have wanted to bury the news of the suffering and cannibalism while those in California reported the stories in graphic detail?
2. What do we learn about the broader history of starvation in the United States? How to public debates about starvation change our thinking about regular access to food?
3. We often think about food as a socially constructed category. In other words, what humans eat and do not eat is defined by social custom. But how does the story of the Donner Party test that idea? Is it more than desperation?

Document 5.5: Gold Rush Food: Selections from Lansford W. Hastings, *The Emigrants' Guide to Oregon and California* (1845) and Elisha Douglas Perkins, *Gold Rush Diary* (1849)

Lansford W. Hastings wrote his guide for emigrants moving to the West in 1845 before the start of the Gold Rush, but the move westward was already underway. In fact, Hastings wrote this guide as a way to entice more people to move to California. His book is a kind of siren call to the western states, complete with exaggerated descriptions of the landscape, weather, and ease of travel. Elisha Douglas Perkins was perhaps swayed by these colorful depictions of California and in 1849 set off from Ohio as part of the Marietta Gold Hunters to make his own fortune in California. The contrast between the stories told in these documents and the Donner Party's fate is striking.

From Hastings, *The Emigrants' Guide to Oregon and California*

In procuring supplies for this journey, the emigrant should provide himself with, at least, two hundred pounds of flour, or meal; one hundred and fifty pounds of bacon; ten pounds of coffee; twenty pounds of sugar; and ten pounds of salt, with such other provisions as he may prefer, and can conveniently take; yet the provisions, above enumerated, are considered, ample, both as to quantity, and variety. It would, perhaps, be advisable for emigrants, not to encumber themselves with any other, than those just enumerated; as it is impracticable for them, to take all the luxuries, to which they have been accustomed; and as it is found, by experience, that, when upon this kind of expedition, they are not desired, even by the most devoted epicurean. The above remarks, in reference to the quantity of provisions, are designed to apply only to adults; but taking the above as the data, parents will find no difficulty, in determining as to the necessary quantum for children; in doing which, however, it should always be observed, that children as well as adults, require, about twice the quantity of provisions, which they would, at home, for the same length of time. This is attributable to their being deprived of vegetables, and other sauce, and their being confined to meat and bread alone; as well as the fact, of their being subjected to continued and regular exercise, in the open air, which gives additional vigor and strength, which, greatly improves the health, and therefore, gives an additional demand for food. I am aware, that an opinion prevails among many, that when arriving in that region in which the buffalo abound, meat can be very readily obtained, and hence, much less meat need be taken; but this is in error, which, unless cautiously guarded against, will be very, apt to prove fatal: for to be found in that wild and remote region, depending upon the buffalo for meat, would, in nine cases out of ten, result in immediate or ultimate starvation, especially, if there should be large body of persons together. It is true, that immense herds of buffalo, are found in that region; but it would be impossible, to kill them in sufficient numbers, to sustain a large party, unless many, persons should devote their entire attention to the business of hunting; and, even then, it could not be done, unless the company should delay for that purpose, which would, in all probability, produce consequences, equally as fatal as starvation; for, unless you pass over the mountains early in the fall, you are very liable to be detained, by impassable mountains of snow, until the next spring, or, perhaps, forever. Then it would seem, that, although the buffalo are vastly numerous, they cannot be relied upon; yet to avoid encumbering himself with the very large quantities of meat which his family would require, the emigrant can drive cattle, which will afford him a very good substitute, not only for the beef of the buffalo, but, also, for bacon; and what is more important, is, that they can be relied upon, under all circumstances.

Very few cooking utensils, should be taken, as they very, much increase the load, to avoid which, is always a consideration of paramount importance. A baking-kettle, frying-pan, tea-kettle, tea-pot, and coffee-pot, are all the furniture of this kind, that is essential, which, together with tin plates, tin cups, ordinary knives, forks, spoons, and a coffee-mill, should constitute the entire kitchen apparatus.

From *The Diary of Elisha Douglas Perkins*

Thursday Aug 30. Morn clear. Night very cold, ice made in considerable quantity was nearly stiffened by sleeping cold, having given some of my bedding to Gilbert. Sunrose hot however and soon thought me out. Wind East.

Had a glorious supper last night. Gilbert bought 12 hot light biscuits of a train camped near for which he paid 5.00! & I broiled some of the best pieces of my last ham, made a pot of tea & having bought 5 lb of sugar a day or two cents of which I had been out for a week or more, paying for it .50 pr LB we sat down to a meal which it is seldom the good fortune of packers to enjoy. & By contrast to our usual fat bacon & hard crackers was delicious. Our living is anything but tempting, the crackers being hard tasteless & somewhat musty from often wedding & drying, & fat bacon toasted on a stick being a dish that at home would have spoil my appetite to look at. However we are glad to get anything to live on. Everybody is shorter provisions at the stage of the journey the result of so much there on the way in the first instance. For some poor bacon which I succeeded in paid 37¢ pr lb & they now ask 50. Crackers 25¢ pr lb. only one train has sugar to sell, which is held as stated above at 50¢ & flour not to be had at all.

Hundreds of foolish man not content with slow progress of their oxen have left their trains & taking four or five days provision on their backs & 25¢ in their pocket start off for California, calculating to speed their way through. How they are to get along I can't conceive, as Gen Moore told me that hardly a day past but he had application from more or less of these footpads for meals, & sometimes though not often wanting to pay for food but was compelled to refuse all alike as he had no more than sufficient for his own consumption. I think some of them must suffer considerably as they reach the land of promise.

Discussion questions

1. Does Hastings suggest that emigrants will need more or less food when they are on the trail west as compared to when they are at home? Why is that? What does this passage reveal about expectations of diet? Does it tell us something about the economic class of emigrants that Hastings was addressing?

2. What does Perkins complaining about the high price of food tell us about their trip? What has the price and scarcity of food done to their tastes? Does this passage tell us something about Perkins's social class? Expectations for the trip?

3. Is there a difference between how people think hunger is going to effect them and how it does? Do we see more evidence in these documents of people making poor predictions of how much food they need to eat? Can we draw any larger insights into history outside of the frontier experience?

Document 5.6: Advertisement for Cyrus McCormick's Mechanical Reaper (1846)

A reaper is a tool that cuts a crop when it is ripe. For centuries this work was done by hand, as a person would walk through a field swinging a large, sharp blade, like a scythe or rake, to harvest a crop, usually a grain like wheat, corn, or rye. As settlers, many first-generation immigrants from Europe moved into the Great Lakes, Midwest, and Plains regions of the country and they quickly established farms on which they produced grains. Many technological advances in the nineteenth century made farm production much more efficient. The steel plow, made popular by John Deere, became very popular in the 1840s. The McCormick Reaper, which appears in the advertisement below, was a great advance because it allowed a farmer to ride on a wheeled cart pulled by two horses. A saw worked back and forth by crank, cutting the grain and laying it to the side of the reaper as it moved.

Discussion questions

1. How does a relatively simple technological advance like the reaper change the eating habits of an American who lives nowhere near the Midwest?
2. How does farm technology affect the crop itself? In other words, how might farmers choose the variety of wheat that they grow after they have purchased a McCormick Reaper?
3. How does the image above refute or endorse the Jeffersonian ideal of agrarianism?
4. If buying a McCormick Reaper made one's farm more efficient, would that push the farmer to expand acreage or decrease acreage? How could a farmer afford an expensive piece of machinery?

Chapter 6   The Civil War (1861–1865)

Document 6.1: Selections from the Diary of Louis Léon (CSA)

Louis Léon's diary was one of the first published memoirs of the experience of a regular Confederate soldier as opposed to an officer. Published in 1913 when Léon was 73, it recalls the mundane day-to-day life of an enlisted man: camping, marching, and eating. In fact, Léon mentions food in many, if not most, of his diary entries, most of the time noting that it was either not available or simply poor. Below are selections that tell us a bit about what soldiers ate, the many ways they found food, and about how officers had to organize soldiers' eating.

April 21, 1861
A few days after that a squad of us were sent out to cut down trees, and, by George! they gave me an axe and told me to go to work. Well, I cut all over my tree until the lieutenant commanding, seeing how nice I was marking it, asked me what I had done before I became a soldier. I told him I was a clerk in a dry-goods store. He said he thought so from the way I was cutting timber. He relieved me—but what insults are put on us who came to fight the Yankees! Why, he gave me two buckets and told me to carry water to the men that could cut.

We changed camp several times, until about the 3d of June, when we marched fifteen miles and halted at Bethel Church, and again commenced

Food and Eating in America: A Documentary Reader, First Edition.
Edited by James C. Giesen and Bryant Simon.
© 2018 John Wiley & Sons, Inc. Published 2018 by John Wiley & Sons, Inc.

making breastworks. Our rations did not suit us. We wanted a change of diet, but there were strict orders from Col. D. H. Hill that we should not go out foraging. Well, Bill Stone, Alie Todd and myself put on our knapsacks and went to the creek to wash our clothes, but when we got there we forgot to wash. We took a good long walk away from the camp, and saw several shoats[1]. We ran one down, held it so it could not squeal, then killed it, cut it in small pieces, put it in our knapsacks, returned to the creek, and from there to camp, where we shared it with the boys. It tasted good.

Our comrade Ernheart did not fare so well. He went to a place where he knew he could get some honey. He got it all right, but he got the bees, also. His face and hands were a sight when he got the beehive to camp.

June 20, 1861
Up until this date there has been nothing worth recording, but to-day got orders to fall in line with two days' rations cooked. Left at 12 M. in box cars. We knocked holes in them to get fresh air. We laid over six hours eight miles from Gerresburg in order to let the passenger cars pass us. Several of our company left the train in quest of supper. We found a house where a lady promised to give us supper for fifty cents each. As we were doing full justice to her supper the train started, we left in a hurry, and did not have time to pay for our meal. I don't suppose she gave us her blessing.

June 21, 1861
We reached Petersburg, Va., this morning at half-past two, and had barely laid down with a brick wall for my pillow when breakfast was announced in the shape of Mack Sample, who told us where we could get it. I ran the blockade with Katz, and went to see Mike Etlinger. He was not at home. Afterward we met Wortheim, and we all went again and got something good to eat. We then returned to our regiment, which is the 53d North Carolina Regiment, infantry, Col. William Owens, commander. We are enlisted for three years, or the war. We fell in line and marched to our camp, which is on Dunn's Hill, just outside of the city.

July 6, 1861
We got orders to march this morning. Left here with two days' rations of corn meal and bacon in our haversacks. We got to Petersburg in the evening—fifteen miles—after a hard march. It is very warm, and we did not rest on the way, as it was a forced march. We camped on Dunn's Hill.

---

[1] Young pigs

March 15, 1863
Laid here all day, with two crackers for our rations, and these we got at night.

June 4, 1863
Got orders to cook three days' rations immediately. We left our camp at 3 this morning, marched fourteen miles and halted. We march one hour and rest ten minutes.

Discussion questions

1. Why would Léon's officer order that the men not forage for food around the camp?
2. What were the effects of foraging and marching on the countryside itself, on plants, animals, and agriculture in general?
3. Imagine you're a soldier. How do you think about the relationship between marching and eating? If you were an officer in charge of getting food to your men, how would your thinking be different?

Document 6.2: The Confederate Right to Impress Food, a selection from "A Bill to Provide Supplies for the Army and to Prescribe the Mode of Making Impressments" (1864)

The Confederate legislature passed this law on May 31, 1864. At that time the momentum of the war was swinging from their side to that of the Union. Confederate armies had suffered key losses and the major battles of the war were now happening on southern soil, which was taking its toll on both the soldiers and those southern families on the homefront.

Sec. 5. If, in addition to the tax in kind and the contribution herein required, the necessities of the army or the good of the service shall require other supplies of food or forage, or any other private property, and the same cannot be procured by contract, then impressments may be made of such supplies or other property, either for absolute ownership or for temporary use, as the public necessities may require. Such impressments shall be in accordance with the provisions, and subject to the restrictions, of the existing impressment laws, except so far as is herein otherwise provided.

Sec. 6. The right and the duty of making impressments is hereby confided, exclusively, to the officers and agents charged, in the several districts, with the assessment and collection of the tax in kind and of the contribution herein required; and all officers and soldiers, in any department of the army, are hereby expressly prohibited from undertaking, in any manner, to interfere with these officers and agents in any part of their duties, in respect to the tax in kind, the contribution, or the impressments herein provided for.

Sec. 7. Supplies or other property taken by impressment shall be paid for by the post quartermasters in the several districts, and shall be disposed of and accounted for by them as is required in respect to the tax in kind and the contribution herein required; and it shall be the duty of the post quartermasters to equalize and apportion the impressments within their districts, as far as practicable, so as to avoid opposing any portion of the community.

Sec. 8. If any one not authorized by law to collect the tax in kind or the contribution herein required, or to make impressments, shall undertake, on any pretence of such authority, to seize or impress, or to collect or receive any such property, or shall, on any such pretence, actually obtain such property, he shall, upon conviction thereof, be punished by fine not exceeding five times the value of such property, and be imprisoned not exceeding five years, at the discretion of the court having jurisdiction. And it shall be the duty of all officers and agents charged with the assessment and collection of the tax in kind, and of the contribution herein required, promptly to report, through the post quartermasters in the several districts, any violations or disregard of the provisions of this act by any officer or soldier in the service of the Confederate States.

Discussion questions

1. Why did the Confederacy have a need for this law? What does this say about the state of the Confederacy and its army in 1864?
2. Why is impressment of food linked to collection of taxes?
3. Why does the law state who may impress food and under what conditions? What can this tell us about the conditions on the ground at this point of the Civil War?

Document 6.3: Photograph of Hardtack

Armies of the North and the South subsisted for long stretches on foods that were easy to prepare, carry, keep, and eat. The most ubiquitous was hardtack, a dry biscuit that looked and tasted like a bland, thick cracker. Made from a simple recipe of flour, salt, fat, and water, hardtack could be baked in large batches, wrapped, and distributed to soldiers who could carry the light food with them in their pockets. Not surprisingly, soldiers on both sides of the war were unceasing in their complaints about the food. These photos depict hardtack that was given as a (probably tongue-in-cheek) gift after the war from one soldier to another. The packaging reads "Army Cracker or Hardtack 1864, John W. Weiser, Ohio Infy."

Discussion questions

1. What made hardtack so common? What were its advantages from the army's perspective?
2. What made hardtack so unpopular with soldiers? Could any food that was given to an army again and again be popular? What if these biscuits had contained more salt or sugar? Would they have been more popular? What can this tell us about taste?
3. Think about the ingredients. What can we learn about supply lines and agriculture from hardtack?

Document 6.4: "A Dangerous Novelty in Memphis," cartoon by Frank Bellew, *Harper's Weekly* (1862)

The Union invaded and seized the Confederate city of Memphis, Tennessee in early 1862. Frank Bellew, a relatively famous illustrator, drew this cartoon depicting the near-riot conditions of the hungry Memphis public shortly after the Union occupation began. The cartoon was read by a predominantly northern audience, as Harper's Weekly *was available and popular across the Union.*

A DANGEROUS NOVELTY IN MEMPHIS.

OFFICER OF THE PROVOST GUARD. "Hi! look here, you Eating-House Keeper. Take that Mutton Chop out of your Window, or we shall have a riot, presently!"

Discussion questions

1. How are the southerners depicted? Keep in mind that Bellew drew this for a northern audience. Did most readers look with pity upon these hungry people? With scorn or hatred?

2. What does the presence of this sole mutton chop suggest about food availability in Memphis? Who had access to good meat like this? Why? What does it tell us about food supply lines among the Union army?

3. Imagine you're the Union soldier in the image. Are you interested in keeping the people of Memphis well fed, or is there an advantage to keeping them hungry?

4. How can food be used as a weapon during war?

Document 6.5: Photographs of Prisoners Liberated from Confederate Prisons (1865)

Though the most infamous of Confederate prisons is Andersonville, the southern armies captured and detained Union soldiers across the region, just as the Union did with captured Confederates. In Andersonville, roughly 45,000 prisoners were held during the course of the war, crowded into a camp designed for many fewer people. There was no suitable supply of fresh water or food and about 13,000 people died in Andersonville alone. Below are two photographs of prisoners after they were liberated from Confederate capture. The first depicts William Smith of Kentucky, who was captured in Virginia and kept in a warehouse prison in Richmond for months. The second is a photograph of William Hattle, a Pennsylvanian, who was likely held in Andersonville for many months near the end of the war.

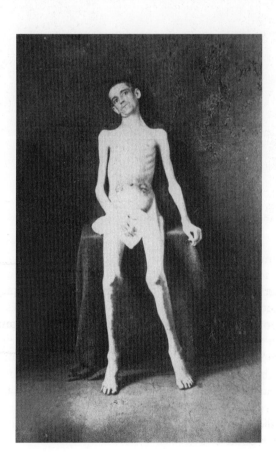

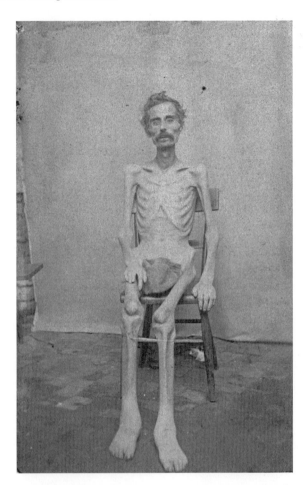

Discussion questions

1. Starvation was certainly a way to torture captured Yankee soldiers, but what other factors could explain these men's appearances?
2. Think about the impact of these photos on magazine and newspaper readers in the North. How do you think they affected the people's ideas about the South and about reconciliation with the region?
3. What is the relationship between our conceptions of bodies and our ideas about food? Do you think it would have been the same in 1865 as it was in 1965?
4. Why would a photographer have been interested in capturing images of these men's bodies?

Chapter 7   Food Reborn: Immigration, Urbanization, and Eating (1857–1905)

Document 7.1: Observations of Food and Cooking in Texas: Frederick Law Olmsted, *A Journey Through Texas* (1857)

Frederick Law Olmsted is best known as the landscape architect who designed Central Park in New York City, but long before then he was known as a writer who specialized in traveling the United States and recording what life was like among average Americans in various places. In 1856 he under-took a trip on horseback through Texas, which was very much the western frontier at the time. His record of life from the banks of the Rio Grande to Houston, San Antonio, and a dozen villages and campgrounds underscores the region's multi-ethnic culture. His observations about food and eating habits both in homes and in hotels and restaurants reveal a clash between his own sense of what constituted good eating and manners, and the reality of Texas shortly before the Civil War.

CORN-BREAD BEGINS.—THE ROADSIDE

We stopped for dinner at a small and unattractive village, and at an inn to which scarcely better terms could be applied. The meal was smoking on the table; but five minutes had hardly elapsed, when "Stage's ready," was shouted and all the other passengers bolting their coffee, and handing their half dollars to the landlord, who stood eagerly in the door, fled precipitately

Food and Eating in America: A Documentary Reader, First Edition.
Edited by James C. Giesen and Bryant Simon.
© 2018 John Wiley & Sons, Inc. Published 2018 by John Wiley & Sons, Inc.

to their seats. We held out a few moments longer, but yielded to repeated threats that the stage was off without us, and mounted our places amid suppressed oaths on all side.

At this dinner I made the first practical acquaintance with what shortly was to be the bane of my life, viz., corn-bread and bacon. I partook innocent and un-suspicious of these dishes, as they seemed to be the staple of the meal, without a thought that for the next six months I shall actually see *nothing else*. Here, relieved by other meats and by excellent sweet potatoes baked and in *pone*, they disappeared in easy digestion. Taken alone, with vile coffee, I may ask, with deep feelings, who is sufficient for these things?

A GRAZIER'S FARM.

It was a log cabin, of one room, fourteen feet by fourteen, with another small room in a "lean-to" of boards on the windward side. There was no window, but there were three doors, and openings between the logs in all quarters....a strong fire was roaring in the great chimney at the end of the room, and we all clustered closely around it, "the woman" alone passing through our semicircle, as she prepared the "pone" and "fry," and coffee for supper....A rough board box, three feet square, with a shelf in it, contained the crockery-ware of the establishment; another similar box held the store of meal, coffee, sugar, and salt, a log crib at the horse-pen held the corn, from which the meal was daily ground, and a log smoke or store-house contained the store of pork. A canopy-bed filled one quarter of the room; a cradle, four chairs seated with untanned deer-hide, a table, a skillet or bake-kettle, a coffee-kettle, a frying-pan, and a rifle laid across two wooden pegs on the chimney, with a string of patches, powder-horn, pouch, and hunting-knife, completed the furniture of the house. We all sat with hats and over-coats on, and the woman cooked in a bonnet and shawl....

AUSTIN.

Austin has a fine situation upon the left bank of the Colorado. Had it not been the capital of the state, and a sort of bourne to which we had looked forward for a temporary rest, it would still have struck us as the pleasantest place we had seen in Texas....

We had reckoned upon getting some change of diet when we reached the capital of the state, and upon having good materials not utterly spoiled, by carelessness, ignorance, or nastiness, and cooking. We reckoned without our host.

We arrived in a norther, and were shown, at the hotel to which we had been recommended, into an exceedingly dirty room, in which two of us slept with another gentleman, who informed us that it was the best room in the house.... When the breakfast-bell rung, we all turned out in haste, though our boots were gone and there was no water....When finally we got to breakfast, and had offered us—but I will not again mention the three articles—only the "fry" had been changed for the worse before it was fried—we naturally began to talk of changing our quarters...Never did we any wholesome food on that table. It was a succession of burnt flesh of swine and bulls, decaying vegetables, and sour and mouldy farinaceous glues, all pervaded with rancid butter. After a few days, we got a private room, and then, buying wheat-bread of a German baker, and other provisions of grocers, cooked what was necessary for ourselves, thus really coming back to caravansarism.

Discussion questions

1. Why the ubiquity of pone? What was this foodstuff and what was it about its ingredients and preparation that made it so common?
2. Think about regional cuisine for a moment. Do you think Texans at this time and place complained about the "vile coffee" and pone as much as Olmsted did? Was it his palette, which was used to food in bigger cities in the northeast, that objected to these foods or do you think the food in Texas was objectively bad?
3. How does Olmsted link his opinions of food in Texas with his other observations? Do his comments about the people, the weather, and the housing influencing readers' thinking about food in the West? How do our own ideas about food link to ideas about the environment and culture?

Document 7.2: Documents on Irish Immigration from Mary Anne Sadlier, *Bessy Conway; or, The Irish Girl in America* (1885) and John O'Hanlon, *The Irish Emigrant's Guide for the United States* (1861)

In the middle of the nineteenth century, the population of Ireland fell by nearly one-quarter, attributable to the tragedy of the Great Famine, which is sometimes called the "Irish Potato Famine." Approximately one million Irish citizens died and another million emigrated, many of whom came to the United States. The following two documents give us a window into both the famine and the experience of the émigrés to America. First, you will read an excerpt from a fictionalized account of an Irish girl who came to America. The author, Mary Anne Sadlier, tells the story of Bessy Conway and the Irish famine. The second selection comes from John O'Hanlon's 1861 book The Irish Emigrant's Guide for the United States. Hanlon's book is intended to warn Irish travelers of the harsh realities of life in America. As he writes, "The Utopia of our imagination, is not the United States of our experience."

From *Bessy Conway; or, the Irish Girl in America*

We will now leave Bessy Conway for awhile, and return to the old home-stead she left behind…[the sun's] slanting rays rested on the straw-thatched roof of Denis Conway, but there was no beauty in the picture, for the look of comfort and neatness that belonged to the place in former days was gone, and had left scarce a trace behind. The thatch so trim and smooth in those bygone days was broken in many places, and covered with patches of moss, whilst chicken weed and darnel flaunted their unwelcome verdure on the gable-tops…The haggard was empty, and so was the byer—the horse was gone from the stable, and even the sty had lost its tenants—the overgrown sow was no longer there with her squeaking brood, nor the well-cared bacon pigs, which, in other days, furnished so important a share of the winter's store for the family. The fowl were gone from the barn door, for no grain was there to gather them round it. The discordant chorus of the farm yard was no longer heard; the very hum of the bees in the adjacent garden had ceased, and silence sat brooding over Denis Conway's cottage. Decay, too, was there, and, beneath its withering touch, all things were hastening to ruin.

This was the aspect of affairs without, and within it was nothing better. The same look of desolation was everywhere visible, but its saddest imprint was on the people. Famine and disease had found their way into that happy household, and misery sat on the threshold. The aged father and mother sat opposite each other in their old straw chairs, by the dull, flickering fire, watching with dis-tended eyes the unsavory mess which Nancy was making for the family supper, consisting of water and nettles, with a handful or so of oatmeal. Nancy herself as she bent over the pot was a living picture of hunger, and the low, suppressed moans which came at irregular intervals from a straw "shakedown" in the corner indicated the presence of one who suffered bodily pain. It was Ellen, the bright-eyed, dark-haired fairy, whose laugh used to ring the loudest, whose foot spring the lightest in days not long gone by. But the terrible fangs of hunger had fastened on her vitals, and disease was wearing her young life away.

"Nancy dear!" said the mother, "go and see what Ellen wants. I think she's speaking."

"What is it, astore?" said the elder sister bending over the straw pallet.

"Something to eat," murmured Ellen, only half conscious. "I'm hungry."

"You'll have it in a minute, darling in one minute," and Nancy hastened back to her miserable cooking, and squatted down on the hearth to fan the expiring embers into something like a blaze. The tears ran down the mother's face, and she clasped her hands and looked up to heaven in silent anguish

"Don't grieve, Bridget, don't grieve, *achorra*!" said her husband; "God is good, you know, and He'll never desert us."

"Well, father ! we're far enough gone now," said Nancy in a faint, dejected voice.

"Never mind, dear, never mind!" still said Denis; "ifs only tryin' us He is—He'll change His hand with us when He sees fit. Have you the broth ready for Ellen, Nancy?—God help us! it's poor stuff for a sick weakly stomach!—well! the Lord be praised, anyhow!"

Ellen was raised on her sister's arm, and swallowed with avidity some spoonfuls of the pottage, then looked up in Nancy's face and whispered: "Have you enough for all?"

"Plenty, machree, plenty!—don't be afeard! there's a potful of it!" Ellen's face lighted, and she gulped down some spoonfuls more, then made a sign that she had enough, and sank heavily back on her pillow.

...Truly that was a dismal time in Denis Conway's cottage, and in many a cottage through the length and breadth of Ireland. It was the terrible year of the Famine, as the reader will have guessed, and the ruin which had been progressing rapidly during the previous years of dearth and commercial depression, and the failure of crops, had at length reduced the small farmers of the country, and amongst the rest Denis Conway and his family, to the pitiful state in which we have seen them. What money Denis had had was long since gone, no corn or wheat was ripening in his fields, for in the spring-time he had not the means to purchase seed, the stock could not live without eating, and one after another every hoof was taken to the fair and sold. Milk and butter, of course, went with them, and what was worse than all, the money which they brought—it was little compared with what it would have been at another time.

From John O'Hanlon *The Irish Emigrant's Guide for the United States*

The Passenger Laws of England...declare: "That on board every ship carrying passengers on any such voyage as aforesaid, there shall be issued to the passengers a supply of water, at the rate of at least three quarts for each passenger per day, and that there shall also be issued, at convenient times, not less often than twice a week, a supply of provisions after the rate seven pounds of bread, biscuit, flour, oatmeal, or rice, per week, provided that one-half at least of the supply shall consist of bread or biscuit, and that potatoes being computed as equal to one pound of the other articles enumerated."

The Laws of the United States require each passenger be furnished with a weekly allowance of 6 lbs. of meal, 2½ lbs Navy bread, 1 lb. wheat flour, 1 lb. salt pork, free from "bone." 3 quarts of water per day, 2 oz. of tea, 8 oz. of sugar, 8 oz. of molasses, and vinegar. Children also, under twelve years of age (not including infants) are to be furnished according to the recent Act of Congress, with 7 pounds of bread stuffs per week, including 1 pound of salt pork, half allowance of tea, sugar and molasses, and full allowance of water and vinegar. This supply must consist of wholesome food, in the several items. ... It must be remarked, that although the amount of provision enumerated above, be according to the intention of the Act of Parliament, calculated to keep away want and starvation on a long voyage, it will not perhaps suffice for the sufficient support of the passenger. Hence, he must in addition buy in a supply of food that will be capable of sustaining him, over and above the time requisite for a reasonably long voyage....As to the quality of the food, this will furthermore depend on the preference, habit, taste, means, &c, of the consumer; however, in all instances it should be procured of a wholesome kind, and such as will not be liable to spoil on the voyage. The stores most generally preferred on ship board are potatoes, oatmeal, wheat, flour, fine or shorts, bacon, eggs, butter, &c. in good preservation. The inferior kind of Navy Bread served out on board is considered as hard fare, especially to those not accustomed to it; an excellent kind can be procured at an advanced price. It must be added also, that in a general manner, the pork furnished is not of a good quality. A supply of biscuit is in some degree requisite; since the accommodations necessary for kneading and baking bread are indifferent, or rather not furnished, unless by the ingenuity of the emigrant, who must use, for instance, the lid of one of his traveling chests for a kneading-board.

Discussion questions

1. Why would Sadlier want to include this episode from her character's life in Ireland to explain how she was dealing with life in America? What was formative about the famine for Bessy Conway?
2. Why would there be laws in England and the United States about what food should be furnished to all passengers aboard ships? What does this tell us about the shipping companies and their passengers?
3. Taken together, do these documents suggest something about how Irish-Americans might have a different relationship to food and eating than other ethnic groups in the United States?

Document 7.3: Recipes for "Broth in haste," "Cheap white," and "Tongue, Braised, with Aspic Jelly," from Lafcadio Hearn, *Creole Cookbook* (1887)

As the introduction to Hearn's Creole Cookbook attests, the book is a collection of recipes from around New Orleans, "which is cosmopolitan in its nature, blending the characteristics of the American, French, Spanish,

Italian, West Indian and Mexican." Indeed, the city's cuisine distinguished itself from American and even southern food due to its amalgamation of ingredients, tastes, and cooking techniques brought from around the world. As the author states, the key to great Creole cooking is "economy and simplicity," as will become clear in the recipes selected below.

Broth in Haste

Cut some rare roast meat or broiled steak very fine. To a teacupfull of the cut meet put a pint and a half of boiling water; cover it, And set it on the fire for 10 minutes; season to taste. Roll a cracker fine, and put in with the meat. This broth is both excellent and convenient for invalids or children.

Cheap White Soup

Chop up any remains you may have a cold veal, chicken, game or rabbit roasted dry. Grate them, beat them in a mortar, and rub them through a sieve. Then add to the panada a quart of stock, put it into a stew pan and cook. Pay great attention to skimming as it boils.

Tongue Braised With Aspic Jelly

Boil the tongue until tender, then place it in a stew pan with two onions, a head of celery, four cloves, and salt and pepper; cover it with the liquor it was boiled in; add to it a glass of brandy, a tablespoonful of sugar, a blade of mace, a bunch of thyme, and a bunch of parsley. Let it simmer gently for two hours. Take out the tongue, strain the liquor it was boiled in, and add to it a box of Cox's gelatine which has been soaked in a goblet of cold water. Heat it and pour over the tongue. Serve cold.

Discussion questions

1. Most Americans associate Creole food today with spicy red beans and rice, or jambalaya. But these dishes are different in many ways. How so? What do these three recipes tell us about life in New Orleans in the 1880s?
2. To many cooks who are not from New Orleans, Creole cooking would have seemed exotic in the late nineteenth century. Today, however, Louisiana food can be found almost anywhere. What was exotic about it then and what has happened in American kitchens and restaurants— and society at large—to make it less exotic now?

Document 7.4: Platform of the Populist Party (1892)

The Populist Party (sometimes also known as the People's Party) became a political force in the United States for about 20 years at the end of the nineteenth and early twentieth centuries. Its origin was rural, and farm issues dominated its project. Its 1892 platform below embodies some farmers' distrust of the growing size (and power) of railroads, and their stance that only a strong government could protect the people from powerful corporations, banks, and railroads. Since the growing and shipping of agricultural food products was so central to Populists' complaint about the modernizing country, read the following platform with an eye toward how Americans' food habits were central to this political question.

Platform

We declare, therefore—

First.—That the union of the labor forces of the United States this day consummated shall be permanent and perpetual; may its spirit enter into all hearts for the salvation of the Republic and the uplifting of mankind.

Second.—Wealth belongs to him who creates it, and every dollar taken from industry without an equivalent is robbery. "If any will not work, neither shall he eat." The interests of rural and civic labor are the same; their enemies are identical.

Third.—We believe that the time has come when the railroad corporations will either own the people or the people must own the railroads, and should the government enter upon the work of owning and managing all railroads, we should favor an amendment to the Constitution by which all persons engaged in the government service shall be placed under a civil-service regulation of the most rigid character, so as to prevent the increase of the power of the national administration by the use of such additional government employes.

FINANCE.—We demand a national currency, safe, sound, and flexible, issued by the general government only, a full legal tender for all debts, public and private, and that without the use of banking corporations, a just, equitable, and efficient means of distribution direct to the people, at a tax not to exceed 2 per cent. per annum, to be provided as set forth in the sub-treasury plan of the Farmers' Alliance, or a better system; also by payments in discharge of its obligations for public improvements.

1. We demand free and unlimited coinage of silver and gold at the present legal ratio of 16 to 1.

2. We demand that the amount of circulating medium be speedily increased to not less than $50 per capita.
3. We demand a graduated income tax.
4. We believe that the money of the country should be kept as much as possible in the hands of the people, and hence we demand that all State and national revenues shall be limited to the necessary expenses of the government, economically and honestly administered.
5. We demand that postal savings banks be established by the government for the safe deposit of the earnings of the people and to facilitate exchange.

TRANSPORTATION.—Transportation being a means of exchange and a public necessity, the government should own and operate the railroads in the interest of the people. The telegraph, telephone, like the post-office system, being a necessity for the transmission of news, should be owned and operated by the government in the interest of the people.

LAND.—The land, including all the natural sources of wealth, is the heritage of the people, and should not be monopolized for speculative purposes, and alien ownership of land should be prohibited. All land now held by railroads and other corporations in excess of their actual needs, and all lands now owned by aliens should be reclaimed by the government and held for actual settlers only.

Discussion questions

1   Were politics and food intertwined for the Populists? Were they thinking about food when they were trying to protect land ownership and independent farmers? If not, why not?
2   What is the spirit behind the quote "If any will not work, neither shall he eat"? Might the rural-based Populists have been suggesting something about people in the growing industrial cities?
3   Other than reasons stated here, why were Populists interested in transportation being owned by the government?
4   What do American political parties say about food and agriculture today? Are there any lessons that we can take from the Populists?

Document 7.5: Cooking Utensils for Sale in the 1912 Sears, Roebuck and Co. Catalog

Sears, Roebuck and Co. was the largest single store in the world at the turn of the twentieth century. Its massive catalogs changed the way Americans, particularly those who lived away from cities and large towns, could participate in the booming consumer world of modern America. One could order almost anything through the catalog, from the smallest household items like thread and needles, to stoves, wagons, and even an entire house (sent as a big kit that could be put together on site). We can learn a lot from the catalog if we think about it as a document showing what Americans had and wanted. Below is the detail of a page in the 1912 catalog selling sets of kitchenware.

Discussion questions

1. What does this basic set tell us about the average middle-class American kitchen? What kinds of tools were needed to cook the average meal?
2. What can we learn about ingredients and specifically the forms of those ingredients from these tools? Did home cooks need to perform more labor in the kitchen to prepare meals than they do today?
3. To what degree did aesthetics matter for cookware? Were these purely utilitarian items? What might your answer say about kitchens themselves and their relationship to the rest of the house?

Document 7.6: Ernest H. Crosby, Letter to *The New York Times* on Vegetarianism (1905)

Vegetarianism has existed for thousands of years, but in the late 1800s and early 1900s, it grew in popularity in the United States. Ernest H. Crosby, the author of this letter to the editor of the New York Times, *was a highly educated author who had served in the New York state legislature and traveled the world, even becoming friends with the famous Russian writer Leo Tolstoy. Two years after penning this letter Crosby died at the age of 51.*

To the Editor of the New York Times:

A correspondent in your journal of this morning asks, apropos of the present high price of meat, whether we cannot live without eating flesh. He gives due warning that he wishes to have an answer from some one who can speak with authority, and not from a faddist, which injunction would probably rule me out, but as I happen to have on my table a little treatise by a well-known physician of New York, who is neither a faddist nor a vegetarian, to wit, Dr. Joseph E. Winters, I shall venture to give an answer in his name. The pamphlet to which I refer has just appeared from the press of William Wood, 51 5ᵗʰ Ave., New York, and is entitled "The Food Factor as a Cause of Health and Disease During Childhood."

Dr. Winters shows that the valuable element in meat is that part known as the proteids, and then points out the fact that they can be obtained as well from vegetable products as from flesh food. "The proteids maybe divided into those of animal and those of the vegetable origin. There does not appear to be any essential difference between these two classes. Vegetable proteid is equal in nutritive value to animal proteid. Dr. Winters punctures the popular fallacy that red blood and red cheeks come from a meat diet. "There exists," he says, "an interesting relationship between the blood-coloring matter and the vegetable-coloring matter, and vegetable food is probably the chief factor in the production of blood-coloring matter."..."There is more so-called nervousness, anemia, rheumatism, valvular disease of the heart, and chorea at the present time in children from an excess of meat and its preparations in the diet than from all other causes combined."

The fact that Dr. Winters believes in giving meat to adults adds force to his admission that all the good which exists in meat can be obtained from the vegetable creation. It would be easy to go on and prove that meat is in many ways an unwholesome and unclean food. Take a given cube inch of meat. We know that if the animal had taken violent exercise during the last half hour of its life that that cubic inch would have produced so much sweat. As the exercise was not taken, the sweat is still there. And so with various other excrementitious substances which the body throws off. Every particle of flesh is full of worn-out tissue on its way to the several channels of exit. We have each of us already our own waste tissues to get rid of, and if we load our stomachs with the waste tissue of other animals we give our organs too much work to do, and dyspepsia, kidney disease, and gout are likely to follow.

As to the fact that men can thrive without meat, I could give to your correspondent letters of introduction to several vigorous brain workers who have not tasted meat in over fifty years. I could cite the cases of Elsasser and Pletz, who in 1893 came in first and second in the famous walking match from Berlin to Vienna, beating the fastest meat eater by twenty-two hours, or of Eustace Miles, who last month won again the amateur tennis championship of England, and is besides a successful tutor in the Greek language at Cambridge.

In taking up a vegetarian diet, it is wise to make the change gradually and to be sure to substitute for meat those foods which contain proteids. Peas and beans, the cereals, such as oatmeal and whole-wheat bread, are perfect substitutes for meat, and so are nuts. Eggs and cheese also contain the same necessary elements. With due consideration for these facts, it requires little or no exercise of self-denial for most people to become vegetarians, and after a time the idea of eating meat will probably become disagreeable to the experimenter.

Ernest H. Crosby
Rhinebeck, N.Y.
April 27, 1902

Discussion questions

1. Why is Crosby writing the letter in the first place? Why was the *New York Times* addressing a vegetarian diet? Does his defense of vegetarianism address that reason?
2. How is Crosby's defense of vegetarianism based on understandings of health? Does he claim that meat is unhealthy? Do people need proteids (protein)?
3. What kinds of reasons do vegetarians give today for their eating choices? Are there moral and economic reasons that Crosby ignores? How does the health advice at the heart of this letter still resonate today?

Part IV   Feeding a Modern World:
Revolutions in Farming,
Food, and Famine

Chapter 8   The Progressive Era and Food

Document 8.1: Samuel Gompers, *Meat vs. Rice: American Manhood Against Asiatic Coolieism, Which Shall Survive* (San Francisco: American Federation of Labor, 1901)

Samuel Gompers was the head of the American Federation of Labor. In the early twentieth century, this was the nation's largest and most stable body of unionized laborers. A cigar maker and socialist in his younger days, Gompers shifted his views as he got older and began to espouse, what some have called, bread and butter unionism. He wanted to raise the pay of workers, not change the country's economic system. In Gompers' view, tightly controlled labor markets helped to maintain decent wages and safe conditions. By the 1870s, this meant strong unions that oversaw the supply of workers by limiting the number of people qualified for a position. It also meant control over immigration. In this document, Gompers lays out his support for the Chinese Exclusion Act, which Congress passed in 1879. The measure barred "skilled and unskilled" Chinese laborers from entering the country.

Beginning in the 1840s, a significant number of Chinese laborers, almost all men, started to arrive on the western shores of the United States. They got jobs with the railroads laying track and doing support work, like cooking, for prospectors in the Gold Rush in California. (This marked, by the way, the opening of some of the first Chinese restaurants in the country.) As long as the economy remained robust and jobs plentiful, the grumbling from white workers remained muffled. But in the 1870s in California, however,

Food and Eating in America: A Documentary Reader, First Edition.
Edited by James C. Giesen and Bryant Simon.
© 2018 John Wiley & Sons, Inc. Published 2018 by John Wiley & Sons, Inc.

unemployment rose and wages dropped. White laborers, especially recently arrived Irish laborers, blamed Chinese laborers for the economic slide. They claimed these men would work for just about anything and under whatever conditions were offered, rather than join with white workers and their allies in a show of class solidarity. Gompers pressed for the exclusion of the Chinese from California and later the nation. The goal, in part at least, was to limit the supply of labor and keep wages up.

In 1901, the Chinese Exclusion Act of 1879 was up for renewal in the United States Congress. The following document represents the concluding paragraphs of Samuel Gompers's 40-page brochure where he explained in (racist) detail his support for keeping this act on the books. This is also where he turns to food. Even though rice and meat are only mentioned in these finals sections, these items are, nonetheless still paired in the pamphlet's title and in the labor leader's analysis of the situation and of what he sees as essential and immutable racial differences. Think about why food choices revealed so much to Gompers as you read the document below.

We cannot, perhaps, close this document in any more fitting manner than by concluding with the remarks made by one of the greatest statesmen of this country, Hon. James G. Blaine, on the 14th day of February, 1879, when the bill restraining Chinese immigration was before the U. S. Senate. Mr. Blaine said:

Either the Anglo-Saxon race will possess the Pacific Slope or the Mongolians will possess it. You give them that start today, with the keen thrust of necessity behind them, and with the inducements to come, while we are filling up the other portions of the continents, and it is inevitable, if not demonstrable, that they will occupy that space of country the Sierra and the Pacific Coast.

The immigrants that come to us from the British Isles and from all portions of Europe, come here with the idea of the family as much engraven on their minds and hearts, and in customs and habits, as we ourselves have. The Asiatic cannot go on with our population and make a homogenous element.

I am opposed to the Chinese coming here. I am opposed to making them citizens. I am unalterably opposed to making them voters. There is not a peasant cottage inhabited by a Chinaman. There is not a hearthstone, in the sense we understand it, of an American home, or an English home, or an Irish, or German, or French home. There is not a domestic fireside in that sense; and yet you say it is entirely safe to sit down and permit them to fill our country, or any part of it.

Treat them like Christians, say those who favor their immigration; yet I believe the Christian testimony is that the conversion of Chinese on that basis is a fearful failure; and that the demoralization of the white race is much more rapid by reason of the contact, than is the salvation of the Chinese race. You cannot work for man who must have beef and bread, and would prefer beef, alongside of a man who can live on rice. In all such conflicts, and in all such struggles, the result is not to bring up the man who lives on rice to the beer and bread stand, but it is to bring down the beef-and-bread man to the rice standard.

Slave labor degraded free labor. It took out its respectability and put an odious cast upon it. It throttled the prosperity of a fine and fair portion of the United States in the South; and this Chinese, which is worse than slave labor, will throttle and impair the prosperity of a still finer and fairer section of the Union on the Pacific Coast.

We have this day to choose whether we will have for the Pacific Coast the civilization of Christ or the civilization of Confucius.

Discussion questions

1. The Senator's—and by implication Gompers'—stance on Chinese immigration is clear, he is strongly opposed to it. But what does food and what do food choices have to do with how Chinese workers allegedly "degraded free labor"?
2. What does he mean when talks about men who must have "beef and bread"? Who are these men and what do they value?
3. What sort of man lives on rice? How does this man threaten the world that Samuel Gompers wanted to create?
4. The law was renewed. Why do you think the notion of meat vs. rice was a successful argument? Who is Gompers appealing to in this document?
5. Can you think of other situations where food traditions are used as a way to explain and justify discrimination and racial prejudice?

Document 8.2: The Pure Food and Drug Act of 1906 (34 Stat. 768)

In 1904, the socialist activist and journalist, Upton Sinclair, lived and worked alongside laborers in Chicago's massive meatpacking plants for nearly two months. His experience on and off the job became the basis for his classic novel, The Jungle. *This book told the story of a fictional family of Lithuanian immigrants who came to America full of hope for a better future and full of strength and vigor. From this upbeat start, the family descends into a modern version of Dante's hell. They lose their jobs and their home, sink into poverty, watch their bodies fall apart, and are driven by their circumstances into homelessness, alcoholism, and prostitution.*

The turn-of-the-century writer Jack London, called The Jungle, *"The Uncle Tom's Cabin of wage slavery." Like Sinclair, London hoped that the book would spark a new abolitionist movement aimed at ending this oppression and curtailing the exploitation of labor in America's emerging capitalist*

economy. But that movement never really took shape. Instead, an outraged
public, horrified by Upton Sinclair's graphic and gross depictions of rancid
meat and of fingers and excrement making their way into hot dogs
and sausage, sparked a consumer revolt. Food buyers demanded that the
government regulate the meatpackers and other supplies. "I aimed at
the public's heart," lamented Sinclair about the reception of his novel, "and
by accident I hit it in the stomach."
*   In 1906, in response to Sinclair's book and the outrage it sparked, the*
United States Congress passed the Meat Inspection Act and the Pure Food
and Drug Act. The text below is from the latter law.

An Act for preventing the manufacture, sale, or transportation of adulterated or misbranded or poisonous or deleterious foods, drugs, medicines, and liquors, and for regulating traffic therein, and for other purposes.

Be it enacted by the Senate and the House of Representatives of the United States of America in Congress assembled, That it shall be unlawful for any person to manufacture within any Territory or the District of Columbia any article of food or drug which is adulterated or misbranded, within the meaning of this Act; and any person who shall violate any of the provisions of this section shall be guilty of a misdemeanor, and for each offense shall, upon conviction thereof, be fined not to exceed five hundred dollars or shall be sentenced to one year's imprisonment, or both such fine and imprisonment, in the discretion of the court, and for each subsequent offense and conviction thereof shall be fined not less than one thousand dollars or sentenced to one year's imprisonment, or both such fine and imprisonment, in the discretion of the court.

Sec. 3. That the Secretary of the Treasury, the Secretary of Agriculture, and the Secretary of Commerce and labor shall make uniform rules and regulations for carrying out the provisions of this Act, including the collection and examination of specimens of foods and drugs manufactured or offered for sale....

Sec. 7. That for the purposes of this Act an article shall be deemed to be adulterated:

In the case of drugs:

First. If, when a drug is sold under or by a name recognized in the United States Pharmacopoeia or Natural Formulary, it differs from the standard or strength, quality, or purity, as determined by the test laid down in the United States Pharmacopoeia or National Formulary official at the time of the investigation: *Provided,* That no drug defined in the United States Pharmacopoeia or National Formulary shall be deemed to be adulterated under this provision if the standard of strength, quality, or purity be plainly stated upon the bottle, box, or other container thereof although the standard may differ from that determined by the test laid down in the United States Pharmacopoeia or National Formulary.

Second. If its strength or purity fall below the professed standard or quality under which it is sold.

In the case of confectionery:

If it contains terra alba, barytes, talc, chrome yellow, or other mineral substance or poisonous color or flavor, or other ingredient deleterious or detrimental to health, or any vinous, malt or spirituous liquor or compound narcotic drug.

In the case of food:

First. If any substance has been mixed and packaged with it so as to reduce or lower or injuriously affect its quality or strength.

Second. If any substance has been substituted wholly or in part for the article.

Third. If any valuable constituent of the article has been wholly or in part abstracted.

Fourth. If it be mixed, colored, powdered, coated, combined in a manner whereby damage or inferiority is concealed.

Fifth. If it contain any added poisonous or other deleterious ingredient which may render such article injurious to health: *Provided*, That when in the preparation of food products for shipment they are preserved by any external application applied in such manner that the preservative is necessarily removed mechanically, or by maceration in water, or otherwise, and directions for the removal of said preservatives shall be printed on the covering or the package, the provisions of this Act shall be construed as applying only when said products are ready for consumption.

Sixth. If it consists in whole or part of a filthy, decomposed, or putrid animal or vegetable substance, or any portion of an animal unfit for food, whether manufactured or not, or if it is the product of a diseased animal, or one that has died otherwise than by slaughter.

Sec. 8. That the term "misbranded," as used herein, shall apply to all drugs, or articles of food, or articles which enter into the composition of food, the package or label of which shall bear any statement, design, or device regarding such article, or the ingredients or substances contained therein which shall be false or misleading in any particular, and to any food or drug product which is falsely branded as to the State, Territory, or country in which it is manufactured or produced.

That for the purposes of this Act an article shall also be deemed to be misbranded:

In the case of food:

First. If it be an imitation of or offered for sale under the distinctive name of another article.

Second. If it be labeled or branded so as to deceive or mislead the purchaser, or purport to be a foreign product when not so, or if the contents of the package as originally put up shall have been removed in whole or in part and other contents shall have been placed in such package, or if it fail to bear a statement on the label of the quantity or proportion of any morphine, opium, cocaine, heroin, alpha or beta eucaine, chloroform, cannabis indica, chloral hydrate, or acetanilide, or any derivative or preparation of any substances contained therein...

Fourth. If the package containing it or its label shall bear any statement, design, or device regarding the ingredients or the substances contained therein, which statement, design, or device shall be false or misleading in any particular.

Discussion questions

1. Was Upton Sinclair right? Did he hit the American stomach with his book? How was the Pure Food and Drug Act evidence of both the success and failure of his novel?
2. Who and what are regulated by the Pure Food and Drug Act? What and who isn't regulated?
3. What sorts of mechanisms for enforcement are put in place by the law?
4. Historians have often identified the Pure Food and Drug Act as a hallmark of Progressive Era legislation. What makes this a Progressive measure? What is the difference between Progressivism and Socialism?
5. Is the Pure Food and Drug Act still relevant? Do we still need the government to regulate our food? Why?
6. How do you know what's in your food? Why is this important?

Document 8.3: "Riots in Newark Over Meat Boycott," *The New York Times* (April 15, 1910)

Immigrants from the British Isles, especially Ireland, and Eastern, Central, and Southern Europe flocked to the United States between 1880 and 1914. According to the noted historian of immigration, Hasia Diner, most crossed the Atlantic not so much because they yearned for freedom or democracy, but because they couldn't get enough to eat at home. They "hungered," as she puts it, for America. Even though most immigrants worked in the burgeoning factories of the United States and were not paid particularly well, they did have enough money for food, certainly more than they had had in their home countries. They celebrated their relative plenty by buying meat, something that before coming to the United States they typically ate only at holiday meals and local festivals. But in America where meat was cheaper and jobs more plentiful, people ate meat just about every day. Italians ate spaghetti at home, but as Hasia Diner's research reveals, spaghetti and meatballs was an American invention. This was also true for the Irish and for Jews—in America, they supplemented and altered traditional dishes with meat.

This article talks about what happened in one American city—Newark, New Jersey, a city of factories and immigrants—in 1910 when meat prices rose. Read carefully to see how people reacted to this development, who they blamed, and why.

Riots in Newark Over Meat Boycott.

Hundreds of Women Turn Out and Join in Attacks on the Butcher Shops. Rabbi Severely Beaten.

Threat of a General Retail Closing Until the Wholesalers Reduce Beef Prices.

Marching Down Prince Street, Newark, last night a mob of 5,000 men, women, and children, who have declared a boycott on the price of food, defied the police to stop them. Many who attempted to hold open-air meetings were frustrated by the police. Some of the agitators who wished to address the crowd got up in the second floor of the houses, and did their speaking from the windows. The police made five arrests, two women and three men.

About 8 PM a man came out of a grocery store carrying a basket filled with packages. A group of rioters stood outside of the place, and when he came out they demanded to know whether he had any meat. He paid no attention to the crowd, and went on his way. Mrs. Ida Jacob of 273 Prince Street was arrested as she grabbed the basket from the man. Its contents were thrown into the street. The rioters then attempted to rescue the woman. The crowd walled in about the patrolman, and he was carried along for nearly 2 blocks.

At 9:30 o'clock the crowd became so great that patrolmen were called in from outlying districts. Late in the night a mob of rioters captured a grocery and meat wagon in Sixteenth Avenue, and poured kerosene oil over the orders of meat that were in the vehicle. Attempts were made to set fire to the wagon, but the prompt arrival of the police prevented it.

Prince Street, which is the centre of the boycott, was turbulent all day. The demonstrations started early in the morning when the proprietors of the meat markets opened up their shops.

The first trouble of the day that the police reserves had to contend with was at the butcher shop of Benjamin Nowick, at 124 Prince Street. Nowick sold some of his stock of meat to several customers, and as soon as they appeared in the streets their packages were wrested from them.

In some cases, the customers were roughly handled and their clothing torn. About that time Morris Yatlowsky, President of the Retail Butchers' Association, arrived on the scene with Benjamin Amade, Issac Schoening, and Herman Menson. Nowick explain to them that he was trying to sell out his stock, intending to close his place last night.

The crowd of rioters gathered in front of the place, and when the women heard Nowick say he was going to sell his stock they charged at him. During the scuffle Nowick had his coat and vest torn off. When the police arrived it was found that he had a stab wound in his right hand. The police made short work of the mob by using their clubs.

A rabbi, Moses Grossbard, of 119 Prince Street, was so badly beaten by a mob that he had to be removed to his home. He had forced his way into a crowd that gathered about the stands of the Roosevelt Market, at 122 Prince Street, and pleaded with the people to return to their homes and not create any disturbance. This talk did not meet with the approval of the crowd, and he was struck down. He was rescued by the police.

At the Uptown Meat Market, 124-126 Prince Street, a crowd made up principally of women entered the place and in spite of the protests of the owners poured kerosene oil on the meat on the counters. Five policemen, led by Roundsman Henry Siepel, fought their way into the place, and made no arrests.

Morris Yatkowsky, head of the Butchers' Association, said that every butcher shop would be closed inside of twenty-four hours, and stay closed until the wholesale dealers lowered the prices of meat.

In the fight against the high price of meat in the city yesterday women attacked two butcher shops. Two pickets of the Women's Progressive Union, organized to fight the high prices, overturned a small barrow filled with cuts of meat, which the son of Abraham Ritzky, a butcher at 913 Longwood Avenue, the Bronx, was taking to his father's market early in the morning. Magistrate Krotel in the Morrisania Court fined them $3 each later, and as the women did not have the money they were locked up. They said they were Fannie Halpern of 491 East 174th Street and Molly Boritz of 1491 Brook Avenue, both of the Bronx.

In the Harlem Court Magistrate House fined Mrs. Mary Israel of 251 East 119th Street $3 for leading a rush into the butcher shop of Morris Friedman at 218 East 112d Street.

Discussion questions

1. Why do you think the people of Newark were so angry about the jump in the price of meat?
2. Who, and be as specific as possible, led the protests? Why was this group at the forefront of the protests?
3. Why do you think these protests took the form(s) they did? Why a boycott? What is a boycott? Who is being boycotted? And what is the significance of the violence associated with the protests? Who is targeted for attack?
4. What were the protesters trying to achieve?
5. In 1910, Newark had a sizable Jewish population. In fact, about 17% of the city was Jewish. Prince Street mentioned in the opening sentence of the article made up the heart of the city's Jewish neighborhood. Most of the protesters were, in fact, probably Jewish. Why, then, did they beat up a Rabbi? What does this incident tell us about Jewish life in the New World?
6. What surprises you the most about this article?

Document 8.4: "Girls' Canning Clubs" from the *Wyoming Farm Bulletin* (April, 1914)

During the Progressive Era (1906–1916), farm families received all kind of advice from others deemed to be experts. One of these expert voices was the Wyoming Farm Bulletin. *This publication was written by university-based extension agents, and their advice centered on efficiency and the everyday application of science. One of the new sciences of the era was the emerging field of nutrition. The document below is an example of this advice and this faith in nutrition as an essential part of foods and a healthy diet. As you read it, think about what the experts are telling rural people? What are the problems they identify and how is canning seen as a solution?*

A few Girls' Canning Clubs have been organized in Wyoming this year. The members are going at the work earnestly and it is very probable that some results will be shown in the fall. It is hoped that every club and many individuals will have exhibits at the State Fair, and so far as possible at the local County Fairs. As home canning the fruits and vegetables becomes better understood, more and more families are taking it up, and the time will come when nearly every family will have a home canner and instead of the daily menu of bread, butter, eggs, meat and potatoes the fare will be varied by the addition of fruits, vegetables and greens, which will keep the children more healthy and there will be less need for the patent medicine laxatives that are now so largely used in the home.

A Department of Agriculture specialist says, that many Americans suffer from indigestion, constipation and rheumatism, and a simple change of the daily menu would go a long way toward remedying these evils. He recommends that every family provide a diet of fruit and vegetables for every day in the year. He says that if every family kept on hand enough canned products so that there might be a can of vegetables for every day during the winter the health of the family would be a great deal better and there would also be great economy in the substitution of inexpensive foods for more expensive ones.

More home canning done at the proper season would save a large amount of food that goes to waste every year. It is estimated that 50% of all vegetables, greens, fruit, and berries that grow in this country go to waste and are actually lost to those that need them. This is because housewives have not learned to care for those surplus products efficiently and to make them available for the winter months by canning.

That home canning may also reduce the cost of living is not generally appreciated. Those who use canned goods often paid transportation charges on the same for long distances, when they could just as well can these products at home at one half or one-third the cost. Canned tomatoes are a good illustration of this. Nearly everyone uses canned tomatoes and on the shelves of any store in Wyoming one may see cans of tomatoes that have been put up in Utah, Maryland or California. The average price is about 15 cents per can. In many parts of the state tomatoes could be put up at home for about 5 cents a can, thus a great saving would be made. There need be no fear of the home canneries hurting the business of the commercial factories as there will always be many who have neither the time nor the inclination to do their own canning. On the contrary, more home canning will accustom people more and more to using canned products.

It is the aim of the Agricultural College and the Department of Agriculture, through the Girls' Canning Clubs to bring the canning industry into the home and this in one more way bring something better of life into the farm home.

It is true that some canning is done in many homes and many say that a regular canning outfit is not necessary. This may be true but often the loss of one lot of fruit or vegetables would easily pay for a home canning outfit. A good home canning outfit can be purchased for as little as $6.00.

Practical experiments have been made by the Bureau of Plant Industry which shows that home canning is profitable. Hey Canning laboratory which is nothing more than an ordinary farm house kitchen, is used for the work. Here recipes that are applicable for every home have been tested and are furnished free to any housewife on application. Farmers' Bulletin No. 521 also contains descriptions of several canning outfits that are suitable for the home, and also valuable suggestions on tomato canning which are applicable to other canned goods. Definitions of canning terms are also included which should be valuable to house wives not familiar with some of the more technical terms. This bulletin may also be obtained free by application to the Department of Agriculture, Washington D.C.

Teachers and others interested in the organization of girls canning clubs or home canning work may get circulars of information and other assistance by writing the Boys' and Girls' Club Department, University of Wyoming, at Laramie.

Discussion questions

1. Who is the intended audience for the article? Why? What does this tell us about gender and homework?
2. According to this article, what will canning do for rural people?
3. How does the article reflect the "progressive" values of efficiency and faith in experts? Point to specific passages.
4. Why do the authors of this short essay single out patent medicines and laxatives? Why aren't these items deemed to be "progressive" or part of the proper and modern application of home economics?

Document 8.5: Lyrics to the Song, "Hoover's Goin' to Get You!" (1918)

Northfield, Minnesota's Mabel L. Clapp's song, "Hoover's Goin' to Get You!" appeared in The Norwegian American *on January 25, 1918. At the time, the United States had just entered World War I and President Woodrow Wilson had recently appointed Herbert Hoover as the United States Food Administrator. Before that, Hoover had led the worldwide effort to feed Belgium after Germany had invaded the country in 1914 and cut off many of its supply routes. Food was clearly a factor in the war and Hoover's position was clearly an important one. As important as it was, however, Hoover's new post came with only limited powers. He did not have the authority, for instance, to ration food. Nor could he set farm prices for commodities or retail prices for foodstuffs for consumers. He could, though, use his position to persuade people about their food buying and eating habits.*

"Food," Hoover asserted over and over again in newspapers articles and in newsreels, "would win the war." One way to secure victory, he insisted, was

through conservation. If people on the homefront ate less, and ate smarter, there would be more food for the troops overseas and the besieged citizens of Europe. The future President urged housewives to eliminate waste and promoted events like wheatless Wednesdays and meatless Mondays. Many Americans, in turn, called their patriotic and voluntary efforts at food conservation, "Hooverizing." How does Clapp's song capture the Hoovering moment?

The "great old Hoover Pledge" has
come to our house to stay;
To frown our breakfast bacon down,
and take our steak away;
It cans our morning waffles, and our
sausage, too, it seems,
And dilates on the succulence of corn,
and spuds and beans,
So skimp the sugar in your cake
and leave the butter out!
Or Hoover's goin' to get you if you
Don't Watch Out!

O, gone now are the good old days of
hot cakes, thickly spread;
And meatless, wheatless, sweetless
days are reigning in their stead;
And gone the days of fat rib roasts,
and two-inch T-bone steaks,
And doughnuts plump and golden
brown, the kind that mother makes
And when it comes to pies and cake,
just learn to cut it out.
Or Hoover's goin' to get you if you
Don't Watch Out!

So spread your buckwheats sparingly,
and peel your taters thin;
And tighten up your belt a notch, and
don't forget to grin.
And, if, sometimes, your whole soul
yearns for shortcake high and wide,
And biscuits drenched with honey, and
chicken, butter fried,
Remember then that Kaiser Bill is
short on sauerkraut.
And Hoover's goin' to get him if we'll
All Help Out!

Discussion questions

1. Was it a political victory for Hoover that Clapp wrote this song and named it after him? How did this effort help Hoover to become President in 1928? Interestingly enough, this seemed to backfire on Hoover later when Hoovervilles, where the homeless of the Great Depression lived, were named after him, doesn't it?
2. While this is a song about conserving food, how does it also document the foods American liked and wanted to eat at the time? What does Clapp tell us about the American diet? What are the principle American foods? The description of the diet in the song borders on gluttony. Why do you think this is the case?
3. Hoover relied officially on voluntary compliance in his food conservation programs. But is that what Clapp describes here? Think about the title of the song. How was food conservation enforced?
4. How, according to the song, did food conservation contribute to the war effort?
5. Some have suggested that food conservation isn't really about food; it is about national unity or creating national unity. Do you agree? Think about where—the actual outlet—this song was published in. What does that tell you about the United States in 1918 and some of the challenges it faced waging war?

Document 8.6: Excerpts from Christine Frederick, "The New Housekeeping," *Ladies' Home Journal* (1912)

Frederick Winslow Taylor is largely forgotten today. Yet in the first decades of the twentieth century, he was remarkably famous. He was widely known for developing the idea of scientific management, the study of work and the organization of work, measuring with a stopwatch each movement a laborer made and how long it took this person to perform an appointed task. He was trying to figure out exactly how a job could be most efficiently organized and thus profitable. His insights revolutionized business and industry, and countless other areas of American life, including, as this document suggests, the kitchen and the household.

Christine Campbell was born in Boston in 1883. She grew up and matured, then, in the era of Taylorism. At the age of 20, she married George Frederick, a Boston businessman and devotee of Taylor and the gospel of efficiency. One day, as she tells it in this document, her husband and an associate were sitting in the family library having a lively discussion about the home and about domestic labor. Their talk quickly turned to time motion studies and efficiency. Overhearing the conversation, Christine Frederick scoffed, "Why I suppose you smart men...will soon try to tell me...that washing dishes can be standardized." That is exactly what they had in mind. And that is exactly what Frederick addresses in this document from 1912.

Ch. One. Efficiency and the New House-Keeping

I was sitting by the library table, mending, while my husband and a business friend were talking, one evening about a year ago. I heard them use several new words and phrases so often that I stopped to listen.

"Efficiency" I heard our caller say a dozen times; "standard practice," "motion study," and "scientific management," he repeated over and over again. The words suggested interesting things, and as I listened I grew absorbed and amazed.

"What are you men talking about?" I interrupted. "I can't help being interested. Won't you please tell me what 'efficiency' is, Mr. Watson? What were you saying about bricklaying?"

"Your husband and I were just discussing this new idea developed in business, called 'efficiency,' or 'scientific management'," Mr. Watson replied. "A group of men, Emerson and Taylor among others, have come to be known in the business and manufacturing world as 'efficiency engineers.' These men are able to go into a shop or factory, watch the men at work, make observations and studies of motions, and from these observations show where waste and false movements occur and why the men lose time. Then they go to work to build up the 'efficiency' of that shop, so that the men do more work in less time, with less waste and greater output or gain to the owners, while the workers have shorter hours, higher pay, and better working conditions."

"Just how do they find out what is wrong?" I asked, laying my sewing on the table, and listening eagerly, "and how do they actually increase this 'efficiency'?"

"Well, for instance" answered Mr. Watson, "this is how they improved the method of laying bricks: Formerly a workman stood before a wall, and when he wanted to lay a brick he had to stoop, pick a brick weighing four and a half pounds from a mixed pile at his feet, and carry it to the wall. Suppose he weighed one hundred and eighty pounds; that worker would have to lower his one hundred and eighty pounds four feet every time he picked up each of the two thousand bricks he laid in a day! Now an efficiency expert, after watching bricklayers at work, devised a simple little table which holds the bricks in an orderly pile at the workman's side. They are brought to him in orderly piles, proper side up. Because he doesn't need to stoop or sort, the same man who formerly could lay only one hundred and twenty bricks an hour can now lay three hundred and fifty bricks, and he uses only five motions, where formerly it required eighteen."

"That sounds like a fairy tale" I laughed skeptically. "What else wonderful can they do with this magic wand of 'efficiency'?"

"It does sound like magic" Mr. Watson replied, "but it is only common sense. There is just one best way, one shortest way to perform any task involving work done with the hands, or the hands and head working in cooperation. These efficiency men merely study to find that one best and shortest way, and when they have found it they call that task 'standardized.' Very often the efficiency is increased because the task is done with fewer motions, with better tools, because of even such a simple thing as changing the height of a work-bench, or the position of the worker."...

"Why, I suppose you smart men and efficiency experts will soon try to tell me and all the other women that washing dishes can be 'standardized,'" I bantered, "or that we could save a million dollars if we would run our homes on 'scientific management'!"

"Now, Mrs. Frederick" replied Mr. Watson seriously, "that is really not too much to imagine. There is no older saying than 'woman's work is never done.' If the principles of efficiency can be successfully carried out in every kind of shop, factory, and business, why couldn't they be carried out equally well in the home?"

"Because" I answered, "in a factory the workers do just one thing, like sewing shoes, or cutting envelopes, and it is easy to standardize one set of operations. But in a home there are dozens, yes, hundreds, of tasks requiring totally different knowledge and movements. There is ironing, dusting, cooking, sewing, baking, and care of children. No two tasks are alike. Instead of working as she would in a factory, at one task, the home-worker peels potatoes, washes dishes, and darns stockings all in the same hour. Yes, and right in the midst of peeling the potatoes she has to drop her knife, and see why the baby is crying.

"You men simply don't understand anything about work in a home" I continued, heatedly. "One day a woman sweeps and dusts, and the next she irons, and the next she bakes, and in-between-times she cares for babies, and sews, answers call bells and 'phones, and markets, and mends the lining of her husband's coat, and makes a coconut cake for Sunday!

"Perhaps she can afford one maid—perhaps she belongs to the fortunate but very small class that can afford two. But even then she has to see that servants don't waste, that they work the best way, and, in addition, put up with their foibles, which is almost as bad as having to do all the work herself.

"Do you mean to tell me that so many kinds of household tasks could be 'standardized,' or that the principles of scientific management could be applied in the home?" I concluded a little triumphantly. "I've talked with numbers of maids, and they all have the same plaint: that there are too many kinds of work to be done by the same person, that they never have any dependable 'off hours,' and that no two families do the same task in the same way. That is why they prefer to work in factories where one set of operations can be standardized; and there you have the whole crux of the servant question."

Mr. Watson shifted his chair with a realization that he had been put up against no simple problem, nor one in which he had experience. Then he answered, "Well, I hadn't considered the idea before, but I believe so strongly in the principles of efficiency and have seen them work out so satisfactorily in every kind of shop where there are different kinds of work and where the owners have said just what you say, that I absolutely know that these principles must have application to any kind of work, and that they could be carried out successfully in the home if you women would only faithfully apply them.

"I must leave now, but I tell you what I'll do. I'll come over some evening to talk to you, and see what we can figure out on home efficiency. I certainly don't see why you couldn't work out some of its principles in a mighty interesting way. Suppose you read this book on scientific management?"

After Mr. Watson had gone, I turned eagerly to my husband. "George" I said, "that efficiency gospel is going to mean a great deal to modern housekeeping, in spite of some doubts I have. Do you know that I am going to work out those principles here in our home! I won't have you men doing all the great and noble things! I'm going to find out how these experts conduct investigations, and all about it, and then apply it to my factory, my business, my home."

The more I thought about it, the stronger hold the idea took upon me. Just a few days previous I had been reading an article by a prominent clubwoman who was solving the servant problem by substituting expensive household equipment in place of her three servants. Another review discussed the number of women who were living in apartments and boarding-houses, and who refused to shoulder the burdens of real homemaking. A third writer enlarged on the lack of youthful marriages, a lack which he claimed was due to the fact that young women of this era refuse to enter the drudgery of household tasks. On all sides it was the problem of the home, the problem of housekeeping and homemaking.

The home problem for the woman of wealth is simple: it is solved. Money, enough of it, will always buy service, just as it can procure the best in any other regard. The home problem for the women of the very poor is also fairly simple. The women of the poor themselves come from the class of servants. Their homemaking is far less complex, their tastes simple, and society demands no appearance-standard from them. Added to this, organized philanthropy is by every means teaching the women of the poor how to keep house in the most scientific, efficient manner. Settlements, domestic science classes, model kitchens and tenements, nursing stations, slum depots, charity boards, health boards, visiting nurses, night schools, and mission classes are teaching, free, the women of the poor how to transmute their old-world ignorance into the shining knowledge of the new hemisphere.

The problem, the real issue, confronts the middle-class woman of slight strength and still slighter means, and of whom society expects so much—the wives of ministers on small salary, wives of bank clerks, shoe salesmen, college professors, and young men in various businesses starting to make their way. They are refined, educated women, many with a college or business training. They have one or more babies to care for, and limited finances to meet the situation.

The soaring cost of living and the necessity for keeping up a fair standard of appearances obligatory on the middle class prevent any but the more than "average" well-to-do from employing regular help. Among ten average families I know (scattered the country over) whose incomes range from $1,200 to $2,500 a year, the occupations range as follows:

Two high-grade mechanics
One salesman in photo supplies
One salesman in office equipment
One artist and illustrator
One young doctor
One lawyer
One advertising man
One literary man...

I determined then to give this gospel of efficiency a fair trial, but first I wanted Mr. Watson, himself an efficiency engineer, to explain it thoroughly.

"Now, Mr. Watson" I said a few evenings later, "I want you to explain the principles of efficiency to me—the how, the why—so that I and all the other homemakers can understand it fully."

"Gladly"" replied Mr. Watson; "I'll begin by stating the twelve principles on which the science of efficiency rests:

1.   Ideals
2.   Common Sense
3.   Competent Counsel

4. Standardized Operations
5. Standardized Conditions
6. Standard Practice
7. Dispatching
8. Scheduling
9. Reliable Records
10. Discipline
11. Fair Deal
12. Efficiency Reward

"You notice that the first principle is that of 'ideals.' The first thing an efficiency expert finds out when he wishes to improve the standard of a plant is, what are its ideals? What is it running for? These experts say it is astounding how many people are running businesses and don't know why they are running them! I sometimes think that many women don't consciously know why they are running their homes. The ideal should be so strong, so clearly kept in mind, that it will overweigh any present petty difficulties. Ideals look to the future, they are the 'something' that guides, directs, propels the whole machinery, whether of business or the home—do you get my meaning?

"Women *do* have ideals as to why they run their homes," Mr. Watson continued "only they are not always concretely expressed to themselves. It may be health, it may be spotless cleanliness, social progress, or something else. I know a woman who takes her babies out for a morning's airing and leaves the parlor undusted, even though she dislikes untidiness. But her ideal of health comes first. Then another woman has turned her guest-room over to her two boys for their wireless and electricity apparatus. You know what a pretty guest-room means to a woman! But this mother has such a strong ideal of the future training and habits of her boys that she is willing to sacrifice a present pleasure for a remote end. Ideals can be so strong as to buoy up, overweigh difficulty, and be a vital spur to effort, in the home particularly. The clearer a woman's ideals, the easier her work, the greater her strength and success. She must know the 'why' of her business.

"Common Sense is the next principle, and some people think this homely term covers all the principles. It is only common sense not to stoop for a pot if you can hang it where you don't need to stoop—and it is efficiency as well."

"And what does 'competent counsel' mean?" I questioned.

"Competent Counsel means expert advice and help. The efficiency engineers who are called in to large factories to find what is wrong, or suggest better methods, are one kind of competent counsel."

"Yes, but there are no efficiency experts in housekeeping, are there?" I inquired.

"If the housewife would only realize it, there is more expert advice being offered her free than is being offered any manufacturer. Take the pages in all the best publications devoted to the science of home management. The finest specialists and experts are retained by magazines to tell women how to care for babies, prepare foods, how to economize and how to make clothing. Both the booklets and the advertisements of various advertisers inform the housewife of new methods, recipes, devices, materials....

"Then comes Standardized Operations, which includes the oft-mentioned 'motion study,'" Mr. Watson continued. "The homemaker takes countless steps and motions in every task, many of which are entirely avoidable. She may walk twenty feet to hang up the egg-beater; she may wash dishes in a way that wastes time and effort; or she lifts separately each piece of laundry from the basket at her feet, when the efficient thing would be to place the whole basket at her own level. Standardized conditions mean the right height of work-table, proper light, ventilation, and the correct tool for the purpose...

"What is this next point of 'Dispatching'?"...

"...Planning and arranging work come under these points... Applied to housework it would mean that there was a definite regular time for each task, so that each task was done at a certain time in relation to other tasks....

"Ninety per cent. of servant troubles are at bottom the fault of the mistress" Mr. Watson declared. "Now if a woman knew and applied scientifically the principle of 'fair play' her help wouldn't leave her, sick, in bed, as I have heard some maids have done. An efficient mistress would handle her help as scientifically as the manager of a big shop. She will use the principle of 'efficiency reward' with her helpers, and know how to secure from them that 'initiative'—that something over and above mere work which is essential, while at the same time she improves the conditions under which they work."

"If efficiency in the home can accomplish all you make me believe it can" I replied, "a new housekeeping will have come, and homemaking will be the greatest profession."

Discussion questions

1. Why does Christine Frederick, according to her account, resist, at first, the application of the principles of scientific management to the household?
2. Why does she change her thinking? Why does she begin to call her household a business?
3. What sorts of big and small changes does she make as she introduces "science" into her household?

4. As discussed earlier, most conversations about food, about cooking, and about household management, are really conversations about gender. How do ideas about gender, about the supposed true "nature" of men and women, get woven through this document? How is scientific management portrayed as male? According to Frederick, how do women's bodies and natures get in the way of efficiency? How, does she think, women could become more scientific, efficient, and ultimately modern?

Document 8.7: LuAnn Jones, "Work Was My Pleasure: An Oral History of Nellie Stancil Langley" (1991)

Historian and museum curator LuAnn Jones wanted to learn more about the lives of rural women in the American South in the first half of the twentieth century. She quickly discovered that these were not the kinds of people who showed up in the newspapers or left behind large collections of papers and documents that ended up in university archives and research libraries. If she was going to find about these people, about their daily lives and their social histories, she was going to have to sit down with them and talk with them.

Born in 1918 in Wilson County, North Carolina, in the eastern and more rural sections of the state, Nellie Stancil Langley spent much of her life growing food, preparing food, and selling food. In this interview, she tells Jones about her family's attitude towards food and consumption. In particular, she talks about the chickens they raised and sold and how these efforts shaped her family's household economy. As you read, think about the differences between now and then, about where our food comes from and our relationship to the food supply. Also think about the role of women in food systems.

We raised everything. We used to raise our popcorn. We did. We didn't have to buy nothing. You know, we didn't have to buy Christmas trees or Christmas decorations. We made 'em. Mama used to go in the woods and cut a lot of holly, string it and put it all over the windows and decorate with holly. I know this sounds crazy, but we used to have to loop tobacco on a stick. When we'd take that tobacco off dry to grade it and tie it, we'd save them tobacco twines and make round balls. About a week before Christmas we'd soak those balls in kerosene. We would strike a match to them and throw them to each other. It's a wonder we didn't hurt ourselves. We called them fireballs. That was our Christmas.

If we didn't raise it, we didn't eat it. I know we used to dry apples and we used to pick peas and we'd hang them up in the top of the barn in a sack down on a string where the rats couldn't climb down that string. What peas we couldn't eat green and can green, we would pick them and sheet them up in cotton sheets, and when we got caught up on the farm we'd beat them peas out and put them in bags and hang them up in a barn. But now you can't; when I dry my apples I have to put them in the freezer.

We had chickens all over the back yard. You couldn't walk out there without getting in chicken stuff. The hog pen come right up there next to the house. We had mule stables out here. We had a log corn barn, and we had two log tobacco barns. We had a milk cow and a place out for the cow to stay. Okay, we'd milk the cow, we'd put the milk in pans and then let the cream come on top. We'd skim that cream off, shake it in a big gallon fruit jar and make butter. Then if you wanted to keep the milk 'til the next day, we'd have to let it down in that open well on a rope and it hung down in that cold water all day long.

We used to kill a lot of hogs. Back then we had no freezer, we couldn't freeze anything. We would can it. I don't know why in the world it didn't kill us. We'd fry us a sausage and put it in big quart jars and fill it full of the sausage grease. We done lean meat the same way. And sometimes when we'd kill hogs we would put a bunch of the fresh sausage at the bottom of a lard stand and then fill it up with lard. And sometimes we would hang sausage up in the smokehouse to dry so it wouldn't spoil.

Biddies in the House

Back then when Mama was living, you didn't buy biddies [baby chicks]. You raised them. You'd save your prettiest, biggest eggs and set them under a chicken hen. You'd have nests, you know. You started out mostly in the spring of the year to set your hens. I don't know why, but you could always tell when one set on a nest two or three days you felt like she'd be a good mama so you'd put fifteen or sixteen eggs under her. I think it took twenty-one days [for the eggs to hatch]. Sometimes she'd hatch them all, and then again there'd be two or three under there no good. And she'd come off the nest with the biddies. You'd see them all in the yard, a chicken hen with fifteen or sixteen little biddies going behind her. If it rained, she'd run and get under a shelter or bush or something.

If Mama had a hen hatch in the winter time, you couldn't leave them out there so she'd bring the biddies in the house. We had a great big fireplace in our living room. She'd get a big pasteboard box and put paper or a big old rag at the bottom. You'd have to clean it out every day. We'd raise them in here in boxes until they got maybe half a pound or a pound. You can imagine how this house smelled. I mean, biddies in pasteboard boxes in the house. People wouldn't do it no more. Sometimes at night you'd wake up and they'd be running all over the floor. (I've done it, too, so we'd have some early chickens to eat, some fryers.)

Then Mama built little chicken houses out of tobacco sticks and put a piece of tin or a plank across the top so when it rained it wouldn't rain on them.

They just raised theirself in the yards. Sometimes she'd have corn shelled and cracked [to feed them]. And scraps, pour the scraps out. They'd eat up your collards or what turnips you didn't have covered up or anything green that was growing in a garden. They more or less looked after their selves.

On Sunday is when we had fried chicken. She'd get up that morning and kill two and clean them. She had a big bucket full of boiling water. She'd kill the chicken—just wring its neck. She'd stick the chicken down in that hot boiling water and you could stand right there and pull all the feathers off. Then take a piece of paper and get the paper on fire and hold the chicken and get the yellow fuzz off. Swinge them, they called it, [meaning to singe them]. Swinge them. Clean it good on the outside and cut the head off and the feet. I used to love the feet; don't ever see a chicken foot no more. Clean the feet and then you put it in another bucket of clean water and scrape it and gut it and go all over it again. You got good, clean chicken then.

Yes, chickens were a whole lot better back then. You didn't see no black bones then. Can't you buy chickens now that you see the bones turned a little bit dark? But they say that's because of being raised so quick. Back then it took a long while. They say you can do it now in six to eight weeks, but back then it used to take us six months, 'cause they won't on a floored pen and they just picked up what they could find out in the yard to eat. They just had a better taste.

You had them coming off all during the year. All different sizes. You'd see some just been hatched; you'd see some about like a big ball and then you'd have some just right to eat and some too big to eat. We always tried to make chicken salad out of the big roosters. Then we'd have the pretty hens we were saving, you know, to lay and hatch.

We got more eggs in the summertime, because in the wintertime it would get cold. Seems like chickens didn't lay good when it got cold back then. But I guess since they've got them in houses they lay about all the time. In the wintertime we'd kind of have to save the eggs up for Christmas or Thanksgiving so we'd be sure to have enough to make cakes with. The cakes turned out prettier. They were more yellow than they are now. Egg yolks made the cake more yellow.

A long time ago there used to be men selling fish traveling up and down the road. We'd trade them three eggs for a piece of ice or three eggs and a salted down hog head for a mess of fish. Or if we had enough eggs we could get us a cold drink. They'd put them in there and carry them to where they could sell them. That's the first [soft] drink we ever had; a man come by selling drinks. The [fish man] that used to come by here so much used to come from Wilson. There used to be a lot of that up and down the road, but it's not any more. And our mailman would stop here and buy eggs.

We'd carry them to the store we traded at, we sure did. But we didn't get nothing for them. We'd carry ten or twelve dozen up there at a time and try to pay on our bill, so we could get us at least a piece of cheese to eat. It was Christmas if we could get a piece of cheese; we thought that was something.

Discussion questions

1. What do you think Langley's foodscape looked like? In other words, where did she get her food from, what did she grow, and what did she buy? How and where did she make her food?
2. What is Langley's attitude towards food and the purchase of food? How does she structure her consumer choices and what her family eats?
3. How does the family raise its chickens? What details about this process stick out to you? Going back to question one, how are these chickens indicative of Langley's larger food world?
4. Langley doesn't say much about men in her account, does she? Why not? What role do you think that men played in the household economies of procuring and making food in rural America in the early twentieth century?
5. How does this form of production differ from what we have today?
6. What are the strengths of this system of growing meat? What are the drawbacks? Think big here.

Document 8.8: "HOT Hamburger: Just Off the Griddle," January 1, 1926, from Josh Ozersky, *The Hamburger: A History* (New Haven: Yale University Press, 2008), 21

In 2008, Josh Ozersky, the longtime food editor for New York Magazine, *published a book entitled,* The Hamburger: A History. *In it, he called Edgar Waldo "Billy" Ingram, the founder of the White Castle chain, the "Henry Ford of hamburgers." Like Ford, Ingram standardized the food and made it relatively affordable and widely available. He started his chain of eateries selling five cent burgers in 1921 in Wichita, Kansas, at the start of "The Roaring Twenties." Five years later, Ingram and his associates started a newsletter called "Hot Hamburger." In the first installment, one article insisted that the hamburger had become "A STABILIZED FOOD PRODUCT."*

THE HAMBURGER AS A STABILIZED FOOD PRODUCT.

When the word "hamburger" is mentioned one immediately thinks of the circus, or carnival, or the county fairs, or even of the dirty, dingy, ill-lighted hole-in-the-wall, down in the lower districts of the city.

The day of the dirty, greasy hamburger is passed. No more shall we be privileged to taste the hamburger at the circuses and carnivals only, for a new system has arisen, the "White Castle System."

The hamburger contains the three main items of the American diet, namely bread, meat and vegetables, properly proportioned in exact amounts to make a nutritious sandwich.

A revelation in the eating business has come. Instead of having to go to a restaurant and wait half an hour before the noon lunch, one may step into a nearby hamburger establishment and partake of a hot, juicy hamburger, prepared instantaneously.

They may be taken out in parcels to the homes, on pleasure trips, picnics, etc. And as a well-known St. Louis magazine puts it, "The sandwiches are not alone as cheap as they were ever served but a better and more palatable sandwich than was served several years ago."

The materials used are selected and purchased from establishments who specialize in their particular line, and are served by men who have served their apprenticeship in the hamburger business.

Through constant study and application of all concerned the lowly hamburger is gradually winning its way and has become one of the most economical foods available to the public.

Discussion questions

1. What do the people from White Castle mean when they call the "hamburger a stabilized food product?" Why is this a good thing? How does this relate to standardization, even scientific management, and to the related value of predictability? Why are these things important to chains, and really to modern eating?
2. Why does the document draw a comparison between White Castle burgers and the burgers found at the county fair? What are the virtues of White Castle (and again of chains)?
3. What is the importance of price here? Is this about cheapness or about relative prosperity? Think here about the times, i.e. the 1920s. What do you know about the economy of the 1920s?
4. What makes the hamburger "an American" food? What does it say about America, its culinary traditions and its diverse population?
5. The newsletter predicts that White Castle will be a "revelation in the eating business?" Was this claim correct? How so? How does White Castle anticipate McDonald's? How does McDonald's take things to another level?

Chapter 9   The Great Depression

Document 9.1: Oscar Heline, farmer from Iowa, interviewed by Studs Terkel in *Hard Times* (New York: Pantheon, 1970, 217–21)[1]

Studs Terkel was one of the great chroniclers of American life. Relying largely on oral histories, he recounted in his books and on his Chicago-based radio show, the everyday experiences of ordinary Americans at home, at war, and at work. In Hard Times, *he related the stories of the Great Depression.*

In 1970, Terkel sat down with 78-year-old Oscar Heline at his home, set back from a gravel road in Marcus, Iowa, a small town of 1,200 residents in the northwest corner of the state. The longtime hog farmer told him about "the struggles" he and others who produced the nation's food had to go through during the 1930s. As you read this passage, think about how the deep economic crisis that we call the Great Depression affected farmers. How did they respond? How were they changed by what they experienced during in this decade-long period of economic collapse and crisis?

The farmers became desperate. It got so a neighbor wouldn't buy from a neighbor, because the farmer didn't get any of it. It went to the creditors. And it wasn't enough to satisfy them. What's the use of having a farm sale?

[1] Excerpt from *Hard Times: An Oral History of the Great Depression* - Copyright © 1970, 1986 by Studs Terkel. Reprinted by permission of The New Press. www.thenewpress.com

Why do we permit them to go on? It doesn't cover the debts, it doesn't liquidate the obligation. He's out of business, and it's still hung over him. First, they'd take your farm, then they take your livestock, then your farm machinery. Even your household goods. And they'd move you off. The farmers were almost united. We had penny auction sales. Some neighbor would bid a penny and give it back to the owner.

Grain was being burned. It was cheaper than coal. Corn was being burned. The county just east of here, they burned corn in their courthouse all winter.'32,'33. You couldn't hardly buy groceries for corn. It couldn't pay the transportation. In South Dakota, the county elevator listed corn as minus three cents. *Minus* three cents a bushel. If you wanted to sell'em a bushel of corn, you had to bring in $.03. They couldn't afford to handle it. Just think what happens when you can't get out from under....

We had lots of trouble on the highway. People were determined to withhold produce from the market—Livestock, cream, butter, eggs, what not. If they wouldn't dump the produce, they would force the market to a higher level. The farmers would man the highways, and cream cans were emptied in ditches and eggs dumped out. They burned the trestle bridge, so the trains wouldn't be able to haul grain. Conservatives don't like this kind of rebel attitude and aren't very sympathetic. But something had to be done.

I spent most of my time in Des Moines as a lobbyist for the state cooperatives. Trying to get some legislation. I wasn't out on the highway fighting this battle. Some of the farmers probably didn't think I was friendly to their cause. They were so desperate. If you weren't out there with them, you weren't a friend you must be a foe. I didn't know from day to day whether somebody might come along and cause harm to my family. You have bridges burned, accidents, violence, there may have been killings, I don't know.

There were some pretty conservative ones, wouldn't join this group. I didn't want to particularly, because it wasn't the answer. It took that kind of action, but what I mean is it took more than that to solve it. You had to do constructive things at the same time. But I never spoke harshly about those who are on the highway.

Some of the farmers with teams of horses, sometimes in trucks, tried to get through. He was trying to feed his family, trying to trade a few dozen eggs and a few pounds of cream for some groceries to feed his babies. He was desperate, too. One group tried to sell so they could live and the other group tried to keep you from selling so they could live.

The Farmer is a pretty independent individual. He wants to be a conservative individual. He wants to be an honorable individual. He wants to pay his debts. But it was hard. The rank-and-file people of the state—who were brought up as conservatives, which most of us were—would never act like this. Except in desperation.

There were a few who had a little more credit than the others. They were willing to go on as usual. Mostly the ones who tried to break the picket lines. They were the ones who gained at the expense of the poor. They had the money to buy when things were cheap. There are always a few who make money out of other people's poverty. This was a struggle between the haves and the have-nots.

The original bankers who came to the state, for instance. When my father would borrow $100, he would get $80. And when it was due, he'd pay back the $100 and a premium besides that. Most of his early borrowings were on this basis. That's where we made some wealthy families in this country.

We did pass some legislation. The first thing we did was stop the power of the judges to issue deficiency judgment. The theory was: the property would come back to you some day. The next law provided for committees in every county: adjudication committees.... People got time. The land banks and insurance companies started out hard-boiled. They got the farm, they got the judgment and then found out it didn't do them any good. They had to have somebody to run it. So they'd turn around and rent it to the fella who lost it. He wasn't a good renter. The poor fellow lost all his capacity for fairness, because he couldn't be fair. He had to live. All the renters would go in cahoots. So the banks and companies got smart and stopped foreclosing.

Through a federal program we got a farm loan. A committee of twenty-five of us drafted the first farm legislation of this kind 35 years ago. We drew it up with Henry Wallace. New money was put in the farmers' hands. The federal government changed the whole marketing program from burning 10-cent corn two 45-cent corn. People could now see daylight and hope. It was a whole transformation of attitude. You can just imagine…

It was Wallace who saved us, put us back on our feet. He understood our problems. When we went to visit him, after he was appointed Secretary, he made it clear to us he didn't want to write the law. He wanted the farmers themselves to write it. "I will work with you," he said, "but you're the people who are suffering. It must be your program." He would always give his counsel, but he never directed us, the program came from the farmers themselves, you betcha.

Another thing happened: we had twice too many hogs because corn'd been so cheap. And we set up with people called Wallace's Folly: killing the little pigs. Another farmer and I helped develop this. We couldn't afford to feed 45-cents corn to a $3 hog. So we had to figure out a way of getting rid of the surplus pigs. We went out and bought 'em and killed 'em. This is how desperate it was. It was the only way to raise the price of pigs. Most of 'em were dumped down the river.

The hard times put farmers' families closer together. My wife was working for the County Farm Bureau. We had lessons in home economics, how to make underwear out of gunny sack, flour sacks. So some good things came out of this. Sympathy toward one another was manifest. There were personal values as well as terrible hardships.

The real boost came when we got into the Second World War. Everybody was paying on old debts and mortgages, but the land values were going down. It's gone up now more than ever in the history of the country. The war…(A long pause.)

It does something to your country. It's what's making employment. It does something to the individual. I had a neighbor just as the war was beginning. We had a boy ready to go to service. This neighbor one day told me what we needed was a damn good war, and we'd solve our agricultural problems. And I said, "Yes, but I'd hate to pay with the price of my son." Which we did. (He weeps.) It's too much of a price to pay…

In'28, I was chairman of the farm delegation which met with Hoover. My family had always been Republican, and I supported him. To my disappointment. I don't think the Depression was all his fault. He tried. But all his plans failed, because he didn't have the government involved. He depended on individual organizations.

It's a strange thing. This is only 35 years ago—Roosevelt, Wallace. We have a new generation in business today. Successful. It's surprising how quickly they forget the assistance their fathers got from the government. The Farm Bureau, which I helped organize in this state, didn't help us in'35. They take the same position today: we don't need the government. I'm just as sure as I'm sitting here we can't do it ourselves. Individuals have too many different interests. Who bailed out the land banks when they were busted in the 30s? It was the federal government.

What I remember most of those times is that poverty creates desperation, and desperation creates violence. In Plymouth County—LeMars—just west of us, a group met one morning and decided they were going to stop the judge from issuing anymore deficiency judgments. This judge had a habit of very quickly okaying foreclosure sales. These farmers couldn't stand it anymore. They'd see their neighbors sold out.

There were a few judges who would refuse to take the cases. They'd postpone it or turn it over to somebody else. But this one was pretty gruff and arrogant: "You do this, you do that, it's my court." When a bunch of farmers are going broke every day and the judge sits there very proudly and says: "This is my court"; They say: "Who the hell are you?" He was just a fellow human being, same as they were.

These farmers gathered this one particular day. I suppose some of them decided to have a little drink, and so they developed a little courage. We'll go down and teach that judge a lesson. They marched into the court room, hats on, demanded to visit with him. He decided he would teach them a lesson. So he says: "Gentlemen, this is my court. Remove your hats and address the court properly."

They just laughed at him. They said, "We're not concerned whose court this is. We came here to get redress from your actions. The things you're doing, we can't stand to have done to us anymore." The argument kept on, and got rougher. He wouldn't listen. He threatened them. So they drug him from his chair, pulled him down the steps of the courthouse, and shook a rope in front of his face. Then, tarred and feathered him.

The governor called out the National Guard. And put the farmers behind barbed wire. Just imagine...(he weeps)...in this state. You don't forget these things.

Discussion questions

1. How do Heline and the people around him on the countryside and on the farms experience the Great Depression? How were their experiences different in terms of food from people living in the cities?
2. Why did people burn their crops?
3. Heline says that he spent much of his time during the 1930s in Des Moines, Iowa's capital city, as a lobbyist for the state cooperatives. How would a cooperative act as a break against the Great Depression? What resistance did Heline encounter in his cooperative work?
4. Who did Heline say saved the nation's farmers? How were the farms saved? What was the impact of government policies?
5. Why did Heline switch his political affiliation during the 1930s? What did he see as the purpose of government?
6. Several times during the interview, Terkel says that Heline "weeps." What made him cry as he remembered the Great Depression?

Document 9.2: John Steinbeck, "The Harvest of Gypsies," *San Francisco Chronicle* (October 5, 1936)

John Steinbeck told the stories of twentieth-century America. Born into a middle-class family from Salinas, California, a small town on the edge of California's sprawling empire of massive factory farms, Steinbeck honed a brand of gritty fiction that captured the heartbreak and fleeting triumphs of the Golden State's field hands, fisherman, and factory operatives. With thick description and pinpoint detail, his fiction served as an emotive literary counterpoint to the documentary photographs of Dorothea Lange and the filmmaking of John Ford from the same Depression-marred era.

Steinbeck's most famous novel, The Grapes of Wrath, *told the story of the Joad family who were pushed off their farm in Oklahoma by unscrupulous bankers and relentless dust storms. They ended up scraping together a living picking peaches and filling up bales of cotton in California's Central Valley. This wasn't the first time Steinbeck wrote about the trials of the so-called Okies. In 1936, in what in retrospect looks like a prequel to the novel, he researched and wrote a series of newspaper articles about itinerant agricultural workers for the* San Francisco Chronicle, *which he called "The Harvest Gypsies." The following article is the first installment in the six-part series.*

At this season of the year, when California's great crops are coming into harvest, the heavy grapes, the prunes, the apples and lettuce and the rapidly maturing cotton, our highways swarm with the migrant workers, that shifting group of nomadic, poverty-stricken harvesters driven by hunger and the threat of hunger from crop to crop, from harvest to harvest, up and down the state and into Oregon to some extent, and into Washington a little. But it is California which has and needs the majority of these new gypsies. It is a short study of these wanderers that these articles will undertake. There are at least 150,000 homeless migrants wandering up and down the state, and that is an army large enough to make it important to every person in the state.

To the casual traveler on the great highways the movements of the migrants are mysterious if they are seen at all, for suddenly the roads will be filled with open rattletrap cars loaded with children and with dirty bedding, with fire-blackened cooking utensils. The boxcars and gondolas on the railroad lines will be filled with men. And then, just as suddenly, they will have disappeared from the main routes. On side roads and near rivers where there is little travel the squalid, filthy squatters' camp will have been set up, and the orchards will be filled with pickers and cutters and driers.

The unique nature of California agriculture requires that these migrants exist, and requires that they move about. Peaches and grapes, hops and cotton cannot be harvested by a resident population of laborers. For example, a large peach orchard which requires the work of 20 men the year round will need as many as 2000 for the brief time of picking and packing. And if the migration of the 2000 should not occur, if it should be delayed even a week, the crop will rot and be lost.

Thus, in California we find a curious attitude toward a group that makes our agriculture successful. The migrants are needed, and they are hated. Arriving in a district they find the dislike always meted out by the resident to the foreigner, the outlander. This hatred of the stranger occurs in the whole range of human history, from the most primitive village form to our own highly organized industrial farming. The migrants are hated for the following reasons, that they are ignorant and dirty people, that they are carriers of disease, that they increase the necessity for police and the tax bill for schooling in a community, and that if they are allowed to organize they can, simply by refusing to work, wipe out the season's crops. They are never received into a community nor into the life of a community. Wanderers in fact, they are never allowed to feel at home in the communities that demand their services.

Let us see what kind of people they are, where they come from, and the routes of their wanderings. In the past they have been of several races, encouraged to come and often imported as cheap labor; Chinese in the early period, then Filipinos, Japanese and Mexicans. These were foreigners, and as such they were ostracized and segregated and herded about.

If they attempted to organize they were deported or arrested, and having no advocates they were never able to get a hearing for their problems. But in recent years the foreign migrants have begun to organize, and at this danger signal they have been deported in great numbers, for there was a new reservoir from which a great quantity of cheap labor could be obtained.

The drought in the middle west has driven the agricultural populations of Oklahoma, Nebraska and parts of Kansas and Texas westward. Their lands are destroyed and they can never go back to them.

Thousands of them are crossing the borders in ancient rattling automobiles, destitute and hungry and homeless, ready to accept any pay so that they may eat and feed their children. And this is a new thing in migrant labor, for the foreign workers were usually imported without their children and everything that remains of their old life with them.

They arrive in California usually having used up every resource to get here, even to the selling of the poor blankets and utensils and tools on the way to buy gasoline. They arrive bewildered and beaten and usually in a state of semi-starvation, with only one necessity to face immediately, and that is to find work at any wage in order that the family may eat.

And there is only one field in California that can receive them. Ineligible for relief, they must become migratory field workers.

Because the old kind of laborers, Mexicans and Filipinos, are being deported and repatriated very rapidly, while on the other hand the river of dust bowl refugees increases all the time, it is this new kind of migrant that we shall largely consider.

The earlier foreign migrants have invariably been drawn from a peon class. This is not the case with the new migrants.

They are small farmers who have lost their farms, or farm hands who have lived with the family in the old American way. They are men who have worked hard on their own farms and have felt the pride of possessing and living in close touch with the land.

They are resourceful and intelligent Americans who have gone through the hell of the drought, have seen their lands wither and die and the top soil blow away; and this, to a man who has owned his land, is a curious and terrible pain.

And then they have made the crossing and have seen often the death of their children on the way. Their cars have been broken down and been repaired with the ingenuity of the land man.

Often they patched the worn-out tires every few miles. They have weathered the thing, and they can weather much more for their blood is strong.

They are descendants of men who crossed into the middle west, who won their lands by fighting, who cultivated the prairies and stayed with them until they went back to desert.

And because of their tradition and their training, they are not migrants by nature. They are gypsies by force of circumstances.

In their heads, as they move wearily from harvest to harvest, there is one urge and one overwhelming need, to acquire a little land again, and to settle on it and stop their wandering. One has only to go into the squatters' camps where the families live on the ground and have no homes, no beds and no equipment; and one has only to look at the strong purposeful faces, often filled with pain and more often, when they see the corporation-held idle lands, filled with anger, to know that this new race is here to stay and that heed must be taken of it.

It should be understood that with this new race the old methods of repression, of starvation wages, of jailing, beating and intimidation are not going to work; these are American people. Consequently we must meet them with understanding and attempt to work out the problem to their benefit as well as ours.

It is difficult to believe what one large speculative farmer has said, that the success of California agriculture requires that we create and maintain a peon class. For if this is true, then California must depart from the semblance of democratic government that remains here.

The names of the new migrants indicate that they are of English, German and Scandinavian descent. There are Munns, Holbrooks, Hansens, Schmidts.

And they are strangely anachronistic in one way: Having been brought up in the prairies where industrialization never penetrated, they have jumped with no transition from the old agrarian, self-containing farm where nearly everything used was raised or manufactured, to a system of agriculture so industrialized that the man who plants a crop does not often see, let alone harvest, the fruit of his planting, where the migrant has no contact with the growth cycle.

And there is another difference between their old life and the new. They have come from the little farm districts where democracy was not only possible but inevitable, where popular government, whether practiced in the Grange, in church organization or in local government, was the responsibility of every man. And they have come into the country where, because of the movement necessary to make a living, they are not allowed any vote whatever, but are rather considered a properly unprivileged class.

Let us see the fields that require the impact of their labor and the districts to which they must travel. As one little boy in a squatters camp said, "When they need us they call us migrants, and when we've picked their crop, we're bums and we got to get out."

There are the vegetable crops of the Imperial Valley, the lettuce, cauliflower, tomatoes, cabbage to be picked and packed, to be hoed and irrigated. There are several crops a year to be harvested, but there is not time distribution sufficient to give the migrants permanent work.

The orange orchards deliver two crops a year, but the picking season is short. Farther north, in Kern County and up the San Joaquin Valley, the migrants are needed for grapes, cotton, pears, melons, beans and peaches.

In the outer valley, near Salinas, Watsonville, and Santa Clara there are lettuce, cauliflowers, artichokes, apples, prunes, apricots. North of San Francisco the produce is of grapes, deciduous fruits and hops. The Sacramento Valley needs masses of migrants for its asparagus, its walnuts, peaches, prunes, etc. These great valleys with their intensive farming make their seasonal demands on migrant labor.

A short time, then, before the actual picking begins, there is the scurrying on the highways, the families in open cars hurrying to the ready crops and hurrying to be first at work. For it has been the habit of the growers associations of the state to provide by importation, twice as much labor as was necessary, so that wages might remain low.

Hence the hurry, for if the migrant is a little late the places may all be filled and he will have taken his trip for nothing. And there are many things that may happen even if he is in time. The crop may be late, or there may occur one of those situations like that at Nipomo last year when twelve hundred workers arrived to pick the pea crop only to find it spoiled by rain.

All resources having been used to get to the field, the migrants could not move on; they stayed and starved until government aid tardily was found for them.

And so they move, frantically, with starvation close behind them. And in this series of articles we shall try to see how they live and what kind of people they are, what their living standard is, what is done for them and to them, and what their problems and needs are. For while California has been successful in its use of migrant labor, it is gradually building a human structure which will certainly change the State, and may, if handled with the inhumanity and stupidity that have characterized the past, destroy the present system of agricultural economics.

Discussion questions

1. About halfway through the article, Steinbeck writes, "And because of their tradition and their training, they are not migrants by nature. They are gypsies by force of circumstances." Why does Steinbeck draw a distinction between migrants and gypsies, nature and circumstances? And what were the traditions of the these people?

2. What were the circumstances, including the food circumstances, that brought this group to California? Can big agriculture exist without these gypsies/migrants? Why are they so crucial to the process of growing food? And why were people willing—is willing the right word?—to work for such low wages and in such bad conditions? How are they kept in place politically and socially? How, according to Steinbeck, were they trying to change their circumstances?

3. What does the history of gypsies have to do with the history of food? What does this article tell us about the food chain in the United States in the 1930s and beyond? (The food chain represents all the links and all the people and laws and regulations that get our food from the fields to our forks.)

4. What conditions do you think Steinbeck would find today if he went to the Central Valley? What has changed? What hasn't changed? And what does this say about our food supply?

Document 9.3: Excerpt from Kathy Mays Smith, *Gold Medal: CCC Company 1538, A Documentary* (Paducah, Kentucky: Turner Publishing Company, 2001)

Started in 1933, when unemployment in the United States stood at 25 percent, the Civilian Conservation Corps (CCC) quickly became one of the most popular New Deal programs. The idea behind it was to give unemployed urban youth a job, a place to live, clothes to wear, and food to eat. That way that would not compete with others for work and they would not, in their downtime, wreak havoc on city streets. Between 1933 and 1942, three million young men served in the CCC. Generally, CCC members worked outdoors planting trees, building pathways, clearing away dangerous brush, digging irrigation ditches, constructing fire lookout towers, and smoothing out access roads.

Tributes to the CCC often celebrate the "tree soldiers'" contributions to conservation, an important and new source of emphasis in New Deal policy. But at the time, in the 1930s, much of the discussion of the CCC centered on food, especially on how much CCC men—and they were almost always men—ate while they were in the camps. Camp directors boasted about how many calories—often as many as 4,500 a day—they fed the men in their platoons. In her book, Gold Medal, *Kathy Mays Smith chronicles the history of a Kentucky CCC Company. One of the chapters in the book is entitled "Chow." It lists how much food was purchased each month and what was served for holiday meals. Like most accounts of the CCC, it also talks about how much weight the men in the company gained.*

In a tongue-in-cheek article appearing in *The Independent Herald*, October 5, 1934 reference was made that "four men who did not appear on the company roster" were going home with the 85 officially listed, honorably discharged enrollees from Camp Wyoming. This revelation was based on the physical examinations given the men before they left. The physical showed that the 85 men had accumulated a grand total of 613 pounds of flesh during their stay in camp. Taking 150 pounds as the average weight of a man, this excess would equal slightly more than four extra men. Seventy-six men showed gains of from 1 to 21 pounds. The average gain was 6 to 8 pounds per man. Only eight men lost weight, five of whom were overweight at the time of enrollment. Only one man showed no change. The average length of service by these 85 men was five months.

The Independent Herald continued, "from these figures it can readily be seen that CCC camp life is excellent as a bodybuilder in the vast majority of cases. Plain, wholesome food, regular hours of sleep, vigorous outdoor work, and instruction in sanitation and personal cleanliness all contribute to the increase in the physical well-being of the enrollees. And since a healthy man is much less likely to be a liability to society than a sickly one, the bodybuilding activities of the camp may be accepted as a contribution toward better citizenship."

Discussion questions

1. Today we have reality television shows like Fit Club that celebrate weight *loss*. Why did the CCC, a government agency, make weight *gain* such a top priority? What does this tell us about this time, the health of the nation, and the priorities of the government?
2. Think about the years of the CCC's existence. What is going on, not just in the United States, but also around the rest of the world? What are the men of the CCC being groomed (and fed) to do?
3. What did an unhealthy and a healthy body look like to the leaders of the CCC?
4. What connections are made in the document between citizenship and the CCC? Why is an unhealthy man seen as a liability? What made someone a good citizen? Do we have the same ideas about eating, bodies, and citizenship today? What makes for a healthy citizenry in this day and age? Is the government today still interested in the size and shape of people's bodies?

Document 9.4: Lynn-Pgh, Recipe for "Depression Cake" (circa 1935), available at allrecipes.com/recipe/8214/depression-cake-i

At the height of the Great Depression in 1932, a quarter of all Americans were unemployed and another quarter of the workforce was underemployed. The loss of jobs and the loss of wages put tremendous pressures on household economies, and housewives especially. Almost without fail, women were the people in charge of procuring and preparing food. In order to help their families weather the storm of the Great Depression, they had to make do with less through performing, as someone said at the time, "endless little economies" at the store, in the garden, and in the kitchen. They turned leftover bones and vegetables into hearty soups, flour and water into filling biscuits, and dandelions into salads.

But making "endless little economies," also meant learning how to cook in new ways. The document below is a recipe for a "Depression Cake." Take a look at this recipe and study the ingredients.

"This was my mother's...It's from the Depression-era."

Ingredients
1 cup shortening
2 cups water
2 cups raisins

1 teaspoon ground cinnamon
1 teaspoon ground nutmeg
1 teaspoon ground allspice
1/2 teaspoon ground cloves
2 cups white sugar
3 cups all-purpose flour
1 teaspoon baking soda

Directions

1. In a saucepan combine the shortening, water, raisins, cinnamon, nutmeg, allspice, cloves and sugar. Simmer for 10 minutes. Remove from heat and let stand until cool.
2. Preheat oven to 350 degrees F (175 degrees C). Grease one 9x13 inch baking pan.
3. Stir the flour and baking soda into the cooled raisin mixture and mix until just combined. Pour batter into the prepared pan.
4. Bake at 350 degrees F (175 degrees C) for 45 minutes.

Discussion questions

1. Examine the recipe. What ingredients usually found in a cake are missing?
2. What does the fact that there is a recipe for a "Depression Cake" tell you about the times? In the face of on-going need, why do families still "need" to have dessert?
3. Do a "compare and contrast." Search the internet for a Betty Crocker recipe from the 1950s. Note in most cases there remains an emphasis on frugality, but how has the idea and practice of food frugality changed?
4. In general, what can recipes tell us about the past? Are they useful historical sources? Can you think of a contemporary recipe that reveals something about current tastes and economic needs?

Document 9.5: President Franklin D. Roosevelt, "Address" (May 14, 1935)

When Franklin Delano Roosevelt assumed the presidency in March 1933, the country had hit the rock bottom of the Great Depression. Perhaps no group was suffering more than farmers. In many ways, the nation's economic crisis had started in the countryside, where hard times began earlier and lasted longer. Starting in the mid-1920s, farmers confronted what economists call a "crisis of overproduction." They were, in a sense, victims of their own success. Aided by new chemical fertilizers and more efficient equipment, farmers produced more cotton, wheat, tobacco, and hogs than ever before. In fact, over the course of the decade they had produced too much for the market to absorb. As a result, prices of agricultural products began to tumble. Cotton, what President Roosevelt grew on the small farm next to his second home in Warm Springs, Georgia, cost between six and seven cents a pound to plant, cultivate, and get to market. By 1933, as Roosevelt notes in his speech, it was selling for 4.5 cents a pound. Hoping that the price would rise, farmers sometimes carried over crops, meaning that they didn't sell them, to the next year, but often, this just led to more downward pressure on cotton, wheat, and corn prices. As the President insisted in this speech, the drop in income for farmers rippled through the entire economy, adding to the nation's larger problem of underconsumption. There just weren't enough people in 1933 with enough money to spend to keep the factories humming and the economy moving forward.

The farm crisis was at the very top of Roosevelt's list of things of do when he came into office. As part of the first wave of New Deal legislation, in May 1933, Congress passed the Agricultural Adjustment Act (AAA). "Adjustment," to the market, was the key term here as the Roosevelt administration pursued a bold initiative of "planned scarcity." Under AAA guidelines, farmers were encouraged to grow fewer crops. The theory was that reduced supply would lead to increased prices. But how to do this? The AAA paid farmers to destroy some of their crops and farm animals and keep some lands bare and uncultivated. The program was financed by a tax on food processors. In 1933 alone, $100 million was paid out to cotton farmers to plow under crops already in the ground. Perhaps most famously, the government bought and slaughtered six million pigs. Some of the meat was canned and given to the unemployed, but some just went to waste. Many Americans had a hard time accepting this policy of destruction and subsidies, especially as people were going hungry. Opponents of Roosevelt and the New Deal derided the AAA as idiocy and—even worse—as socialism. In 1935, two years after the program was started, Roosevelt defended the initiative.

I am glad to welcome you to Washington. We can think of this occasion as a kind of surprise birthday party because it was exactly two years and two days ago that the Agricultural Adjustment Act became a law. I pretty well remember the occasion over there in the Executive Offices, and the fine group of representatives of farmers from every part of the country who stood around me when I signed the Act.

After that took place, and in record time, you and thousands of other farmers took hold. You set up the machinery to control your affairs and you put the new law to work.

I remember, too, the many—what shall I call them—the high and mighty people who said you could not do it, who said it was no use for you to try, intimating clearly that their only remedy to improve your situation was to let the sheriffs' sales go on. That was the old familiar way, the high and mighty way of balancing farm production with demand. Those people, my friends, did not understand and many of them do not understand today that, if the farm population of the United States suffers and loses its purchasing power, the people in the cities in every part of the country suffer of necessity with it. One of the greatest lessons that the city dwellers have come to understand in these past two years is this: Empty pocketbooks on the farm do not turn factory wheels in the city.

Let us go back for a minute to that spring of 1933 when there was a huge carryover. Let us take some examples. There was a carryover of almost thirteen million bales of cotton and a price, because of that carryover, of six cents a pound. Henry Wallace insists it was six and a half cents a pound, but I know that I got only four and a half cents for my cotton. You and I know what six cent cotton means to the purchasing power of the Cotton Belt. And you and I remember that there was a huge carryover of tobacco and that the price of tobacco during the preceding six months was the lowest on record for a great many years. Wheat had a carryover of nearly four hundred million bushels and a price of thirty-five cents on the farm or less; corn, a price of fifteen cents a bushel on many farms – and I knew some farmers who sold it at nine cents; hogs, a price of three cents a pound.

You and I know what those figures meant in the way of purchasing power for forty million Americans.

When we came down here to Washington that spring we were faced with three possible ways of meeting the situation. The first method that was suggested involved price fixing by Federal decree. We discarded that because the problem of overproduction was not solved thereby.

The second plan was to let farmers grow as much as they wanted of everything, and to have the Federal Government then step in, take from them that portion of their crop which represented what we called the exportable surplus and, in their name and on their behalf, dump this surplus on the other Nations of the world. We discarded that plan for a good many reasons and one was because the other Nations of the world had already taken steps to stop dumping. From that time on, with increasing frequency they were raising their tariffs, establishing quotas and clamping on embargoes against just that kind of proposition. And that is why we discarded that.

Therefore, we came to the third plan—a plan for the adjustment of totals in our major crops, so that from year to year production and consumption would be kept in reasonable balance with each other, to the end that reasonable prices would be paid to farmers for their crops and unwieldy surpluses would not depress our markets and upset the balance.

We are now at the beginning of the third year of carrying out this policy. You know the results thus far attained. You know the present price of cotton, of wheat, of tobacco, of corn, of hogs and of other ham products today. Further comment on the successful partial attainment of our objective up to this time is unnecessary on my part. You know.

I want, for a moment, to emphasize that word "adjustment." It is almost a forgotten word just as some of you, once upon a time, were forgotten men. As you know, a great many of the high and mighty, with special axes to grind, have been deliberately trying to mislead people who know nothing of farming by misrepresenting—no, why use a pussyfoot word?—by lying about the kind of farm program under which this Nation is operating today.

A few leading citizens have gone astray from other causes—such as ignorance. I must admit that. For example, a few years ago in the countryside where I live, I was driving with a prominent city banker. Everything was brown. The leaves were off the trees. And all of a sudden we passed a beautiful green field. He asked me what it was. I told him it was winter wheat. He turned to me and said, "That is very interesting. I have always wondered about winter wheat. What I don't understand is how they are able to cut it when it gets all covered up with snow."

The other example was down in Georgia. An editor of a great metropolitan paper was visiting me down there in the summertime when I showed him my farm with 40 or 50 acres of cotton, when the cotton was nearly grown but before the bolls had formed. Looking out over the cotton fields he said to me:

"What a large number of raspberries they grow down here."

Well, raspberries was right. Because, at four and a half cents a pound for cotton his mistake was, perhaps, a natural one.

I was speaking to you about that word adjustment. I think it is your duty and mine to continue to educate the people of this country to the fact that adjustment means not only adjustment downward but adjustment upward. If you and I agree on a correct figure for a normal carryover in a basic crop, it means that if we have a bumper crop one year we will, by mutual consent, reduce the next year's crop in order to even up that carryover. At the same time, if we get a short crop in a given year, you and I agree to increase the next year's crop to make up the shortage. That is exactly what we are doing in the case of wheat this year.

Yes, it is high time for you and for me to carry, by education, knowledge of the fact that not a single program of the AAA contemplated the destruction of an acre of food crops in the United States, in spite of what you may read or what you may have been told by people who have special axes to grind.

It is high time for you and for me to make clear that we are not plowing under cotton this year—that we did not plow it under in 1934 and that we only plowed some of it under in 1933 because the Agricultural Adjustment Act was passed by that Congress at that famous Special Session after a huge crop of cotton was already in the ground.

It is high time for us to repeat on every occasion that we have not wastefully destroyed food in any form. It is true that the Relief Administrator has purchased hundreds of thousands of tons of foodstuffs in order to feed the needy and hungry who have been on the relief rolls in every part of the United States.

The crocodile tears shed by the professional mourners of an old and obsolete order over the slaughter of little pigs and over other measures to reduce surplus agricultural inventories deceive very few thinking people in this country, and least of all the farmers themselves.

I have always supposed, ever since I was able to play around, that the acknowledged destiny of a pig is sausage, or ham, or bacon or pork. It was in those forms—as sausage, ham, bacon or pork—that millions of pigs were consumed by vast numbers of needy people who otherwise would have had to do without them.

Let me make one other point clear for the benefit of the millions in cities who have to buy meats. Last year the Nation suffered a drought of unparalleled intensity. If there had been no Government program, if the old order had obtained in 1933 and 1934, that drought on the cattle ranges of America and in the corn belt would have resulted in the marketing of thin cattle, immature hogs and the death of these animals on the range and on the farm, and if the old order had been in effect those years, we would have had a vastly greater shortage than we face today.

Our program—we can prove it—saved the lives of millions of head of livestock. They are still on the range, and other millions of heads are today canned and ready for this country to eat.

I think that you and I are agreed in seeking a continuance of a national policy which on the whole is proving successful. The memory of old conditions under which the product of a whole year's work often would not bring you the cost of transporting it to market is too fresh in your minds to let you be led astray by the solemn admonitions and specious lies of those who in the past profited most when your distress was greatest.

You remember and I remember that not so long ago the poor had less food to eat, and less clothes to wear, at a time when you had practically to give away your products. Then the surpluses were greater, and yet the poor were poorer than they are today when you farmers are getting a reasonable, although still an insufficient, price.

I have not the time to talk with you about many other policies of your Government which affect the farm population of the country. I have not the time, although I would like to do it, to go into the practical work of the Farm Credit Administration which, in all of its ramifications, has saved a million farms from foreclosure and has accomplished the first great reduction in exorbitant interest rates that this country has ever known.

It is because what you stand for is so just and so wholly reasonable that no one today has had the temerity to question the motives of this grand "march on Washington." It is a good omen for Government, for business, for bankers and for the city dwellers that the Nation's farmers are becoming articulate and that they know whereof they speak.

I hope you have enjoyed your stay in Washington. Seeing your Government at first hand, seeing the immensity of government which, after all, is not surprising when you think of the immensity of the country—seeing all that at first hand, you have a better idea why sometimes our efforts in the National capital seem lumbering and slow and complicated. On the other hand, you may have seen, in this visit of yours, that we are moving faster, that we are accomplishing more practical results than you have been led to believe by the high and mighty gentlemen of whom I have spoken.

We haven't quite got the engine tuned up yet but it is a mighty fine engine. I think after it has run a total of about a thousand miles it will be the best engine we have ever had.

I want to thank you for your patience with us, your Government. I want to pledge to you not only our wholehearted cooperation as you go forward, but our continued deep interest in a problem that is not just a farmer's problem because, as I have said before, your prosperity is felt in every city home, in every bank and in every industry in the land.

Discussion questions

1. Why was it so important for President Roosevelt to address the farm crisis right away? How, according to Roosevelt, did the problems in the agricultural economy affect the rest of the economy in 1933?

2. In this address, Roosevelt talks about some of the other options proposed for dealing with declining farm prices and huge carryovers of crops. What were these options and what does Roosevelt suggest are the problems with these alternatives to his plan?

3. Like all good politicians, Roosevelt deliberately chose his words and phrases with great care. Why, for instance, does he use the word "adjustment" instead of buying up or subsidy? What does he call his opponents? What does he mean by the phrase "crocodile tears shed by professional mourners?"

4. What are the successes of the AAA according to Roosevelt?

5. While some of Roosevelt's opponents called him a socialist, some historians have said that he saved capitalism from itself. What do they mean by this argument? What do you think? Can you have something like the AAA and still have capitalism? What are the benefits and liabilities of such a "mixed economy"?

6. Do farm subsidies still exist? Are they a good or bad thing for the economy?

Chapter 10   World War II and the Food and Government Revolution

Document 10.1: Office of Price Administration, "How to Use Your War Ration Book" (1943)

During World War II, a shopper couldn't just walk into the corner store or the local butcher and buy as much sugar or butter or meat as she/he wanted or could afford. That's because there were widespread shortages throughout the conflict. The war generated restrictions on imported goods and disrupted global supply chains. Gasoline and rubber were in short supply, which put limits on the transportation of goods, including foods. At the same time, the government diverted agricultural products and canned goods to troops at home and abroad.

Most government officials in the United States concluded that voluntary conservation along the lines deployed during World War I did not work. As an alternative, the Office of Price Administration (OPA)—the agency in charge of controlling the cost of key goods during the war—introduced a mandatory rationing system for scarce items, including foods, so that everyone, at least in theory, got a fair share, but not more.

But what is a fair share and how could the government ensure that everyone had an equal amount of essential goods? The OPA answered these questions by issuing ration books. These came with removable coupons. If a consumer wanted, for instance, a pound of butter, she/he presented the coupon from the book to the storekeeper. She couldn't buy the rationed item

Food and Eating in America: A Documentary Reader, First Edition.
Edited by James C. Giesen and Bryant Simon.
© 2018 John Wiley & Sons, Inc. Published 2018 by John Wiley & Sons, Inc.

*without a coupon. When she was out of coupons, she was, at least theoreti-
cally, out of butter or some other item until the next month when the
government issued a new ration book. The document below was put out by
the OPA in 1942 to explain how rationing would work. Imagine you are the
person in charge of buying and cooking food in your household. What would
you think of the government plan and program for rationing?*

Your first ration book has been issued to you, originally containing 28 war
ration stamps. Other books may be issued at later dates. The following
instructions apply to your first book and will apply to any later books,
unless otherwise ordered by the Office of Price Administration. In order to
obtain a later book, the first book must be turned in. You should preserve
War Rations Books with the greatest possible care.

1. From time to time the Office of Price Administration may issue Orders
    rationing certain products. After the dates indicated by such Orders,
    these products can be purchased only through the use of War Rations
    Books containing valid War Ration Stamps.
2. The Orders of the Office of Price Administration will designate the
    stamps to be used for the purchase of a particular rationed product, the
    period during which each of these stamps may be used, and the amounts
    which may be bought with each stamp.
3. Stamps become valid for use only when and as directed by the Orders of
    the Office of Price Administration.
4. Unless otherwise announced, the Ration Week is from Saturday mid-
    night to the following Saturday midnight.
5. War Ration stamps may be used in any retail store in the United States.
6. War Ration stamps may be used only by or for the person named and
    described in the War Ration Book.
7. Every person must see that this War Ration Book is kept in a safe place
    and properly used. Parents are responsible for the safekeeping and use
    of their children's War Ration Book.
8. When you buy any rationed product, the proper stamp must be detached
    in the presence of the storekeeper, his employee, or the person making
    the delivery on his behalf. If a stamp is torn out of the War Ration Book
    in any other way than above indicated, it becomes void. If a stamp is
    partly torn or mutilated and more than one half of it remains in the
    book, it is valid. Otherwise it becomes void.
9. If your War Ration Book is lost, destroyed, stolen or mutilated, you
    should report that fact to the local Ration Board.

10. If you enter a hospital, or other institution, and expect to be there for more than 10 days, you must turn your War Ration Book over to the person in charge. It will be returned to you upon your request when you leave.
11. When a person dies, his War Ration Book must be returned to the local Ration Board, in accordance with the regulations.
12. If you have any complaints, questions, or difficulties regarding your War Ration Book, consult your local Ration Board.

Discussion questions

1. After closely reading the document, do you understand the program? In March 1943, a Gallop poll asked Americans if they understood how food rationing worked. Seventy-six percent of women said, Yes. Only fifty-three percent of men answered, Yes. Would you have been one of those who understood the program?
2. What are the government's goals here? What are officials—judging from the rules—most worried about?
3. Can you think of ways around the rules? In fact, there was a huge black market for all kinds of goods during the war. Didn't the government, in some ways, create this black market? Was someone who bought an extra pound of butter to make a birthday cake unpatriotic, were they a criminal?
4. Think about rationing and the ideological goals of the war. The war was a war for democracy, at least in part, right? What are the values of democracy that rationing espouses? Or did rationing and the limiting of consumer choices threaten democracy? Did the rationing program, as some argued at the time and then later, set a dangerous precedent of postwar government action?

Document 10.2: Clive McCay, "Eat Well to Work Well: The Lunch Box Should Carry a Hearty Meal," in War Emergency Bulletin No. 38 (1942)

Fighting Word War II—a war being waged on multiple fronts thousands of miles away from the homefront against huge and well-equipped armies— required a massive mobilization of people and resources. Through posters, radio broadcasts, and grainy newsreels, the government urged Americans to enlist in the armed services, buy war bonds, limit gossip ("Loose Lips Sink Ships"), get to work on time, and stay focused on the job of building tanks, planes, and guns.

Food was a prime focus of wartime propaganda. Citizen soldiers were urged to plant victory gardens, conserve meat (and make more soups and fewer roasts), and drink orange juice for vitamin C so they wouldn't miss a shift at the factory.

Look at the bulletin below with its stark contrasts between "Helping Hitler" and "Helping Uncle Sam." How does the text for this poster define eating as a key aspect of wartime citizenship?

WORKER

Are You Helping Hitler?

Then:

Eat a poor lunch every day so that you will have many accidents, spoil much material, and keep your fellow-workers from getting their work done while you quarrel with them.

Eat only white bread—never whole-wheat or enriched. White bread has the fewest vitamins and will keep down your pep.

Don't eat eggs, liver, green vegetables, and yellow fruit; then the vitamin A in your eyes will be low. This will insure more accidents, because you see poorly. It may help you to smash your head or cut off your fingers.

Instead of thick sandwiches with good fillings, eat only a cake or a doughnut and some coffee for lunch. This may give you a headache by the end of the shift.

Don't eat oranges, tomatoes, cabbage, green peppers, or other fruits or vegetables in your lunch. Then you may get scurvy and your teeth may loosen. Dentists will then get too much of your pay check.

Let the other fellow drink your pint of milk each day. He will benefit from the calcium, protein, and vitamins in milk, and probably will do his work so well that the company will keep him busy after the war is over.

Don't eat sandwiches filled with peanut butter, liver, eggs, salmon, cheese, pork, beef, or chicken. These foods would keep your muscles in good condition, and you might feel as strong as a prize fighter and get more work done.

Don't drink much water; then the waste products in your body will accumulate in the blood and make you dopey. If you sweat a lot, don't eat extra salt—then you really will feel fatigued. This will keep you fighting with your boss so that he will not recommend you for promotion.

Don't wash your hands before eating; then you can get your peck of dirt. Swallow your food as fast as you can. You may have an iron stomach now but later on it may corrode and give you a goat's breath.

Don't learn anything about foods. If you do, you might choose a better diet, be able to forget your constipation, and quit fighting with your wife.

WORKER
Are You Helping Uncle Sam?

Then:

Eat a hearty lunch every day to help to keep you in top-notch physical condition, to make you feel like doing your job and "playing ball" with your fellow workers.

If possible, use whole-wheat bread. If you use white, be sure it is enriched with vitamins and iron. The slight extra money you pay is well worth the extra pep you get.

Keep your vision clear by eating plenty of green and yellow vegetables and fruits, salmon, and liver. These foods contain the vitamin A needed for good eyesight.

Make your lunch so hearty that it provides a large part of your day's need for vitamins, minerals, and proteins. The lunch period falls in the middle of your work day, and you need a good one to help you carry on. A good lunch is a good investment.

Include fruit in your lunch every day, such as an orange, apple, peach, or banana. Fresh or canned tomatoes and oranges help to protect you from scurvy.

Drink plenty of milk even if you feel that it is expensive. Remember it has many times the food value of any other drink.

Peanut butter, liver, eggs, salmon, cheese, pork, ham, beef, and chicken are muscle-building foods. Get one or two of these in your lunch every day. They will help to increase your capacity for work

Plenty of water every day helps to flush waste products from the body. If you sweat a lot, drink extra water and eat extra salt to prevent fatigue.

Get plenty of rest and fresh air. Chew your food and eat slowly. Eat lunch with company you enjoy. Remember, no matter how good your lunch it cannot give the best results if mixed with dirt and bacteria.

Learn about food values. Regulate your diet and thus enjoy good health and live to a ripe old age. You will have little trouble with constipation if your meals contain the vitamins in good meat, milk, and bread, as well as the roughage of vegetables and whole-grain cereals.

Discussion questions

1. This document talks about two kinds of Americans. How are the two Americans portrayed?
2. Why is this document, put out by the United States government, aimed at workers? What role did workers play in the war and in wartime mobilization?
3. What foods are identified as "good" foods (helping Uncle Sam) and what are identified as "bad" food (helping Hitler)?
4. What do these distinctions tell us about ideas about nutrition in the 1940s? How have these ideas changed and how have they remained the same?
5. According to this bulletin, what are the obligations of citizenship when it comes to food? Can you think of any other examples from other moments in American history when eating and citizenship get conflated?

Document 10.3: World War II Era Advertisement, "Have a 'Coke' = Good Winds Have Blown You Here" (1943)

At first, World War II seemed like bad news for the Coca-Cola Company of Atlanta, Georgia. In 1939, Coke sold its drinks in 44 countries around the world, some of whom would align themselves with the Axis powers. This led to some transport and supply and demand problems for the soda company. Think also about rationing in this context. As Document 10.1 explained, not long after the United States entered the war, the government began to ration sugar, a major ingredient in Coke. Despite these challenges, the soft drink maker managed to emerge from the war stronger, bigger, and more popular than ever.

Marketing and strategic political connections saved Coke. Just after the United States entered the war, Company President Robert Woodruff announced "every man in uniform gets a bottle of Coke for 5 cents, wherever he is and whatever it costs to the company." That promise won the company a hefty dose of favorable patriotic public relations. Coke got another boost from the Supreme Commander of Allied Forces in Europe,

Have a "Coke" = Good winds have blown you here

... a way to say "We are friends" to the Chinese

In far-off places, when Coca-Cola is on hand, you find it cementing friendships for our fighting men. China knew Coca-Cola from Tientsin to Shanghai, from Hong Kong to Tsingtao. To Chinese and Yank alike, *Have a "Coke"* are welcome words. They belong with friendliness and freedom. From Atlanta to the Seven Seas, Coca-Cola stands for *the pause that refreshes* — has become a symbol of good will among the friendly-minded.

*   *   *

Our fighting men are delighted to meet up with Coca-Cola many places overseas. Coca-Cola has been a globe-trotter "since way back when". Even with war, Coca-Cola today is being bottled right on the spot in over 35 allied and neutral nations.

"Coke" = Coca-Cola

It's natural for popular names to acquire friendly abbreviations. That's why you hear Coca-Cola called "Coke".

Coca-Cola
· the global high-sign

Dwight D. Eisenhower. Looking for a way to maintain morale, the five-star general made sure his troops always had access to a Coke. Aided by government support, Coke sold five billion bottles of the sugary drink during the war.

And it wasn't just American GIs who got a taste for the drink. Coke gained millions of new customers in countries around the world occupied by the United States during the war as soldiers left behind and shared their Cokes with locals. These people wouldn't lose their taste for the drink when the fighting stopped.

Coke also helped its sales through a steady flow of glossy magazine advertisements. The ads reminded consumers, who had well-paying jobs and money in their pockets for the first time since the Great Depression, to pick up a Coke at the drug store and local food markets. But the advertisements did more than that. They linked Coke to America, and to American values, not just in the United States, but also around the world. Study the advertisement below. Look at the image closely and carefully read the text.

Discussion questions

1. According to the advertisement, what is the power of Coke?
2. What is the source of the "good" winds blowing here? How is the United States represented in the advertisement? Who isn't in the picture?
3. Some commentators have maintained that Coke is not only an agent of globalization, but also an agent of the related, but more partisan process, of Americanization. What does that mean? What are the values that the ad associates with the United States?
4. What is the significance of the Chinese here? What is the role of China in the war? (You may need to do some additional research to answer this question.)
5. This advertisement is in English. Presumably, then, the main audience is American consumers. How is the ad geared towards them? Why should they feel good about drinking Coke? Do you think this is an effective advertisement?

Document 10.4: "The Official Bracero Agreement," For the Temporary Migration of Mexican Agricultural Workers to the United States (August, 1942)

Food, as we have seen in a number of the documents in the collection, was crucial to the war effort, but food was, and never is, just about production. Food is also about labor, about who will harvest, pack, and process the things we eat. Despite the essential nature of food, food work is rarely well paid work and rarely anyone's first choice of a job. These dynamics became clear, again, in the early 1940s.

World War II created an acute labor shortage in the United States. The draft pulled eight to nine million men between the ages of 18 and 45 out of the factories and fields into the military and away from mines and oilrigs. In response, women, like Rosie the Riveter, took jobs in airplane plants and rubber factories. African American who picked cotton in the South moved north to well-paying jobs in Pittsburgh and Detroit. In this environment of intense competition for workers, who, then, was going to pick and package the foods that would win the war?

In response to this labor shortage, the United States and Mexican governments made a deal. Mexico with its surplus of underemployed, undereducated laborers would legally send workers north to work, temporarily, in the fields of the United States, doing tasks that American laborers depended on, but had largely abandoned. In exchange, the United States would suspend its immigration laws and provide some protection for these temporary laborers. This program became known as the "Bracero Program." In Spanish, bracero literally means arm, but it translates also as manual labor.

Over the course of the war, more than 150,000 Mexican laborers legally entered the United States to work in the fields. The program didn't end with the war and neither did labor shortages in the fields. In 1951, after nearly a decade in existence, amidst new concerns about labor shortages as a result of the United States' entry into the Korean conflict, Congress moved to formalize the Bracero Program with Public Law 78. The program would continue until 1964, bringing some 4.5 million Mexicans to the United States to work and live (and as some of the documents below will suggest change the taste profile of America). See below for the original formal agreement that provides a legal path for Mexican laborers to come and work in American fields.

General Provisions

1. It is understood that Mexicans contracting to work in the United States shall not be engaged in any military service.

2. Mexicans entering the United States as result of this understanding shall not suffer discriminatory acts of any kind in accordance with the Executive Order No. 8802 issued at the White House June 25, 1941.

3. Mexicans entering the United States under this understanding shall enjoy the guarantees of transportation, living expenses and repatriation established in Article 29 of the Mexican Federal Labor Law as follows:

Article 29.- All contracts entered into by Mexican workers for lending their services outside their country shall be made in writing, legalized by the municipal authorities of the locality where entered into and vised by the Consul of the country where their services are being used. Furthermore, such contract shall contain, as a requisite of validity of same, the following stipulations, without which the contract is invalid.

I. Transportation and subsistence expenses for the worker, and his family, if such is the case, and all other expenses which originate from point of origin to border points and compliance of immigration requirements, or for any other similar concept, shall be paid exclusively by the employer or the contractual parties.

II. The worker shall be paid in full the salary agreed upon, from which no deduction shall be made in any amount for any of the concepts mentioned in the above sub-paragraph.

III. The employer or contractor shall issue a bond or constitute a deposit in cash in the Bank of Workers, or in the absence of same, in the Bank of Mexico, to the entire satisfaction of the respective labor authorities, for a sum equal to repatriation costs of the worker and his family, and those originated by transportation to point of origin.

IV. Once the employer established proof of having covered such expenses or the refusal of the worker to return to his country, and that he does not owe the worker any sum covering salary or indemnization to which he might have a right, the labor authorities shall authorize the return of the deposit or the cancellation of the bond issued.

It is specifically understood that the provisions of Section III of Article 29 above-mentioned shall not apply to the Government of the United States notwithstanding the inclusion of this section in the agreement, in view of the obligations assumed by the United States government under Transportation(a) and (c) of this agreement.

4. Mexicans entering the United States under this understanding shall not be employed to displace other workers, or for the purpose of reducing rates of pay previously established.

In order to implement the application of the general Principles mentioned above the following specific clauses are established:

(When the word "employer" is used hereinafter it shall be understood to mean the Farm Security Administration of the Department of Agriculture of the United States of America; the word "sub-employer" shall mean the owner or operator of the farm or farms in the United States on which the Mexican will be employed; the word "worker" hereinafter used shall refer to the Mexican Farm laborer entering the United States under this understanding.)

Contracts

a. Contracts will be made between the employer and the worker under the supervision of the Mexican Government. (Contracts must be written in Spanish.)

b. The employer shall enter into a contract with the sub- employer, with a view to proper observance of the principles embodied in this understanding.

Admission

a. The Mexican health authorities will, at the place whence the worker comes, see that he meets the necessary physical conditions.

Transportation

a. All transportation and living expenses from the place of origin to destination, and return, as well as expenses incurred in the fulfillment of any requirements of a migratory nature shall be met by the Employer.

b. Personal belongings of the workers up to a maximum of 35 kilos per person shall be transported at the expense of the Employer.

c. In accord with the intent of Article 29 of Mexican Federal Labor Law, quoted under General Provisions (3) above, it is expected that the employer will collect all or part of the cost accuring (sic) under (a) and (b) of Transportation from the sub- employer.

Wages and Employment

a. (1)Wages to be paid the worker shall be the same as those paid for similar work to other agricultural laborers under the same conditions within the same area, in the respective regions of destination. Piece rates shall be so set as to enable the worker of average ability to earn the prevailing wage. In any case wages for piece work or hourly work will not be less than 30 cents per hour.

b. (2)On the basis of prior authorization from the Mexican Government salaries lower than those established in the previous clause may be paid those emigrants admitted into the United States as members of the family of the worker under contract and who, when they are in the field, are able also to become agricultural laborers but who, by their condition of age or sex, cannot carry out the average amount of ordinary work.

c. The worker shall be exclusively employed as an agricultural laborer for which he has been engaged; any change from such type of employment or any change of locality shall be made with the express approval of the worker and with the authority of the Mexican Government.

d. There shall be considered illegal any collection by reason of commission or for any other concept demanded of the worker.

e. Work of minors under 14 years shall be strictly prohibit (sic), and they shall have the same schooling opportunities as those enjoyed by children of other agricultural laborers.

f. Workers domiciled in the migratory labor camps or at any other place of employment under this understanding shall be free to obtain articles for their personal consumption, or that of their families, wherever it is most convenient for them.

g. The Mexican workers will be furnished without cost to them with hygienic lodgings, adequate to the physical conditions of the region of a type used by a common laborer of the region and the medical and sanitary services enjoyed also without cost to them will be identical with those furnished to the other agricultural workers in the regions where they may lend their services.

h. Workers admitted under this understanding shall enjoy as regards occupational diseases and accidents the same guarantees enjoyed by other agricultural workers under United States legislation.

i. Groups of workers admitted under this understanding shall elect their own representatives to deal with the Employer, but it is understood that all such representatives shall be working members of the group.

The Mexican Consuls, assisted...[by]...Mexican Labor Inspectors, recognized as such by the Employer will take all possible measures of protection in the interest of the Mexican workers in all questions affecting them, within their corresponding jurisdiction, and will have free access to the places of work of the Mexican workers, The Employer will observe that the sub-employer grants all facilities to the Mexican Government for the compliance of all the clauses in this contract.

j. For such time as they are unemployed under a period equal to 75% of the period (exclusive of Sundays) for which the workers have been contracted they shall receive a subsistence allowance at the rate of $3.00 per day.

Should the cost of living rise this will be a matter for reconsideration.

The master contracts for workers submitted to the Mexican government shall contain definite provisions for computation of subsistence and payments under the understanding.

k. The term of the contract shall be made in accordance with the authorities of the respective countries.

l. At the expiration of the contract under this understanding, and if the same is not renewed, the authorities of the United States shall consider illegal, from an immigration point of view, the continued stay of the worker in the territory of the United States, exception made of cases of physical impossibility.

Savings Fund

a. The respective agencies of the Government of the United States shall be responsible for the safekeeping of the sums contributed by the Mexican workers toward the formation of their Rural Savings Fund, until such sums are transferred to the Wells Fargo Bank and Union Trust Company of San Francisco for the account of the Bank of Mexico, S.A., which will transfer such amounts to the Mexican Agricultural Credit Bank. This last shall assume responsibility for the deposit, for the safekeeping and for the application, or in the absence of these, for the return of such amounts.

b. The Mexican Government through the Banco de Crédito Agrícola will take care of the security of the savings of the workers to be used for payment of the agricultural implements, which may be made available to the Banco de Crédito Agrícola in accordance with exportation permits for shipment to Mexico with the understanding that the Farm Security Administration will recommend priority treatment for such implements.

Numbers

As it is impossible to determine at this time the number of workers who may be needed in the United States for agricultural labor employment, the employer shall advise the Mexican Government from time to time as to the number needed. The Government of Mexico shall determine in each case the number of workers who may leave the country without detriment to its national economy.

General Considerations

It is understood that, with reference to the departure from Mexico of Mexican workers, who are not farm laborers, there shall govern in understandings reached by agencies to the respective Governments the same fundamentals principles which have been applied here to the departure of farm labor.

It is understood that the employers will cooperate with such other agencies of the Government of the United States in carrying this understanding into effect whose authority under the laws of the United States are such as to contribute to the effectuation of the understandings.

Either Government shall have the right to renounce this understanding, given appropriate notification to the other Government 90 days in advance. This understanding may be formalized by an exchange of notes between the Ministry of Foreign Affairs of the Republic of Mexico and the Embassy of the United States of America in Mexico.

Discussion questions

1. Why was this agreement important? What sorts of jobs did these temporary workers perform? Is this stipulated in the agreement?
2. How were workers screened? What rights for workers are safeguarded? What responsibilities do employers have to these workers?
3. What benefits does the Mexican government get from this agreement? As you answer this, think about the many restrictions and provisions in the agreement from age stipulations to transportation to savings.
4. Who do you think benefits the most from this agreement and subsequent laws allowing Mexican nationals to be hired for temporary agricultural work in the United States? Is it just the employers who benefit? What about American consumers?
5. Did the war set an important precedent? Why did the program continue *after* the war? How did this program shape US–Mexican relations? What did it mean to have Mexican citizens continually working in the United States? Think about the Okies discussed in Document 9.2. This is a pattern familiar around the United States and the rest of the world. Food is often produced and processed by the most vulnerable and mobile people in society. Is there something significant about that?

Document 10.5: Excerpt from Jeanne Wakatsuki Houston and James D. Houston, *Farewell to Manzanar* (Boston: Houghton Mifflin, 1973), 35–38[1]

The bombs dropped on Pearl Harbor had barely cooled before rumors started to swirl around the West Coast of the United States. People whispered that Japanese Americans and Japanese immigrants planned to sabotaged munitions plants and mount a campaign of terror. By the spring of 1942, President Roosevelt signed Executive Order 9066, authorizing the physical removal by the War Department of the Japanese from their homes and communities. Eventually the government established ten internment camps in California, Arizona, Utah, Wyoming, Colorado, Idaho, and Arkansas. From the start, tensions stirred in the camps about everyday freedoms, including speech, self-government, housing, work, and of course, food.

Jeanne Wakatsuki Houston's memoir, Farewell to Manzanar, *tells the story of one family's struggles to cope with forced removal from its home and forced detention. On her first day at the camp, she got in the "chow line" with her family. "Caucasian servers," she wrote, "plopped" down a meal of "Vienna sausage, canned green beans, steamed rice that had been cooked too long, and on the top of the rice a serving of canned apricots." Among the Japanese, Wakatsuki Houston explained, rice is never eaten with sweet food. But no one protested, they just didn't eat the "inedible concoction."*

Later in her book, in the passage below, Wakatsuki Houston talks about another camp foodway that knocked up against Japanese and Japanese American traditions and would shape her family for years to come.

At seven I was too young to be insulted. The camp worked on me in a much different way. I wasn't aware of this at the time, of course. No one was, except maybe Mama, and there was little she could have done to change what happened.

It began in the mess hall. Before Manzanar, mealtime had always been the center of our family scene. In camp, and afterward, I would often recall with deep yearning the old round wooden table in our dining room in Ocean Park, the biggest piece of furniture we owned, large enough to seat twelve or thirteen of us at once. A tall row of elegant, lathe-turned spindles separated this table from the kitchen, allowing talk to pass from one room to the other. Dinners were always noisy, and they were always abundant with great pots of boiled rice, platters of homegrown vegetables, fish Papa caught.

He would sit at the head of the table, with mama next to him serving and the rest of us arranged around edges according to age, down to where Kiyo and I sat, so far away from our parents it seemed at the time, we had our own enclosed nook inside this world. The grownups would be talking down at their end, while we two played our secret games, making eyes at each other when Papa gave the order to begin to eat, racing with chopsticks to scrape the last grain from our rice bowls, eyeing papa to see if he had noticed who won.

Now in the mess halls, after a few weeks had passed, we stopped eating as a family. Mama tried to hold us together for a while, but it was hopeless. Granny was too feeble to walk across the block three times a day, especially during heavy weather, so May brought food to her in the barracks. My older brothers and sisters, meanwhile, began eating with their friends, or eating somewhere blocks away, in the hopes of finding better food. The word would get around of the cook over in Block 22, say, really knew his stuff, and they would eat a few meals over there, to test the rumor. Camp authorities frowned on mess hall hopping and tried to stop it, but the good cooks liked it. They like to see long lines outside their kitchens and would work overtime to attract a crowd.

Younger boys, like Ray, would make a game seeing how many mess halls they could hit in one meal period—be the first in line at Block 16, gobble down your food, run to 17 by the middle of the dinner hour, gulp another helping, and hurry to 18 to make the end of that chow line and stuff in the third meal of the evening. They didn't *need* to do that. No matter how bad the food might be, you could always eat till you were full.

Kiyo and I were too young to run around, but often we would eat in gangs with other kids, while the grown-ups sat at another table. I confess I enjoyed this part of it at the time. We all did. A couple of years after the camps opened, sociologists studying the life noticed what had happened to the families. They made some recommendations, and edicts went out that families must start eating together again. Most people resented this; they griped and grumbled. They were in the habit of eating with their friends. And until the mess hall system itself could be changed, not much could really be done. It was too late.

My own family, after three years of mess hall living, collapsed as an integrated unit. Whatever dignity or feeling of filial strength we may have known before December 1941 was lost, and we did not recover it until many years after the war, not until after Papa died and we began to come together, trying to fill the vacuum his passing left in all our lives.

The closing of the camps, in the fall of 1945, only aggravated what had begun inside. Papa had no money then and could not get work. Half of our family had already moved to the East Coast, where jobs had opened up for them. The rest of us were relocated into a former defense workers' housing project in Long Beach. In that small apartment there never was enough room for all of us to sit down for a meal. We ate in shifts, and I yearned all the more for our huge roundtable in Ocean Park.

Soon after we were released I wrote a paper for a seventh-grade journalism class, describing how we used to hunt grunion before the war. The whole family would go down to Ocean Park beach after dark, when the grunion were running, and build a big fire on the sand. I would watch Papa and my older brothers splash through the moonlit surf to scoop out the fish, then we'd rush back to the house where Mama would fry them up and set the sizzling pan on the table, with soy sauce and horseradish, for a midnight meal. I ended up with this sentence: "The reason I want to remember this is because I know we'll never be able to do it again."

Discussion questions

1. "It began in the mess hall," Wakatsuki Houston writes. What does "it" refer to here?
2. How did the mess halls in Manzanar differ from the dining room and dinner table of the Wakatsuki household before internment?
3. How did the camp change the family dynamics? Were these changes permanent or temporary?
4. Despite the confinement, what sorts of new freedoms did the camps offer?
5. When the camp put out an edict saying that families had to eat together, what happened? What does the entire section say about the power of the camp authorities? Was their power total? What were some of the limits to their power?
6. Why are meals and mealtimes so important, both then and now, to families?

Chapter 11 The Postwar Food Revolution(s) of Suburban America

Document 11.1: Photograph of Super Giant Supermarket, Rockville, Maryland (1964)

The United States emerged from World War II as the world's preeminent military and economic power. By the middle of the century, the country had begun a 20-year run of unprecedented growth and prosperity. Unemployment was at a historic low. Hourly wages and rates of unionization were higher than ever. Aided by the G.I. Bill, veterans returned from the war, got married, and had kids. The new families, especially the white ones, left the cities for the suburbs.

The suburbs, Fortune *magazine reported in 1950, were growing at ten times the rate of the cities. All of these young couples and their young kids in their new ranch houses needed sedans and station wagons, roads and schools, churches and synagogues. And they needed places to shop for clothes and food. This robust demand further fueled the already strong economy.*

The suburbs created more than just a building and industrial boom, they also represented a new spatial arrangement. In the city, the corner store, the fruit vendor, and the butcher shop were down the street from the apartment. The workplace was a couple of blocks or a trolley ride away. In the suburbs

Food and Eating in America: A Documentary Reader, First Edition.
Edited by James C. Giesen and Bryant Simon.
© 2018 John Wiley & Sons, Inc. Published 2018 by John Wiley & Sons, Inc.

everything had its own separate place. There was the city or the industrial park for jobs, the shopping center for clothes and furniture, and the supermarket for food.

A&P on the East Coast and Ralphs on the West Coast opened the nation's first supermarkets in the 1920s. The idea was to keep prices low by stacking items high and selling them in bulk and in volume. The concept took off in the 1950s as people had more money and more room to store food. Eventually the supermarket would be reimported into the cities and exported around the world.

The picture below appeared in Life Magazine *in 1964. It is, of course, a modern supermarket, the Super Giant supermarket in Rockville, Maryland. Located just outside Washington, DC, Rockville was a typical postwar suburb. While it was established long before the war, the area mushroomed with new homeowners in the middle of the twentieth century. It got its first shopping center in 1954 and a self-serve supermarket soon after that. Study the picture. What does it tell us about the postwar era in the United States?*

Discussion questions

1. What are the economic and social differences between the supermarket and the corner store? How and why does the supermarket become the dominant form of food distribution in the postwar era?
2. What details stick out in this photograph? What surprises you?
3. Generally in the early part of the twentieth century, as we saw in Document 8.3 on meat boycotts, woman were in charge of food consumption? What has changed here? What does this tell you? Is this progress?
4. What does this image tell you about the suburbs? About postwar America? What's the significance of the store's name?
5. What kinds of foods are for sale? Use your imagination. The supermarket, obviously, changes people's shopping habits, but does it also lead to changes in diet?
6. What has changed about the supermarket since this photograph was taken?

Document 11.2: Excerpt from Emily Post, "Restaurant Etiquette" in *Etiquette: The Blue Book of Social Usage* (New York: Funk and Wagnalls, 1957, 55–61)

As mentioned in the introduction to the document about the supermarket (11.1), in the wake of World War II, America became, in the words of the historian David Potter, a "people of plenty." The evidence of opulence was everywhere. Men and women celebrated their new status by getting married sooner and having more kids. They purchased oversized cars decorated with useless fins and streaks of chrome. They bought new homes and filled them with televisions, dishwashers, and refrigerators. Teenagers stayed in school for more years and out of the workforce longer, but they still had money for records, magazines, and the latest fashions. And families used their newfound material comfort to fund trips to the beach, national parks, and theme parks such as Disneyland.

Closer to home, the burgeoning American middle class began to change the way they ate. Perhaps most remarkably, they began to regularly eat meals out of the home. Many went to McDonald's to give mom a night off from cooking. But at the same time, they spent special occasions at fancier downtown restaurants and in hotel dining rooms. For those born during the Great Depression and raised in immigrant and working-class households, this was a new experience and it required learning new codes of behavior.

Born in 1898, Emily Post became America's foremost etiquette coach. In her best-selling books and newspaper columns, which appeared in hundreds of outlets across the country, she taught people how to behave in unfamiliar situations. She instructed them on how to set a table for an informal lunch and for a formal dinner. She told them what to wear and how to greet people. The passage below is about restaurants and how to behave in them and it comes from the 1957 edition of her book, Etiquette: The Blue Book of Social Usage.

In a fashionable restaurant a man leaves his hat and coat in the coat room or checks them at the entrance of the restaurant. A woman leaves her wrap in the dressing room—or, if she prefers, she goes into the dining room and sits down at the table as she is. She then merely throws the shoulders of her wrap back of her, over her chair.

In the daytime she wears a hat and keeps it on, of course. In spite of the vagaries of transient fashion, a hat is correct with a street dress, just as boots are correct with a riding habit. At night she wears a hat if in daytime clothes, an evening hat if she chooses with semi-evening clothes, and no hat ever if in formal evening dress. The fee to the maid in the dressing room—given when she returns the coat check and is helped on with her wrap—is twenty-five cents—in every restaurant or hotel that can be called luxurious. In a very simple hotel, one whose clothes are equally simple usually gives ten cents. The fee to the check-rack boy or girl who takes care of a man's hat and coat is ten cents—or in a super-smart restaurant a little more.

When entering a restaurant or hotel dining room, always stand near the door. The head waiter or waitress will show you where to sit. If you are staying at an American-plan hotel, you usually sit at the same table in the dining room, and after your first entrance you go to your place at table without waiting to be shown—although the head waiter will hurry, if he can, to pull your chair out for you. In a restaurant, even though you have the same special table reserved for you, you are always shown to your place by the head waiter or one of his assistants—very often both.

The waiter always pulls out the choice seat first (the seat which he considers choice because it is facing the room or the view or whatever is supposed to be of interest). A woman dining with the man naturally takes it, unless for some reason she definitely prefers another, in which case she stands beside the other chair, saying "I'd rather sit here." A woman who has invited another woman to lunch or dine with her naturally lets her guest go first and take the choice seat.

When a woman is lunching or dining with two men, they will of course seat her between them. A man lunching or dining with two women will sit between two who are not related to him, but he will sit opposite his wife. In a restaurant that has sofa seats the women always sit against the wall (or partition), and a man or men sit on the chairs facing them.

If a woman and two men are lunching or dining in an alcove (a table with benches) the woman takes her place first against the wall; the man who is not related to her sits beside her, and her husband or brother sits opposite. If this number is reversed, the two women sit next to the wall and the man sits beside her who is not related to him.

AT A DINNER GIVEN IN A RESTAURANT

The women always follow the head waiter and the men follow them. If a man is giving a party of six or more, the women stand at the table until told by their host where to sit. If they are only four and neither woman is married, the women seat themselves facing each other without direction.

Also, if Mary Lone and John Batchler dine with the Joneses, it is better that Mary and Mrs. Jones sit opposite—in spite of the taboo of seating a wife next to her husband—in order to let Mary sit next to Batchler instead of between the Joneses. When the Joneses and the Gaylings dine together, husbands and wives sit opposite each other.

It is said that in certain localities husbands and wives are purposely seated together when out in company. This, if true, is certainly contrary to all precepts of etiquette!

In all first-class restaurants each dish is presented to the host or hostess as soon as it arrives from the kitchen. The host is not expected to help himself, but merely to approve of its preparation. He nods "all right" and the waiter then serves it, or passes it to the guests.

ORDERING THE MEAL

When invitations are given beforehand to a lunch party or to a dinner in a restaurant, the host or hostess should order the meal in advance, and the guests eat what is put before them exactly as at a dinner in someone's house. But when the dinner has been made up at the spur of the moment, or when one woman lunches with another or dines with a man and the meal has not been ordered, and a host or hostess asks what the guests would like, it is better frankly to name a dish or two than to answer, "oh, anything," which means nothing whatever and leaves the host helplessly staring at that utterly impersonal dictionary of dishes, and *à la carte* menu.

But don't ask the waiter for explanations of every dish and change your order so that he has to rub it out as fast as he writes it down. And unless you know that your hostess is fabulously rich, you should show some consideration and not choose caviar, terrapin, breast of guinea-hen, and so on!

A GIRL DINES IN A RESTAURANT WITH A MAN

When a girl lunches or dines in a restaurant with a man, she takes the seat the headwaiter holds for her. This is usually the seat facing the door—if near the door—or possibly the view. She is supposed to sit opposite—at a small table—or on his right on a sofa seat against the wall. But this "on the right" rule is not important in the United States and they sit where they choose.

On occasion a man who may want to order a special dish—or dishes—gives this order beforehand. Usually, however, the man, the girl and the waiter hold a three-sided conversation, something like this:

MAN	"What would you like? Fruit cocktail? Oysters?"
WAITER	"Our shrimps are particularly fine."
MAN TO GIRL	"Would you like shrimps?"
GIRL	"Yes, very much," or else, "I'd rather have oysters."
MAN TO WAITER	"Bring one order of shrimps, one of oysters."
MAN TO GIRL	"Soup?"
GIRL	"No, I'd like just one dish, chicken—or something like that, and a desert."

Or when asked what she would like, she says in the beginning what she wants. Or she says nothing except "very nice" to whatever he suggests. One point: unless she knows the man is very well off, or the restaurant is a *table d'hote* one, the girl ought to show some consideration for her companion's purse. A young woman who says sweetly "yes" to his necessary suggestions of "hors d'oeuvres?" "Soup?" "Fish?" "Entrée?" "Roast?" "Salad?" "Dessert?" "Coffee?" is not very likely to be asked to dine with him soon again—if ever!

At a *table d'hôte*, each person usually gives her or his individual order to the waiter—or waitress.

TABLE D'HÔTE OR À LA CARTE

Table d'hôte (the table of the host) means a set price for each meal, irrespective of how many courses you order. "Club" breakfasts and lunches, "blue plate" dinners or any meals at fixed prices, whether $.50 or $5 a cover, are *table d'hôte*. *À la carte* means that you order "according to the card," and you pay for each dish ordered.

"American plan" means so much a day for room, including *table d'hôte* meals.

In the "European plan" hotel the prices of rooms include no food. And the restaurant charge is so much for each dish ordered....

There is one word of warning against mistaking an *à la carte* menu without prices printed on it for a *table d'hôte* bill of fare. But this need concern you only if you patronize those few among the highest-priced restaurants which, copying those for which Paris is famous, present you with a menu without prices printed on it. Should you encounter this, you can remember that it is entirely correct to hand it back—as does every European—and say, "bring me the menu with prices."

In an *à la carte* restaurant, the check—meaning a list of what you have ordered with the price of each item and the total of the bill—is brought to you by the waiter who serves you. In first-class restaurants it is always turned face down on a plate or a small silver tray. You turn it over and pay the waiter. He then brings your change, and you give him a tip.

DE LUXE RESTAURANT TIPS

It is impossible to give you definite schedules for tipping, because it all depends upon where you go, and upon what you order, and upon the service given you—or that you exact.

The conventional ten percent of a restaurant bill was correct in the days when people ordered an excessive amount of food. But today, when most people go to the other extreme and "rations vie with diets" in limiting your order, ten per cent of your bill must be qualified as "ten percent if *above the minimum* tip for the class of restaurant you are in" and for the class of person you *appear* to be. That is, if you patronize restaurants of greatest luxury and wear obviously expensive clothes with valuable accessories or if you are critical and difficult to please, greater "compensation" is expected than if your appearance were simpler and your manners more kind.

In New York at an ultra-smart restaurant of greatest luxury, the smallest tip you can give is thirty-five cents if you lunch alone, twenty per cent of a bill of three dollars or less, seventy-five cents on a total of five cents and ten per cent above this. For two persons, add about fifteen cents to each of these sums. The tipping system may be a bad plan and the trend is up! But in restaurants of this type the waiters depend upon tips for their wages. A lunch or dinner-party tip would be a minimum of twenty-five cents a person and ten per cent in addition to this base.

In an average first-class restaurant a reasonably accurate base is a minimum tip of twenty-five cents, whether for one person or two, for a bill that totals less than two dollars; thirty-five cents for one up to three dollars; forty cents for one from three dollars to four dollars. And a minimum of twenty cents a person for a lunch or dinner party.

194 Food and Eating in America

If you're having a party of ten or twelve or more, ten per cent would be quite enough divided between the waiters to serve you, if the bill comes to two dollars a person or more. Otherwise you would give two dollars, or two dollars and a half, and perhaps as much again to the head waiter if he has taken particular pains to have the service efficient or if he made you a special per-person price. On the other hand, if he does nothing for you, you give him nothing. Some people are very unfair in that the tips they give to waitresses are less than those given to waiters.

In a bare-tabled café or tea room, a tip of fifteen or even ten cents is possible for a dollar meal. In a restaurant with tablecloths, you would add five cents (laundry?) tip.

American-plan-hotel meal cards are often bought at the hotel desk. Country hotels sometimes ask you to register and pay for the meal later, but sometimes the check is paid to the waiter or waitress as in a restaurant. It is always easy enough to ask whoever serves you, "Where do I pay?" In any event you tip the one who served you, unless the management is one that forbids tipping. In this case a ten per cent fee is added to the bill. You pay the check at the cashier's desk and leave nothing on the table.

PREPAYING THE RESTAURANT CHECK

Not so very long ago a host—as well as a hostess—found the moment when the waiter presented the check embarrassing. In fact, the hostess who had no charge account either ordered the meal ahead of time and paid for it (which was impractical because no one could count on how many would, or would not, take cocktails or cigarettes or cigars). Many hostesses made it a practice to have the bill brought to them at the door of the ladies' dressing room.

Today, however, all questions of payment are taken as a matter of course—even when a man alone is dining with the woman. In this case, if possible, she takes him to her club, where she necessarily signs the voucher, and there can be no question about the propriety of her paying. But if they dine in a restaurant where she has no charge account, there is no reason why a man should feel embarrassed to have a woman friend who, let us say, has dined with him time and again take the check and pay it. In other words, Mrs. Grundy has lost nearly all of her influence during the war. If a woman who wants to return a man's many invitations to her would like to ask him to dine with her, he can decline (ungenerously) if he chooses. But if he accepts her invitation, he must *not* make her and himself conspicuous by refusing to accept the situation in a matter-of-fact way.

When a woman gives a dinner of any size, she usually makes the man she knows best her banker by giving him the money beforehand. He pays the bills and makes an accounting to her afterwards.

RESTAURANT MANNERS

When one lady, passing another seated at a table in a restaurant, stops and shakes hands, the one who is seated does not rise unless she is very young and the one passing is quite old. All the gentleman at the table of course rise and stand until the visiting lady has departed, whether she is known to them or not.

This detail of behavior is one that every lady should take seriously, since every gentleman MUST stand as long as she stands. It doesn't change the situation a bit for her to say, "Please sit down," because a man who is seen sitting and eating while a "lady" stands is automatically proclaimed "no gentleman" by each person who catches a glimpse of this behavior.

Very expert waiters save the situation by instantly placing a chair behind the knees of any woman inclined to linger. As soon as she sits, the men may sit—and continue eating. If the visitor sits down, she is introduced to the two or three others at a very small table, or to those next her at a large one; but should she merely stand, the friend with whom she stops to speak does not make any introduction, unless she *knows* that one of those at the table and the visitor are for some reason anxious to meet each other.

If the ladies are introduced, the ones at the table do not rise—unless very young and the visitor very elderly.

Gentlemen at table do not rise when another gentleman stops at the table unless there is a great difference in age. All younger men rise for a really old gentleman.

CONSIDERATION FOR THOSE WHO SERVE US

Lack of consideration for those who in any capacity serve us —whether in restaurants or hotels or stores, or in public places anywhere—is always on evidence of ill-breeding as well as inexcusable selfishness....It is only those who are afraid that someone may encroach upon their exceedingly insecure dignity who show neither courtesy nor consideration except to those whom they think it would be to their advantage to please.

Discussion questions

1. Who is the typical reader of Emily Post's book? How do you think they will feel after reading this passage about going to a formal dining room? Will they be more comfortable or more anxious?
2. Why are restaurants such important spaces? What do they teach us? What do you need to know to navigate them? Why do we need these skills?

3. Beyond the obvious, what is Post teaching her readers, about, for instance, tipping? Gender? Other issues? How does Post deal with larger social relations?

4. If Post were to write an etiquette guide now to formal dining, what would she say? What has changed and what has stayed the same?

Document 11.3: Excerpt from Rachel Carson, *Silent Spring* (Boston: Houghton Mifflin, 1962)[1]

Noted author and marine biologist, Rachel Carson, published, Silent Spring, in 1962. Despite its title, the book immediately generated a tremendous amount of buzz. With a muckraker's sense of outrage and disgust, Carson stirred up the dirt at the bottom of big agriculture and big science and exposed the hazardous effects of pesticides, like DDT, on the environment and on food stuffs. She pointed to the nation's compromised ecosystems and worried aloud about the development of chemically resistant pests and bugs. In other places in the book, she talked about the health risks, including cancer, associated with repeated exposure to pesticides.

In the bold tradition of Uncle Tom's Cabin and The Jungle, Silent Spring doesn't just tear off the veil of silence, it also looks for culprits. Carson pointed fingers at the chemical industry and the government, accusing them of lies and subterfuge, and of compromising the health of plants, animals, and humans in the search for profit. But even more, Carson's book questioned the abiding postwar faith in science and technology as the surest path to progress and the best answer to any and all social problems. In the excerpt below, Carson discusses the presence of DDT in the nation's food supply. What risks does she identify?

The question of chemical residues on the food we eat is a hotly debated issue. The existence of such residues is either played down by the industry as unimportant or is flatly denied. Simultaneously, there is a strong tendency to brand as fanatics or cultists all who are so perverse as to demand that their food be free of insect poisons. In all this cloud of controversy, what are the actual facts?

It has been medically established that, as common sense would tell us, persons who lived and died before the dawn of the DDT era (about 1942) contained no trace of DDT or any similar material in their tissues. As mentioned in chapter 3, samples of body fat collected from the general population between 1954 and 1956 averaged from 5.3 to 7.4 parts per million of DDT. There is some evidence that the average level has risen since then to a consistently higher figure, and individuals with occupational or other special exposures to insecticides of course store even more.

Among the general population with no known gross exposures to insecticides it may be assumed that much of the DDT stored in fat deposits has entered the body in food. To test this assumption, a scientific team from the United States Public Health Service sampled restaurant and institutional meals. *Every meal sampled contain DDT.* From this the investigators concluded reasonably enough that "few if any foods can be relied upon to be entirely free of DDT."

The quantities in such meals may be enormous. In a separate Public Health Service study, analysis of prison meals disclosed such items as stewed dried fruit containing 69.6 parts per million and bread containing 100.9 parts per million of DDT!

In the diet of the average home, meats in any products derived from animal fats contain the heaviest residues of chlorinated hydrocarbons. This is because these chemicals are soluble in fat. Residues on fruits and vegetables tend be somewhat less. These are little affected by washing—the only remedy is to remove and discard all outside leaves of such vegetables as lettuce or cabbage, to peel fruit and use no skins or outer covering whatever. Cooking does not destroy residues.

Milk is one of the few foods in which no pesticide residues are permitted by Food and Drug Administration regulations. In actual fact, however, residues turn up whenever a check is made. They are heaviest in butter and other manufactured dairy products. A check of 461 samples of such products in 1960 showed that a third contained residues, a situation which the Food and Drug Administration characterized as "far from encouraging."

To find a diet free from DDT and related chemicals, it seems one must go to a remote and primitive land, still lacking the amenities of civilization. Such a land appears to exist, at least marginally, on the far Arctic shores of Alaska—although even there one may see the approaching shadow. When scientists investigated the native diet of the Eskimos in this region it was found to be free from insecticides. The fresh and dried fish; the fat, oil, or meat from beaver, beluga, caribou, moose, oogruk, polar bear, and walrus; cranberries, salmonberries and wild rhubarb all had so far escaped contamination. There was only one exception—two white owls from Point Hope carried small amounts of DDT, perhaps acquired in the course of some migratory journey.

When some of the Eskimos themselves were checked by an analysis of fat samples, small residues of DDT were found. The reason for this was clear. The fat samples were taken from people who had left their native villages to enter the United States Public Health Service hospital in Anchorage for surgery. There the ways of civilization prevailed, and the meals in this hospital were found to contain as much DDT as those in the most populous city. For their brief stay in civilization the Eskimos were rewarded with a taint of poison.

The fact that every meal we eat carries its load of chlorinated hydrocarbons is the inevitable consequence of the almost universal spraying or dusting of agricultural crops with these poisons. If the farmer scrupulously follows the instructions on the labels, his use of agricultural chemicals will produce no residues larger than are permitted by the FDA. Leaving aside for the moment the question whether these legal residues are as "safe" as they are represented to be, there remains the well-known fact that farmers very frequently exceed the prescribed dosages, use the chemical too close to the time of harvest, use several insecticides where one will do, and in other ways display a common human failure to read the fine print.

Even the chemical history recognizes the frequent misuse of insecticides and need for educational farmers. One of the leading trade journals recently declared that "many users do not seem to understand that they may exceed insecticide tolerances if they use higher dosages than recommended. And haphazard use of insecticides on many crops may be based on farmers' whims."

The files of the FDA contain records of a disturbing number of such violations. A few examples will serve to illustrate the disregard of directions: a lettuce farmer who applied not one but eight different insecticides to his crop within a short time of harvest, a shipper who had used the deadly parathion on celery in an amount five times the recommended maximum, growers using endrin—most toxic of all the chlorinated hydrocarbons—on lettuce although no residue was allowable, spinach sprayed with DDT a week before harvest.

There are also cases of chance or accidental contamination. Large lots of green coffee in burlap bags have become contaminated while being transported by vessels also carrying a cargo of insecticides. Packaged foods in warehouses are subjected to repeated aerosol treatments with DDT, lindane, and other insecticides, which may penetrate to packing materials and occur in measurable quantities on the contained foods. The longer the food remains in storage, the greater the danger of contamination.

To the question "But doesn't the government protect us from such things?" the answer is, "Only to a limited extent." The activities of the FDA in the field of consumer protection against pesticides are severely limited by two facts. The first is that it has jurisdiction only over foods shipped in interstate commerce; foods grown and marketed within a state are entirely outside its sphere of authority, no matter what the violation. The second and critically limiting factor is the small number of inspectors on its staff—fewer than 600 men for all its varied work. According to a Food and Drug official, only an infinitesimal part of the crop products moving in interstate commerce—far less than 1 per cent—can be checked with existing facilities, and this is not enough to have statistical significance. As for food produced and sold within a state, the situation is even worse, for most states have woefully inadequate laws in this field.

The system by which the FDA establishes maximum permissible limits of contamination, called "tolerances," has obvious defects. Under the conditions prevailing it provides mere paper security and promotes a completely unjustified impression that safe limits have been established and are being adhered to. As to allowing a sprinkling of poisons on our food—a little on this, a little on that—many people contend, with highly persuasive reasons, that no poison is safe or desirable on food. In setting a tolerance level the FDA reviews tests of the poison on laboratory animals and then establishes a maximum level of contamination that is much less than required to produce symptoms in the test animal. This system, which is supposed to ensure safety, ignores a number of important facts. A laboratory animal, living under controlled and highly artificial conditions, consuming a given amount of a specific chemical, is very different from a human being whose exposures to pesticides are not only multiple but for the most part unknown, unmeasurable, and uncontrollable. Even if 7 parts per million of DDT on the lettuce in his luncheon salad were "safe," the meal includes other foods, each with allowable residues, and the pesticides on his food are, as we have seen, only a part, and possibly a small part, of his total exposure. This piling up of chemicals from many different sources creates a total exposure that cannot be measured. It is meaningless, therefore, to talk about the "safety" of any specific amount of residue.

And there are other defects. Tolerances have sometimes been established against better judgment of FDA scientists…or they have been established on the basis of inadequate knowledge of the chemical concerned. Better information has led to later reduction or withdrawal of the tolerance, but only after the public has been exposed to admittedly dangerous levels of the chemical for months or years. This happened when heptachlor was given a tolerance that later had to be revoked. For some chemicals no practical field method of analysis exists before a chemical is registered for use. Inspectors are therefore frustrated in their search for residues. This difficulty greatly hampered the work on the "cranberry chemical," aminotriazole. Analytical methods are lacking, too, for certain fungicides in common use for the treatment of seeds—seeds which if unused at the end of the planting season, may very well find their way into human food.

In effect, then, to establish tolerances is to authorize contamination of public food supplies with poisonous chemicals in order that the farmer and the processor may enjoy the benefit of cheaper production—then to penalize the consumer by taxing him to maintain a policing agency to make certain that he shall not get a lethal dose. But to do the policing job properly it would cost money beyond any legislator's courage to appropriate, given the present volume and toxicity of agricultural chemicals. So in the end the luckless consumer pays his taxes but gets his poisons regardless.

What is a solution? The first necessity is the elimination of tolerances on the chlorinated hydrocarbons, the organic phosphorus group, and other highly toxic chemicals. It will immediately be objected that this places an intolerable burden on the farmer. But if, as is now the presumable goal, it is possible to use chemicals in such a way that they leave a residue only 7 parts per million (the tolerance for DDT), or of 1 part per million (the tolerance for parathion), or even of only 0.1 part per million as is required for dieldrin on a great variety of fruits and vegetables, then why is it not possible, with only a little more care, to prevent the occurrence of any residues at all? This, in fact, is what is required for some chemicals such as helptachlor, endrin, and dieldrin on certain crops. If it is considered practical in these instances, why not for all?

But this is not a complete or final solution, for a zero tolerance on paper is of little value. At present, as we have seen, more than 99% of the interstate food shipments slip by without inspection. A vigilant and aggressive FDA, with a greatly increased force of inspectors, is another urgent need.

The system, however—deliberately poisoning our food, then policing the result—is too reminiscent of Lewis Carroll's White Knight who thought of a "plan to dye one's whiskers green, and always use so large a fan that they could not be seen." The ultimate answer is to use less toxic chemicals so that the public hazard from their misuse is greatly reduced. Such chemicals already exist: the pyrethrins, rotenone, ryania, and others derived from plant substances. Synthetic substitutes for the pyrethrins have recently been developed and some of the producing countries stand ready to increase the output of the natural product as the market may require. Public education as to the nature of the chemicals offered for sale is sadly needed. The average purchaser is completely bewildered by the array of available insecticides, fungicides, and weed killers, and has no way of knowing which are the deadly ones, which reasonably safe.

In addition to making this change to less dangerous agricultural pesticides, we should diligently explore the possibilities of nonchemical methods. Agricultural use of insect diseases, caused by a bacterium highly specific to certain types of insects, is already being tried in California, and more extended tests of this method are underway. A great many other possibilities exist for effective insect control by methods that will leave no residues on foods. Until a large-scale conversion to these methods has been made, we shall have little relief from a situation that, by any common-sense standards, isn't tolerable. As matters stand now, we are in little better position than the guests of the Borgias.

Discussion questions

1. How did DDT help to create modern food? How did it make things cheaper? How prevalent is the problem of DDT in the food supply? And what kinds of food does it affect the most and why?
2. Who benefits from this system? Who doesn't? For a clue, think of Carson's reference to prison food.
3. Why didn't the government protect consumers from chemicals in the food supply? Can the government alone safeguard food? What complicates things according to Carson?
4. How can the food and agricultural systems be made safer? Do you think these issues have been addressed and corrected? What sort of social order is Carson advocating in her book?

Document 11.4: Swanson Advertisement, "Everybody Wins" (1963)

Gerald Thomas, a Swanson and Sons executive, badly overestimated turkey consumption for Thanksgiving 1953. He found himself with ten refrigerator trucks full of turkeys and he needed to figure out something to do with the leftovers. Not long after, he thought about his next move on a plane ride. As he sat in his seat, the flight attendant handed him a silver tray of food with meat in one compartment, vegetables in another, and dessert in yet another. That's it, he thought, let's fill a bunch of trays with turkey and gravy, buttered peas, and sweet potatoes and freeze them. Now people can have Thanksgiving all year long. And they could eat these meals in front of their television sets.

Thomas wasn't the first person to think of TV dinners. Initially previewed at the New York World's Fair in 1939, television as a business and form of entertainment exploded after the war as Americans yearned to get back to normal and spend the money they had in their pockets for the first time since the Great Depression. The postwar period was, again, one of robust prosperity. Harvard University historian Lizabeth Cohen has dubbed the 1950s, "A Consumers' Republic." By 1955, three quarters of all Americans had TVs in their houses, increasingly their own houses in the suburbs. The television became the center of the household, a place for the family to gather together or to sit alone. It also transformed eating, with parents and children sometimes moving the dinner table into the living room.

Emerging from a pack of competitors, Swanson established itself as the nation's number one TV dinner company. It did so largely through advertising and even by using the design of the television right on its packaging. By the 1960s, as television reached nearly 90 percent of American households, Swanson began to sharpen its advertising to better target and capitalize on the hopes and desires of its audiences.

Swanson Night... everybody wins!

Each one can pick his favorite meal (like this golden shrimp) and join in the after-dinner fun.

"Gee, this sauce makes the shrimp extra-good."

LOOK

Swanson gives you tangy cocktail sauce as an extra "home style" touch!

SWANSON FROZEN FRIED SHRIMP DINNER

- Swanson Shrimp—fried crispy on the outside, *juicy* and tender on the inside.
- Young green peas in seasoned butter sauce.
- "Crinkle-cut" potatoes for more crispness. Carefully fried to keep them light and tender.
- The perfect complement for fried shrimp —a tart, tangy, tomato cocktail sauce.

Have a Swanson Night soon!

Trust Swanson

"TV" and "TV Dinner" are registered trademarks of Campbell Soup Company

Discussion questions

1. In the advertisement above, who is the target of the marketing? Think about the composition of the advertisement. Pay particular attention to the photograph. What's the message here? What does this say about the ideal of the American family? Why are they pictured at a table, do you think, instead of in front of a television?
2. What does the slogan, "Everyone wins," mean? Who wins what? What do the kids win? What does the mom win?
3. Imagine that you are an archaeologist and that you discovered this TV dinner in a long lost freezer. What would this meal tell you about American civilization in the 1960s? What did people want from their food? What did this society value in terms of taste and time? Why is the food described in this way? What isn't said about the food?
4. What would an advertisement for a "TV dinner" look like today? Would it be called a laptop dinner? Who would be the target of the ad? What foods would be served? How would the food and its qualities be described? What do these imagined changes suggest?

Document 11.5: Excerpts from Norman Borlaug's lecture "The Green Revolution, Peace, and Humanity," Delivered Upon Receiving the Nobel Peace Prize December 11, 1970)

Through much of the twentieth century, Americans invested a tremendous amount of faith, much of it uncritical, in science. Science could make life easier in cities, in the kitchen, and at work. Science would allow people to live longer and healthier lives. Science would take us to the moon, and science would feed people in the developing world.

That's certainly what an American scientist named Norman Borlaug believed. In 1944, the Mexican government, with funds provided by the Rockefeller Foundation, hired Borlaug to help make the country self-sufficient in terms of agricultural production and output. In other words, Mexico wanted to produce enough food for its own citizens on its own land. He painstakingly went about his work. Eventually, Borlaug and his team developed a strain of dwarf wheat that thrived in the Mexican heat. This genetically modified strain of wheat was resistant to most diseases and produced high yields. When combined with heavy doses of fertilizer, often made by US companies from petroleum and other products, the new strains of wheat produced tremendous yields, made food more plentiful, and helped to avert famine across the country.

By the 1960s, the US Agency for International Development started to do additional research and make available "miracles seeds" of wheat, rice, and

*corn in India and other parts of Asia. As in Mexico, increased outputs
required heavy reliance on irrigation and chemical fertilizers, but the
techniques worked, at least in the aggregate, as food production soared and
people avoided starvation. The director of the US Agency for International
Development, William Gaud, called the rapid growth in output, "The Green
Revolution." In 1970, Borlaug won the Nobel Prize for his contribution to
this transformation. Below, you will read an excerpt from Borlaug's acceptance speech, which he titled, "The Green Revolution."*

It is a sad fact that on this earth at this late date there are still two worlds, "the privileged world" and "the forgotten world." The privileged world consists of the affluent, developed nations, comprising twenty-five to thirty percent of the world population, in which most of the people live in a luxury never before experienced by man outside the Garden of Eden. The forgotten world is made up primarily of the developing nations, where most of the people, comprising more than fifty percent of the total world population, live in poverty, with hunger as a constant companion and fear of famine a continual menace.

When the Nobel Peace Prize Committee designated me the recipient of the 1970 award for my contribution to the "green revolution," they were in effect, I believe, selecting an individual to symbolize the vital role of agriculture and food production in a world that is hungry, both for bread and for peace. I am but one member of a vast team made up of many organizations, officials, thousands of scientists, and millions of farmers—mostly small and humble—who for many years have been fighting a quiet, oftentimes losing war on the food production front.

During the past three years spectacular progress has been made in increasing wheat, rice, and maize production in several of the most populous developing countries of southern Asia, where widespread famine appeared inevitable only five years ago. Most of the increase in production has resulted from increased yields of grain per hectare, a particularly important development because there is little possibility of expanding the cultivated area in the densely populated areas of Asia.

The term "The Green Revolution" has been used by the popular press to describe the spectacular increase in cereal-grain production during the past three years. Perhaps the term "green revolution" as commonly used, is premature, too optimistic, or too broad in scope. Too often it seems to convey the impression of a general revolution in yields per hectare and in total production of all crops throughout vast areas comprising many countries. Sometimes it also implies that all farmers are uniformly benefited by the breakthrough in production.

These implications both oversimplify and distort the facts. The only crops which have been appreciably affected up to the present time are wheat, rice, and maize. Yields of other important cereals, such as sorghums, millets, and barley, have been only slightly affected; nor has there been any appreciable increase in yield or production of the pulse or legume crops, which are essential in the diets of cereal-consuming populations. Moreover, it must be emphasized that thus far the great increase in production has been in irrigated areas. Nor have all cereal farmers in the irrigated areas adopted and benefited from the use of the new seed and the new technology. Nevertheless, the number of farmers, small as well as large, who are adopting the new seeds and new technology is increasing very rapidly, and the increase in numbers during the past three years has been phenomenal. Cereal production in the rain-fed areas still remains relatively unaffected by the impact of the green revolution, but significant change and progress are now becoming evident in several countries.

Despite these qualifications, however, tremendous progress has been made in increasing cereal production in India, Pakistan, and the Philippines during the past three years. Other countries that are beginning to show significant increases in production include Afghanistan, Ceylon, Indonesia, Iran, Kenya, Malaya, Morocco, Thailand, Tunisia, and Turkey.

Before attempting to evaluate the significance of the green revolution one must establish the point of view of the appraiser. The green revolution has an entirely different meaning to most people in the affluent nations of the privileged world than to those in the developing nations of the forgotten world. In the affluent, industrialized nations giant surpluses of wheat, maize, and sorghum are commonplace; cattle, swine, and poultry are fed and fattened on cereal grains; meat, milk, eggs, fruits, and vegetables are within the economic reach of most of the population; well-balanced diets are more or less automatically achieved, and cereal products constitute only a modest portion of the "daily bread." Consequently, most of the people in such societies have difficulty in comprehending and appreciating the vital significance of providing high-yielding strains of wheat, rice, maize, sorghum, and millet for the people of the developing nations. Understandably then, the majority of the urbanites in the industrialized nations have forgotten the significance of the words they learned as youngsters, "Give us this day our daily bread." They know that food comes from the supermarket, but only a few see beyond to the necessary investments, the toil, struggle, and frustrations on the farms and ranches that provide their daily bread. Since the urbanites have lost their contact with the soil, they take food for granted and fail to appreciate the tremendous efficiency of their farmers and ranchers, who, although constituting only five percent of the labor force in a country such as the United States, produce more than enough food for their nation.

Even worse, urbanites often vociferously criticize their government for attempting to bring into balance the agricultural production of its farmers with the domestic and foreign market demands for farm products, and attempting thereby to provide the consumer an abundant food supply at reasonable cost and also to assure a reasonable return to the farmer and rancher.

Contrasting sharply, in the developing countries represented by India, Pakistan, and most of the countries in Asia and Africa, seventy to eighty percent of the population is engaged in agriculture, mostly at the subsistence level. The land is tired, worn out, depleted of plant nutrients, and often eroded; crop yields have been low, near starvation level, and stagnant for centuries. Hunger prevails, and survival depends largely upon the annual success or failure of the cereal crops. In these nations both under-nutrition and malnutrition are widespread and are a constant threat to survival and to the attainment of the genetic potential for mental and physical development. The diet consists primarily of cereals, which provide from seventy to eighty percent of the calories and sixty-five to seventy percent of the protein intake. Animal proteins are so scarce and expensive as to be beyond the economic reach of the vast majority of the population. Although many of these nations were self-sufficient and some were exporters of cereals before the Second World War, they are now net importers, victims of population growth's outrunning agricultural production. There is little possibility in these countries of expanding the cultivated area to cope with the growing demand. The situation worsens as crop yields remain stagnant while human numbers continue to increase at frightening rates.

For the underprivileged billions in the forgotten world, hunger has been a constant companion, and starvation has all too often lurked in the nearby shadows. To millions of these unfortunates, who have long lived in despair, the green revolution seems like a miracle that has generated new hope for the future.

... There are no miracles in agricultural production. Nor is there such a thing as a miracle variety of wheat, rice, or maize which can serve as an elixir to cure all ills of a stagnant, traditional agriculture. Nevertheless, it is the Mexican dwarf wheat varieties, and their more recent Indian and Pakistani derivatives, that have been the principal catalyst in triggering off the green revolution. It is the unusual breadth of adaption combined with high genetic yield potential, short straw, a strong responsiveness and high efficiency in the use of heavy doses of fertilizers, and a broad spectrum of disease resistance that has made the Mexican dwarf varieties the powerful catalyst that they have become in launching the green revolution. They have caught the farmers' fancy, and during the 1969–1970 crop season, fifty-five percent of the six million hectares sown to wheat in Pakistan and thirty-five percent of the fourteen million hectares in India were sown to Mexican varieties or their derivatives. This rapid increase in wheat production was not based solely on the use of Mexican dwarf varieties; it involved the transfer from Mexico to Pakistan and India of a whole new production technology that enables these varieties to attain their high-yield potential. Perhaps seventy-five percent of the results of research done in Mexico in developing the package of recommended cultural practices, including fertilizer recommendations, were directly applicable in Pakistan and India. As concerns the remaining twenty-five percent, the excellent adaptive research done in India and Pakistan by Indian and Pakistani scientists while the imported seed was being multiplied, provided the necessary information for modifying the Mexican procedures to suit Pakistani and Indian conditions more precisely.

Equally as important as the transfer of the new seed and new technology from Mexico to India and Pakistan was the introduction from Mexico of a crop-production campaign strategy. This strategy harnessed the high grain-yield potential of the new seed and new technology to sound governmental economic policy which would assure the farmer a fair price for his grain, the availability of the necessary inputs - seed, fertilizers, insecticides, weed killers, and machinery—and the credit with which to buy them. Collectively these inputs and strategy became the base from which the green revolution evolved.

Never before in the history of agriculture has a transplantation of high-yielding varieties coupled with an entirely new technology and strategy been achieved on such a massive scale, in so short a period of time, and with such great success. The success of this transplantation is an event of both great scientific and social significance. Its success depended upon good organization of the production program combined with skillful execution by courageous and experienced scientific leaders.

Experimentation with dwarf Mexican varieties was initiated in both India and Pakistan in 1963 and continued in 1964. Results in both countries were highly promising....During the past three years, wheat production has risen spectacularly in both countries. Using as a base the pre-green revolution crop year 1964–1965, which produced an all-time record harvest in both countries, the production in Pakistan increased from the 1965 base figure of 4.6 million tons to 6.7, 7.2, and 8.4 millions of tons, respectively, in 1968, 1969, and 1970. West Pakistan became self-sufficient in wheat production for the first time in the 1968 harvest season, two years ahead of our predictions. Indian wheat production has risen from the 1964–1965 pre-green revolution record crop of 12.3 million tons to 16.5, 18.7, and 20.0 million tons during 1968, 1969, and 1970 harvests, respectively. India is approaching self-sufficiency and probably would have attained it by now if rice production had risen more rapidly, because, with a continuing shortage of rice, considerable wheat is being substituted for it.

The revolution in wheat and rice production in India and Pakistan has not only greatly increased food production, but it also has had many indirect effects on both the farmer and the economy. It is estimated that Indian and Pakistani farmers who are cultivating the new Mexican dwarf-wheat varieties under the recommended management practices have increased their net income from thirty-seven dollars per hectare with the local varieties to 162 dollars with the dwarf Mexican varieties. During the past three harvests, a total of 1.4 billion dollars and 640 million dollars have been added to the gross national product (G. N. P.) of India and Pakistan, respectively, from the increase in wheat production above the record 1965 base. The injection of this large increase in purchasing power into the economies has had many effects.

Mechanization of agriculture is rapidly following the breakthrough in wheat production. Prior to the first big wheat crop in 1968, unsold tractors accumulated at the two factories then in production; at present, prospective purchasers must make written application for them and wait one or two years for delivery. Although five factories, with an output of eighteen thousand units per year, are now producing tractors, thirty-five thousand units were imported in 1969–1970.

The traditional method of threshing by treading out of the grain with bullocks, followed by winnowing, is now inadequate for threshing the increased volume of wheat before the onset of the monsoon rains. Consequently, hundreds of thousands of small threshing machines have been produced and sold by hundreds of small village machine shops during the past three years, thus avoiding the loss of much of the crop after harvest and also providing additional employment in many new small-village industries.

Moreover, mechanization has had another very important indirect effect on the intensification of cereal production. When small mechanical threshers replace bullocks for threshing, the bullocks are released for use in the timely preparation of the land for the next (summer) crop. This need for timely preparation of land is also one of the main reasons for the surge in demand for tractors. Before the adoption of the new wheat and rice varieties, in combination with heavy applications of chemical fertilizer, the time of sowing was relatively unimportant because yields were limited primarily by the low level of available plant nutrients. Most farmers would expect to harvest about one metric ton of wheat during the winter (rabi) season and about one and a half metric tons of rice during the summer (kharif) season, or a total of two and a half metric tons of grain per hectare per year. But by using the high-yielding varieties, fertilizing heavily, sowing at the right time, and managing the fields properly, the same farmer can now harvest five tons of wheat and seven tons of rice per hectare from the same land, a total of twelve metric tons of food grain per hectare per year, as contrasted with the two and a half tons which he obtained with the old varieties and methods. If plantings are not done at the optimum time, however, the yield of wheat may drop to three tons and that of rice to four tons per hectare, a total production of seven tons per year instead of the twelve tons when all operations are proper and timely. A few of the most progressive farmers now use triple cropping, involving wheat – mung beans – rice, or wheat – rice – potato, or three consecutive crops of rice during the same year. By increasing the intensity of cropping, both food production potential and employment are increased. Yields must then be calculated on the basis of kilos per hectare per year rather than on the basis of kilos per hectare per crop.

The increased mechanization in cereal production has tended thus far to increase rather than decrease the employment opportunities for labor, and above all it has helped to reduce drudgery and increase the efficiency of human energy, especially in India.

Millions of farmers who have successfully grown the new wheat, rice, and maize varieties have greatly increased their income. And this has stimulated the rapid growth of agro-industry by increasing the demand for fertilizers, pumps, machinery, and other materials and services.

Farmers in many villages are investing in better storage facilities. In some locations, brick houses are beginning to replace those made of rammed earth. More electricity is being used to light the houses and to drive the motors on the wells. There also has been a rapid increase in demand for consumer goods. The purchase of transistors and radios for use in the villages has increased rapidly, and thereby the government for the first time can effectively reach the remote villages with educational programs. Sewing machines, bicycles, motor scooters, and motorcycles are coming to the villages, and truck and bus service between villages is improving.

In summarizing the accomplishments of the green revolution during the past three years, I wish to restate that the increase in cereal production, rice, maize, and wheat, especially in wheat, has been spectacular and highly significant to the welfare of millions of human beings. It is still modest in terms of total needs. Recalling that fifty percent of the present world population is undernourished and that an even larger percentage, perhaps sixty-five percent, is malnourished, no room is left for complacency. It is not enough to prevent the currently bad situation from getting worse as population increases. Our aim must be to produce enough food to eradicate all present hunger while at the same time striving to correct malnutrition. To eliminate hunger now in the developing nations, we would need to expand world cereal production by thirty percent.

I am convinced that if all policymakers would take sufficient interest in population control and in aggressively employing and exploiting agricultural development as a potent instrument of agrarian prosperity and economic advancement, many of the social ills of the present day could soon become problems of the past. The tropics and subtropics have abundant sunlight and other great biological assets, and it will be criminal to delay further the conversion of these assets into wealth meaningful to the poor and hungry.

Some critics have said that the green revolution has created more problems than it has solved. This I cannot accept, for I believe it is far better for mankind to be struggling with new problems caused by abundance rather than with the old problem of famine. Certainly, loyalty to the status quo in food production—when being pressured by population growth—cannot break the chains that have bound the peasant to poverty and hunger. One must ask: Is it just to criticize the green revolution, with its recognized accomplishments, for failure to correct all the social-economic ills of the world that have accumulated from the days of Adam and Eve up to the present? Change we must, or we will perish as a species, just as did the dinosaurs in the late Cretaceous.

… The green revolution has won a temporary success in man's war against hunger and deprivation; it has given man a breathing space. If fully implemented, the revolution can provide sufficient food for sustenance during the next three decades. But the frightening power of human reproduction must also be curbed; otherwise the success of the green revolution will be ephemeral only.

Most people still fail to comprehend the magnitude and menace of the "Population Monster." In the beginning there were but two, Adam and Eve. When they appeared on this earth is still questionable. By the time of Christ, world population had probably reached 250 million. But between then and now, population has grown to 3.5 billion. Growth has been especially fast since the advent of modern medicine. If it continues to increase at the estimated present rate of two percent a year, the world population will reach 6.5 billion by the year 2000. Currently, with each second, or tick of the clock, about 2.2 additional people are added to the world population. The rhythm of increase will accelerate to 2.7, 3.3, and 4.0 for each tick of the clock by 1980, 1990, and 2000, respectively, unless man becomes more realistic and preoccupied about this impending doom. The ticktock of the clock will continually grow louder and more menacing each decade. Where will it all end?

Malthus signaled the danger a century and a half ago. But he emphasized principally the danger that population would increase faster than food supplies. In his time he could not foresee the tremendous increase in man's food production potential. Nor could he have foreseen the disturbing and destructive physical and mental consequences of the grotesque concentration of human beings into the poisoned and clangorous environment of pathologically hypertrophied megalopoles. Can human beings endure the strain? Abnormal stresses and strains tend to accentuate man's animal instincts and provoke irrational and socially disruptive behavior among the less stable individuals in the maddening crowd.

We must recognize the fact that adequate food is only the first requisite for life. For a decent and humane life we must also provide an opportunity for good education, remunerative employment, comfortable housing, good clothing, and effective and compassionate medical care. Unless we can do this, man may degenerate sooner from environmental diseases than from hunger.

And yet, I am optimistic for the future of mankind, for in all biological populations there are innate devices to adjust population growth to the carrying capacity of the environment. Undoubtedly, some such device exists in man, presumably *Homo sapiens*, but so far it has not asserted itself to bring into balance population growth and the carrying capacity of the environment on a worldwide scale. It would be disastrous for the species to continue to increase our human numbers madly until such innate devices take over. It is a test of the validity of *sapiens* as a species epithet.

Since man is potentially a rational being, however, I am confident that within the next two decades he will recognize the self-destructive course he steers along the road of irresponsible population growth and will adjust the growth rate to levels which will permit a decent standard of living for all mankind. If man is wise enough to make this decision and if all nations abandon their idolatry of Ares, Mars, and Thor, then Mankind itself should be the recipient of a Nobel Peace Prize which is "to be awarded to the person who has done most to promote brotherhood among the nations."

Then, by developing and applying the scientific and technological skills of the twentieth century for "the well-being of mankind throughout the world," he may still see Isaiah's prophesies come true: "... And the desert shall rejoice, and blossom as the rose...And the parched ground shall become a pool, and the thirsty land springs of water..."

And may these words come true!

Discussion questions

1. What does Norman Borlaug see as the greatest triumphs of the Green Revolution? How was this achieved? What techniques were used? Why is this development historically so significant? What are the rollover effects of more food?

2. What does he mean by the "population menace?" Isn't the Green Revolution as much a part of the problem as the solution when it comes to population growth? What does Borlaug say? Do you agree with him?

3. By the 1990s, some people were criticizing the Green Revolution. Why do you think that was?

4. Some critics have charged that the Green Revolution led to the rapid decline of small farmers. In some cases, farmers killed themselves by drinking the pesticides they purchased for their crops. Is this fair? Is this simply the price of progress as some have said?

5. Did the Green Revolution make countries both more and less dependent on the developed world? (Remember while output soared, as some pointed out, farmers depended on fertilizers from wealthy multinational corporations.) What are the environmental implications of the Green Revolution? Are the trade-offs worth it?

Document 11.6: Margaret Visser, "A Meditation on the Microwave," *Psychology Today* (December, 1989)

"The way we treat food and the manner in which we consume it," declares Margaret Visser, a classics professor, "are expressions of our goals and values." Like others, she wants us to pay close attention to our eating habits and the settings for our meals. (Compare this with Document 10.5's description of Japanese internment.) Both how we eat and where we eat, as she makes clear, interact all the time with new tools and new technologies. Food habits, of course, changed drastically with the advent of fire and home ovens. Writing in 1989, she thinks that the American kitchen stands at yet another historic watershed with the wide introduction of the affordable microwave oven.

Once we braised, broiled, fried and poached our food. Today we zap and nuke it. The social historian who wrote *Much Depends on Dinner* searches for the meaning of our changing meals.

When the members of a family, or of a college fraternity, regularly eat meals together, they are not only nourishing themselves, they are also creating and reinforcing personal and cultural attitudes and expectations. If they decide to eat irregularly and apart—each are consuming a different dish, for example, or dining in silence or in different rooms of the house—they just as infallibly enact and symbolize a different series of values and preferences.

The way we treat food and the manner in which we consume it are expressions of our goals and values. Eating choices and rituals help to shape and control daily life and human relationships. These are matters of particular relevance today, because in just two decades a new and astonishingly efficient technology has arisen that promises (or threatens) radical change in the relationship to cooking, to dining and hence to each other.

Today more than 70% of the households in the United States have microwave ovens in their kitchens, and a vast industry has grown up to provide these customers with microwave meals. Fast foods are hardly new, of course, but these are the first designed to create the illusion of home-cooked food and intended to take the place of traditional family meals.

Beyond that, the speed with which they can be prepared—perhaps seven minutes, as compared to 45 minutes for regular frozen food—eliminates the necessity for family members to eat at the same time, or even the same food. This unmatched efficiency is transforming the way we eat. But before we can begin to appreciate how these changes may be affecting us, it is necessary to understand the traditions it is supplanting.

Finishing School: What We Learn in the Dining Room

The most widespread and important of these is probably the family meal, which in some ways has defined the family for nearly three centuries. This communal eating ritual has never been associated with any particular country or cuisine. But it is virtually synonymous with a piece of furniture: The dining-room table has been a potent symbol of Western attitudes towards living together since the 18th Century. (Before that, most people drew up benches to the hearth and sat down in relays to eat. The rich used rough planks to set up temporary trestle tables.)

The dining-room table stands, solid and immobile, in a room of its own. Its size is the size of the family group; when anyone leaves home or is away, the table provides a mute but constant reminder of the absentee, of the space no longer filled. Even a silent, deserted dining-room table seems haunted by memories of numberless family dramas that once took place around it.

In our culture the dining-room table also represents a distinctive view of the family as a close-knit, independent and extremely disciplined entity. Viewed historically and cross-culturally, to insist on everyone in the family being present round the table daily is highly unusual behavior. To sit, in a chair, in a special room for eating, with the edge of a table-top close to your midriff, with your arms close to your sides and to agree to touch food only by means of specialized metal instruments, is to undergo a degree of physical constraint that is quite rare in the history of human mealtimes.

At the table, people wait until everyone is ready to begin and never leave until everyone has finished. They are served, or serve themselves, pass condiments to those who request them and refrain from taking more than their share.

Children learn at the table "how to behave," to express themselves, to listen, to catch conversational nuances. The table also provides a controlled setting where family relations, in all their ambiguity, can safely be played out. Indeed, social researchers have long studied the ubiquitous, revealing dinner-table drama in order to explore the dynamics of group interaction.

Cooking vs. Zapping

The traditional meal, then, is time-consuming, intricate, openly hierarchical and communal—its rituals hallowed by tradition and respect for tradition. By contrast, nothing could more perfectly symbolize the aims as well as the stresses of modernity than the vast proliferation of fast foods: their "anti-hierarchical" uniformity, not only of foods but of venues to eat them in; their sweet and bland flavors (nothing strong enough to displease anyone); the obsessive concern with wrapping and packaging (suggesting technological control and the atmosphere of a children's party with presents); the relaxed and egalitarian way in which they are eaten (while walking along, using plastic cutlery or one's hands).

Above all, fast foods embody cleanliness, a modern Western version of the ancient concept of ritual purity. Most frozen microwavable meals for the home look hygienic, carrying the message that what is inside is protected, controlled, clean and safe.

Foods are, in fact, a new version of one other extremely ancient phenomenon. Ever since people began living in cities, most of them have had to depend on food vendors to feed themselves. In ancient Rome, for example, ordinary people lived in apartment buildings called *insulae* and were prevented by safety regulations from building fires for cooking. Instead, they went out into the streets to buy ready-cooked food. Anyone lucky enough to be asked to dinner in a wealthy household with its own kitchen would return home afterwards with parcels of food as a treat for the family.

Thus, if microwaved fast foods do become our daily home fare, we shall be turning the clock back, not forward. But history never repeats itself exactly, and here the peculiar impersonality of microwave technology is important. The future, as seen by microwave and microwaveable-food producers, contains refrigerators, but no stoves, plenty of shelves and more than one microwave per family.

The warm stove, our last connection to the sustaining hearth fire, would disappear, as would the slow, sweet smells of cooking that we associate with it. Those qualities of the family meal, the ones that imparted feelings of security and well-being, might be lost forever in a world where food is "zapped" instead of cooked.

Accepting ready-cooked microwaveable foods for daily family meals also spells freedom, of course—not only from having to cook, but from regular mealtimes and having to share. The scarcest commodity of all in modern life is time. Though we like to imagine that society is devoted to providing us all with leisure, Americans work longer hours, with shorter holidays, than almost any people on earth.

But with the microwave, there is no waiting at all, let alone waiting your turn. This allows women—on the assumption that kitchen work is ineluctably female work and invariably distasteful—finally to escape from the kitchen. This liberation has much to recommend it, but it has been estimated that by the year 2000, the majority of adults will have become so dependent on prepared microwaveable meals that they will no longer know how to cook a meal for themselves.

The Age of Instant Gratification

Microwave meal containers already have plastic strips that turn blue when the food is hot, and we are promised still better strips to relieve all remaining necessity for thought by transmitting cooling instructions directly to the oven. With cooking reduced to pushing a button, the kitchen may wind up as a sort of filling station. Family members will pull in, push a few buttons, fill up and leave.

To clean up, all we need do is throw away the plastic plates. We would receive freedom from social complexity and the fulfillment of the primitive longing to have everything magically available at the flick of a switch, an electronic cornucopia.

Beyond this continuing, infantile desire for instant gratification, market researchers say they have detected in us the equally childlike want to buy food that looks good before we heat it and eat it. For instance, we don't like food that looks raw, so many best-selling microwave products are coated in pre-yellowed crumbs. Coatings are very big in the microwave business—they provide protection and cover a multitude of sins. They emphasize the self-sufficiency of each little object.

Microwaves happen to prefer food in smallish pieces, but that "clear, clean, separate" appearance potently symbolizes the image we entertain of ourselves. We are individuals, if all comfortingly alike: We do not cling, stick or mingle. We do not need to share, to talk, to interrelate.

Many of the attitudes toward food, however, are not babyish at all, and mass acceptance of microwaveable food depends in part on a highly culture-specific puritanical streak. This is the reason that microwave-food producers have made much of the preordained low-fat, low-cholesterol status of many of their offerings. Thus, they wed our extreme physical discipline and knowledge about health and diet to our longing for somebody else's control, by offering us portion management. This means that when you buy precut pieces, say of apple pie in its plastic cover, the slice is severely limited in size so that you can't eat too much of it.

The old dining-room table required each individual to give up some personal autonomy and bow to the dictates of the group and the social system. If we stop eating together, we shall save time for ourselves and achieve mealtime self-sufficiency. But being free inevitably entails deciding from what and for what we want to be free.

In the case of food, we should perhaps first consider whether, in saving time and effort by accepting microwaved fast foods as daily fare, we would, in fact, be more healthy, more content, better adjusted. The communal meal is the primary ritual for encouraging the family to gather together every day. If it is lost to us, we shall have to invent new ways to be a family. It is worth considering whether the shared joy that food can provide is worth giving up.

Discussion questions

1. Why is the advent of the microwave, in Visser's mind, so divisive and troubling? What's the relationship between technology and culture? Is it the technology that makes the microwave so important or is it what it enables people to do (or not do) that matters?
2. What possibilities and pitfalls does this new way of cooking allow for according to Visser?
3. What social institution is most endangered by the microwave? At the same time, think about what social values—values that alarm Visser—that this new form of cooking reflects. Do you agree with Visser's argument?
4. If everyone got rid of their microwaves tomorrow would this fix the problems that Visser sees looming on the horizon?
5. If Americans worked less and ate slower, would they create stronger family ties? Can you think of other examples of technology shaping the social experience of eating, for the worse and perhaps for the better?

Chapter 12   Eating Civil Rights

Document 12.1: Announcement of New Segregated Restaurant Law, *Birmingham Age-Herald* (December 15, 1914)

In the South, segregation of black and white Americans had been a custom since the end of slavery, and in the late nineteenth century, this custom became backed by law. Restaurants were no exception. Indeed, the white southerners who controlled the state laws and most of the region's businesses, objected to black and white southerners eating in close proximity. However, the separation of people based on race in a restaurant meant different things in different places and at different times. After all, in many restaurants black cooks and kitchen workers were preparing the food for white customers and most whites didn't object to that. At thousands of establishments across the region, white and African American diners ate in the same restaurants though rarely were they seated at the same table or even in the same sections of the restaurant. This gave rise to blacks-only doors at the rear of restaurants and to segregated lunch counters at some larger establishments.

As historian Angela Jill Cooley has explained, in Birmingham, Alabama, the municipal laws regulating race in restaurants changed for the worse without much fanfare in 1914. Below is an article from a local newspaper explaining a new segregation ordinance for the city's restaurants. Segregation itself was nothing new—those laws were already on the books—this new code just took things one step farther. As Cooley explains, this law suggests that merely separating whites and African Americans

Food and Eating in America: A Documentary Reader, First Edition.
Edited by James C. Giesen and Bryant Simon.
© 2018 John Wiley & Sons, Inc. Published 2018 by John Wiley & Sons, Inc.

within the same room was not enough, that physical separation of eating spaces was imperative. In other words, whites and African Americans could no longer eat in separate parts of the same room, rather they had to eat in rooms divided by a permanent, fixed wall. Birmingham whites believed that "interracial eating," Cooley argues, "might contribute to racial mixing and thereby challenge racial purity." The proposal for the ordinance passed without objection.

To Stop Serving of Whites and Blacks in Same Restaurant
Judge Lane Will Introduce Ordinance Today Prohibiting Black and Tan Lunch Rooms

An ordinance to abolish restaurants or lunch rooms in which white and negroes eat in the same room will be introduced by Judge A. O. Lane, commissioner in charge of police.

It is stated that this practice has become deleterious to the peace and happiness of the community and therefore it is to be stopped. What will be the position of the other two commissioners is unknown. There are many such lunch rooms, especially those where negroes eat on one side and whites on another, which will be put out of business by the new ordinance.

Discussion questions

1. What exactly does this law do that the previous segregation code did not?
2. This ordinance was a municipal code, meaning a law of the local Birmingham city government, and it fell in a category of laws governing health. What does this classification tell us about how segregationists understood food and eating in the South? At the same time, what does it tell us about how they saw health?
3. Imagine you're an African American motorist from the North driving through the South for business or a vacation to visit family members. How would you know where you could stop and what the local customs would be?
4. Note the headline here and its reference to "Black and Tan Lunch Rooms." What questions does this prompt? Do you think lunchrooms that usually closed mid-afternoon and did not serve supper or dinner, created a particular problem for segregationists? In other words, does the noon meal itself allow for people to get together in a way that is less common at other times of day?

Document 12.2: Mississippi Freedom Democratic Party, "Food for Fight for Freedom" (1965)

Historian James Silver declared in 1964 that his home-state of Mississippi was a "closed society." White residents, he noted, were committed to maintaining segregation and white supremacy—a system that preserved social privilege, economic opportunity, and political power for whites only. Anyone who tried to buck that system would be harassed in hopes of silencing them.

In the 1960s, the Civil Rights Movement came to Mississippi, as it did to all places in the segregated South and the North. African American students, religious leaders, and working people protested against legal discrimination at lunch counters, stores, and other public places, and struggled to end the exclusion of blacks from schools and voting booths.

In the summer of 1964, inspired by sit-ins, freedom rides, and marches on seats of political power, civil rights activists, white and black, from Mississippi and around the country, launched a campaign to break down the state's Jim Crow system of politics. For decades after Reconstruction, white leaders had used a combination of poll taxes, easily manipulated rules like the so-called understanding clause, and outright intimidation to keep blacks from voting. They were largely successful. In 1960, 45 percent of the Mississippi's population was African American, but only five percent of African Americans were registered to vote. Blocked from joining the state's official white's only Democratic Party (at the time, the Republican Party was all but nonexistent in the state), Civil Rights supporters established, the Mississippi Freedom Democratic Party (MFDP).

In 1964, after spending a "Freedom Summer" signing up tens of thousands of supporters, the MFDP traveled to Atlantic City to the Democratic National Convention, where Lyndon Johnson would receive the nomination for President. They demanded to be seated in place of the state's all-white regular Democratic Party delegation. They were largely rebuffed and returned to Mississippi disappointed, but determined to keep up the fight. As James Silver might have predicted, the MFDP knocked up against the hard walls of his state's closed society, against the fierce determination of many whites to hold onto power.

As this document shows, one of the ways that this white elite punished the forces of change was with food. Actually, they used the government to starve dissident communities. For much of the twentieth century, the federal government distributed basic food supplies— flour, milk, and blocks of cheese— to the poor. They did so through local government agencies. In response to pressure from national liberals and Civil Rights leaders, federal authorities in 1965 demanded that state and local agencies appoint African Americans to the administrative boards that handled food relief and other matters. Mississippi leaders—drawn from the all-white electorate of the all-white official Democratic Party—refused and the federal government withheld the food supplies. But this was exactly what Mississippi officials wanted. They wanted to cut off food from African Americans pushing for change. It was the poor in Mississippi, sharecroppers and rural laborers, who backed the MFDP and who suffered from the intransigence of state and local officials.

Faced with a food crisis, the MFDP and its allies called a conference at Mount Beulah, Mississippi in 1965 to figure out what to do to alleviate suffering and hunger. This document announced that meeting and its intentions.

JOIN WITH THE

FREEDOM DEMOCRATIC PARTY

FREEDOM LABOR UNION

DELTA MINISTRY

AND

FIGHT
for
FOOD
for
FREEDOM

TO THE POOR PEOPLE OF MISSISSIPPI:

Do you know there can be FOOD for you Here in Miss.?

Do you know there can be PAYING JOBS for you giving this food to your brothers and sisters?

IT IS TRUE!   There can be FOOD for <u>you</u> and WORK for <u>you</u>.

BUT YOU WILL HAVE TO <u>ORGANIZE</u> AND <u>FIGHT</u> FOR IT!

2 MONTHS AGO the Department of Agriculture said it
was sending 24 million dollars worth of commodity foods to
feed Mississippi poor people for six months. The Office of
Economic Opportunity - the federal agency that runs the War
on Poverty - said it was giving over 1½ million dollars
to pay for passing out this food.

The Food and Money are late in coming because local
Mississippi officials are always against helping the poor.
Federal officials are afraid to talk directly to poor people.

BUT WHO GETS THIS FOOD AND THIS MONEY?

The food and money are going to the State of Mississippi
through the Department of Public Welfare. The Walfare
Department calls this program "Operation HELP." This same
department that discriminates against poor Negroes in
welfare payments and throws Negores off welfare for trying
to register to vote - this same department says they will
take the money and the food and help poor people.
Who does "Operation HELP" really help?
Your County Board of Supervisors will help control
the program.
This means that in your community the rich white boss
man who throws you out of work and then calls you no-good
and lazy will get MORE POWER OVER YOU from food and money
sent to help you.
Racist politicians who fight to keep you from voting,
going to good schools, and working at decent jobs will
decide who gets the food and the jobs.

BUT WHAT ABOUT POOR PEOPLE?

All over the Delta and in other parts of the state Negro poor people are being thrown off plantations and fired from jobs.

The white boss man says they can't have a living in his white society.

Many poor Negroes are leaving their Mississippi homes because the white man will not let them earn a living.

And now, the federal government plans to help the white boss by giving him control over food and money for poor people.

Can poor people win anything by asking help from the boss man who wants to keep them poor ? ?

We think it's time that the poor people organized THEIR OWN "Operation HELP."

The Welfare Department, County Board of Supervisors, and all other white bosses can't be trusted with this program.   Only POOR PEOPLE can be trusted to help other poor people.   Poor People know what poor people need.

That food is OUR Food.

Giving it to poor people is OUR job. WE NEED TO GET TOGETHER AND FIGURE OUT HOW TO GET OUR FOOD AND OUR MONEY AND HELP OUR PEOPLE !

COME to MT. BEULAH

We want every poor person who wants to organize and

fight for a real FREEDOM program to come to the Mount

Beulah campus - Delta Ministry headquarters near Edwards -

This FRIDAY - January 28

Let's all get together and plan

How to Get   OUR FOOD

OUR JOBS

OUR FREEDOM /
.

Bring Blankets,   Call Jackson 352-9128

bedding,   or Edwards 852-2622

and YOUR NEIGHBORS.

Prepare to stay several days.

If you have no transportation, rides will be

arranged from your area.

TO GET TO MT. BEULAH:

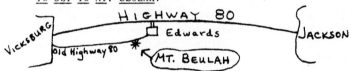

Exit from Highway 80 at Edwards.
Mt. Beulah Center is 3 miles west of Edwards.

Discussion questions

1. Who do you think wrote this document? What is the tone? How is the MFDP approaching those in power in Mississippi?
2. What does this have to say about the Civil Rights Movement and how it changed people?
3. According to the document, what is the problem? Why isn't there enough food available in Mississippi?
4. Again according to the document, who is targeted by food polices of the time? Why are they targeted? Is this evidence of the "closed society"?
5. Who do the authors of this document think should be in charge of food policy in Mississippi?

6. By saying that it is "our food," what claims are the authors of the pamphlet making? How are they making a claim about their place in society?

7. Think for moment about American politics and about ideas about states' rights. How have ideas about states' rights (e.g. who is in control of local agencies like the one that distributed food in Mississippi) worked against change? What sorts of tensions exist between states' rights and equality?

Document 12.3: Black Panther Party, "To Feed Our Children," *The Black Panther* (March 26, 1969)

The non-violent protests at lunch counters in Greensboro and Nashville in 1960, the rallies in the streets of Birmingham and Jackson in 1962 and 1963, and the massive March on Washington in 1963 made an impact. In 1964, Congress passed a landmark Civil Rights Act. The legislation made segregation in public places illegal. African Americans could go where they wanted, stay overnight where they wanted, and eat where they wanted. Yet as more than one activist pointed out, "we could sit at the lunch counter, but we couldn't afford a hamburger." That was the dilemma that the Civil Rights Movement faced in the middle of the 1960s. Martin Luther King Jr. and his allies had ended legal segregation, but their efforts had done little to address African American poverty and powerlessness.

Organizations like the Black Panther Party, founded in Oakland, CA in 1966, addressed the issues faced by urban African Americans: crime, drugs, unemployment and underemployment, and police violence. They developed a revolutionary critique of America and of American imperialism. They insisted that only black people could free themselves and that freedom would require the overthrow of the American government. But the Panthers also formulated practical solutions to deal with everyday poverty and oppression. They set up health, dental, and optometry clinics. They gave away shoes and furniture and started a free bus service to nearby prisons to help people to travel to see family members behind bars. The Panthers' most successful activity was its Free Breakfast for School Children Program. By 1970, the group fed 10,000 poor children across the country every morning before school.

In many ways, the Free Breakfast for School Children Program became the basis for the federal government's free breakfast program, minus, of course, the revolutionary rhetoric. Read the document below. How did the Black Panther Party explain itself and its politics and the role that food played in social change?

According to David Hilliard, a leader in the Black Panther Party, "Police raided the Breakfast for Children Program, ransacked food storage facilities, destroyed kitchen equipment, and attempted to disrupt relations between the Black Panthers and local business owners and community advocates, whose contributions made the programs possible." Why did it face this kind of backlash? Think about this as you read the document.

To Feed Our children

The Free Breakfast for School Children is about to cover the country and be initiated in every chapter and branch of the Black Panther Party. This program was created because the Black Panther Party understands that our children need a nourishing breakfast every morning so that they can learn.

These breakfasts include every nutrient that they need for the day. For too long have our people gone hungry and without the proper health aids they need. But the Black Panther Party says that this type of thing must be halted, because we must survive this evil government and build a new one fit for the service of all the people. This program is run through donations of concerned people and the avaricious businessmen that pinch selfishly a little to the program. We say that this is not enough, especially from those that thrive off the Black Community like leeches. All of the avaricious businessmen have their factories etc. centered in our communities and even most of the people that work in these sweat shops are members of the oppressed masses.

It is a beautiful sight to see our children eat in the mornings after remembering the times when our stomachs were not full, and even the teachers in the schools say that there is a great improvement in the academic skills of the children that do get the breakfast. At one time there were children that passed out in class from hunger, or had to be sent home for something to eat. But our children shall be fed, and the Black Panther Party will not let the malady of hunger keep our children down any longer.

The Breakfast Program has already been initiated in several chapters, and our love for the masses makes us realize that it must continue permanently and be a national program. But we need your help and that means money, food, and time. We want to turn the programs over to the community, but without your efforts and support we cannot.

Discussion questions

1. Who is the audience for this document? Members of the Black Panther Party?
2. What are the practical and political goals of the program? What is the link between food and learning?

3. Why do the Black Panthers put such a stress on food and learning? Why is education so important to them?
4. The Black Panther Party was known as a revolutionary group. What is revolutionary here?
5. On May 15, 1969, in an internal memo, FBI Director J. Edgar Hoover wrote: "The Breakfast for Children Program represents the best and most influential activity going for the BPP (Black Panther Party) and, as such, is potentially the greatest threat to efforts by authorities to neutralize the BPP and destroy what it stands for." What do you think of Hoover's assessment? Why did he and others see the Breakfast Program as such a threat?
6. Does a healthy breakfast still matter to learning and public health? How come?

Document 12.4: Eliseo Medina, "Why A Grape Boycott?" (circa 1969)

Most people who work in factories or offices or who sit down to lunch or dinner at home in cities and towns don't think about where their food or drink comes from. They don't think a whole lot about who made it or who picked it in the fields or processed it in a plant. They buy what they want and what they can afford at a supermarket or a restaurant, cook it and clean it and put on the table. That changed in the United States in the second half of the 1960s.

In September 1965, a group of Filipino grape pickers frustrated with their low pay and harsh working conditions went out on strike in California. They reached out to Caesar Chavez, who at the time was organizing Mexican and Mexican American agricultural laborers, for support. Chavez quickly determined that the strikers could not win their protest in the fields. The well-connected growers had too much power, and easily mobilized striker-breakers, often from other ethnic groups, to cross the picket lines and get the grapes off the vines and into the supermarkets.

Beginning in December 1965, Chavez decided to shift tactics and broaden the campaign. Borrowing a course of action successfully deployed by Martin Luther King, Jr. and his allies in the Civil Rights Movement, he called on consumers to boycott California grapes until growers from the state agreed to recognize the union and improve pay and conditions. Eventually, Chavez's tactic succeeded. He and his allies got enough people, especially young people and members of the nation's growing freedom movements, to stop eating the grapes. In 1970, California grape growers finally agreed to a contract with the United Farm Workers and the boycott was called off, though subsequent boycotts against other producers would be called over the next ten years.

The document below comes from this fight and is aimed at consumers far from the grape fields of California.

In nearly every major city of the United States today there are California-based union farmworkers. They are there, they hope temporarily, to promote the boycott against California grapes and seek broad understanding and support from the consumer community.

They are far from their homes and most of their relatives. They are away from their friends, living in strange places under difficult conditions. Why do they do it? Because there is no other way forward. The alternative is to stand still, and in so doing to hand down to their children the bleak frustration they have lived with, with no security, no dignity, and very little hope. To get from where they are to where they want to be, they must go together. They must organize, and for workers that means to unionize.

This is not the first effort to unionize among farmworkers. It is simply the first one that has succeeded, and it is succeeding, slowly but surely. To understand the significance of the progress that has been made, one only needs to know that previous efforts of farmworkers ended in bitterness and often bloodshed.

A reasonable person might ask, "Aren't their (sic) legal procedures for determining the rights and the wishes of workers with respect to having unions?"

The answer is "yes" for millions of American workers—but not for farmworkers! They are specifically excluded from the coverage of the federal law that assures and protects the rights of other workers to organize and bargain collectively. And give them some equal treatment where these rights are concern.

Such a proposition sounds reasonable. As a matter of fact, hundreds of priests, rabbis, ministers, professors, industrialists, and others have thought so, and have offered their services as third-party participants. The employers have turn down every such effort.

Denied the protection and procedures under the Federal law and faced with the growers' refusal even to discuss the matter of union recognition, the workers were forced to choose between striking and crawling. They said they would no longer be the last vestige of the "crawling American." In 1965 they struck.

The built-in pitfalls of farm labor strikes became immediately apparent. Local courts went into action. Judges and public officials who have long been a part of the power structure in agriculture-dominated communities are "soft" on growers. Injunctions were quick and devastating.

The gates that these injunctions opened in the picket lines were soon filled with masses of strike-breakers, green-card visa holders from Mexico, who had easy entrance into the United States because of the laxity of the government in enforcing its immigration policy. The green-carders flooded the strike-bound fields, often in buses provided by growers and escorted by local police, ready and willing to undercut their brothers because of economic conditions in Mexico that make US farm wages, however miserable by American standards, look very, very good.

Another technique, one familiar to those in the civil rights movement, was to try to break the back of the union by raising wages and cleaning up the camps of the farm laborers, but without union recognition or any contract. The "reforms" of course lasted only as long as the company wished. One grower increased wages to $1.30 an hour but with no contract; wages were reduced again after a few months. Those who traveled in the South just prior to the Supreme Court decision regarding school segregation will recall the new schools for Negroes which blossomed all over the landscape. This sudden effort to make the dual school system "equal" might, it was hoped, enable it to survive.

Faced with such limitations on the strike's effectiveness, the farm worker reinforced his strike activities by introducing the boycott, which he realized was his last best hope of success.

The current boycott was started against one company, Giumarra Vineyards Corporation in the Bakersfield area of California, probably the Nation's largest shipper of fresh table grapes.

To frustrate the boycott, the Giumarra Company started shipping its grapes in cartons bearing the labels of its competitors. Whereas Giumarra normally shipped under a half dozen labels, suddenly there were 50 or 60 labels available to them, lent by their "competitors." Under such conditions the union had no alternative but to include all of the "competitors" in the boycott, thus the action against all California grapes.

That is where it stands today and that is why California farm workers—Mexican-American, Filipino-American, Negro-American and "Anglos"—can be found in Boston, New York, Washington, Chicago, Cleveland, Seattle, and the other big cities rallying support for the "Don't Buy Grapes" campaign.

Here, in Chicago, the boycott had been very effective until Jewel Food Stores started to buy grapes, once again, in June. Jewel officials, as usual, claimed neutrality. It wasn't until a couple of weeks ago that we really knew just how "neutral" they were. Examples are:

On May 20, 1969, one month before they started to buy grapes, they wrote a letter to Congressman Charles Melvin Price, requesting legislation that would give farm workers the right to have union elections but which would also prohibit strikes, boycotts and would subject farm workers to compulsory arbitration.

They are also pushing a bill, to be introduced by Rep. James "Pate" Phillips in the next session of the Illinois General Assembly, which would prohibit picketing by more than three people and impose a $500 fine and six months in jail as punishment. It was specifically drawn up against the grape boycott but can be applied to anybody.

On June 24, 1969, they put out a mass mailing to all their managers giving them grower anti-union literature and telling them that these were the true facts.

With Jewel, the name of neutrality is money.

So we ask the public to support us by not shopping at Jewel Food Stores. Every person that refuses to shop at Jewel is a vote for social justice.

The growers have complained about having the boycott used against them, but in at least one instance they had no scruples about applying boycott pressure against a fellow grower. The grower in question had a franchise for cars and tractors and a seed company. He was told by the other growers that they would no longer buy these products from him if negotiated a contract with the union.

The first series of boycotts were against the wine grape growers. By and large these were successful. The union now has contracts with approximately 70% of the wine grape growers. The next step has been to win union recognition from the growers of table grapes, beginning with Giumarra, one of the largest; the union began by seeking union recognition from them. They got nowhere even after they succeeded in 1967 in organizing 95% of the strike breakers brought in by Giumarra after the initial strike. The union requested a meeting with the company to discuss a union election. When, after many delays, a meeting was finally held, those present said they could not speak for the company. Again as had been the case with the wine grape growers, the only course open to the union was the boycott. The boycott against Giumarra began well over a year ago.

We are determined to continue our struggle until we win. As the great revolutionary Mexican leader Emiliano Zapata said, "It is better to die on your feet than to live on your knees". We have lived on our knees long enough; now we are demanding justice and we will not turn back.

Discussion questions

1. Who is Eliseo Medina? Where is he located? What is his role in the boycott? How does he make the grape workers' fight the fight of middle-class urbanites?
2. What does he mean when he contrasts "crawling" with "striking"?
3. Why did the strikers turn to the boycott as a tactic? What laws hampered their efforts? What does this tell you about the power of the growers, not just in the fields, but also in the political arena?

4. Is eating or not eating always a political act? When is it? When it is not?
5. In the 1960s, there was a lot of talk about the "personal as political". How, then, is Medina's document a product of its time, and of the everyday personalization of politics?

Document 12.5: Ralph Johnson and Patricia Reed, "What's Wrong with Soul Food," *The Black Collegian* (December, 1980/January, 1981)

Even after dramatic marches led to the landmark legislative triumphs of the 1960s, the Civil Rights Movement continued. It didn't end with the raised fists of Black Power or the riots that tore through the nation's cities. It continued in quieter, but still persistent, ways. Activists looked to create equality in schools and in businesses, in the media and in sports. And of course, the Civil Rights struggle considered food and power in American society.

African American activists had long talked about what was "black" food or "soul" food, what was good for their community and what wasn't good for them and their children. In the early 1960s, for example, Elijah Muhammad, the leader of the Nation of Islam, the organization that Malcolm X belonged to for many years, wrote down a list of foods to be avoided. He counseled his followers to avoid all kinds of scavenger seafoods, including halibut, catfish, and carp. No pork, he said. And no fried foods or canned meats or vegetables.

In this essay from the 1980s, Ralph Johnson and Patricia Reed urge African American college students to rethink "soul food," its origins and its place in their community. Essentially, they question whether or not this food is part of the authentic black experience and the true black past. In fact, the authors go a step further and link these foods to pressing problems in African American public health. In a sense, they are linking the ongoing and long-term battle for equality to food choices.

Black Americans are under the illusion that their cultural food is soul food. This misconception about soul food has been perpetuated from generation to generation. Black Americans rarely question the history of the origin of this so-called "soul food." The lack of knowledge in this area has kept Blacks unaware of the health problem associated with this form of food. Like many other areas of study concerning Black Americans, the study and history of "soul food" has for long been overlooked and neglected. We offer the following information so that Black Americans can finally examine and reevaluate their dietary habits and health status.

Being Black Americans, Negros, or even slaves, we were West Africans. As West Africans, we enjoyed the various foods from the land provide for us by our mother country. These foods helped to keep the Africans healthy and strong. Such foods included sorghum, millet, teff, West African rice, guinea yams, cow peas, okra, nuts seeds, spinach, peppers, fresh fruits and vegetables, and grains.

With the arrival of the Europeans, West Africans' health and dietary habits started to deteriorate. Having been kidnapped, beaten, and having had their villages destroyed, a once mighty and proud people found themselves being treated like wild animals. Along with the cruel and inhuman treatment given to animals, came the food fed to animals. These foods barely kept the Africans alive and caused many to die. Africans who refused to eat this racist food were either beaten or tortured until they ate or died. The diet on the slave ships consisted of horsebeans, Indian corn, yams and rice, all ground up into mush. Most eventually died from malnutrition and those who survived found themselves with numerous deficiencies and illnesses. This food was eaten for 1–3 months, depending upon the length of the voyage.

Once in America, the Africans found themselves cruelly examined, sold and carried off to a planation. Stripped of their native land, families, culture, lifestyle, and foods, the Africans were forced to live and eat like animals. The eradication of African cultural and dietary habits, forced the African Americans to accept the non-nutritional foods given to them by slave owners. After having such foods as fresh vegetables, fruits, grains, herbs, seeds, nuts, and wild game, this new form of food was a physical and mental shock to the Africans' body and mind. The slave owners only provided such foods as white refined rice, corn meal, potatoes, pig fat, salt pork, grits, and sweet potatoes. These foods were the cheapest and easiest for the slave owners to supply. Only those who worked received their rations and they weren't even enough to fill one's stomach. On fresh vegetables, no dairy, no fowl or fish, no grains, etc. caused the most severe deficiencies and diseases and numerous deaths. Deficiencies in the B vitamins, protein, and other essential nutrients, made the African tired and weak. This caused the slave owners to stereotype them as lazy, slow, and no good—a stigma which still persists today. Mothers passed these deficiencies on to their babies and they in turn passed them on to their babies, thus the decline in the health was passed down from generation to generation.

The African slaves eventually adopted and culturally justified these foods and called them their own. This combination of food and style of cooking became known as "soul food." After slavery, Black Americans continued to eat these foods, believing them to be their native food, but it nothing more than slave food. Add to this slave food the chemicalized, refined sugary, fast convenience foods of our modern society, and you have quite a deadly combination.

The cumulative effects of malnutrition have caused great health problems for Black Americans as can be seen by looking at recent statistics from the American Cancer Society and the American Heath Association. (1) High blood pressure is 50 % more prevalent in Blacks than in whites. (2) Blacks suffer from more strokes at an earlier age with more severe results than for whites. (3) 32% of the Black females and 31% of the Black males suffer from hypertension. (4) The cancer mortality rate for Blacks has increased only 25%, while for whites it has increased only 5%! (5) The overall cancer rate for Blacks went up 8%, while for whites it went down 3%! (6) Blacks have significantly higher rates of hypertensive heart disease, thus causing a higher mortality rate than for Whites. These are disturbing statistics that Blacks most face.

Recent studies by Dr. Dennis Burkitt show how today's rural Africans do not suffer from such western diseases as cancer, appendicitis, constipation, obesity, heart disease, diabetes, and diverticulitis. Rural Africans still consume the foods and crops of their ancestors. Black Americans can start to reverse those health statistics and gain back their health by utilizing the West African diet, which is rightfully ours to begin with! Black Americans should unchain their dietary habits and let "soul food" die along with the concept of slavery!

The following foods are recommended for those who wish to take the turn back towards the unrefined food of their African ancestors. These foods are health-providing and come as close to the African diet as possible. All are easily accessible in the local markets or in the health food stores (as indicated):

1. Fruits – all kinds, raw and dried.
2. Vegetables – all kinds. Green leafy, squashes, root vegetables, etc. Cook them as little as possible – steam, stir fry, raw (as in salads), is best.
3. Grains – brown unrefined rice, millet (found in health food store), barley, buckwheat groats, oats, corn, rye, and wheat berries. Many recipes can be found in natural cook books.
4. Beans – all kinds. Many recipes can be found.
5. Nuts and seeds – sunflower seeds, almonds, cashews, pecans, brazil nuts, sesame seeds, pumpkin seeds, walnuts, etc.
6. Cut down on meat eating as much as you can. Cut out all fatty parts of meat. Chicken and turkey and white fish are leanest.
7. Eat whole grain bread made with whole wheat flour and add bran to your recipes where ever you can.

Discussion questions

1. Why do the authors of this article think that Black Americans should reevaluate their diets?
2. The authors talk about "racist food". What do they mean by this term? Can a food be racist? How do the authors say that foods fueled stereotypes? Can you think of any examples of food and racism in the past or today?
3. How did the black community come to adopt soul food as its comfort food? Can foods that were forced on communities in the past become a part of a community going forward?
4. Do you agree with the authors' arguments about soul food and public health?
5. What do they recommend as a model for a new black diet, in a sense a new "soul food"? What does this say about their politics and their perspective on race relations? And what does it say about their sense of healthiness? Is health a political issue?
6. What would happen if you reexamined your comfort foods? What would you find? Where do they come from? How have they changed over time?

Document 12.6: "Marlon Brando, S.F. Cleric Arrested for Fishing Illegally," *Seattle Daily Times* (March 2, 1964)

Inspired by the sit-in movement where African American Civil Rights activists walked up to whites-only lunch counters in the South and asked to be served and wouldn't leave until they either got their food or were arrested, Native Americans in the Pacific Northwest launched a series of "fish-ins" beginning in the early 1960s. These demonstrations were protests against what Native Americans saw as violations of treaties signed in the late nineteenth century by the federal government and their tribal nations. Under these accords, Native Americans ceded (under some duress) much of their land to the federal government, but they reserved the right to fish as they always had in waters beyond the boundaries of their tiny reservations. In the intervening years, the state of Washington, in this case, tried to enforce other fishing and hunting rules on these lands. To protest, Native Americans would fish—often for salmon, trout, and steelhead—in defiance of newly enacted laws, especially the ones that required a state fishing license. They would also use nets and traps— as Native Americans traditionally had used— again in defiance of the law.

The fish-ins gained national attention in 1964, when the Academy Award winning actor Marlon Bando joined in the protests and got arrested for fishing without a license. Over the next ten years, the demonstrations continued as Native Americans and their allies proclaimed their pride in their heritage and asserted their treaty rights. In 1974, a federal court ruled in the Boldt Decision that tribes were entitled to act alongside the state as co-managers of fish and wildlife and to continue harvesting them in accordance with the various treaties that the United States had signed with the tribal nations many decades earlier.

The following is a newspaper article reporting on the fish-in in 1964.

Marlon Brando, actor, and the Rev. Canon John Yaryan of San Francisco went fishing with an Indian in the Puyallup River this morning and were arrested by a representative of the State Game Department.

Brando, 39, Canon Yaryan, 48, of the staff of the Grace Episcopal Cathedral in San Francisco and Bob Satiacum, a Puyallup Indian from Fife, put their nets in the water from a long boat just north of Highway 99 at the Tacoma city limits.

The three caught two steelhead as they drifted a short distance down the river. Representatives from the State Game Department were waiting on the bank when the long boat reached the shore.

Brando and Yaryan were taken to the Pierce County jail to be charged with illegal fishing. But Pierce County Prosecutor John McCutcheon ordered both released and said he would not press charges.

"We think this is just window dressing for the Indian's cause," McCutcheon said, "Brando's no fisherman. He was here to make a point. He made his point—90 percent of it anyway. There is no use prolonging this."

The prosecutor was asked whether his action voided the arrest tickets issued to Brando and Canon Yaryan on the river bank.

McCutcheon did not give a direct answer.

"There is no charge, no criminal charge, until I file something," he said, "We are releasing them without charge. I think that explains everything."

Satiacum was not arrested.

The Game Department said Satiacum will likely be arrested tomorrow on a warrant showing him violation of a court injunction forbidding Indians to fish in the river.

Brando said he was pleased with the prosecutor's action, as he left the jail about 12:30 o'clock in the afternoon.

Brando said he wants to confer with the State Attorney General John J. O'Connell, and "come to some understanding."

"I feel the pressure (on the Indians) comes from the attorney general," Brando said.

Brando showed irritation when asked if his participation in the "fish-in" was a publicity stunt.

"The first thing people do is accuse you of that," he said. But when you are out raising money for children or something like that they don't call it a publicity stunt."

Brand said money will be raised to finance an independent scientific study to determine the effect Indian fishing here has on fishery-conservation programs.

Another "fish-in," scheduled for the Nisqually River this morning, was postponed...after a bankside powwow with Brando. The fishermen were Nisquallys who are under suspended sentences for illegal fishing.

"Your purpose is to openly defy the state law?" the Game Department representative Ellsworth Sawyer, asked Brando when the arrest was made.

"My purpose is to help these Indians," Brando replied.

Brando told the law-enforcement officer he was merely "helping some Indian friends fish."

The Game Department representative told Brando: "I won't argue with you. You should have your day in court. I think that's what you're looking for."

Brando, who was carrying one of the fish he caught, handed it to an Indian friend and climbed into the Game Department car. A Game Department man took the fish.

An estimated 200 Indians who were waiting on the river bank glowered at the Game Department officials.

"You can't do this to us. We have a treaty," one Indian woman yelled.

"What are you going to do with the fish, give them to some white man?" a young Indian mother with a baby strapped to her back shouted.

"To hell with you," another Indian woman shrieked at the officers.

The Indians clambered to look in the Game Department car, where Brand and the canon were being held.

"Just push those old white men out of your way. They won't let you through," one woman advised another.

Brando told newsmen he was not purposely looking for publicity, but merely helping the Indians maintain their treaty rights.

"They have little left," he said. Everything has been taken from them. They intend to hang on to these fishing rights.

Canon Yaryan, who had gone to the banks of the Nisqually River earlier in the morning for the "fish-in" there, said he was "more sad than mad," about the fishing situation.

"Today the whole world seems to want to be twentieth century Anglo-Saxon," Canon Yaryan said, "All these people want is to be twentieth century Indians."...

The next step in the Indians' campaign to preserve their treaty rights will be at the state Capitol in Olympia tomorrow. Governor Rosellini has agreed to meet the group at 11 o'clock. Leaders, who estimate from 1,000 to 5,000 Indians will attend, plan to present a "proclamation of protest."

Discussion questions

1. Who is Marlon Brando? What is significant about his participation in this protest? What does this tell us about protest and the press? Would the press have covered this event if Brando hadn't shown up?
2. What are the key issues here? What do Indians want? What groups were the Game Department trying to protect? Why are they at odds?
3. What do you think about the tone of the reporting here? Is it fair and balanced? How are Indians portrayed? Pay attention to the quotes. What are the Native American women quoted in the article saying? Why isn't the Native American man who fished with Brando quoted in the article?
4. What do food and fish represent here? What civil rights issues are at stake?
5. Is race an issue here, how? A few weeks after the Brando was arrested, several white men held an anti-Indian protest where they said, "We are fed up with Indians catching fish planted with our money." What are they saying?
6. If race isn't the issue, is this a battle over tradition and modernity? Think about the quote from Canon Yaryan where he says, "All these people want is to be twentieth century Indians."

Document 12.7: Vietnamese Fishermen's Association, et al., Plaintiffs, v. The Knights of the Ku Klux Klan, et al., Defendants. Civ. A. No. H-81-895. United States District Court, S. D. Texas, Houston Division (July 15, 1981)

The Vietnam War did not end when the fighting on the battlefields in Southeast Asia stopped in 1975. Like all wars, this one came home. One place it landed was Galveston Bay, Texas, a commercial fishing area and waterway connected to the Gulf of Mexico.

With the fall of Saigon, tens of thousands of Vietnamese supporters of the defeated pro-United States South Vietnamese government and army, fearing reprisals from the new Communist regime they had battled against for years, fled the country. After spending time in refugee camps in Thailand and Indonesian, some ended up in the United States. Looking to make a living, a

*number of these refuges settled along the Texas coast, bought small boats
and began to shrimp to earn a living —something some of them had done
back in Vietnam.*

*Meanwhile, a number of white Texas fishermen had also served in
Vietnam. They came home and hoped to make their living shrimping as well.*

*But there was only so much shrimp to be harvested and that's where the
conflict started.*

*"There were a lot of vets working down here at the time," one longtime
area resident told a news reporter, "and I think they saw in these new people
all the people they'd been fighting."*

*When a battle over shrimping rights broke out in the late 1970s, the
Vietnamese fought back. They armed themselves and declared that they, too,
had a right to these waters. On the night of August 3, 1979, in the town of
Seadrift, several Vietnamese boats were burned and a vacant Vietnamese
house was firebombed. That same night, a fistfight between white and
Vietnamese fishermen broke out and ended with the fatal shooting of a
white man.*

*In the aftermath of that murder, Louis Beam, the Grand Dragon of the
Texas Ku Klux Klan, showed up to protect the "real Americans" from, as he
put it, "little web-footed gooks." Armed Klansmen began cruising the
harbors in boats to intimidate Vietnamese fishermen.*

*The Vietnamese, in turn, sought legal protections in their new homeland.
The document below is from a case filed in a United States District Court
in Texas.*

VIETNAMESE FISHERMEN'S ASSOCIATION, et al., Plaintiffs,
v.
The KNIGHTS OF the KU KLUX KLAN, et al., Defendants.

Civ. A. No. H-81-895.

United States District Court, S. D. Texas, Houston Division.

July 15, 1981.

Introduction

This is an action filed on April 16, 1981 by an organization of Vietnamese
Fishermen and individual Vietnamese fishermen against the Knights of the
Ku Klux Klan, the Grand Dragon of the Ku Klux Klan in the State of
Texas, certain unknown members of the Ku Klux Klan, the American
Fishermen's Coalition, various alleged members of that coalition, and sev-
eral individual American fishermen alleging violations of various federal
and state statutes.

Specifically, the plaintiffs allege that the defendants have violated their rights under several civil rights statutes…the Thirteenth and Fourteenth Amendments to the United States Constitution; the Sherman Act…the Racketeer Influenced and Corrupt Organizations Act (RICO), and the common law torts of assault, trespass to personal property, the intentional infliction of emotional distress and intentional interference with contractual relations. In addition, the plaintiffs allege in their Second Amended Complaint that defendants Louis Beam and the Knights of the Ku Klux Klan have violated their rights under Tex. Rev. Civ. Stat.…This suit has been certified as a class action….

The plaintiffs seek a preliminary and permanent injunction enjoining the defendants generally from engaging in any activity, including unlawful acts of violence or intimidation, conducted for the purpose of interfering with the rights of the Vietnamese fishermen prior to and during the shrimping season, which begins on May 15, 1981. In particular the plaintiffs request this Court to restrain the defendants from undertaking:

a. activities undertaken with the purpose of interfering with the rights of the plaintiff class at issue in this case;
b. unlawful acts of violence or intimidation against the plaintiff class;
c. engaging, or inciting others to engage in acts of boat burning, armed boat patrols, assault and battery, or threats of such conduct;
d. maintaining or conducting or attending military or paramilitary camps and giving or receiving military or paramilitary training except from military institutions operated by the state of Texas or United States government.

The plaintiffs also request this Court to require the conspicuous posting of all Orders as the Court may issue at all meetings and meeting places of any or all of the defendants and to appoint additional United States Magistrates and deputies to prevent the violation of any Orders of this Court.

The plaintiffs' class of Vietnamese fishermen was certified by agreement of all parties on May 8, 1981. The class is defined as "all Vietnamese fishermen in the Galveston Bay, Texas area"….The defendants' Motion to Dismiss has previously been denied by Order of this Court on May 11, 1981. The testimony and documentary evidence received during the hearing on the Motion for Preliminary Injunction makes it absolutely clear that the claims are justiciable.

THE FACTUAL SETTING
On or about January 24, 1981, defendant Fisher was introduced to defendant Louis Beam, Grand Dragon in the State of Texas of the Knights of the Ku Klux Klan (hereinafter KKK or Klan), by defendant James Stanfield a

member of the Original Ku Klux Klan of America....The admitted purpose
for this introduction was for defendant Fisher to secure support of Louis
Beam and the Klan in order to further the purposes of a group of American
fishermen who were ostensibly concerned about "over fishing" in the
Kemah-Seabrook area of Texas. Defendant Fisher considered that the Klan
was an organization that had the "courage" to stand by their convictions
and would provide needed publicity to draw the attention of various governmental agencies he felt had failed to address his concerns. This meeting
resulted in a rally that was held on February 14, 1981 on the property of
defendant Joseph Collins that is located in Santa Fe, Texas. Defendant
Joseph Collins leased this property for that purpose for a $1.00 payment
from Mr. Stanfield. He stated in substance that he would give the government 90 days to rectify the situation, (referring to the presence of the
Vietnamese fishermen in the Kemah-Seabrook area) and if that was not
accomplished the Klan would take action stating it "may become necessary
to take laws into our own hands." He admitted stating in his speech that it
was necessary to "fight fight fight" and see "blood blood blood" if this
country was to survive. That rally was covered extensively by the news
media. At that same rally, Beam demonstrated how to burn a boat. A cross
propped with the aid of a pickup truck of defendant Joseph Collins was also
burned at the rally. On that evening, defendant Beam offered to train
American fishermen at one of the "military camps."

On March 15, 1981, a "boat ride" was held in the waters surrounding the
Kemah- Seabrook area. The boat was owned by defendant Joseph Collins
and was navigated by defendant David Collins. The boat was the shrimping
boat used by defendant Joseph Collins in his business, and by his own
admission it is hardly a "pleasure craft." Several persons who were on that
shrimp boat on March 15, 1981 wore robes of the KKK, some also wore
hoods and most were visibly armed. The boat was equipped with a small
cannon and a figure hung in effigy. Defendant Stanfield was present on the
boat and wore a Klan robe and hood. Other persons who viewed, participated in or heard of this boat ride acknowledged that this display would be
fearful and intimidating to Vietnamese fishermen. Indeed, Joanne Oliphant-
Curren, a reporter who was invited by David Collins to join them in the
boat ride testified that she was "scared." By way of explanation she stated
that the presence of robed, armed Klansmen on the boat might incite others
to respond in a violent way and acknowledged that if she were a Vietnamese
fishermen she would be afraid by such a display. She reported that "Collins
steered the boat out into the bay well past the mile marker and the Klansmen
fired their small cannon...Everybody else had their fingers in their ears,
but I was snapping pictures and the cannon blast left me nearly deaf for

a few moments." The account in the newspaper further related the following: "Let's hear it for the American fishermen, David Collins shouted and the fishermen cheered."

Defendant David Collins acknowledged that the purpose of the boat ride was to gain media attention, asserting "violence sells stories." Defendant Fisher testified that defendant Beam had informed him that one of the persons on this boat ride was a Klansman involved in the Greensboro, South Carolina shooting during which members of the Communist Workers Party were killed during a confrontation with members of the Ku Klux Klan.

Members of the class who testified by deposition also expressed fear because of the presence of the shrimp boat loaded with robed and armed Klansmen. Colonel Nam Van Nguyen testified that he was especially frightened by the weapons that were carried by the persons on the boat and the figure that was hanging in effigy on the boat...He also testified that the boat came right to his dock and stopped there for about four or five minutes and someone on the boat gestured toward his house...Colonel Nam's sister-in-law, Phuong Pham, was present in his house when the boat approached and she saw persons wearing white robes. This so frightened her that she took her infant niece and ran from the house to a nearby relative's home. Although Miss Pham had previously lived with Colonel Nam, since this incident, she testified that she is too fearful to spend the night in that house.

Mr. Jerry Walzel, State Game Warden for the Texas Department of Parks and Wild life testified that "fortunately" he was not on duty on the day of the boat ride; fortunate because if he had been in the area, undoubtedly he would have received a complaint of possible violations of water safety regulations and if he had tried to board the boat it would have been "like throwing a spark on gasoline." He explained that he would be the spark and the armed Klansman the gasoline. In his opinion, the presence of armed Klansmen aboard shrimp boats would cause violence.

Chief Kerber testified further that the tension between Vietnamese and American fishermen did not stem solely from fishing conflicts. According to Chief Kerber, some American fishermen believe there are just too many Vietnamese people in Kemah-Seabrook and therefore these individuals will only be satisfied when some of the Vietnamese leave the area.

Mr. Louis Beam, the Grand Dragon of the Knights of the Ku Klux Klan of Texas testified about the history of his organization. Mr. Beam stated that the Knights of the Ku Klux Klan of Texas opened a public information center in Pasadena, Texas in 1975. Prior to that time, he originally joined the United Klans of America in and about April of 1969 immediately after returning from Viet Nam. According to Mr. Beam's testimony, the United Klans of America was "destroyed" by "government subversion" in 1971.

Consequently, in 1973, Mr. Beam helped organize the Original Ku Klux Klan in the state of Texas (hereinafter referred to as the "Original Klan").

At trial, Mr. Beam testified that the Original Klan received permission from now former Grand Dragon of Louisiana, Robert W. Fuller, to use the Original Ku Klux Klan of Louisiana's charter. Mr. Beam testified that although the aims of the Louisiana and Texas organizations were different, the Original Klan was incorporated under the laws of Louisiana.

Sometime in late 1974 or early 1975 Mr. Beam advised all the members of the Original Ku Klux Klan of Texas to withdraw their membership from that Klan and affiliate themselves with David Duke's Knights of the Ku Klux Klan out of Metairie, Louisiana (hereinafter referred to as "the Knights"). Mr. Beam subsequently abandoned the charter the Original Klan had operated under and adopted the charter utilized by the Knights. The Knights of the Ku Klux Klan is a national organization and David Duke's group is incorporated under the laws of Louisiana.

The record is replete with provocative statements made by various defendants in this action. Defendant David Collins testified by way of deposition and reaffirmed at trial that he planned to have an armed Klansman on his boat on May 15, 1981. Jim Craig owner of the Old Harbor Seafood House testified that he has 43 boats owned by Vietnamese fishermen docked at his establishment, referred to as the "Saigon Harbor". He testified about a conversation during the Fall of 1980 with defendant Fisher. According to Mr. Craig, Mr. Fisher told him to "watch your boats they're easy to burn."

It is uncontroverted that defendant Fisher stated that it would not bother him if the Klan burned all of the (Vietnamese) boats; further adding that the Klan were the only ones with the courage of their convictions. He added that a certain number of Vietnamese boats would have to be taken out of the water and destroyed. At the rally on February 14, 1981, defendant Fisher publicly stated that "we're going to help (Vietnamese fishermen) to control themselves."

A woman who lives in the Galveston Bay area had allowed a Vietnamese fisherman to use one of her docks for approximately two years. She testified that in January, 1981 she received a card in the mail, signed by the Knights of the Ku Klux Klan which read: "You have been paid a 'friendly visit' do you want the next one to be a 'real one.'" She also received three threatening phone calls. The first asked if she knew where her children were; the second was a threat to burn her boat; the third, stated that she would die that night. Mr. Dang, a Vietnamese fisherman, testified that approximately four weeks ago an American pointed a gun at him while he was on his shrimp boat. Miss Do Thi Doi who is a shrimp seller and married to a Vietnamese fisherman testified that six weeks ago two American men drove up in a truck and pointed a gun at her. She testified that unless there is some solution to the conflict between the American fishermen and the Vietnamese fishermen her husband will not take out their shrimp boat on May 15, 1981 because she is afraid that he will be killed.

The plaintiffs have alleged that defendants Beam and the Knights of the Ku Klux Klan have operated one or more military or paramilitary training camps in the State of Texas in violation of Tex.Rev.Civ.Stat.Ann. The plaintiffs introduced a videotape depicting defendant Beam instructing persons dressed in military type uniforms in the art of psychological warfare, ambush and counter ambush, reconnaissance patrol and other types of military movements. Defendant Beam has referred to the group of persons who will receive his training as the "Texas Emergency Reserve."

Defendants testified that the primary purpose for inviting the Ku Klux Klan to speak on the behalf of American fishermen, was merely an attempt to gain media attention of the plight of the American fishermen because state, federal, and local officials had attempted to "whitewash," the complexity of the nature of the conflict between the American and Vietnamese fishermen. The defendants stated that over the past year and a half to two years they had attempted to present their concerns to Austin with the hope that the Texas legislature would enact legislation designed to curtail the number of boats allowed to fish in the Galveston Bay. According to the defendants, such legislation would significantly decrease the amount of tension that exists between the American and Vietnamese fishermen, and would diffuse any explosive situation that may exist in Kemah-Seabrook.

TORTIOUS INTERFERENCE WITH CONTRACTUAL RELATIONSHIPS

The plaintiffs have alleged that the actions of the defendants constituted the tort of intentional interference with contractual relationship...interference with their commercial fishing business.

It is well established that a wrongful or malicious interference with the performance or the formation of a contract or the right to pursue a lawful occupation constitutes a tort for which damages may be recovered....Texas courts recognize a cause of action for improper interference with contractual relationships....Under Texas law a party has the right to be free from malicious interference with the right to conduct negotiations that have a reasonable probability of resulting in a contract....Texas courts have also recognized a cause of action for tortious and wrongful interference with advantageous business relationships.

The elements of the tort of wrongful interference with a prospective contract right are as follows: the plaintiff must show that (1) there was a "reasonable probability that he would have entered into a contractual relationship; (2) the defendant acted maliciously by intentionally preventing the relationship from occurring with the purpose of harming plaintiff; (3) the defendant was not privileged or justified, and (4) actual harm or damage occurred as a result." As the plaintiffs have stated, the commercial fishing business is essentially contractual in nature. Moreover, the commercial fishing business is a lawful occupation which the plaintiffs have a right to pursue without wrongful interference on behalf of the defendants. The evidence adduced at the hearing clearly established that the defendants acted intentionally to impede and prevent the plaintiffs from pursuing their lawful occupation. As a result of the defendants' actions, many members of the plaintiff class have agreed to sell their shrimping boats and many have been reluctant to pursue their lawful occupation. In light of these facts and the Court's earlier discussion...there is a substantial likelihood that the plaintiffs will prevail on this tort claim.

THE COMMON LAW TORT OF ASSAULT

The plaintiffs also alleged that the defendants had committed the common law torts of assault, trespass to personal property, and the intentional infliction of emotional distress. The cause of action for the tort assault recognizes a plaintiff's right to be free from apprehension of a harmful or offensive contact. Any act of such a nature as to excite an apprehension of a battery may constitute an assault....It is an assault to hold a weapon in a threatening position, or to surround an individual with a display of force....As a rule, however the defendant's act must amount to an offer to use force, and there must be an apparent ability and opportunity to carry out the threat immediately. There is no assault where the defendant is too far away to do any harm. With respect to weapons, when the defendant presents the weapon in such a manner as to indicate that it may immediately be made ready for use, the threat becomes sufficiently imminent to constitute an assault.

Under Texas law, a person commits an assault if he intentionally or knowingly threatens another with imminent bodily injury....The definition of assault is the same whether it is the subject of a criminal prosecution or of a civil suit for damages....An assault can only be committed when the act is coupled with the ability to commit a battery. For example, if the parties are too far separated for the accused to commit violence with the means used, there is no assault.

At the hearing, Miss Do Thi Toi testified that two American men pointed a gun at her. Mr. Dang, another member of the plaintiff class, also testified that an American pointed a gun at him while he was on his shrimp boat. Although these acts may constitute an assault, none of the actions of these Americans could be attributed directly to the defendants.

Several members of the plaintiff class also testified that when they witnessed the "boat ride" on March 15, 1981 they became frightened. Although
there were several armed persons on this "boat ride", there was no testimony that any of these individuals were in close enough proximity to any of
the plaintiffs to actually commit a battery. It is certainly clear that the actions
of the defendants created an atmosphere conducive to the commission of
violence and that such violent acts were the foreseeable natural cause of the
calls for violence, especially those of defendants Beam and Fisher and acqui-
esced in by the remaining defendants. At this stage of the proceedings, the
Court will not foreclose the plaintiffs from introducing such evidence and
further evidence of a direct connection between the defendants and actual
acts of assault and battery; however, insufficient evidence has been adduced
to demonstrate a likelihood of success on the merits and therefore, the
request for preliminary injunctive relief will be denied.

THE INTENTIONAL INFLICTION OF EMOTIONAL DISTRESS

The plaintiffs' Original Complaint also sought relief from the defendants'
alleged intentional infliction of emotional distress. The elements of a prima
facie case of this intentional tort are: 1) an act by the defendant(s), 2) intent,
3) extreme and outrageous conduct, 4) causation and 5) damages.

The evidence adduced at trial demonstrated a substantial likelihood
that the "boat ride" constituted extreme and outrageous conduct on
the part of defendants David Collins, James Stanfield and several, as yet,
unidentified members of the Ku Klux Klan. Colonel Nam's young sister-
in-law, Phuong Pham, testified that she was so frightened by the sight of
armed and robed Ku Klux Klan members, on the "boat ride," that she ran
from Colonel Nam's home and is now afraid to spend the night there.
Ordinarily under Texas law, damages for mental anguish and fright are
not recoverable unless they result from or are accompanied by physical
injury....However, Texas plaintiffs have a damage action for mental/emo-
tional suffering, unaccompanied by physical injury, "when the wrong
complained of is a willful one intended by the (defendant) to produce
mental anguish or from which such result should be reasonably anticipated as a natural consequence."...Here, the plaintiffs produced sufficient
evidence to establish a substantial likelihood that the defendants intended,
or at least could have reasonably anticipated that the "boat ride" would
cause plaintiff distress.

Nevertheless, the facts of this case as well as the governing law need to be
more fully developed for the plaintiffs to show a likelihood of success. The
plaintiffs have failed to cite any Texas authority allowing a damage action
for mental anguish, unaccompanied by some other intentional tort such as

trespass or assault. Moreover, the evidence adduced at the hearing failed to establish that any member of the plaintiff class suffered a mental and/or emotional injury severe enough to maintain a cause of action for the intentional infliction of emotional distress. Phuong Pham is not a member of the plaintiff class. The plaintiffs, therefore, have not demonstrated a substantial likelihood that any of the class members would be entitled to recovery of damages for Ms. Pham's emotional distress.

Discussion questions

1. Before going to the KKK, how had white fishermen tried to resolve matters? Is fishing a right? Should access to fishing waters be regulated or open to everyone? How can fishing waters be regulated? How can nature be controlled and harvested?
2. What was the goal of the KKK? What tactics did they use? Make a list. How did they define America and the rights of Americans? Who are the Americans here? Are white veterans of the war entitled to more rights than non-whites who still fought on the same side?
3. How would you feel if you were one of the Vietnamese fishermen? How about if you were one of the white fishermen?
4. How did the court rule in this case? Do you agree with its decision?
5. Think about the previous document. Also about fishing. History is full of conflicts over food and national identity, and about who has a right to food and the right to make a living from food. Why is that?

Document 12.8: Press Release: "T.G.I. Friday's® to Bring 'Magic' Brand of Restaurants to Urban Communities" (February 9, 1998)

After winning a national college basketball championship at Michigan State University, Earvin "Magic" Johnson decided to turn professional. He was the first player taken in the 1979 National Basketball Association draft by the Los Angeles Lakers. For the next 13 years, he engineered the team's famed "Showtime" offense and led them to four NBA championships. In 1991, Johnson abruptly retired after an emotional press conference where he revealed that he had contracted HIV. He would return to the Lakers in 1996 for half of a season, only to retire again.

With his basketball career over, Johnson reinvented himself. He became an important spokesperson for safe sex and HIV/AIDs prevention. At the same time, he became an entertainer, an entrepreneur, and a prominent businessperson. He tried his hand at movie making and even had a television show for a short time. But the thrust of Johnson's early business

*efforts—especially after riots ripped through Los Angeles in 1992 in the
wake of the acquittal of the police officers who beat Rodney King, an African
American motorist, and who were caught on video tape—were to bring
what he called middle-class amenities to "urban," largely underserved
communities. "We deserve the best," Johnson said about his efforts to open
eateries, movie houses, and coffee shops in African American sections of
major American cities. In this document, his company announces the
opening of a handful of T.G.I. Friday's restaurants, a chain of bars and
eateries. Think about what Johnson and his partners are promising. Can
a restaurant be more than a business? What can it represent?*

"Friday's Hospitality Worldwide Inc. Teams Up with Earvin 'Magic' Johnson in Unprecedented Urban Development Agreement"

Friday's Hospitality Worldwide Inc., the worldwide leader in the casual dining industry, today announced an agreement with Earvin "Magic" Johnson and his company, Johnson Development Corporation, which calls for the development of T.G.I. Friday's® restaurants in underserved urban communities throughout the United States. Designed to bring jobs, vitality and entertainment opportunities to America's underserved urban communities, this partnership combines Friday's famous heritage with Earvin "Magic" Johnson's vision for improving urban infrastructure and lifestyle.

"Over the next five years, we plan to open T.G.I. Friday's restaurants in Atlanta, Baltimore, Houston, Los Angeles and Washington, D.C.," said Earvin "Magic" Johnson. "We plan to bring T.G.I. Friday's to those cities which are also targeted for Magic Johnson Theatres to create a vibrant entertainment center," added Ken Lombard, president of Johnson Development Corporation and Magic Johnson Theatres. According to Lombard, the restaurants will be in close proximity to the movie theatres, which are developed by Johnson Development Corporation in partnership with Sony Retail Entertainment and are targeted for underserved urban communities throughout the United States that are not currently serviced by movie theatres or national chain restaurants, such as T.G.I. Friday's.

"The viability of inner city neighborhoods is a critical issue to building a strong America. T.G.I. Friday's partnering with Johnson Development Corporation is a positive step forward in providing quality, family-oriented restaurant alternatives to these urban communities," Johnson said.

The development of the restaurants is a true partnership with each company contributing and owning a 50 percent share without any government funds involved, according to Wallace B. Doolin, president and chief executive officer of Friday's Hospitality Worldwide Inc., parent company of TGI Friday's Inc.

"This opportunity with Earvin and Johnson Development Corporation offers us a new domestic expansion opportunity in market areas that we are not currently serving," said Steve King, chief operating officer of Friday's domestic operations. "We are proud to be associated with Earvin and look forward to our partnership and the positive results which we can achieve in these urban areas."

The restaurants will feature the same core menu, decor and atmosphere of T.G.I. Friday's, with the addition of artifacts representing local culture and history as well as other adaptations to make them more a part of the community in which they are developed. They will also highlight T.G.I. Friday's partnership with Earvin "Magic" Johnson, along with featuring various sporting memorabilia.

"Magic Johnson and T.G.I. Friday's restaurants are both American icons. It makes perfect sense for us to become partners," said Doolin.

Discussion questions

1. What do you think of the logic here? Can a chain restaurant deliver "unprecedented urban development"?
2. What gains does the press release promise will accompany the opening of T.G.I. Friday's in Atlanta, Baltimore, Houston, Los Angeles, and Washington, DC.?
3. Is this largely a symbolic gain? How can a restaurant bring about economic development? Do you think the opening of a T.G.I. Friday's led to additional development?
4. What are the costs of this strategy? How will these new businesses affect existing businesses?
5. Johnson often referred to his work of opening businesses in urban areas as a form of "retail justice," giving the poor and underserved the same buying options as the white middle-class. He even talked about it as an extension of the Civil Rights Movement. Do you agree with him? Is equal buying a form of justice? Are communities without a T.G.I. Friday's somehow oppressed?

Chapter 13 The Counterculture and the Lunch Counter

Document 13.1: Excerpts from Gordon and Phyllis Grabe, *The Hippie Cookbook or Don't Eat Your Food Stamps* (1970)

In the 1960s, the counterculture questioned everything about America, its core values, its propensity for war making, its wanton consumption, and its straitlaced sexuality. Its legion of adherents also questioned how the nation ate and what values were reflected in its food choices. What did it mean to develop a countercuisine and alternative modes of eating? How did a member of the counterculture know what was the correct countercultural approach to eating. Hippies, as the members of the counterculture were called, needed help. Some people needed advice on just how to be a proper and right-eating hippie. Like others before and after them in search of new ways of eating, they turned to cookbooks.

In 1970, Gordon and Phyllis Grabe published a cookbook for the Age of Aquarius, as some referred to the 1960s. It had recipes for brown rice and brown bread, commune beans, moratorium (or antiwar) march muffins, and peace pancakes. It also featured recipes for "I Ching noodles" and "Mother's astrological antique chile enchiladas." One section offered advice on "cooking in the nude." Contrary to public opinion, explained the Grabes, "nude cooking is good for your head, your body." Making food for company while completely undressed, they predicted, will "keep them interested." But they cautioned against frying bacon or potatoes without clothes, and added, "be sure to cook enough for unexpected guests if downtown San Francisco overlooks your kitchen."

Food and Eating in America: A Documentary Reader, First Edition.
Edited by James C. Giesen and Bryant Simon.
© 2018 John Wiley & Sons, Inc. Published 2018 by John Wiley & Sons, Inc.

Below is the introduction to The Hippie Cookbook. *As you read through this passage, think about what this tells you about what hippies—or the counterculture of the 1960s and early 1970s – valued and cared about the most. Pay close attention to the words and tone of this piece.*

Introduction

Any decent Hippie knows that the establishment does weird things to their food, and since most grocers are over 30, the first step in good Hippie cooking is to plant a vegetable garden. You'll need lots of table or chicken coop scrappings for good healthy plants. Plow your furrows unevenly, and use some imagination with weeds and free form. This will confuse the golphers [sic] and discourage your landlord from evicting you and commandeering the place just because it looks good.

Be sure to plan enough for bugs, birds, and gophers, and enough to feed the commune. If you don't have a commune, don't be discouraged, you soon will. If you don't have room for a garden, move.

Any Hippie can tell you what to plant, and that the Panama Red always goes in the neighbor's garden.

Next, go to the Salvation Army or local junk store and replace all your plastic dishes and cookware with good stuff. Plastic is bad for your head.

On your way home from the goodwill store, stop by the dumps and pick up an old-time wood stove. These may be a little hard to find because of the recent outbreak of antique freaks who sit them out in their gardens and plant geraniums in them. Throw away your gas or electric stove. (They are not only expensive to run, but they inhibit the growth of important groovy vibrations in good healthy food.) Also shop around for other groovy things like mattresses (for the commune), old clothes, old furniture and mason jars.

If you're hitchhiking, hide the mattresses and other junk in the stove. When the Volkswagon (sic) stops, distract the driver by asking him where he's going, what route he's taking, and if he's seen any of your friends along the way. In the meantime, the friends you made at the dump have been making a trailer out of washing machine gears and a bathtub, and have it loaded up and hooked on to the car with a bent soup ladle which you can use later.

Cooking in the Nude

Contrary to public opinion, nude cooking is good for your head, your body, and your food. While your pores are flashing on the air, the rest of you will get behind turning on the food, and it'll taste like it. Remember, your body needs your food and your food needs your body.

It is always more satisfying when all your friends get behind it, but don't let the social worker bring you down. If you're cooking food that's a drag, washing up before dinner will excite anybody's appetite, and making it nude will keep them interested.

A few helpful notes:

Nude cooking is a trip in the summer months, but it's always quicker in cold weather. Also, avoid frying bacon or french fries, and be sure to cook enough for unexpected guests if downtown San Francisco overlooks your kitchen.

Moratorium March Muffins

These are very filling and ought to last you all day. If nobody likes muffins they might last you for years.

1½ C whole wheat flour
1 C what germ
2 eggs
1½ C milk
½ C vegetable oil
1 tsp salt
1 tsp brown sugar

Beat the egg yolks with a wooden spoon. Add salt, sugar, and oil and mix together. Stir in the milk. Mix in the flour and wheat germ. Beat the egg whites until they are stiff and fold them into the batter. Pour into oiled muffin tins and bake at 350 for about 40 minutes. These are good with jelly or preserves or with white sauce poured over them.

Brown Bagging for Peace Marchers

It must be made clear before beginning your march to hide all diuretic type foods such as teas, beer, and soft drinks. An uptight bladder can turn the most ardent head towards the nearest one.

Fruit that will last all day, and better yet all night, is essential. Dried fruits and rice cakes are good examples.

For protective food, two loaves of Northridge bread stuffed in your shirt will protect against sword-like jabs from night sticks. And when a sit-in tends to drag on, it will protect against hunger pangs.

Commune Beans

2 lbs pinto beans
2 large cloves fresh garlic

1 large onion
salt and pepper
2½ T bacon fat
1½ T chilli powder
¾ lb Monterey jack cheese

Discard the shriveled and discolored beans and rinse the remainder with cold water. Place them in a 6–8 quart pot and cover with five or 6 inches of water. Add garlic and onion minced finely. Salt and pepper to taste. (It usually needs lots of salt.) Stir in the bacon fat and chilli powder. And stir until all the cheese is melted. Serve over brown rice, corn chips or with tortillas or cornbread on the side.

Discussion questions

1. What kinds of "weird things" does the establishment do to food and why can't they, according to the Grabes, be trusted?
2. How do they recommend procuring food?
3. What's wrong with plastic? (Do you know the line from the famous film of this era, *The Graduate*, about plastics?) What do plastics symbolize? What do junk stores, the Salvation Army, and mason jars, on the other hand, mean to hippies?
4. Why do they recommend using a wood stove?
5. Go back to the introduction to this document for a moment. What do the recipes in the book—just their titles—tell you about the politics of hippies and their politics of food? Why do they think that brown products are better? What does brownness symbolize here?
6. What does Panama Red refer to?
7. What is the imagined community of people here as reflected in the introduction and in the recipes?

Document 13.2: Kit Leder, "Women in the Communes," *Women: A Journal of Liberation* (1969)

The men wore beads and sandals and the women wore flowers in their hair and flowing dresses. They were the hippies, the counterculture of the 1960s. But they were about more than style or thumbing their noses at established elites. The counterculture believed that the personal was political; that what you wore, the length of your hair, the music you listened to, and what you said mattered; that to quote John Lennon, if you say you want a revolution, you had to change yourself first.

Just as there were radical wings to the antiwar movement and the black freedom struggle, there were radical counterculturists. And like their counterparts in other movements, by the end of the 1960s, these radicals questioned whether the establishment in the United States would ever change. Some answered the question with an emphatic, NO. Their response, to quote a slogan of the day, was "to tune in, turn on, and drop out." With the latter in mind, communes—or alternative societies—popped up across the United States in the 1960s. The goals of the communes were to live free from and free of the constraints and misplaced priorities of mainstream society. In the Utopian tradition, they were attempts to build alternative models of how people could live. But building a new world was never easy. Parts of the old world were hard to get rid of and tensions were inevitable.

Kit Leder dropped out and joined one of these communes. While there, as the document below suggests, she learned other lessons about gender, power, and the organization of society. Food, once again, proved to be a point of conflict and of consciousness raising.

Something approximating such a chance occurred this summer for a small group of people living on a farm commune. There were twelve of us, give or take a few, for most of the summer, doing the work which consisted of planted, weeding, pulling trees, and harvesting, as well as chopping wood, cooking over an open fire, washing clothes, and keeping the tents and the camp clean. There was no running water, which made housekeeping chores a little more difficult, and no electricity, which meant that some of the work like washing the dinner dishes, was usually done in the dark.

Even though there was no society-dictated division of labor, even though we had complete freedom to determine the division of labor for ourselves, a well-known pattern emerged immediately. Women did most of the cooking, all of the cleaning up, and of course, the washing. They also worked in the fields all day—so that after the farm work was finished, the men could be found sitting around talking and taking naps while the women prepared supper. In addition to that, one of the women remained in camp every day in order to cook lunch—it was always a woman who did this, never a man. Of course, the women were excused from some of the tasks: for example, none of us ever drove the tractor. That was considered too complicated for a woman. We never would have had to haul wood or chop it if we hadn't wanted to.

Does this story sound exaggerated? I think it is true that even men who verbally condone the liberation of women would tend to react the same way in a similar situation, as the result of conditioning. It is true that to some extent our group was free of the dictates of society last summer—but of course we weren't free of our cultural conditioning, which exists outside of society's institutions, and is, in fact, embodied in the individual. The men in our group were exhibiting a collective system of belief based on early training.

The women, too, had much to overcome, and we had to consciously organize ourselves to face the oppressive conditions which we were partially responsible for creating. We were a minority, and most of us were unattached; we were all between the ages of fifteen and twenty-four; all of us had thought and read, in varying degrees, about the problems which women face. We began holding private caucuses in the woods, far enough from camp so that we could feel free from any stray masculine ears. These meetings were not held in secret, though we said little about them, but they were considered a declaration of war by the men in the camp, and in a sense we considered them a sign of secession from the normal order of life as predetermined by the men, and by our own maimed outlooks.

In the meetings, we discussed day to day experiences in the camp, related them to what we had gleaned from the past and the condition of women in general and began to educate ourselves by reading and sharing knowledge. Our strategy was a total reorientation of our images of what we could and could not do.

One of tactics was complete non-response to hostility on the part of the men. We had to learn to differentiate between a legitimate attempt to discuss women's liberation, and sheer harassment. To the former we would willingly respond: the latter met with neutral silence. In order to forcibly shift the division of labor, we began doing other chores around dinner time. Collecting and chopping wood was an activity which was often neglected in the course of the day, so after our regular farm work, we would turn to the wood instead of the pots. We tried to discover and do things that needed to be done for the maintenance of the camp—building rather than cleaning.

If a tense situation arose, where a sister was uncertain how to react, there was usually another sister nearby, and a smile, a hand on the arm, or just the knowledge of concern, helped everyone keep calm. We felt that consistency and complete discipline in regard to our willingness to work were of utmost significance in showing the males that our intent was not to humiliate them, but to work toward a more healthy environment for everyone concerned.

Our experiment was a colossal failure. In analyzing what went wrong, it is unfair to place the blame completely on the man's inability to understand. Yet, as a woman, that is the only conclusion I can come to. A lot of dusty old myths were dragged out and shoved in our faces...you don't work fast enough; a man can't even get a decent meal around this place unless he cooks it for himself; before you can learn to drive a tractor, learn to get the dishes clean (I don't want you fucking with *my* tractor, baby); is there something wrong with your sex life? [Y]ou want to be just like a man...

For several weeks we lived in two separate camps. If we went gathering wood at dinner time, the men cooked...for themselves only. They washed their own dishes, but never the pots and pans that the food had come from. In the field we were a separate women's brigade—all day we worked together and talked liberation, separate from men.

Those were happy days! Left alone, we taught ourselves, feeling free to be clumsy at first, knowing that we wouldn't laugh at each other. I think we all began to develop confidence in our ability to do things, and my own physical endurance increased tremendously—I had no reason to let a man take over, ever. I think my sisters and I learned to love and value each other as women seldom can when they are divided from each other and forced to compete for recognition by the men in their lives—forced to compete much in the same way that capitalism forces men to compete against each other. In each case, it is the best position in the pecking order that determines how people act toward each other.

The fact that half of the women involved with the farm commune project are no longer there, and that the other half are consciously compromising in order to insure the success of the farm, is a testimony to the long fight which we all face. The inability of the men to respond to our attempts to liberate ourselves seems to be indication that now is the time to isolate, to learn, to build, and if necessary, when we have the strength to force a change that must come if we are to be free. Cultural change, through the breaking of the boundary conditions on behavior, will have to occur, and can only occur, through a conscious re-orientation of our own self-images.

Discussion questions

1. What was the gendered division of labor at the commune at the start?
2. How did these arrangements raise Leder's consciousness? How did they make her aware of her own oppression as a woman?
3. What is the long fight that she refers to at the end of the essay?
4. Why is the organization of household labor, inside and outside of the communes, so important?
5. Why is food so often defined as "women's work" in the United States and most other societies? How does this shape other relationships?

Document 13.3: Excerpt from Carol Adams, *The Sexual Politics of Meat: A Feminist-Vegetarian Critical Theory, 20th Anniversary Edition* (New York: Bloomsbury, 2010)[1]

In 1974, Carol Adams was a Yale Divinity School student living in Cambridge, Massachusetts. She had just become a vegetarian and was learning how to cook meals without meat. On a crisp fall day, while she was out for a walk, she had what she later described as an epiphany, one that would change her life and reshape her career. Eating meat, she determined was not just wrong, it was murder. But even more that, she concluded that day, meat was an expression of violence against women and an emblem of their oppression at the hands of men.

Over the following decade or so, Adams continued to think about the troubling connections between eating and gender, meat and maleness. Eventually her ideas became the basis of her important and influential book, The Sexual Politics of Meat, *which was originally published in 1990. This would become a widely debated and discussed statement of gender politics and food politics. In this book, which might also be thought of as a manifesto, Adams argued that there was a link between ideas of manliness and meat eating that together relied on the objectification of women and animals and the marginalization and denigration of the value of both groups to society. Male power, in other words, went hand in hand with meat eating.*

The excerpt below comes from a section of the book that Adams titled "Gender Inequality/Species Inequality?"

The men...were better hunters than the women, but only because the women had found they could live quite well on foods other than meat.
—Alice Walker, The Temple of My Familiar

What is it about meat that makes it a symbol and celebration of male dominance? In many ways, gender inequality is built into the species inequality that meat eating proclaims, because for most cultures obtaining meat was performed by men. Meat was a valuable economic commodity; those who controlled this commodity achieved power. If men were the hunters, then the control of this economic resource was in their hands. Women's status is inversely related to the importance of meat in non-technological societies:

The equation is simple: the more important meat is in their life, the greater relative dominance will the men command.... When meat becomes an important element within a more closely organized economic system so that there exist rules for its distribution, then men already begin to swing the levers of power....Women's social standing is roughly equal to men's only when society itself is not formalized around roles for distributing meat.

Peggy Sanday surveyed information on over a hundred nontechnological cultures and found a correlation between plant-based economies and women's power and animal-based economies and male power. "In societies dependent on animals, women are rarely depicted as the ultimate source of creative power." In addition, "When large animals are hunted, fathers are more distant, that is, they are not in frequent or regular proximity to infants."

Characteristics of economies dependent mainly on the processing of animals for food include:

- sexual segregation in work activities, with women doing more work than men, but work that is less valued
- women responsible for child care
- the worship of male gods
- patrilineality

On the other hand, plant-based economies are more likely to be egalitarian. This is because women are and have been the gatherers of vegetable foods, and these are invaluable resources for a culture that is plant-based. In these cultures, men as well as women were dependent on women's activities. From this, women achieved autonomy and a degree of self-sufficiency. Yet, where women gather vegetable food and the diet is vegetarian, women do not discriminate as a consequence of distributing the staple. By providing a large proportion of the protein food of a society, women gain an essential economic and social role without abusing it.

Sanday summarizes one myth that links male power to control of meat:

> The Mundurucu believe that there was a time when women ruled and the sex roles were reversed, with the exception that women could not hunt. During that time women were the sexual aggressors and men were sexually submissive and did women's work. Women controlled the "sacred trumpets" (the symbols of power) and the men's houses. The trumpets contained the spirits of the ancestors who demanded ritual offerings of meat. Since women did not hunt and could not make these offerings, men were able to take the trumpets from them, thereby establishing male dominance.

We might observe that the male role of hunter and distributer of meat has been transposed to the male role of eater of meat and conclude that this accounts for meat's role as symbol of male dominance. But there is much more than this to meat's role as symbol.

Discussion questions

1. In the first line of the section, Adams writes, "What is it about meat that makes it a symbol and celebration of male dominance?" How does she answer her own question? What does she use for evidence? What do you think of her use of history?
2. What is the "simple equation" she talks about in this section?
3. What are the chief characteristics of a meat-based society? What do you think of her list? Is anything missing from this list?
4. Why, according to Adams, are plant-based economies more likely to be less stratified and have fewer gender hierachies? What do you think of this analysis?
5. After *The Sexual Politics of Meat* was first published in 1990, Adams became a frequent lecturer on college campuses. During her presentations, she showed a set of slides about how meat was marketed and sold (for examples, see http://caroljadams.com/examples-of-spom). She often likened meat sales campaigns to pornography, rape, and battery. Take a look at the images featured in the link above. What do you see in these images? Do you see the exploitation and de-humanization of women? Is your analysis of these images the same as Adams's analysis? Is this what perpetuates the gender inequalities that Adams is concerned with in her book and lectures?
6. Is there still a link between gender and eating, meat and masculinity? Can you think of some foods that are coded as "male" and some others that are coded as "female"? How does this happen?

Document 13.4: Hanna Rosin, "The Evil Empire: The Scoop on Ben & Jerry's Crunchy Capitalism," *The New Republic* (September 19, 1995)

The Sixties were certainly an era of protest and political change, about saying and showing which side you were on. They were, at the same time, about changing desires and changing tastes. Almost by accident, the decade created new markets for new things that hippies and others wanted, things like Native American jewelry, rock and roll music and concerts and stereo systems, peace symbols, blues jeans, and clothes made with natural fabrics, and purer, more authentic, and just plain more fun foods.

When it came to food, hippies and their allies looked for alternatives to the processed corporate foods found at the supermarket and at McDonald's. They wanted handmade brown bread instead of mushy and predictable Wonder Bread. They wanted organic carrots and peas instead of vegetables drenched in pesticides. And they wanted healthier, more unadulterated foods as well as foods with more adventuresome tastes.

Companies that catered to hippies also maintained that they could use business profits to make the world a better place. This impulse has been called "countercultural" capitalism and it survived the fading of the counterculture itself in the 1970s. As it did, it sold a riff on the countercultural notion that the personal is political, suggesting you are what you buy and if you buy the best and most natural products that you are more-informed, more caring, cooler, and in some ways, a better person than those who opted for more ordinary things. Buying also became a stand-in for politics itself. If you buy products that help, or say they help, to save the environment, then you are an environmentalist.

One of the companies most identified with countercultural capitalism, or what Hanna Rosin in the essay below calls "Crunchy Capitalism," was the ice-cream maker, "Ben & Jerry's." Ben Cohen, the public face of the firm, looked the part. He dressed more like an aging hippie than a corporate titan. He preferred tie-dyed T-shirts over gray flannel suits, and high-top Converses over wing-tips. And he spoke a different language than most Wall Street businessmen. He insisted that a company could be both profitable and socially responsible, that there is no contradiction between serving investors and the larger community.

In the essay below, journalist Hanna Rosin takes a close look at both the rhetoric and practice of Ben & Jerry's and the legacy of the 1960s.

Ben Cohen, the crankier half of Vermont's ice cream duo, opens his company's June shareholder meeting with some bad news: "Nineteen-ninety-four, my friends, will forever live in ignominy as the year of our first loss." As the gloom sinks in, a breeze blows through the tent, throwing open the flaps to reveal a stunning view of Vermont's Green Mountains. The tent walls are festooned with a collage of cheery posters, some uplifting (what we cannot do alone we can do together) and some just bubbly (smooth—no chunks!). Many of the 2,000 loyalists have driven here from as far away as Chicago, and they do not want Arcadia spoiled. Their needs are not lost on Ben. "You know," he picks up, "people talk about how our social mission is affecting our profits negatively. But I want you to know that's a false dichotomy. Our social mission does not detract from our profits. Our social mission adds to our profits. This year is a test. But we will stay true to our roots, true to our soul, true to our dreams for the common good."

The mood lifts; the crowd bursts into applause. Emboldened, Ben begins to holler, his chubby sunburned face turning a shade redder. "I refuse to see another weapons system or space rocket launch and keep my mouth shut.... How do you look a hungry child in the face, coming home to a garbage-strewn neighborhood where gunshots are an everyday occurrence and say that you don't have the money to protect those streets?...Our country, the last remaining superpower on earth, needs to learn to measure its strength not in terms of how many people it can kill but how many people it can feed, clothe and house."

The crowd is on its feet. By the end of Ben's speech, anyone concerned about the fate of the sagging stock has forgotten all about it. A middle-aged woman runs up to the microphone, her giggling sons in tow: "Ben," she asks, "my boys and I just wanted to know, when are you going to run for president?" Another woman, pregnant under her yellow sundress, is crying when her turn comes. "Ben, Jerry, Ben," she weeps. "It's such a beautiful thing, what you're doing." The man sitting next to me sees me taking notes and solemnly offers his story: "I've been a shareholder since they made their first offering, and I want you to know that I have never, ever tasted even one spoon of Haagen-Dazs."

Before their recent dip, Ben and Jerry's Homemade Ice Cream Inc. was considered nothing short of an economic miracle. In the annals of business history, they are recorded as the first company to turn a profit while behaving like a nonprofit. Their story is almost legendary: the two high-school friends, with a $4,000 loan, opened their first scoop shop in an abandoned Burlington gas station in 1978. As sales grew, the hippie capitalists were consumed with guilt. "We worried we were becoming a cog in the economic machine, whose values we had detested all our lives," Ben recalls in The Inside Scoop, a company biography published last year. Jerry Greenfield couldn't take it and, in 1982, moved to Arizona. But Ben stayed behind and invented The Third Way, a path he called "Caring Capitalism."

How does it work? "Detached from values, money may indeed be the root of all evil," Ben now explains in the inspirational speeches he gives to college students and businessmen. "But linked effectively to social purpose, it can be the root of opportunity." To ease his guilt, Ben repented. On the company's first anniversary he gave away free cones to the hippies who flocked to the Vermont shop. A few years later, he vowed to buy milk from Vermont's flagging dairy farms, above market prices. When he hit the $10 million mark, he founded the Ben and Jerry' s Foundation, through which the company gave away 7.5 percent of its pre-tax profits to charity, the highest of any American company (the average is 1 percent). But the lost cash also saved millions on advertising. "[I]nspirational ice cream," gushed The New York Times, in one of hundreds of fawning articles. In fifteen years, the $140 million company with barely 500 employees built up the brand-name recognition of a company ten times its size....

Their customers, of course, love quick and easy activism, a lesson Ben and Jerry learned early. In 1983, the company decided to expand into Boston, to see if they could compete in an urban market. The business expansion fast became a populist crusade. They plastered the city with posters announcing, "two crazy Vermont hippies invade Boston with their ice cream." Haagen-Dazs, which then held a monopoly on superpremium ice cream, threatened distributors who carried Ben and Jerry's that they would lose their business, a prospect no distributor could afford. So Ben and Jerry started a movement. They took out a classified ad in Rolling Stone asking readers to "help two Vermont hippies fight the giant Pillsbury corporation." Jerry doggedly picketed the Pillsbury headquarters in Minneapolis, handing out pamphlets asking, "what's the doughboy afraid of?" The Doughboy hotline was flooded with outraged callers, expressing such sentiments as, "Corporations like yours really make me sick!" and threatening to form gangs of Doughboy busters. The guerrilla warfare achieved its goal: Ben and Jerry's conquered the market and in a few years owned their own giant corporation.

That irony aside, the campaign was based on a kernel of untruth. Ben and Jerry's has always defined itself as the polar opposite of Haagen-Dazs: their competitor is "worldly and elegant," they are the underdog, "funky and unpretentious." "Do you think the Doughboy is afraid of the The American Dream?" B&J's pamphlets taunted. But, as B&J know, no one embodies the American Dream better than Reuben Mattus, founder of Haagen-Dazs, a high-school dropout from Poland who started by hawking homemade ices in the Bronx from a horse-drawn cart. (He made up the name Haagen-Dazs because he thought it sounded Danish, and he put a map of Scandinavia on the lid.) B&J's scraggly hipness, by contrast, is only skin deep. Their first idea for a company, after all, was United Bagel Service, which would home-deliver bagels and lox with The New York Times on Sundays. And Ben only recently gave up his Saab for a pick-up truck, at the same time he went on a rice-and-beans diet in solidarity with the Third World.

Paeans to the oppressed seem to be Ben's forte. At the shareholders' meeting, he declared himself committed to a "diverse organization in a diverse society," after introducing the new CEO. This summer, he signed the fashionable petition to stay the execution of death-row prisoner Mumia Abu-Jamal. And, in the last year, Ben has been seen wearing baggy pants, high-tops and a baseball cap turned backward, blasting rap music from his office. His latest idea, hatched on a recent visit to Harlem, is to have one black and one Korean driver on every delivery truck, to encourage inter-racial harmony.

Still, peel off the gangsta-wear and Ben's politics are utterly conventional, if not Wall Street Republican: "Business is the most powerful force in the world," Ben preaches, echoing Andrew Mellon-era capitalists. The company's direct inner-city initiatives are all model Republican workfare programs, such as a Partnershop in Harlem, a franchise run by a local businessman where scoopers from a nearby drug rehab center follow strict work and dress codes. Another of the company's proudest projects is a partnership with the Greyston Bakery, where homeless people bake brownies to be used in Chocolate Fudge Brownie frozen yogurt and, as the annual report trumpets, "transform their relationship to work." [This] cult of business visionaries lives by Ben's universal dichotomy: money is the root of all evil or the font of all good. Entrepreneurs are saints or predators. Merely by declaring solidarity with their movement, a businessman's actions are beyond question: CEOs are admitted to the Social Venture Network by invitation only, and they are never asked to leave. "The distance between our rhetoric and our actions is the field in which we labor," is the group's motto, a foolproof shield from critics.

It would never occur to them to apply that motto to those outside the group. If Mobil launches a clean air campaign, it is assumed to be a cynical ploy. In fact, some of the most innovative environmental solutions have come from the worst polluters, responding purely to fear of punishment, as Entine points out in a recent paper. When the chemical company Monsanto discovered it was cheaper to recycle sludge than dispose of it, the innovation revolutionized toxic-waste disposal and had a far greater effect on the environment than a Save the Rainforest campaign. When GM signed the ceres principles to protect the environment, it paved the way for other corporate giants.

Caring capitalism is perhaps best left to larger enterprises. Ben and Jerry's ultimate contribution is a more conservative one: translating the spirit of the'60s into ad copy: "You know it will sell, because Dead paraphernalia always sells," wrote the two anonymous hippies who suggested calling a new flavor Cherry Garcia. And sell it did. Ben and Jerry printed up bumper stickers in psychedelic neon that read, "what a long, strange dip it's been." Aging baby-boomers bought it by the carton. But the story is not without its ironies. When Ben and Jerry sent a pint to Jerry Garcia, they got back a letter from his lawyer demanding royalties. Still, Ben forgives. "Jerry Garcia inspired us and lifted our spirits," Ben laments on the occasion of the legend's death. And, as always, there's a happy ending: as soon as his death was announced, sales of Cherry Garcia frozen yogurt shot through the roof.

Discussion questions

1. How does Rosin define "crunchy capitalism" and "caring capitalism"? How would her definition differ from Ben Cohen's definition?
2. What does Rosin mean when she says that, "Caring capitalism is perhaps best left to larger enterprises"?
3. If "crunchy capitalism" is more a marketing ploy than a commitment to social good, as Rosin suggests, than why does it work? What is it about "the spirit of the'60s," as she calls it, that sells? What are people buying when they buy the 1960s? What other companies use this spirit to sell things? How do they do it?
4. Are other companies better at "crunchy capitalism" than Ben & Jerry's? The same? Is "crunchy capitalism" an inherently false promise? If so, why?
5. What do you think of the tone of Rosin's essay? Is she fair to the company? Is Ben & Jerry's the same as Häagen-Dazs? Are businesses really only about making money? What are the alternatives to "crunchy capitalism?" Can people pursue politics and build a better world through purchasing rather than boycotts, for instance? Can the world be changed at the cash register or does it need to be done at the ballot box?

Document 13.5: Bryant Simon, "Why Starbucks Lost its Mojo," *Christian Science Monitor*, July 28, 2005

Along with Ben & Jerry's Ice Cream and Whole Foods grocery stores and a number of other chains, Starbucks represents an example of countercultural capitalism and its long and rather complicated history. The company was started in 1971 by three San Francisco college graduates interested in selling genuine and natural products. They thought about opening a cheese shop, but decided instead on coffee. At their original Seattle store, they sold only whole bean coffee to make at home; they gave away the drinks to get people to taste the "real" coffee. In 1987, Howard Schultz became the CEO of the company and began to emphasize the selling of espressos and cappuccinos and opening hundreds and then thousands of new stores each year.

By the mid-1990s, Starbucks was opening a new store somewhere around the world every six hours. Cartoonists and commentators joked that the coffee giant would soon begin to launch new stores right next to old ones or when it ran out of space on the street it would open new outlets in its own bathrooms. Even as Starbucks grew, though, it insisted that it was a different kind of company, a company built around the core values of quality, community building, diversity, and social responsibility.

*By 2005, however, Starbucks had begun to experience serious growth
pains. See below for an article by historian Bryant Simon, author of*
Everything But the Coffee: Learning about America From Starbucks *and
co-editor of this book, on the slowing down of Starbucks and what this says
about consumer politics, tastes, and desires.*

How Starbucks Lost its Mojo

Bad news has been pouring down on Starbucks for a year.

The price of the company's stock has been cut in half—and then some.
Fewer people come through store doors and those who do buy less.

Still when Starbucks, that longtime engine of growth, announced that it
planned to close 600 US stores—50 of them by the end of July—and lay off
12,000 employees, company watchers reacted with surprise. One journalist
called it the "sudden shocking end to the long and gilded age of Starbucks."

As the shock wore off, the explanations came. Pundits and analysts
blamed stock prices, the mortgage crisis, competition from McDonald's and
Dunkin Donuts, along with real estate blunders, like putting stores on opposite corners of the same intersection. But they had it mostly wrong. This
economic logic was too narrow and not culturally informed enough to
explain Starbucks' fall.

The company thrived throughout the past 15 years by giving middle-class
Americans exactly what they thought they wanted—and this wasn't really
about coffee. It was about creating a product that allowed doctors and lawyers, IT specialists and travel writers, and then their imitators, to portray
themselves as they wanted to be seen. That's how products work in the
world we live in. We buy things to announce something about ourselves.

For the most part, the products that sell the best are the ones that communicate most effectively. That's what Starbucks did with their coffee.

Really, then, they sold not coffee but elevated status. Just by buying the
coffee and speaking the company's made-up lingua franca, you became a
cup-carrying member of the upper class. And that made Starbucks, over-
priced as it was, an affordable form of status making.

It was, after all, cheaper than a BMW, a Kate Spade bag, an Armani suit,
or a Colorado ski vacation, but it projected "upscale" in the same way.
That's why it was valuable, maybe even a bargain at $4 a cup.

I once asked a woman who graduated from community college and
worked as a dental hygienist why she went to Starbucks several times a
week; she answered, "I don't really like the coffee, but I go because successful people go there and I hope it rubs off on me."

This was not a phenomenon unique to the United States. I once talked with a 30-something man who was sipping a grande iced coffee in Singapore. Why do you like Starbucks, I asked him. Why don't you go to a local cafe where the coffee costs a quarter as much?" "It is cool," he responded; "I'm cool when I'm drinking it."

That sense of success—that sense of cool—is what is gone now.

It is gone because Starbucks violated the economic principles of cultural scarcity. Once something becomes too common, it can't keep generating cool or envy or status.

Now that there are Starbucks stores everywhere, in Tokyo and Terre Haute, London and Lancaster (PA and CA), it is too ordinary. Once the soundtrack promoted in stores changed from Miles Davis and Buena Vista Social Club to Kenny G. and Paul McCartney, it seemed too commonplace. When cappuccinos turned into Frappuccinos—a trademarked phrase by the way—the brand didn't seem as sophisticated. And now that Cosi and Panera—not to mention some airport lounges—look like Starbucks, it just doesn't look so special anymore either.

Even the company's much touted bluish values of doing good seemed to get scarcer, or at least spread thinner. Over the last year, Ethiopian officials accused Starbucks of something close to coffee colonialism; judges charged the company with unfair labor practices and putting its hand in tip jars; and environmentalists wondered loudly how green the firm could be when it used all of those throw-away paper and plastic cups.

Now Starbucks is just a coffee (and frothy milk and sugar) seller. In many ways, the company has no one to blame but itself. It wanted to grow and grow and force itself into the mainstream.

It succeeded. But that was the tipping point. At its height, consumers could no longer distinguish themselves from one another anymore. And the white cup with the green logo was emptied of cultural capital—long before gas prices pushed past $4 or even $3 a gallon.

For Starbucks to make a comeback, it will somehow have to capture that mojo again. And if it does, it won't matter how much a barrel of oil costs or what McDonald's is selling. Status seekers will come back only when Starbucks is a little scarcer and thus a little cooler.

Discussion questions

1. How did Starbucks up until 2005 sell countercultural or slightly liberal values and products?
2. What else was Starbucks selling by this point? What does the author mean when he says that Starbucks sold status? How does this reflect the

times and perhaps the transformation of the values of the 1960s and 1970s? How in other words had hippies become yuppies?

3. Why did Starbucks begin to falter in 2005? Was this about "economics" or "culture"? What is an "aspirational product"? What other food products are "aspirational"? Is that a fulfillment of the counterculture or a negation of the counterculture?

4. If you were giving Starbucks CEO Howard Schultz advice on how to run his company in 2005, and then today, what would you tell him?

Chapter 14   Cheap Food, Cheap Calories

Document 14.1: Centers for Disease Control Maps of the Obesity Trend in the United States (1985–2010)

The United States government established the Communicable Disease Center, later called the Centers for Disease Control and Prevention (CDC), in 1946. Over its six plus decades in operation, the CDC has emerged as the leading federal agency in the fight against disease and in the promotion of public health, not just in the United States, but around the world. According to the its website, "CDC increases the health security of our nation…[and]…saves lives and protects people from health threats. To accomplish our mission, CDC conducts critical science and provides health information that protects our nation against expensive and dangerous health threats, and responds when these arise."

Beginning in the 1980s, the CDC began to pay increased attention to the problem of obesity in the United States. To show the growing problem, it produced a series of maps of the country. Using body mass index (BMI) as a measure—the BMI calculates an adult's weight in relation to his or her height—it showed a steady and dramatic jump in weight gain in the United States over the last four decades. Please note that these maps should be looked at in conjunction with Documents 14.2 and 14.5.

Food and Eating in America: A Documentary Reader, First Edition.
Edited by James C. Giesen and Bryant Simon.
© 2018 John Wiley & Sons, Inc. Published 2018 by John Wiley & Sons, Inc.

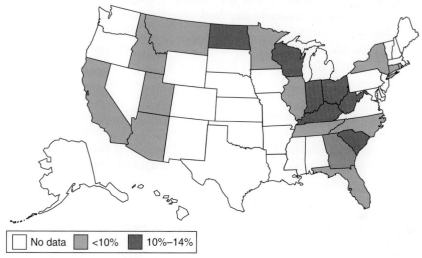

Obesity Trends* Among U.S. Adults
BRFSS, 1985
(*BMI ≥30, or ~ 30 lbs. overweight for 5′ 4″ person)

No data   <10%   10%–14%

Source: Behavioral Risk Factor Surveillance System, CDC.

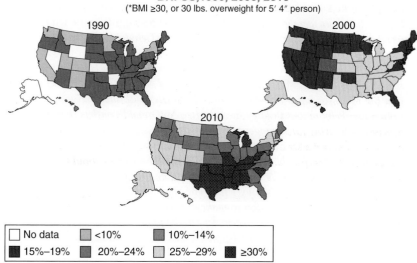

Obesity Trends* Among U.S. Adults
BRFSS,1990, 2000, 2010
(*BMI ≥30, or 30 lbs. overweight for 5′ 4″ person)

No data   <10%   10%–14%
15%–19%   20%–24%   25%–29%   ≥30%

Source: Behavioral Risk Factor Surveillance System, CDC.

Discussion questions

1. Where and in what parts of the country is obesity the most prevalent and why? What factors do you think correlate with increases in rates of BMI? What does wealth or poverty have to do with these numbers?
2. Why did BMI rates increase when they did? What caused the increase? Is it about a change in diet? Is it about individual choices? Is it about changes in living and commuting patterns or still other environmental factors?
3. In its mission statement, the CDC says it "provides health information that protects our nation against expensive and dangerous health threats." Is obesity expensive? Is it a threat to the nation? If yes is your answer, how? And who pays for obesity? Find some data (you might start on the CDC website, cdc.gov) to back up your answers.

Document 14.2: Excerpt from Judge Robert Sweet Opinion in *Pelman v. McDonald's Corp.* (September 3, 2003)

In 2002, Ashley Pelman was fourteen years old. She stood 4 foot, 10 inches tall and weighed 170 pounds. Her neighbor and friend in one of the poorer sections of the Bronx, Jazlyn Bradley, was nineteen years old and 5 foot, 6 inches tall and weighed 270 pounds. They were just two of the millions and millions of kids in the United States who were unhealthy and overweight, and the numbers were growing every year. By the turn of the century, a third of all American teenagers were categorized by the Centers for Disease Control (see the maps in Document 14.1) as obese.

Pelman and Bradley both loved McDonald's. Pelman got a Happy Meal several times a week. Many days, Bradley ordered McMuffins for breakfast and Big Macs for lunch and dinner. Both liked fries with their burgers.

In 2002, Pelman and Bradley sued the two McDonald's outlets that they went to most often for damages related to their obesity. They were the first to do so. They said that the company caused them to be obese because its advertising led them to believe that it sold healthy food. They claimed, moreover, that McDonald's withheld information about the contents of its food. Pelman and Bradley's lawyer told The New York Times, *"Young individuals are not in a position to make a choice after the onslaught of advertising and promotions." Robert Sweet, the judge in the case, dismissed Pelman and Bradley's claims. See below for Sweet's opinion in what came to be known as the "McFat" case.*

OPINION IN PELMAN v. McDonald's BY: ROBERT W. SWEET

Defendant McDonald's Corporation ("McDonald's") has moved pursuant to Rule 12(b)(6) to dismiss the amended complaint of plaintiffs Ashley Pelman, Roberta Pelman, Jazlyn Bradley and Israel Bradley. The plaintiffs have cross-moved for partial summary judgment.

For the reasons set forth below, the motion to dismiss by McDonald's is granted and the motion for partial summary judgment by plaintiffs is denied. Leave to amend the complaint is denied.

Prior Proceedings

The plaintiffs commenced suit by filing their initial complaint on August 22, 2002 in the State Supreme Court of New York, Bronx County. Defendants removed the action to the Southern District of New York on September 30, 2002. By opinion of January 22, 2003, this Court dismissed the original complaint, but granted leave to amend the complaint within 30 days in order to address the deficiencies listed in the opinion. See Pelman v. McDonald's Corp., 237 F. Supp. 2d 512 (S.D.N.Y. 2003).

On February 19, 2003, plaintiffs filed an amended complaint. McDonald's filed a motion to dismiss the amended complaint on April 14, 2003. On May 16, 2003, plaintiffs cross-moved for summary judgment and in opposition to the motion. After submission of briefs, oral argument on both motions was held on June 25, 2003, and the motions were considered fully submitted at that time.

Facts

As befits a motion to dismiss, the following facts are drawn from the allegations in the complaint and do not constitute findings of fact by the Court.

Parties

Ashley Pelman, a minor, and her mother and natural guardian Roberta Pelman are residents of the Bronx, New York.

Jazlyn Bradley, a minor, and her father and natural guardian Israel Bradley are residents of New York, New York.

The infant plaintiffs are consumers who have purchased and consumed the defendant's products in New York State outlets and, as a result thereof, such consumption has been a significant or substantial factor in the development of their obesity, diabetes, coronary heart disease, high blood pressure, elevated cholesterol intake, and/or other detrimental and adverse health effects and/or diseases.

Claims

In the amended complaint, the plaintiffs alleged four causes of action as members of a putative class action of minors residing in New York State who have purchased and consumed McDonald's products. Shortly before oral argument, however, the plaintiffs informed the Court that they are dropping their fourth cause of action, which alleged negligence by McDonald's because of its failure to warn plaintiffs of the dangers and adverse health effects of eating processed foods from McDonald's.

The three remaining causes of action are based on deceptive acts in practices in violation of the Consumer Protection Act, New York General Business Law.

Count I alleges that McDonald's misled the plaintiffs, through advertising campaigns and other publicity, that its food products were nutritious, of a beneficial nutritional nature or effect, and/or were easily part of a healthy lifestyle if consumed on a daily basis.

Count II alleges that McDonald's failed adequately to disclose the fact that certain of its foods were substantially less healthier, as a result of processing and ingredient additives, than represented by McDonald's in its advertising campaigns and other publicity.

Count III alleges that McDonald's engaged in unfair and deceptive acts and practices by representing to the New York Attorney General and to New York consumers that it provides nutritional brochures and information at all of its stores when in fact such information was and is not adequately available to the plaintiffs at a significant number of McDonald's outlets.

The plaintiffs allege that as a result of the deceptive acts and practices enumerated in all three counts, they have suffered damages including, but not limited to, an increased likelihood of the development of obesity, diabetes, coronary heart disease, high blood pressure, elevated cholesterol intake, related cancers, and/or detrimental and adverse health effects and/or diseases.

Discussion

In reviewing the plaintiffs' initial complaint, the Court considered allegations that related to actions taken against McDonald's advertising practices in the late 1980's by state attorney generals from several states, including New York State. At that time, this Court noted that "a review of those advertisements and that state attorney general's analysis of them may assist plaintiffs in shaping a claim." But the Court also warned that "any claim based on the advertisements would likely be time barred."... Despite that warning, plaintiffs have submitted several allegedly deceptive advertisements, promotions and statements that date from those same investigations....

Causation under New York's Consumer Protection Act differs from proximate cause as applied under the common law....("Cases in consumer fraud expand the reach of proximate causation...Causation is thus more broadly construed to carry out state policy against fraud on consumers.") It would therefore be inappropriate to apply the standard from plaintiffs' voluntarily dismissed negligence action to the statutory claims. The plaintiffs need not "establish that the defendant's conduct was a substantial cause in bringing about the harm." Nevertheless, "the causation element is essential: 'The plaintiff...must show that the defendant's material deceptive act caused the injury.'"...In Petitt, the district court first dismissed the plaintiff's negligence claim under the more rigorous standard of proximate causation, and then dismissed the statutory claims because "plaintiffs are unable to show that Celebrity's actions resulted in such injuries, directly or indirectly."

....The absence of a reliance requirement effectively allows plaintiffs to allege a deceptive practice and then to show some connection between that practice and the injury without having to allege specifically that the individual plaintiff was deceived or that the deception was the only reason that the plaintiff purchased the product or, as in the present case, purchased it as frequently as they did.

The absence of a reliance requirement does not, however, dispense with the need to allege some kind of connection between the allegedly deceptive practice and the plaintiffs' injuries. If a plaintiff had never seen a particular advertisement, she could obviously not allege that her injuries were suffered "as a result" of that advertisement. Excusing the reliance requirement only allows the plaintiff to forgo the heightened pleading burden that is necessary for common law fraud claims. It cannot, however, create a causal connection between a deceptive practice and a plaintiff's injury where none has been alleged. Accordingly, this Court required that to state a claim under an amended complaint, plaintiffs would "have to set forth grounds to establish...that they suffered some injury as a result of that particular promotion."

As discussed above, plaintiffs have successfully alleged that they were witness to only one instance of deceptive acts or practices: the various representations by McDonald's that its French fries and hash browns are made with 100% vegetable oil and/or are cholesterol-free, whereas they are actually cooked and processed in beef tallow. Assuming for the purposes of the causation analysis that these acts are deceptive, and granting all inferences in the plaintiffs' favor, the plaintiffs have stated, albeit just barely, a causal connection between the deceptive acts and the plaintiffs' decisions to consume McDonald's food, or to consume it more frequently than they would have otherwise.

Plaintiffs have failed, however, to draw an adequate causal connection between their consumption of McDonald's food and their alleged injuries. This Court noted that the original complaint did not adequately allege the causation of plaintiffs' injuries because it did "not specify how often the plaintiffs ate at McDonald's." In terms of causation, "the more often a plaintiff had eaten at McDonald's, the stronger the likelihood that it was the McDonald's food (as opposed to other foods) that affected the plaintiffs' health."

Unlike the initial complaint, the amended complaint does specify how often the plaintiffs ate at McDonald's. For example, Jazlyn Bradley is alleged to have "consumed McDonald's foods her entire life…during school lunch breaks and before and after school, approximately five times per week, ordering two meals per day." Such frequency is sufficient to begin to raise a factual issue "as to whether McDonald's products played a significant role in the plaintiffs' health problems."

What plaintiffs have not done, however, is to address the role that "a number of other factors other than diet may come to play in obesity and the health problems of which the plaintiffs complain." This Court specifically apprised the plaintiffs that in order to allege that McDonald's products were a significant factor in the plaintiffs' obesity and health problems, the Complaint must address these other variables and, if possible, eliminate them or show that a McDiet is a substantial factor despite these other variables. Similarly, with regard to plaintiffs' health problems that they claim resulted from their obesity…, it would be necessary to allege that such diseases were not merely hereditary or caused by environmental or other factors.

Plaintiffs have not made any attempt to isolate the particular effect of McDonald's foods on their obesity and other injuries. The amended complaint simply states the frequency of consumption of McDonald's foods and that each infant plaintiff "exceeds the Body Mass Index (BMI) as established by the U.S. Surgeon General, National Institutes of Health, Centers for Disease Control, U.S. Food and Drug Administration and all acceptable scientific, medical guidelines for classification of clinical obesity."

In their opposition brief, plaintiffs argue that "surveys and sampling techniques" may be employed to establish causation….While that may be true, it is irrelevant in the present context, where a small number of plaintiffs are alleging measurable injuries. Following this Court's previous opinion, the plaintiffs should have included sufficient information about themselves to be able to draw a causal connection between the alleged deceptive practices and the plaintiffs' obesity and related diseases. Information about the frequency with which the plaintiffs ate at McDonald's is helpful, but only begins to address the issue of causation. Other pertinent, but unanswered questions include: What else did the plaintiffs eat? How much did they exercise? Is there a family history of the diseases which are alleged to have been caused by McDonald's products? Without this additional information, McDonald's does not have sufficient information to determine if its foods are the cause of plaintiffs' obesity, or if instead McDonald's foods are only a contributing factor....

The Advertising Campaign Upon Which Plaintiffs Have Stated Reliance is Not Objectively Deceptive

Even if plaintiffs were able sufficiently to allege that their injuries were causally related to McDonald's representations about its french fries and hash browns, that claim must still be dismissed because the plaintiffs have not alleged that those advertisements were objectively misleading.

In order to demonstrate...that a practice or advertisement is deceptive or misleading, it must be shown objectively that a reasonable consumer would have been misled by the defendant's conduct.... It is appropriate for a court, given particular facts and circumstances, to determine whether or not a given practice is or is not deceptive as a matter of law....

The essence of the plaintiffs' claim of deception with regard to McDonald's french fries and hash browns is that McDonald's represented that its fries are cooked in "100 percent vegetable oil" and that they contain zero milligrams of cholesterol whereas in reality they "contain beef or extracts and trans fatty acids.".... However, the citations in the amended complaint to McDonald's advertisements, and the appended copies of the advertisements, do not bear out the plaintiffs' claims of deception. The first citation is to an advertisement titled "How we're getting a handle on cholesterol," alleged to have commenced in 1987 and to have continued for several years thereafter. The text cited by the plaintiffs states:

> ... a regular order of french fries is surprising low in cholesterol and 4.6 grams of saturated fat. Well within established guidelines for good nutrition.

The text cited in the complaint, however, inexplicably drops several significant words from the text of the advertisement included in the appendix to the amended complaint. The actual advertisement states:

> ... a regular order of french fries is surprising low in cholesterol and saturated fat: only 9 mg of cholesterol and 4.6 grams of saturated fat. Well within established guidelines for good nutrition.

The plaintiffs next allege that beginning on or around July 23, 1990, McDonald's announced that it would change its french fry recipe and cook its fries in "100 percent vegetable oil," a change that rendered its fries cholesterol-free....They allege that from the time of the change until May 21, 2001, McDonald's never acknowledged "that it has continued the use of beef tallow in the french fries and hash browns cooking process." On its website, however, McDonald's is alleged to have "admitted the truth about its french fries and hash browns":

> A small amount of beef flavoring is added during potato processing -- at the plant. After the potatoes are washed and steam peeled, they are cut, dried, par-fried and frozen. It is during the par-frying process at the plant that the natural flavoring is used. These fries are then shipped to our U.S. restaurants. Our french fries are cooked in vegetable oil at our restaurants.

Plaintiffs further allege that McDonald's claims that its french fries and hash browns are cholesterol-free is also misleading because the oils in which those foods are cooked contain "trans fatty acids responsible for raising detrimental blood cholesterol levels (LDL) in individuals, leading to coronary heart disease."...However, plaintiffs have made no allegations that McDonald's made any representations about the effect of its french fries on blood cholesterol levels. As McDonald's argues,

> The contents of food and the effects of food are entirely different things. A person can become "fat" from eating "fat-free" foods, and a person's blood sugar level can increase from eating "sugar-free" foods.

McDonald's representation that its fries are "cholesterol-free" or contain zero milligrams of cholesterol is therefore objectively non-deceptive.

Because the plaintiffs have failed to allege both that McDonald's caused the plaintiffs' injuries or that McDonald's representations to the public were deceptive, the motion to dismiss the complaint is granted....

III. Leave to Amend is Denied

The plaintiffs have not only been given a chance to amend their complaint in order state a claim, but this Court laid out in some detail the elements that a properly pleaded complaint would need to contain. Despite this guidance, plaintiffs have failed to allege a cause of action for violations of New York's consumer protection laws with respect to McDonald's advertisements and other publicity. The plaintiffs have made no explicit allegations that they witnessed any particular deceptive advertisement, and they have not provided McDonald's with enough information to determine whether its products are the cause of the alleged injuries. Finally, the one advertisement which plaintiffs implicitly allege to have caused their injuries is objectively non-deceptive.

Conclusion

McDonald's motion to dismiss the amended complaint is granted. The plaintiffs' motion for partial summary judgment is denied as moot. Plaintiffs' request for leave to amend the complaint is denied.

It is so ordered.
New York, NY
September 3, 2003
ROBERT W. SWEET

Discussion questions

1. How, according to Pelman and Bradley, did McDonald's contribute to their obesity as well as other aliments?
2. Judge Sweet ruled that McDonald's was not responsible for its customers' obesity. Why? Do you agree with his ruling?
3. After the ruling, the judge said, "where should the line be drawn between an individual's own responsibility to take care of herself and society's responsibility to ensure others shield her?" Are these the real issues in the case? Is eating fast food a matter of personal choice? Do people have the information to make independent choices and decisions?
4. What other factors cause obesity? Is it all about fast food?
5. If you think that fast foods contribute substantially to obesity, what should be done about it? Should the government regulate the growth of McDonald's and the foods it and its competitors serve? How? Should it limit their ability to advertise? Should it impose "sin taxes" on these companies? Should fast food firms be treated like cigarette makers and be forced to issue a warning label? What would you put on that warning label?

Document 14.3: Michael Pollan, "Down on the Industrial Organic Farm," *The New York Times Magazine* (July 13, 2001)[1]

By the start of the twentieth century, Michael Pollan had emerged as the most influential and talked about food writer and thinker in the United States. With his best-selling books and thoughtful essays in widely circulated

---

[1] Copyright © 2001 by Michael Pollan. Reprinted by permission of ICM Partners.

magazines and newspapers, he helped to give shape to and consolidate a new American food movement. Perhaps more than anything else, this new movement tried to show consumers where their food came from, what was it in, and how it would affect their bodies. He wrote about the piles of highly subsidized, industrial-produced corn in our fast-food meals. He urged consumers to make smarter choices with their forks and their dollars and to buy fewer processed items and eat more things that looked like food. Organic food benefited from the new food movement. From 1990 to 2009, annual sales of organic food and beverages in the United States jumped from $1 billion to $24.8 billion. As the size of this market grew, what constituted organic was also beginning to change. In this article from The New York Times Magazine, *Pollan takes a visit to an "Industrial Organic Farm." What did he find down on the farm? Was he troubled by what he found? Did he see it as a contradiction?*

IV. Down on the Industrial Organic Farm

No farm I have ever visited before prepared me for the industrial organic farms I saw in California. When I think about organic farming, I think family farm, I think small scale, I think hedgerows and compost piles and battered pickup trucks. I don't think migrant laborers, combines, thousands of acres of broccoli reaching clear to the horizon. To the eye, these farms look exactly like any other industrial farm in California—and in fact the biggest organic operations in the state today are owned and operated by conventional mega-farms. The same farmer who is applying toxic fumigants to sterilize the soil in one field is in the next field applying compost to nurture the soil's natural fertility.

Is there something wrong with this picture? It all depends on where you stand. Gene Kahn makes the case that the scale of a farm has no bearing on its fidelity to organic principles and that unless organic "scales up" it will "never be anything more than yuppie food." To prove his point, Kahn sent me to visit large-scale farms whose organic practices were in many ways quite impressive, including the Central Valley operation that grows vegetables for his frozen dinners and tomatoes for Muir Glen.

Greenways Organic is a successful 2,000-acre organic-produce operation tucked into a 24,000-acre conventional farm outside Fresno; the crops, the machines, the crews, the rotations and the fields were indistinguishable, and yet two very different kinds of industrial agriculture are being practiced here side by side.

In place of petrochemical fertilizers, Greenways's organic fields are nourished by compost made by the ton at a horse farm nearby. Insects are controlled with biological agents and beneficial insects like lacewings. Frequent and carefully timed tilling, as well as propane torches, keeps down the weeds, perhaps the industrial organic farmer's single stiffest challenge. This approach is at best a compromise: running tillers through the soil so frequently is destructive to its tilth, yet weeding a 160-acre block of broccoli by hand is unrealistic.

Since Greenways grows the same crops conventionally and organically, I was interested to hear John Diener, one of the farm's three partners, say he knew for a fact that his organic crops were "better," and not only because they hadn't been doused with pesticide. When Diener takes his tomatoes to the cannery, the organic crop reliably receives higher Brix scores—a measure of the sugars in fruits and vegetables. It seems that crops grown on nitrogen fertilizer take up considerably more water, thereby diluting their nutrients, sugars and flavors. The same biochemical process could explain why many people—including the many chefs who swear by organic ingredients—believe organic produce simply tastes better. With less water in it, the flavor and the nutrients of a floret of organic broccoli will be more concentrated than one grown with chemical fertilizers.

It's too simple to say that smaller organic farms are automatically truer to the organic ideal than big ones. In fact, the organic ideal is so exacting—a sustainable system that requires not only no synthetic chemicals but also few purchased inputs of any kind and that returns as much to the soil as it removes—that it is most often honored in the breach. Yet the farmers who come closest to achieving this ideal do tend to be smaller in scale. These are the farmers who plant dozens of different crops in fields that resemble quilts and practice long and elaborate rotations, thereby achieving the rich biodiversity in space and time that is the key to making a farm sustainable.

For better or worse, these are not the kinds of farms Small Planet Foods does business with today. It's simply more efficient to buy from one 1,000-acre farm than 10 100-acre farms. Indeed, Cascadian Farm the corporation can't even afford to use produce from Cascadian Farm the farm: it's too small. So the berries grown there are sold at a roadside stand, while the company buys berries for freezing from as far away as Chile.

The big question is whether the logic of an industrial food chain can be reconciled to the logic of the natural systems on which organic agriculture has tried to model itself. Put another way, Is "industrial organic" a contradiction in terms?

... One of the most striking ways Small Planet Foods is changing the system is by helping conventional farms convert a portion of their acreage to organic. Several thousand acres of American farmland are now organic as a result of the company's efforts, which go well beyond offering contracts to providing instruction and even management. Kahn has helped to prove to the skeptical that organic—dismissed as "hippie farming" not very long ago—can work on a large scale. The environmental benefits of this educational process shouldn't be underestimated. And yet the industrialization of organic comes at a price. The most obvious is consolidation: today five giant farms control fully one-half of the $400 million organic produce market in California. Partly as a result, the price premium for organic crops is shrinking. This is all to the good for expanding organic's market beyond yuppies, but it is crushing many of the small farmers for whom organic has represented a profitable niche, a way out of the cheap-food economics that has ravaged American farming over the last few decades. Indeed, many of the small farmers present at the creation of organic agriculture today find themselves struggling to compete against the larger players, as the familiar, dismal history of American agriculture begins to repeat itself in the organic sector.

This has opened up a gulf in the movement between Big and Little Organic and convinced many of the movement's founders that the time has come to move "beyond organic"—to raise the bar on American agriculture yet again. Some of these innovating farmers want to stress fair labor standards, others quality or growing exclusively for local markets. In Maine, Eliot Coleman has pioneered a sophisticated market garden entirely under plastic, to supply his "food shed" with local produce all winter long; even in January his solar-heated farm beats California on freshness and quality, if not price. In Virginia, Joel Salatin has developed an ingenious self-sufficient rotation of grass-fed livestock: cattle, chickens and rabbits that take turns eating, and feeding, the same small pasture. There are hundreds of these "beyond organic" farmers springing up now around the country. The fact is, however, that the word "organic"—having entered the vocabulary of both agribusiness and government—is no longer these farmers' to redefine. Coleman and Salatin, both of whom reject the U.S.D.A. organic label, are searching for new words to describe what it is they're doing. Michael Ableman, a "beyond organic" farmer near Santa Barbara, Calif., says: "We may have to give up on the word 'organic,' leave it to the Gene Kahns of the world. To be honest, I'm not sure I want the association, because what I'm doing on my farm is not just substituting materials."

Not long ago at a conference on organic agriculture, a corporate organic farmer suggested to a family farmer struggling to survive in the competitive world of industrial organic agriculture that he "should really try to develop a niche to distinguish yourself in the market." The small farmer replied: "I believe I developed that niche 20 years ago. It's called 'organic.' And now you're sitting on it."

... Still, while it surely represents real progress for agribusiness to be selling organic food rather than fighting it, I'm not sure I want to see industrialized organic become the only kind in the market. Organic is nothing if not a set of values (this is better than that), and to the extent that the future of those values is in the hands of companies that are finally indifferent to them, that future will be precarious.

Also, there are values that the new corporate—and government—construction of "organic" leaves out, values that once were part and parcel of the word but that have since been abandoned as impractical or unprofitable. I'm thinking of things like locally grown, like the humane treatment of animals, like the value of a shorter and more legible food chain, the preservation of family farms, even the promise of a countercuisine. To believe that the U.S.D.A. label on a product ensures any of these things is, as I discovered, naïve.

Yet if the word "organic" means anything, it means that all these things are ultimately connected: that the way we grow food is inseparable from the way we distribute food, which is inseparable from the way we eat food. The original premise, remember, the idea that got [Gene] Kahn (a small organic farmer) started in 1971, was that the whole industrial food system—and not just chemical agriculture—was in some fundamental way unsustainable. It's impossible to read the papers these days without beginning to wonder if this insight wasn't prophetic. I'm thinking, of course, of mad cow disease, of the 76 million cases of food poisoning every year (a rate higher than in 1948), of StarLink corn contamination, of the 20-year-old farm crisis, of hoof-and-mouth disease and groundwater pollution, not to mention industrial food's dubious "solutions" to these problems: genetic engineering and antibiotics and irradiation. Buying food labeled organic protects me from some of these things, but not all; industrial organic may well be necessary to fix this system, but it won't be sufficient.

Many of the values that industrial organic has jettisoned in recent years I find compelling, so I've started to shop with them in mind. I happen to believe, for example, that farms produce more than food; they also produce a kind of landscape, and if I buy my organic milk from halfway across the country, the farms I like to drive by every day will eventually grow nothing but raised ranch houses. So instead of long-haul ultrapasteurized milk from Horizon, I've started buying my milk, unpasteurized, from a dairy right here in town, Local Farm. Debra Tyler is organic, but she doesn't bother mentioning the fact on her label. Why? "My customers can see for themselves what I'm doing here," she says. What she's doing is milking nine pastured Jersey cows whose milk changes taste and hue with the seasons.

"Eat Your View!" is a save-the-farms bumper sticker you see in Europe now. I guess that's part of what I'm trying to do. But I'm also trying to get away from the transcontinental strawberry (5 calories of food energy, I've read, that it takes 435 calories of fossil-fuel energy to deliver to my door) and the organic "home meal replacement" sold in a package that will take 500 years to decompose. (Does that make me a True Natural?) So I've tracked down a local source for grass-fed beef (Chris Hopkins), eggs (Debra Tyler again) and maple syrup (Phil Hart), and on Saturday mornings I buy produce at a farmer's market in a neighboring town. I also have a line on a C.S.A. ("community supported agriculture"), or "subscription farm," a new marketing scheme from Europe that seems to be catching on here. You put up a couple of hundred dollars every spring and then receive a weekly box of produce through the summer. Not all of the farmers I'm buying from are certified organic. But I talk to them, see what they're up to, learn how they define the term. Sure, it's more trouble than buying organic food at the supermarket, but I'm resolved to do it anyway. Because organic is not the last word, and it's not just lunch.

Discussion questions

1. What does organic mean? Does it mean growing food without the use of chemicals? Is it about sustainability? Is there a difference between "big and little organic"? How organic are organic products if they have to be shipped from California to the East coast? In other words, is all organic food the same?
2. What does Pollan find down on the industrial organic farm? What surprised him? Is it, as Pollan says "too simple to say that smaller organic farms are automatically truer to the organic ideal?" But can you have "industrial" organic and it still be organic?
3. What does "beyond organic" mean? How is this a response to the industrial organic farm that Pollan visited?
4. In 2015, the Agriculture and Land-Based Training Association gave farmworkers small plots on which to grow organic crops. Do you think Pollan would applaud this move? However can a series of small plots meet the demand for organic products? Is it better to have organic products priced at a reasonable rate or to have fewer products grown in smaller scale, more "organic" settings?
5. Some writers have accused Michael Pollan and his followers of having a "labor problem." What do you think they mean by that? And how would these critics react, do you think, to this article that you read?

Document 14.4: Avi Solomon, "Working Undercover in a Slaughterhouse: An Interview with Timothy Pachirat," *Boing, Boing* (March 8, 2008)

As a result of falling prices, Americans spent 18 percent less on food during the 1990s than they did during the 1980s. Much of the drop in food prices stemmed from increased efficiencies and output in the food industry. Yet what did these cuts in costs for consumers and jumps in productivity mean to workers, to the people who made and processed our foods?

For five long and cold months in 2004, political scientist Timothy Pachirat worked inside a Nebraska slaughterhouse. What he found there was that the plant produced silence as much as it processed meat. The whole system of industrial evisceration depends, Pachirat came to believe, on making killing invisible, not just for consumers, but also for workers. In 2011, Avi Solomon interviewed Pachirat about his book, Every Twelve Seconds: Industrial Slaughter and the Politics of Sight *(New Haven: Yale University Press, 2013), that chronicled his time spent working undercover in a slaughterhouse.*

Avi Solomon: Tell us a bit about yourself.

Timothy Pachirat: I was born and raised in northeastern Thailand in a Thai-American family. In high school, I spent a year in the high desert of rural Oregon as an exchange student where I worked on a cattle ranch, farmed alfalfa, and—improbably—became a running back for the school's football team. Since then, I've lived in Illinois, Indiana, Connecticut, Alabama, Nebraska, and New York City working as a builder of housing trusses, a pizza deliverer, a behavioral therapist for children diagnosed with autism, a stay-at-home-dad, a graduate student, a slaughterhouse worker, and, for the past four years, as an assistant professor of politics at The New School for Social Research.

Avi: Why did you choose to go undercover in a slaughterhouse?

Timothy: I wanted to understand how massive processes of violence become normalized in modern society, and I wanted to do so from the perspective of those who work in the slaughterhouse. My hunch was that close attention to how the work of industrialized killing is performed might illuminate not only how the realities of industrialized animal slaughter are made tolerable, but also the way distance and concealment operate in analogous social processes: war executed by volunteer armies; the subcontracting of organized terror to mercenaries; and the violence underlying the manufacturing of thousands of items and components we make contact with in our everyday lives. Like its more self-evidently political analogues—the prison, the hospital, the nursing home, the psychiatric ward, the refugee camp, the detention center, the interrogation room, and the execution chamber—the modern industrialized slaughterhouse is a "zone of confinement," a "segregated and isolated territory," in the words of sociologist Zygmunt Bauman, "Invisible," and "on the whole inaccessible to ordinary members of society." I worked as an entry level worker on the kill floor of an industrialized slaughterhouse in order to understand, from the perspective of those who participate directly in them, how these zones of confinement operate.

Avi: Can you tell us about the slaughterhouse you worked in?

Timothy: Because my goal was not to write an exposé of a particular place, I do not name the Nebraska slaughterhouse I worked in or use real names for the people I encountered there. The slaughterhouse employs nearly eight hundred nonunionized workers, the vast majority being immigrants from Central and South America, Southeast Asia, and East Africa. It generates over $820 million annually in sales to distributors within and outside of the United States and ranks among the top handful of cattle-slaughtering facilities worldwide in volume of production. The line speed on the kill floor is approximately three hundred cattle per hour, or one every twelve seconds. In a typical workday, between twenty-two and twenty-five hundred cattle are killed there, adding up to well over ten thousand cattle killed per five-day week, or more than half a million cattle slaughtered each year.

Avi: What jobs did you end up doing there?

Timothy: My first job was as a liver hanger in the cooler. For ten hours each day, I stood in 34 degrees cold and took freshly eviscerated livers off an overhead line and hung them on carts to be chilled for packing. I was then moved to the chutes, where I drove live cattle into the knocking box where they were shot in the head with a captive bolt gun. Finally, I was promoted to a quality-control position, a job that gave me access to every part of the kill floor and made me an intermediary between the USDA federal meat inspectors and the kill floor managers.

Avi: What are the main strategies used to hide violence in the slaughterhouse?

Timothy: The first and most obvious is that the violence of industrialized killing is hidden from society at large. Over 8.5 billion animals are killed for food each year in the United States, but this killing is carried out by a small minority of largely immigrant workers who labor behind opaque walls, most often in rural, isolated locations far from urban centers. Furthermore, laws supported by the meat and livestock industries are currently under consideration in six states that criminalize the publicizing of what happens in slaughterhouses and other animal facilities without the consent of the slaughterhouse owners. Iowa's House of Representatives, for example, forwarded a bill to the Iowa Senate last year that would make it a felony to distribute or possess video, audio, or printed material gleaned through unauthorized access to a slaughterhouse or animal facility.

Second, the slaughterhouse as a whole is divided into compartmentalized departments. The front office is isolated from the fabrication department, which is in turn isolated from the cooler, which is in turn isolated from the kill floor. It is entirely possible to spend years working in the front office, fabrication department, or cooler of an industrialized slaughterhouse that slaughters over half a million cattle per year without ever once encountering a live animal much less witnessing one being killed.

But third and most importantly, the work of killing is hidden even at the site where one might expect it to be most visible: the kill floor itself. The complex division of labor and space acts to compartmentalize and neutralize the experience of "killing work" for each of the workers on the kill floor. I've already mentioned the division of labor in which only a handful of workers, out of a total workforce of over 800, are directly involved in or even have a line of sight to the killing of the animals. To give another example, the kill floor is divided spatially into a clean side and a dirty side. The dirty side refers to everything that happens while the cattle's hides are still on them and the clean side to everything that happens after the hides have been removed. Workers from the clean side are segregated from workers on the dirty side, even during food and bathroom breaks. This translates into a kind of phenomenological compartmentalization where the minority of workers who deal with the "animals" while their hides are still on are kept separate from the majority of workers who deal with the *carcasses* after their hides have been removed. In this way, the violence of turning animal into carcass is quarantined amongst the dirty side workers, and even there it is further confined by finer divisions of labor and space.

In addition to spatial and labor divisions, the use of language is another way of concealing the violence of killing. From the moment cattle are unloaded from transport trucks into the slaughterhouse's holding pens, managers and kill floor supervisors refer to them as "beef." Although they are living, breathing, sentient beings, they have already linguistically been reduced to inanimate flesh, to use-objects. Similarly, there is a slew of acronyms and technical language around the food safety inspection system that reduces the quality control worker's job to a bureaucratic, technical regime rather than one that is forced to confront the truly massive taking of life. Although the quality control worker has full physical movement throughout the kill floor and sees every aspect of the killing, her interpretive frame is interdicted by the technical and bureaucratic requirements of the job. Temperatures, hydraulic pressures, acid concentrations, bacterial counts, and knife sanitization become the primary focus, rather than the massive, unceasing taking of life.

Avi: Is anyone working in the slaughterhouse consciously aware of these strategies?

Timothy: I don't think anyone sat down and said, "Let's design a slaughtering process that creates a maximal distance between each worker and the violence of killing and allows each worker to contribute without having to confront the violence directly." The division between clean and dirty side on the kill floor mentioned earlier, for example, is overtly motivated by a food-safety logic. The cattle come into the slaughterhouse caked in feces and vomit, and from a food-safety perspective the challenge is to remove the hides while minimizing the transfer of these contaminants to the flesh underneath. But what's fascinating is that the effects of these organizations of space and labor are not just increased "efficiency" or increased "food-safety" but also the distancing and concealment of violent processes even from those participating directly in them. From a political point of view, from a point of view interested in understanding how relations of violent domination and exploitation are reproduced, it is precisely these effects that matter most.

Avi: Did the death factories of Auschwitz have the same mechanisms at work?

Timothy: I recommend Zygmunt Bauman's superb book, Modernity and the Holocaust, for those interested in how parallel mechanisms of distance, concealment, and surveillance worked to neutralize the killing work taking place in Auschwitz and other concentration camps. The lesson here, of course, is not that slaughterhouses and genocides are morally or functionally equivalent, but rather that large-scale, routinized, and systematic violence is entirely consistent with the kinds of bureaucratic structures and mechanisms we typically associate with modern civilization. The French sociologist Norbert Elias argues—convincingly, in my view—that it is the "concealment" and "displacement" of violence, rather than its elimination or reduction, that is the hallmark of civilization. In my view, the contemporary industrialized slaughterhouse provides an exemplary case that highlights some of the most salient features of this phenomenon.

Avi: Violence is found hidden in even the most "normal" of lives. How can we spot this pervading presence in our daily life?

Timothy: We—the "we" of the relatively affluent and powerful--live in a time and a spatial order in which the "normalcy" of our lives requires our active complicity in forms of exploitation and violence that we would decry and disavow were the physical, social, and linguistic distances that separate us from them ever to be collapsed. This is true of the brutal and entirely unnecessary confinement and killing of billions of animals each year for food, of the exploitation and suffering of workers in Shenzhen, China who produce our iPads and cell phones, of the "enhanced interrogation techniques" deployed in the name of our security, and of the "collateral damage" created by the unmanned-aerial-vehicles that our taxes fund. Our complicity lies not in a direct infliction of violence but rather in our tacit agreement to look away and not to ask some very, very simple questions: Where does this meat come from and how did it get here? Who assembled the latest gadget that just arrived in the mail? What does it mean to create categories of torturable human beings? The mechanisms of distancing and concealment inherent in our divisions of space and labor and in our unthinking use of euphemistic language make it seductively easy to avoid pursuing the complex answers to these simple questions with any sort of determination.

Months after I left the slaughterhouse, I got in an argument with a brilliant friend over who was more morally responsible for the killing of the animals: those who ate meat or the 121 workers who did the killing. She maintained, passionately and with conviction, that the people who did the killing were more responsible because they were the ones performing the physical actions that took the animal's lives. Meat eaters, she claimed, were only indirectly responsible. At the time, I took the opposite position, holding that those who benefited at a distance, delegating this terrible work to others while disclaiming responsibility for it, bore more moral responsibility, particularly in contexts like the slaughterhouse, where those with the fewest opportunities in society performed the dirty work.

I am now more inclined to think that it is the preoccupation with moral responsibility itself that serves as a deflection. In the words of philosopher John Lachs, "The responsibility for an act can be passed on, but its experience cannot." I'm keenly interested in asking what it might mean for those who benefit from physically and morally dirty work not only to assume some share of responsibility for it but also to directly experience it. What might it mean, in other words, to collapse some of the mechanisms of physical, social, and linguistic distances that separate our "normal" lives from the violence and exploitation required to sustain and reproduce them?

Discussion questions

1. Why is silence so important to manufacturing of inexpensive industrial meat?
2. What was the job like for Pachirat? How did it affect him physically and mentally? (Remember Pachirat was a temporary worker. He is an academic doing on-site research. How did that shape his experiences?)
3. How are workers hidden from the violence of industrial killing? How is the public hidden? How do the laws help to keep things hidden?

4. What do you think about Pachirat's comparison of the Holocaust and industrial meat?
5. Think about the conversation Pachirat has with his "brilliant friend." Who is responsible for the killing of animals? The workers? The owners of the plant? Meat eaters? How much is each of these groups to blame?

Document 14.5: Statement of Sarah C. White, Member, United Food and Commercial Workers Local 1529 (October, 1990)

Like Timothy Pachirat, (see Document 14.4) Sarah White worked behind the scenes making the cheap foods that filled the nation's supermarkets and dinner plates. White was a catfish processing worker in a small town in Mississippi. Like the poultry and pork industries, catfish became a more consolidated and automated industry in the 1980s. As a result, consumers paid less to eat catfish. Key to the equation of cheap food was, of course, cheap, nearly invisible labor.

As an African American woman and single mom with two kids, White, as she explains, got paid just above minimum wage. But by the 1980s, she had had enough of the harsh conditions at the catfish plant where she worked. Looking to get a better deal, she joined a union and demanded some changes to her job.

In the document below, White talks about why she joined the union, but also about the conditions that she and her coworkers faced producing inexpensive foods.

I am Sarah C. White. I have been employed at the Delta Pride catfish processing plant in Indianola, Mississippi for seven and one-half years. I have a nine-year-old son and a six-year-old daughter that I support by myself.

Currently, I work as a "group leader," responsible for making sure that workers are on the processing line at the correct time with the proper supplies. Previously, I worked for five years as a skinner, which involved taking the skin off the fish. As a group leader, I am one of the higher paid workers at the plant. I earn $4.80 per hour. When I first started working at Delta Pride, my pay was $3.45 per hour.

I was involved in efforts to bring the union into the plant, beginning in 1985, along with my friend Mary Young, who is now a representative for the local union. The majority of workers at the plant are women. We had taken a lot of abuse, and Delta Pride was a rough place to work. People got fired over and over. Supervisors would talk to us any way they wanted. When Mary got a union authorization card in the mail, we talked about it and agreed that the way we were being treated didn't make any sense. We decided that we both would sign cards and back each other.

A month later, in December 1985, a union representative arrived and met us. He urged us to talk with our coworkers about signing authorization cards. Beginning in January, we got to work, getting people to sign them in bathroom, and in cars. It was cold. We had the election in October 1986, and we won.

We needed a union because managers didn't treat us like adults. They would talk with us abusively, and because the bathroom stalls didn't have doors, we didn't have any privacy. When we needed to take out babies to the doctor, they would say, "No, you can't go because you have to work." They weren't paying us enough to go to a regular doctor, so we had to go where we could get discounts or to a free clinic.

Since we've had a union, things have changed a lot, but they could be better. The first contract gave us job security, which was one of the main things we wanted. But they're still not paying us enough. We have to dress our babies, pay bills, and have enough money to plan ahead. The wages really are a problem.

Discussion questions

1. This document can be read a number of ways. Think about who White is and who she is talking to in 1990. Is this a civil rights issue or a labor issue?
2. What is significant about the geography of White's life? Where is she from? (How is this similar to the geography of the world that Timothy Pachirat worked in?) Is there a geography to cheap food? In other words, is it produced in some places and not others?
3. The document can also be read as social history. Using the details from White's testimony, describe the conditions workers in the catfish industry faced.
4. Why did they have to sign union cards in the bathroom?
5. What are the demands being made by White and other union members? Higher pay is one of them. What else?
6. What are the costs of cheap food?

Document 14.6: Excerpt from Sarah Wu, also known as "Mrs. Q.," *Fed Up with Lunch: How One Anonymous Teacher Revealed the Truth about School Lunches—And How We Can Change Them!* (2011)[2]

> *Sarah Wu taught in a Chicago elementary school. One day, she didn't bring her lunch and she went to the school cafeteria. She couldn't quite believe what ended up on her plate. In order to better understand what was being*

[2] From *Fed Up with Lunch* © 2011 by Sarah Wu. Used with permission of Chronicle Books LLC, San Francisco. Visit ChronicleBooks.com

served to her students, she went to the cafeteria every day for a year and took pictures. She ate pizza, salty chips, and dishes of brown mystery meats. Over the course of a year, she consumed countless chicken nuggets. By her guess, the nuggets were only 50 percent chicken. The rest was water, salt, dextrose, partially hydrogenated soybean oil, ammonium bicarbonate, monocalcium phosphate, and dimethylpolysiloxane added as an antifoaming agent. The fruit juice had little fruit and lots of sugar, and the vegetables, when there were vegetables, were limp, pale, and overcooked.

The federally funded School Lunch program had been started, Wu discovered, in the 1940s to offer kids a nutritious and hot meal, one that was healthier, it was hoped, than what they typically got at home. But budget cuts and neglect turned school lunches into part of the growing problem of weight gain and unhealthiness, especially for the poorest and youngest Americans.

Obviously, the fatty, salty, and sugary food served in the cafeteria contributed to problems of childhood obesity. But Sarah Wu noticed some other problems at her school and other schools across the country. What were they?

Baby Carrots Can't Go Outside to Play

> After dinner sit a while, and after supper walk a mile
> – English saying

At the end of each weekday, after most of the kids have headed home, teachers often remain at work, while the janitors start sweeping and cleaning. It's always seemed to me that those big open hallways just ache for activity, especially as the weather grows mild and summer approaches. Sometimes, the temptation of those expansive halls is just too much for me and I can't help skipping all the way down the corridor, in big, broad strides. But our kids don't have that option when school is in session. In fact, one day while I was retrieving something from the office, I heard a mom complaining to the assistant principle.

"Why do the kids burst out of school running at the end of the day? Every day my child almost gets pushed aside because all the kids want to get out so fast."

I wanted to jump in and explain, "Ma'am, your child and all the rest of the kids don't get recess. Not even five minutes to run and engage in free play. When you see those kids, so anxious, frantic even, to get outside, it's because their little bodies cannot stand one more minute pent up inside the school."

You read that right: At my school, there is no recess, which is increasingly true of many schools around the country. The only exception to this rule at my school is that preschoolers go out to play for twenty minutes, if the weather is nice. How pervasive is this trend? The journal *Pediatrics*, in a 2009 study, found that 30 percent of third graders, for example, have no recess at their schools.

In the age of growing concerns over childhood obesity, it seems illogical to eliminate recess. But school districts are under pressure to fill students' short days with testing and academics and, taken at face value, recess looks like open space in the day. Practical considerations about staffing the supervision of recess and any liability concerns over playground accidents that might occur also have influenced those decisions. Additionally, with increased attention on schoolyard bullying, the elimination of recess curtails those opportunities. However, by cutting recess, many opportunities to increase positive social skills are missed.

According to the Clearinghouse on Early Education and Parenting, in 2001 nearly 40 percent of the nation's school districts considered modifying or deleting recess, and many new schools in Chicago, Atlanta, and New York are building new schools without playgrounds. A school without a playground sends a message that play is not valuable, which runs counter to my training in graduate school, where I learned that most early learning happens through play. I have found that many social skills cannot be taught but instead are learned through interpersonal interaction. And even a school without a playground can still let kids run around on concrete. Recess can happen anywhere.

Through my blog, I've learned firsthand from parents, teachers, and administrators that even when recess is on the regular schedule, it is the first thing to get bumped in favor of things like tests and other school activities. So another message our students learn is that free, fun exercise apparently has no place at school. But the reality is that kids need spontaneous, free time that's apart from a more structured gym class. Many studies have shown that physical activity actually boosts classroom performance.

Are we going to treat our kids like little adults, or let our kids be kids? Kids need recess, and they also need more than twenty minutes for lunch if we want them to return to class refreshed and ready to learn. I heard from another teacher that there used to be recess at my school. My ears perked up. I asked around and found out that recess was eliminated about fifteen years ago when the school district "closed campus." I didn't know what that meant, but I kept asking the few teachers I knew who had been working at my school for more than twenty years. Students used to have a morning recess, a forty-five-minute lunch period, and a short afternoon recess. When the school district found that at some schools a few kids left school grounds and caused trouble, they "closed the campus," thereby abolishing recess.

So administrators and teachers cut recess from the schedule for all schools, substituting a twenty-minute lunch period and shortening the school day. Now Chicago Public Schools has one of the shortest school days in the country, and the kids are kept inside all day long.

To help kids fill their stomachs in the short twenty minutes they are allotted to purchase and eat their lunches, schools serve foods that are supposed to be "kid-friendly"—foods that fill them up fast, such as Tater Tots. But in matters of food, as in all important matters, shouldn't schools be helping to *guide* children about healthy choices, not catering to assumptions about what children will or won't eat? One of the special things about childhood is that it's a period of life when we are constantly developing, learning at every moment. Lunchtime is at least as important as any other time in the school day. How much time do *you* need to eat lunch? Personally it takes me at least thirty minutes to eat at an unhurried pace.

I love food. When I used to pack lunch for myself before I started with the Fed Up With Lunch project, I tried to eat at a more leisurely pace. I might get through my sandwich and an apple, then eat my yogurt at the end of the day as a snack. Other times instead of a sandwich, I would bring leftovers from dinner the night before, including pasta or rice-based dishes, which I carried in a small plastic container. In 2010, when I started buying school lunch, I rarely had a chance to finish what was on my tray, let alone to enjoy the rare examples of good, healthful food that were served every now and then. Twenty minutes to eat just wasn't enough time.

Let's take the example of a student I used to work with named Jennifer. She has short brown hair and bright brown eyes, and she lives with her parents and a sibling in an apartment not far from school. She loves listening to Justin Bieber and wears glasses, which really bothers her because she so wants to be "cool." Jennifer receives free lunch and eats the same lunches I used to eat during the course of the twenty-minute lunch period. Unfortunately, unlike mine, Jennifer's twenty minutes include lining-up time, which means that, depending on how fast (or not) the line is moving, she is left with a grand total of nine to thirteen minutes to eat, which obviously isn't enough.

Let's say Jennifer has only ten minutes left to eat lunch. This means she faces a choice: Since she can't eat everything on her tray in just ten minutes, what will she choose to eat? The nuggets and Tater Tots are quick and filling, so it's a no-brainer that she would select these, over, say, a bag of baby carrots or an apple. If there's a bag of chips on her tray, she might munch on these while chatting with friends. My point is, in the short times kids have to eat, they aren't going to have time to eat a balanced meal, even if that's what's being offered. I can't tell you how many times I've seen the students at my school drink their chocolate milk, gobble down a bag of chips or a cookie, and then throw out everything else on their trays. How can Jennifer or any other young kid be expected to be alert and ready to learn when their bodies aren't running on the proper fuel? And what does all of this teach kids about the value of eating healthful meals?

Schools are tasked with teaching subjects like reading, writing, mathematics, science, and history. You may think that just because it's not on the curriculum, students are not learning about nutrition at school, but you are mistaken. What's being served in the cafeteria does send a message about nutrition, just not the right one. Further, the lesson being offered via what's on those trays is not one that the Department of Education takes responsibility for. Rather, it's the USDA—the U.S. Department of Agriculture—that decides what goes on the menu.

Offering students a preponderance of processed foods, and little time in which to eat it, is a huge missed opportunity. My heart breaks every day when I think about how I've learned that other countries with equal or far fewer resources are able to provide their students with real food, cooked on-site. Guest bloggers from Japan, Korea, Croatia, and France have contributed lengthy posts with photos of the school lunches their students eat every day. The lunches contain fresh ingredients that are not processed—and the kids are eating foods from their respective food cultures: whitefish, sushi, and rice dumplings in Japan; seaweed and tofu soup with kimchi in Korea; barley soup and bacon pâté in Croatia; and salad, baguette with butter, cordon bleu, and crème caramel for dessert in France. It is evident that each of these countries has robust food cultures, which makes me wonder about my own food culture. Moreover, I have found out that in some countries, students even participate in the making of their school food. That is happening here and there in the United States, in some instances inspired by chef Alice Waters and her Edible Schoolyard program, but it is far from the norm.

Going back to my student, Jennifer, I didn't mention that she is obese. Her mother works at a big fast-food chain, so she eats a lot of fast food for breakfast and dinner. What she's getting at school isn't any better, which makes me worry that Jennifer's long-term health doesn't stand a chance. What lessons about nutrition and health is Jennifer learning from what's being served in the cafeteria? She's learning that fast food is endorsed by school, and that it doesn't matter how food tastes, since you can't taste food in a mere ten minutes. Finally, she is learning that scheduling time for a healthful lunch and for daily physical movement is not important to her school—so why should it be important to her?

At my school, like many schools, kids are expected to sit still and be quiet at lunch. And it's not the lunch ladies who are telling the kids to be quiet, but the teachers and administrators doing lunch duty. It's common to see teachers and administrators yelling at the kids to sit down and be quiet during lunchtime, which I understand, but makes me wonder: If kids don't have recess, and they only get ten minutes to scarf down their lunches, when, exactly are they supposed to get their wiggles out?

Since starting the Fed Up With Lunch project, I've become much more cognizant of the need for children to move. My training at Northwestern University taught me that speech is a fine-motor movement. Think about how fast your tongue and lips have to move and with what precision they need to execute the correct speech sounds. For most kids, it's necessary to wake up the motor system prior to sitting down and practicing fine-motor movements. I'll often start off a speech class by tossing a soft ball around, doing jumping jacks, or having kids form a circle, grabbing onto the edge of a small parachute and moving it up and down. Large-motor games are fantastic instructional tools via which to teach kids how to follow directions, and how to take turns. School administrators and teachers think a lot about reading and math scores, but maybe we don't think enough about things like visual/motor integration skills. I notice that when my students get warmed up, they are almost always more willing to participate in speech therapy activities; when they actively participate, it makes sense they will be more successful. I love seeing how well they focus after having a movement break.

In a 2005 study, *The Journal of School Health* noted that physical movement increases students' abilities to perform in the classroom. It was during my training as a speech therapist that I first learned this principle, but my later experience with students, not to mention common sense, reinforced the idea that increased blood flow to the brain helps a person focus and think more clearly.

Rather than complaining when we see kids letting off steam by running around and otherwise acting like kids, we should think about the fact that without a break during the day for physical activity, and without a nutritious lunch to power them for the rest of the school day, we can't expect them to perform and behave in a productive manner.

All kids, including my son, need time outside to run around and explore. At school, the only chance they have to do this is during gym class. Where I teach, this only happens once a week, which is just not enough to satisfy our kids' desires to move. One hour of gym just doesn't do it!

And if you won't take my word for it, what about the First Lady's?

Parents can use the Let's Move! Web site as a way to hold their school's feet to the fire. The site is filled with great information about the links between regular physical activity (including outdoor time) and the physical and mental health of kids. It is recommended that kids get a full sixty minutes of vigorous physical activity every single day, and via the Healthier US School Challenge, schools that create healthier school environments, promoting better nutrition and increased levels of physical activity, are recognized for their efforts. Now that sounds like something parents can take up and help their local schools to achieve!

At my school, kids look forward to gym class. I'd love to see them get gym twice a week, but I think that would require an additional teaching position and that would be expensive. Adding recess back to the schedule makes sense to me because even though supervision would be necessary (which any school staff member would be qualified to do), I don't believe that schools would need to hire additional personnel. Since research points to kids needing recess before lunch instead of after, I want my students to get a daily recess starting mid-morning or immediately before lunch. A twenty- to thirty-minute unstructured recess would be ideal. In some cases, depending on the size of the school, two ten- or fifteen-minute recesses might better suit the students, with a morning recess of twenty minutes and an afternoon recess of ten minutes.

Discussion questions

1. Why is the lack of recess a problem for school kids? How does recess enhance a school's learning environment and eating environment? How does it help kids eat better and be healthier?
2. What does the lack of recess and the dearth of playground space say to kids?
3. Why did schools stop providing recess? Is this related to food choices in the cafeteria?
4. Sarah Wu also talks about the time provided for lunch. What problems does she associate with fast lunches? How does this contribute to unhealthiness? Why was the hour set aside for lunch eventually cut in half?
5. Do you agree with Sarah Wu? Is recess essential? If you were a school administrator and you had to decide between lunch and more time to learn a language or study math, what would you decide? How would you justify your decision to parents and teachers?

Document 14.7: Excerpt from "Fat Liberation Manifesto" (1973)

As early as the 1970s, public health officials in the United States worried out loud about the sharp jump in obesity across the country. They talked about weight gain not just as a personal wellness issue but as a public concern. Overweight individuals, they insisted, threatened the nation. They were a drain on productivity, public resources, and even the nation's military strength. As these officials looked for answers, they drew parallels to smoking.

After definitively discovering a link between smoking and cancer in the 1950s, Dr. Alton Ochsner of Tulane University declared an all-out war on smoking. In his fight, he targeted smokers. In his popular book, Smoking: Your Choice Between Life and Death, *he tagged smokers as "selfish," calling smoking the "most selfish habit anyone can have." While Ochsner pushed for government warnings on cigarette packs and talked of lawsuits against the nation's tobacco giants, he stressed the individual act of quitting as the first line of defense in the national battle against smoking. If smokers stopped smoking the problem would go away. He recognized it wouldn't be easy, but he insisted that if smokers exercised greater self-control and made the right choices for themselves, for those around them, and for the entire nation, the problem would disappear.*

As more and more experts and policymakers drew a parallel between smoking and overeating, personal choice started to frame the discussion around obesity. Applying Ochsner's approach to public health, experts began to link the problem of weight gain to poor eating decisions. Americans grew heavier, they said, because they were too lazy to cook at home. They chose chips over vegetables. They ate out too much, and when they did, they too often went to fast-food restaurants. And on top of all of that, they didn't exercise enough.

By presenting the problem this way, as a matter of choice, public health officials suggested that there were good citizens and bad citizens, good bodies and bad bodies. Thin was good, and heavy was bad. Further, they suggested that heavy people, not public policy, was the problem. In order to stop being the problem, they had to shed weight.

Written in 1973, the Fat Liberation Manifesto, *tries to push back against the cult of thinness, the notion of bad choices, and what we might call today "fat-shaming."*

---

1. WE believe that fat people are fully entitled to human respect and recognition.
2. WE are angry at mistreatment by commercial and sexist interests. These have exploited our bodies as objects of ridicule, thereby creating an immensely profitable market selling the false promise of avoidance of, or relief from, that ridicule.
3. WE see our struggle as allied with the struggles of other oppressed groups against classism, racism, sexism, ageism, financial exploitation, imperialism and the like.

4. WE demand equal rights for fat people in all aspects of life, as promised in the Constitution of the United States. We demand equal access to goods and services in the public domain, and an end to discrimination against us in the areas of employment, education, public facilities and health services.

5. WE single out as our special enemies the so-called "reducing" industries. These include diet clubs, reducing salons, fat farms, diet doctors, diet books, diet foods and food supplements, surgical procedures, appetite suppressants, drugs and gadgetry such as wraps and "reducing machines".

WE demand that they take responsibility for their false claims, acknowledge that their products are harmful to the public health, and publish long-term studies proving any statistical efficacy of their products. We make this demand knowing that over 99% of all weight loss programs, when evaluated over a five-year period, fail utterly, and also knowing the extreme proven harmfulness of frequent large changes in weight.

6. WE repudiate the mystified "science" which falsely claims that we are unfit. It has both caused and upheld discrimination against us, in collusion with the financial interests of insurance companies, the fashion and garment industries, reducing industries, the food and drug industries, and the medical and psychiatric establishment.

7. WE refuse to be subjugated to the interests of our enemies. We fully intend to reclaim power over our bodies and our lives. We commit ourselves to pursue these goals together.

FAT PEOPLE OF THE WORLD, UNITE! YOU HAVE
NOTHING TO LOSE ....

By Judy Freespirit and Aldebaran
November, 1973

Discussion questions

1. According to the document, how are "fat people" mistreated by commercial interests? What industries benefit from the ridicule of heavier individuals?
2. How does the "reducing" industry benefit from socially constructed attitudes about "fatness?" Do they create, or least foster, these images?
3. What do the authors of this document mean by "mystified 'science'"?

4. By 2010, a new academic and activist field of research called "fat studies" had emerged. According to one practitioner, this is "a field of scholarship that critically examines societal attitudes about body weight and appearance, and that advocates equality for all people with respect to body size. Fat studies seeks to remove the negative associations that society has about fat and the fat body. It regards weight, like height, as a human characteristic." How is this manifesto a kind of first statement of fat studies?

5. What roles do families, the media, advertisers, toy companies, and others play in creating ideal notions of bodies? How can these notions be resisted? Should they be resisted? Is weight-gain a personal matter or a public matter?

Chapter 15   Foodies and the Complexities of Consumption

Document 15.1: Menu from Spago Restaurant (1987)

The classically trained, Austrian-born chef, Wolfgang Puck, first opened Spago on the famed Sunset Strip in West Hollywood, California in 1982. The restaurant made Puck a culinary star, a celebrity chef before people even used the term. Over the next 25 years, Puck would launch a hundred or more other restaurants around the world, write a stack of best-selling cookbooks, and develop a line of cookware sold on late night television. But it all started with the food at Spago; Puck's innovative twist on what he called "California cuisine."

In 2011, Jonathan Gold, the Los Angeles Weekly's *well-regarded restaurant critic, wrote, "The original Spago on Sunset was to New American cooking what* Meet the Beatles *was to rock and roll: it changed the rules." Twenty years earlier, a writer for the* Los Angeles Times *went to check out what all the fuss was about at the original Spago. What struck him even more than the casual interior and lack of white table clothes was what else wasn't there. "Not one French word on the menu," he wrote. Take some time to study the menu below. Remember the timing, the 1980s. This was during the Reagan-era boom, when upscale restaurants in the United States typically featured European cuisine or steaks and seafood. What, then, made Puck's eatery the food equivalent to* Meet the Beatles? *What did he innovate? What is new and novel here?*

Food and Eating in America: A Documentary Reader, First Edition.
Edited by James C. Giesen and Bryant Simon.
© 2018 John Wiley & Sons, Inc. Published 2018 by John Wiley & Sons, Inc.

LISA STALVEY—CHEF

APPETIZERS

Marinated fresh tuna with avocado, kaiware and sweet onions	9.50
Fresh asparagus with watercress vinaigrette	8.50
Salad of field greens with goat cheese sauteed in olive oil	8.50
Cream of wild mushrooms	6.00
Sauteed Pacific oysters with spicy salsa	8.50
Marinated salmon with dill, golden caviar and toasted brioche	11.00
Grilled baby chicken salad with red leaves, mache, walnut oil and aged Italian vinegar	9.50
Sauteed foie gras with arugula and chanterelle mushrooms	12.50
Cold lobster salad with sour cream, tarragon and mint sauce	12.50
Spicy rare beef salad with ginger mandarin vinaigrette	9.50

PASTAS

Lobster ravioli with chardonnay dill butter and julienne of vegetables	11.00
Angel hair noodles with goat cheese, broccoli and basil	9.50
Pink & black peppercorn fettuccini with smoked duck breast	10.50
Wild mushroom ravioli with sauteed chanterelles and cabernet butter	9.50
Black angel hair pasta with shrimp, lobster butter and garden vegetables	11.00

PIZZAS

Pizza with prosciutto, goat cheese, sweet peppers, double blanched garlic and red onions	11.00
Pizza with smoked shrimps, tomatoes, artichokes, basil and garlic	12.00
Pizza with duck sausage, tomatoes, mozzarella, fresh oregano and garlic	10.50
Pizza with artichokes, wild mushrooms, leeks, sweet onions, eggplant and fresh herbs	9.50
Pizza with lamb sausage, coriander, wild mushrooms, garlic and zucchini	9.50
Calzone with goat cheese, wild mushrooms, scallions and sun dried tomatoes	11.00

ENTREES

Grilled tuna with tomato basil vinaigrette	17.50
Grilled free-range chicken with garlic and fresh herbs	16.50
Composition of grilled fish with two vinaigrettes	18.50
Crispy sauteed sweetbreads with turnip greens and pancetta	17.50
Grilled John Dory with eggplant caviar and ginger vinaigrette	17.50
Grilled Alaskan salmon with tomatillos, jalapeno and garlic cream	17.50
Roasted Sonoma baby lamb with lime pesto butter	18.50
Grilled squab with foie gras and vinegar butter	17.50
Roasted Chinese duck with honey and mustard sauce	17.50
Grilled calf's liver with red onion marmalade and mustard seeds	16.50
Grilled veal chop with balsamic vinegar, cilantro butter and roasted radicchio	19.50
Whole fish of the day	

DESSERTS

Marjolaine with raspberry sauce	5.50
Creme brulee with fresh berries	5.50
Apple pie with caramel ice cream	5.50
Pecan pie with banana ice cream	5.50
Parfait of three chocolates and bitter chocolate sauce	5.50
Assortment of homemade ice cream and cookies	5.50
Warm puff pastry with raspberries and caramel sauce	5.50

BEVERAGES

Coffee	2.00
Tea	2.00
Fresh mint tea	2.00
Espresso	2.00

Split 2.00

BARBARA LAZAROFF—Interior design and decor, kitchen and lighting design

Discussion questions

1. Why is it significant that there were no French words on the Spago menu?
2. What sorts of ingredients did Puck utilize to create his dishes? What culinary trends was he anticipating?
3. *The New York Times* said of Puck's menu and of the California cuisine he helped to create that it "unconsciously reflect[ed] broader socialized changes that were taking place." What are these changes? Think not just about the changing demographics of America, though they are certainly important, but also about California and ideas about established traditions as well as new ideas about health and fitness.
4. In 1985, the famed restaurant critic, Ruth Reichl, talked about the "Spagoization" of American restaurants. What do you think she meant by this term? Can you think of other dishes and foods that reflected the changes introduced by Spago?

Document 15.2: Andrew Chan, "'La Grande Bouffe': Cooking Shows as Pornography," *Gastronomica* (Fall, 2003)[1]

Just pick up the remote control to your television and start surfing through the channels. It won't take long before you come across a show with celebrity chefs racing around studio kitchens trying to make lavish meals or outrageous desserts in 30-minutes or less. Other shows walk the audience through intricate recipes of Italian and Indian dishes. Yet underlining this wave of cooking show is a curious contemporary paradox. Cable cooking programs have proliferated at the very moment that Americans cook less at home and eat out more often. In the 1950s, homemakers—and that meant almost exclusively women—spent on average 20 hours a week cooking. By 2010, that number had dropped to 5.5 hours a week. In 1970, Americans ate about 15 percent of their meals out. Today that number has almost doubled.

So what's going on here? Why are Americans watching people cook, while they increasingly don't cook themselves, at least not very much? These are the questions that Andrew Chan is trying to answer in his article.

TV cooking shows today are, in a word, pornography.

As in the contemporary pornographic film industry, the modern TV cooking programs appeal to our hidden or perverse side. They seduce us to desire the virtual, while complicating our relationship to what is real (or desired). Media outlets such as the Food Network cable TV channel provide special insight into the perversity of contemporary American culture, yet the genealogy reaches further back, as brilliantly visualized in Marco Fereri's 1973 film *La Grande Bouffe*, in which four men eat, screw, and fart themselves to death.

Today's TV cooking shows arouse our senses not only through the material shown but in the way it is presented. Food preparation is a form of foreplay in which the ritual of cooking is announced with sensory cues: the sizzle of oil in the frying pan, pots bubbling away, the crescendo of chopping, dicing, and slicing. The chef starts building the viewer's expectations and hunger by his cleaving, stirring, and whisking—every gesture, raised eyebrow, and licked lip a sign of what is to come.

The idealization of cooking is subtly evident in the surreally colored foods, anatomically perfect chickens, and super-sized "vertical" displays of cooking shows, comparable to the cosmetically altered, human sex-toy actors in porno films. Contemporary TV cooking shows create a gap that separates the viewer from the reality of actual cookery. This gap is evident in the setting itself, an environment far removed from the real goings-on of either a professional restaurant kitchen or the everyday domestic kitchen of the viewers. In the TV program's fantasy kitchen there is copious space and ventilation; there also are no dishes to wash, no mounds of trash to throw out, and no impatient waiters checking on orders. Everything has been carefully planned and prepared beforehand to appear spontaneous and effortless on camera. Everything has also been meticulously edited and orchestrated, often to the strains of classical music, so that the master chef and his happy minions can sauté and garnish to the melodies of Vivaldi or Mozart.

Yet these programs only tease us, since the complete steps involved in cooking have been omitted, just as the resulting by-product is never consummated. We are always left wanting more, so there is a reason to tune in again.

If television audiences really knew that went on in kitchens during preparation of food, would they be so receptive to the allure of the visual representation of a recipe? If they saw the pig being slaughtered and butchered prior to making the stuffed pork loins, or the fresh lobsters being drawn and quartered, then—claws still twitching—boiled alive, would they be as enticed by the televised demonstration of the meal? Classic cookery often involves every part of the animal—the entrails, hoofs, tongue, liver, tail, brain, heart—so that nothing is wasted. Indeed, the more aesthetically ugly, the more challenging to beautify. Hence, by its nature, the cooking program is deceptive, because the primary nature of food is disguised or excised.

And the same goes with real life: our sense of reality is always sustained by a minimum of disidentification. Thus the viewer is not only spared the real-life, violent aspects of food preparation, but also cheated of the full extent of the work and physical exertions required to accomplish the results. Often, these shows are edited so that the viewer sees a simplified process, which then cuts to the chef pulling out an already-cooked version of the same dish from a hidden oven.

As in pornography, the abbreviated preparations parallel the brief or non-existent use of foreplay during sexual intercourse before getting to the climax in a porno film, where the usual *modus operandi* is "Wham, bam, thank you, ma'am." But in real-life cooking or lovemaking, foreplay is perhaps the most important part of the process, with the completed dish serving as almost anticlimax. For many people, sex is predicated on the ability of the participants either to "successfully" achieve orgasm (singularly or simultaneously), or, at the very least to stave off ejaculation for as long as possible. In essence, TV's cooks are demonstrating how to fornicate or fuck, and not very well at that, whereas real chefs are engaged in making love—or art, which is how many chefs view their passion and profession.

That they get paid for making meals many times a day does not make professional chefs prostitutes. The television cooking show, however, can be viewed as the illegitimate love child, or even the prostitute, of the real world of gastronomy. Each show offers a virtual form of fast food or a "quickie" instead of a real meal or mutually satisfying experience. This, of course, fulfills the producers' and the networks' needs—by leaving viewers unsatisfied or still hungry, they'll keep coming back for more.

The demonstrative aspect of contemporary TV cooking shows is, in effect, a rehearsal and studied performance. With slick production values, the program itself has less to do with food and cooking and more to do with the manufacture and packaging of the host/chef himself or herself—and the manufacture of emotions surrounding eating. In the BBC's long-running TV series *Gourmet Ireland*, for instance, Jeanne and Paul Rankin—a married couple who are also professional chefs and restaurateurs—travel around Ireland in a Range Rover to visit their homeland's most picturesque landscapes. When the show finally cuts to the studio (which resembles a high-tech disco more than a serious cooking environment) for their recipe demonstrations, the viewer gets to watch the couple "do it," as it were. We watch them banter and chuckle in a type of foreplay as he prepares the meat and she the vegetables and the dessert, reinforcing stereotypical male/female dominant behavior and sexual role-playing as they argue and tease each other over the preparation methods…

... The popularity of the cooking show as fantasy is paralleled by the real-world decline of culinary culture in America. According to Harvard University nutritionist Dr. George Blackburn, the average meal in this country is consumed in less than seven minutes in one of four ways: alone, watching television, on the run, or standing up. Blackburn also notes that because it takes at least twenty minutes for the brain to register that food has been consumed, the body is cheated of its natural mechanism to warn the eater when the stomach is full, and when it is time to stop.

Recent figures from the American Medical Association also show that one in five Americans is clinically obese, and more than half are overweight, statistics that represent a 12 percent increase since 1990. The evidence is all around us: people slouch along the street eating fast food or have pre-cooked meals delivered to their homes—all because they don't cook for themselves. (A recent *New York Times* article featured a Manhattan couple who had their stove removed in order to make room for a bigger fridge—to store their take-out and delivered meals.)

And when modern TV viewers do not eat at home, where they usually eat standing up or in front of the television, they can be found gobbling food at their desks or while in transit. Not only do they claim they have no time to shop and cook, they're too stressed to care about what they consume, factors that not only rationalize why Americans don't make meals but that are also used to explain why they don't get regular exercise.

This might be the down side of TV cooking shows: rather than increase and improve the viewer's joy of cooking, they might make viewers feel inadequate or unconfident in their own culinary prowess (just as porn might create unrealistic expectations or depression about one's own sexual skills). Cooking shows and porn tap into our primal needs. We are all hungry for love, comfort, passion, gusto, and communal experiences, and we are curious about forbidden pleasures—even if we don't act on our curiosity. These are all experiences and needs that can be vicariously acted out, fantasized about, and observed via both cooking shows and porn.

Just as most clients of prostitutes are lonely men looking for more comfort and understanding than sex, so, too, are cooking-show viewers looking for more than a little distraction from the exigencies of modern living such as preparing food. While viewers may not have a naughty Nigella or cheeky Naked Chef to whip up a little love on a plate at home, they can make a date to catch up with them in a lip-licking saucy mood. These video sirens can be found at most hours, somewhere on the tube, with no complaints, excuses, or headaches to impede the pleasure of their company. Culinary pornography? Perhaps, but why not...especially if it leads us to enjoy and partake of such pleasures in our own lives.

Discussion questions

1. What is the appeal of watching other people cook?
2. What do these shows about cooking hide about cooking? Why is the hiding important?
3. Andrew Chan argues that the fascination with television cooking shows stems from something he calls "food porn." What does he mean by this term?
4. Like pornography, cooking shows present the unobtainable—the absolutely perfect meal. What is the appeal of this fantasy? What dangers lie in watching these shows?
5. Do you agree with Chan? Or are these shows simply harmless entertainment? Is there really such a thing as harmless entertainment?

Document 15.3: Rabbi Nahum Ward-Lev and Shelley Mann-Lev, "Keeping Eco-kosher" (1990)[2]

Aaron Rubashkin revolutionized the kosher meat business. Typically, even into the twentieth century, religious Jews got their meat from a nearby butcher or at a supermarket that stocked chicken and ground beef obtained from a regional producer. Rubashkin introduced mass production to the kosher meat market. Based in out-of-the-way Postville, Iowa, his company, Agriprocessors Inc., churned out a quarter-of-billion dollars worth of beef, chicken, and other meats in 2002. Operating on such a massive economy of scale, Rubashkin brought the price of kosher meats down to historic lows. Customers flocked to his brand.

Rubashkin's empire of kosher meat came crashing down on May 12, 2008. Early that morning, agents from United States Immigration and Customs Enforcement raided his plant. They arrested 309 workers, most of them Guatemalan nationals, who had entered the country illegally. They were charged with using false documents. After investigating the company for months, federal authorities accused Agriprocessors of immigration violations, sexual assault, and child labor abuses.

The accusations against Agriprocessors rocked the orthodox Jewish community in the United States. What, they asked, did kosher mean? What

---

[2] Reprinted with permission from 'Keeping Eco-kosher' by Rabbi Nahum Ward-Lev and Shelley Mann-Lev. In Context #24 - Earth & Spirit (Winter 1990), http://www.context.org/iclib/ic24/ward/. Copyright © 1990, 1996 by Context Institute, www.context.org.2.

did it mean for animals? What did it mean for the people who processed the meat? How could the rules of kosher be updated to meet changes in industry and daily life? In search of answers, some in the orthodox community turned to the ideas of Eco-kosher, which had been around for more than a decade at the time of the Agriprocessors controversy. The document below lays out the fundamentals of Eco-kosher. How is this a response to industrial food and to religious ideas?

Our relationship with eating is one of our most intimate experiences of the earth. When we eat, we take another life into our own. We consume life in order to live. How do we do this with respect? How do we take life, and yet maintain our sensitivity to life?

Kashrut—rooted in the Bible, and developed by the Rabbis—is the Jewish tradition's clearly delineated response to this challenge. *Kashrut* sets limits on what foods we can eat: for example, we can only eat certain (primarily domesticated) animals, and we must slaughter them in the least painful, most respectful way. The blood must be drained and buried, because the life is in the blood and must be returned to the earth. There are also prohibitions against eating shellfish, and the mixing of meat and milk products.

We felt a need to expand this traditional understanding of *Kashrut* to include global environmental and social issues which the Rabbis of two thousand years ago did not face. In conversation with Jewish people in many communities, we have developed the following tentative guidelines for a *Kashrut* which speaks to our planetary concerns.

1. **We are concerned about the earth as a living being, including the soil, water, air and all the planet's living systems.** It is important to choose foods which are produced, transported and packaged in a way that is sustainable and not harmful to the earth. For us this means buying organic foods even when they cost more, and we also try to choose foods grown locally—or grow our own! This minimizes transportation and connects us to the earth's natural cycles.

2. **We are concerned not only with how animals are slaughtered, but also how they are raised.** Animals are often treated as commodities, to be "manufactured" as efficiently as possible for maximum profit. The resulting "factory farms" are appalling places, filled with unspeakable suffering. Upon reading John Robbins' description of them in *Diet for A New America*, we decided to avoid all animal products that have not been raised humanely and respectfully.

3. *We are concerned about the health of our bodies.* We are responsible for taking good care of the bodies that God has given to us. Too much food can be destructive to our systems—especially if it is full of fat and sugar. Tobacco, alcohol, caffeine and other drugs can also be harmful. We eat mostly whole grains, fresh fruits and vegetables, legumes and nuts. We try to pay attention to how our bodies feel about the food we are eating and to make our meals as nourishing and pleasing as possible.

4. *We are concerned about the people who produce and prepare our food.* We have extended Kashrut to include concern for how the people who grow and harvest it are treated. We use our food dollars to support growers and producers who demonstrate concern for their workers (and we avoid, for example, commercially produced grapes in response to the United Farm Workers' boycott). We also use the Council for Economic Priority's guide *Shopping For A Better World* to identify and support socially responsible producers.

5. *We are concerned that all people have enough to eat.* This concern motivated both of us to become vegetarians years ago. We learned from Frances Moore Lappé's book, *Diet for A Small Planet*, that animals are an extremely wasteful source of protein: more food would be available for everyone if people ate much less meat. The increasing production of nonessential foods for export from many Third World countries also contributes to the lack of basic foods for their inhabitants, so we try to avoid specialty items such as coffee and summer fruits out of season.

6. *We are concerned that our dietary practice should not separate us from other people.* While our system of *Kashrut* is very important to us, so are our connections with people. We try to balance our commitment to keeping kosher with an openness to breaking bread with others. There are some foods we aren't willing to eat, like meat—but we try to remain flexible for the sake of community. We communicate our guidelines to people who invite us into their homes, and we enjoy sharing the meaning of our dietary practices with people who come into ours.

Traditional *Kashrut* offers people clear and consistent rules to live by. Today, however, we are not in a position to formulate rules for a planetary *Kashrut*. Instead we need to articulate the questions to be asked, the issues to be considered. These questions do not always lead to clear answers—in the real world, we must often weigh one concern against another. But asking questions and making conscious choices about the food we eat leads to an awareness of our relationship to the life around us. Our practice of *Kashrut* continues to teach us much about our ties to the living world, and the sanctity of all life.

Discussion questions

1. How, as the authors suggest, does "asking questions" about the food we eat lead to greater awareness? What are the questions we should ask about our food?
2. What are the main principles of *Kashrut*? How does Eco-kosher retain the spirit of kosher while updating it?
3. The authors draw on several nonreligious and non-Jewish texts as they outline the ideas of Eco-kosher. Why?
4. How would the proponents of Eco-kosher respond, do you think to the Agriprocessor's Inc. scandal? How would their principals have prevented this from happening?
5. Can the ideas of Eco-kosher become a template for ethical eating in our current moment, not just for Jews, but for others as well?

Document 15.4: Mill Creek Farm's Mission Statement and Values (2017)

By the start of the twenty-first century, many Americans suffered from a new phenomenon called the paradox of plenty. For the first time in history, the problem wasn't that people had too little to eat, at least not generally, and at least not in the United States. Instead, they had too much of the wrong kinds of foods; foods that were cheap in cost, low in grains and fibers, and high in fat, salt, and sugar. As a result of the new diet of plenty, poorer Americans were growing less healthy and heavier all the time. According to a study by the Children's Hospital of Philadelphia, "There is a strong relationship between economic status and obesity, especially among women." Children in these poor, urban households face a higher risk for heart disease, high blood pressure, diabetes, especially type 2 diabetes, and later in life, joint problems, respiratory issues, and even breast, colon, and gallbladder cancer.

At the same time, the most distressed corners of American cities were losing population. First, middle-class whites moved from immigrant enclaves and row houses to the suburbs, and then middle-class people of color fled in another wave of suburban succession. That left some corners of the city depopulated with blocks of empty houses and scores of abandoned lots.

Founded in West Philadelphia at the corners of 49th and Brown Streets in 2005, Mill Creek Farm sought to meet the challenges of the paradox of plenty, while taking advantages of the opportunities of emptiness. Mill Creek Farms was special but not unique. Over the last couple of decades, urban farms have cropped up across the country. Read the farm's statements about its values and purposes to get a sense of what these organizations were trying to achieve.

Mission

Mill Creek Farm is an educational urban farm located in West Philadelphia that is dedicated to improving local access to fresh produce, building a healthy community and environment, and promoting a just and sustainable food system.

Vision

We envision a world in which everyone has access to affordable, healthy, culturally appropriate food, and where local communities work collaboratively to build a food system that is socially just and environmentally and economically sustainable.

Value Statement

We value:

The neighborhood in which we farm. We work with our neighbors to strengthen our community.
Experiential education. We provide hands-on, farm-based learning opportunities.
Our environment. We demonstrate innovative ways to foster sustainable living.
Community and collaboration. We work with and exchange ideas with others.
Urban food production. We foster the connection between people and the food they eat.
Equity and justice. We believe healthy, affordable food is a basic human right.

History

A Little Taste of Everything (ALTOE) is a non-profit agency whose mission is to increase access to nutritious, affordable foods and provide food system education for low-income populations in Philadelphia. ALTOE grew out of a youth-driven project at University City High School (UCHS) in conjunction with the Urban Nutrition Initiative (UNI) and received its non-profit status in 2005. ALTOE evolved from previous efforts to improve food security in West Philadelphia communities through school gardens and farmers' markets.

ALTOE's mission is put into action through the Mill Creek Farm (MCF), an educational urban farm project. The Mill Creek Farm (MCF) is located at 4901 Brown Street in the Mill Creek Neighborhood of West Philadelphia.

The Mill Creek runs under the land we work on and was enclosed in a sewer 100 years ago. Housing was built on fill that was not stable for the foundations and began to subside. It was eventually torn down in the 1970s. Since that time there has been a community garden on the western portion of the block, but the eastern portion sat vacant except for trash and weeds until 2005. In August 2005, the Philadelphia Water Department awarded ALTOE 1.5 acres of vacant land, at 49th and Brown Streets in the Mill Creek Neighborhood of West Philadelphia, on which to start the project. Initial funding for MCF came from Pennsylvania Department of Environmental Protection's Growing Greener Grant for Stormwater Management and the Pennsylvania Horticultural Society (PHS). The Mill Creek Farm had a successful first season in 2006, and has continued to grow and progress as a model for local food system development and sustainability education in succeeding years.

Our activities and educational programs

In addition to growing food for local distribution, MCF is an interactive educational center, giving tours to groups and hosting field trips and community skill-share workshops. In the summer months the farm offers a market internship position as well as employs high-school youth in a leadership development job training program.

The farm partners with the existing community garden to facilitate intergenerational exchange between young people and elders.

The farm's innovative toolshed demonstrates green building and reuse techniques including cob, solar electric, living roof, compost toilet, graywater collection, and found object mosaic. As well the farm is home to a bee apiary, a fruit orchard, and a children's garden.

Discussion questions

1. Where did Mill Creek Farm get its name?
2. Summarize Mill Creek Farm's values. Are these your values about the food chain? How are they similar? How do they differ?
3. Do some research in the census and on Google Maps. How would you characterize the area around the farm?
4. What would a "socially just food system"—what Mill Creek Farm is trying to achieve—look like? How would it operate?
5. Can an organization like Mill Creek Farm solve the paradox of plenty? Is it an answer to the inequities in the food system? If not, why not?

Document 15.5: Excerpt from Gustavo Arellano, *Taco USA: How Mexican Food Conquered America* (New York: Scribner, 2014)[3]

Gustavo Arellano, a fourth generation Mexican-American, began writing the witty and satirical column, "!Ask a Mexican!" for the Southern California OC Weekly in 2004. Readers would write in with questions like, "Why do Mexicans put on their Sunday best to shop at Wal-Mart, Kmart, and Target?" or "Why do you always see Mexicans lying under trees?" Arellano would answer the racially tinged, even racist, questions with humor and frankness. In response to the question about Mexicans lying under trees, he wrote, "Mexicans…are good public citizens who know that parkland is best used for whittling the afternoon away underneath an oak with a salsa-stained paper plate and an empty six-pack of Tecate tossed to the side."

Food, Arellano knew, stood at the center of the Mexican experience in the United States, and how Americans experienced the Mexican-ness around them. As he pointed out in his book, Taco USA: How Mexican Food Conquered America, *the history of Mexican and Mexican-inspired foods north of the border, like other ethnic food imports to the United States, is full of twists and turns and curious ironies. Perhaps not surprisingly the first widespread audience for the burrito in the United States was among the braceros, migrant workers who entered America to work in the fields from the 1940s through the 1960s. (For more about this, see Document 10.4.) One of the pioneers of prepackaged Mexican dinners in the United States was William Gebhardt, a German immigrant. By 2009, at Taco Bell's headquarters in Irvine California, the cafeteria had stopped serving tacos for lunch. By that point, most Mexican and Mexican-American families bought their tortillas the same way as everyone else did, at the grocery store. And perhaps most remarkably, as Arellano points out, salsa now outsells ketchup as the most popular condiment in the United States.*

The excerpt below explores salsa's triumph and what it means to the American experience.

"Here's a fact about American life that may illustrate as much as any census finding," NPR *Weekend Edition* host Scott Simon stated in his clipped, stentorian voice on February morning in 1992, as sales figures released earlier that year disclosed the country's new normal. "Salsa – as in picante, enchilada, and taco sauce, English for salsa—now outsells ketchup in the United States." People repeated this as an article of faith and amazement—how is it that something so un-American, so Mexican, now outsells ketchup, the condiment as American as chili?

But salsa's march to American dominance didn't start in earnest until 1947, when a transplant to San Antonio discovered what the company he formed still calls the "syrup of the Southwest." David Pace was the son of Monroe, Louisiana, born into a syrup-producing family that expected him to continue the family business. World War II took him to Alamo City, and here Pace espied Mexican-style sauce for the first time: not relishy like most salsa, but concentrated into a thick liquid and not as vinegary as American-style hot sauces. Intrigued by the business opportunities, especially for Anglos such as he reticent to indulge in the hot stuff Mexican restaurants offered, Pace figured he'd bottle his own concoction, call it "picante sauce" (*picante* being the Spanish word for "spicy"), and stock it in grocery stores.

The original picante sauce wasn't much, more pureed tomato than pepper. In a city such as San Antonio, where Mexican families and restaurants made their own salsa at home, the public met picante sauce with indifference. Luckily for Pace, the country was preparing to love the taco.

Tacos are delicious things, but they demand a condiment. Mexicans always have drizzled salsa on their tacos, but the condiment's fiery nature wasn't yet ready for American palates. Mexican food in this country has been, if anything, eminently mutable to match demand, so some wily businessman concocted "taco sauce": salsa shorn of its heat. It was first marketed in 1948 by the Mountain Pass Canning Company, an El Paso firm that turned it into the name we know it by today: Old El Paso....

As late as 1977, the *Washington Post* still felt the need to describe salsa to readers as "piquant relish used extensively with Mexican foods." But the 1980s saw the exponential ascendency of salsa in the American market, a raise so sudden that American food companies were caught off guard and forced to play catch-up. It just wasn't the continued immigration of Mexicans into the United States or even the spread of Chi-Chi's (which bottled its own salsa and sold it commercially starting in the 1970s): that decade saw the rise of an informed American gastronome more accepting of ethnic flavors than ever before, and willing to replicate them at home. Also important, however, was the health-food craze, which took to salsa like aerobics: in the freshness of a proper salsa—its many vegetables, the low use of sodium, the lack of preservatives— was a reflection of a lifestyle. Its enlivening taste was almost beside the point: here was a new condiment, one much better than sodium- and sugar-heavy ketchup. "The business exploded when the hippies came along," Pace told reporters years later. "No question but this stuff made the whole category explode."

The trendiness of salsa convinced bigger players to enter the market. Campbell's Soup introduced their own line; even Chesebrough-Pond's, most famous as the manufacturer of Vaseline, debuted Montera salsa in 1983 with a $20 million advertising campaign larger than Pace's profits that year. The company, however, was unfazed. "We just have to keep up our quality," remarked Kit Goldsbury, son-in-law to David Pace, as the big boys invaded Texas.

And they did. In 1979, only Goldsbury and Pace worked the day-to-day operations of the company. Under the guidance of Pace's daughter, Linda, and her husband, Goldsbury, the company strategized to further sales and reach. They added other flavors—mild, hot, and thick and chunky—to expand from the classic picante-sauce recipe. Pace created special-order six-pack containers, urging purchasers to "send someone the taste of Texas." The company also secured a contract with the armed forces as the military's salsa provider, ensuring a customer base that sought the stuff upon returning from their stint. By the mid-1980s, Pace became American's top-selling hot sauce, a position it has rarely relinquished since.

As Pace succeeded, so did its competitors. The Southwestern food movement also encouraged people to experiment with fruit salsas, sweet salsas – anything involving tomato and heat. Even Heinz entered the salsa game, since its own numbers showed the market was taking over the country; in 1988, 16 percent of American households purchased salsa; by 1992, a third of the country did. That was the year when analysts surmised that salsa became America's top-selling condiment; one reporter called the victory "the manifest destiny of good taste." And in the ultimate indicator of its victory, Campbell's bought out Pace for $1.15 billion in 1994 after years of courtship, a move and a price that sparked national headlines....

Incredibly, Pace had reaped millions of dollars in revenue from selling mostly in the Southwest and hadn't yet penetrated the rest of the country. Company execs gingerly tested their product for a national audience in the form of commercials that tweaked the Johnny-come-latelys who had followed in Pace's wake.

In the ad, cowboys sit around a campfire. One of them spoons the last chunk of Pace's sauce and asks the cook for more "picante sauce," pronouncing it with the nasal *a* of a Chicagoan, garbling his Spanish so the word sounded like "pecany." The white-haired cook tosses him another brand. "This ain't Pace Picante sauce!" the younger cowboy exclaims.

"What's the difference," the coot mumbles. The younger cowboy launches into a soliloquy extolling Pace Picante, most importantly because it's "made in San Antonio...by people [who] know what picante is supposed to taste like!"

Another cowboy reads the alien sauce's label. "This stuff's made in New York City?!" he exclaims.

"New York City?" everyone yells, now surrounding the old cook. The commercial ends with another young buck looking directly into the camera, deadpanning, "Get a rope."

It played for laughs, but the Pace commercial also served as a powerful allegory. Gone were the days of taco sauce masquerading as authentic Mexican salsa. Americans expected heat and authenticity, even if its producers were Americans. Pace's commercials became wildly popular, helping the company earn record profits. And across the country, other salsa-savvy entrepreneurs dreamed.

Discussion questions

1. What does it say about the American way of eating that something, as NPR's Scott Simon reported in 1992, "so un-American, so Mexican [as salsa], now outsells ketchup"?
2. What demographic and social factors, according to Arellano, account for salsa's triumph? Can you think of any factors that he may have overlooked?
3. How did taco sauce help pave the way for the triumph of salsa?
4. Think about the last couple of paragraphs of this document. How did Pace advertise its products? Why did it work? Why is "authenticity" so important to food products? Why did it matter to consumers that their salsa came from San Antonio (in the United States, not Mexico) rather than New York?
5. How can changes in taste preferences be explained in cultural terms? How do we acquire our tastes? Is this a biological or social process? Why do more Americans use salsa and hot sauce now than ever before? Is this about a changing palate? Is it about advertising? Again, how do we account for taste differences, and preferences, across time and space?

Document 15.6: Rachel Kuo, "The Feminist Guide to Being a Foodie Without Being Culturally Appropriative," from everydayfeminism.com (2015)

The term foodies first came into use in the late twentieth century. At the start, it was a term used to refer to a person who was into food, and paid attention to how meals were prepared and what was in their dishes. But by the turn of the twenty-first century, "foodies" referred even more to food explorers, people who sought out new and different foods. As the meaning of the term shifted and came into more common use, it became at once a badge of honor and a put-down. In 2005, an online contributor at urbandictionary. com defined a foodie, as "A person that spends a keen amount of attention and energy on knowing the ingredients of food, the proper preparation of food, and finds great enjoyment in top-notch ingredients and exemplary preparation. A foodie is not necessarily a food snob, only enjoying delicacies and/or food items difficult to obtain and/or expensive foods; though, that is a variety of foodie." Sociologists Josée Johnston and Shyon Baumann defined a foodie, in their book of the same title, as someone who possesses a "democratic" impulse and appreciates "hole in the wall" ethnic eateries and working-class food trucks, while rejecting the snobbery of fancy and formal restaurants. But at the same time, they recognized that foodies use food to maintain and reproduce social inequalities. They show off their knowledge and financial standing through their food choices. A 2007 contributor to urbandictionary.com joked about foodie culture, "This newest repackaging of Third World-derived ingredients in the latest Trader Joe's product is ever so delicious and different, it's really made for all you foodies out there to BUY NOW!"

In the article below, blogger, activist, and journalist Rachel Kuo applies a rigorous analytical lens to foodie culture. How does this impulse for urban adventure contribute to mainstream ideas about race and about dominance, she asks?

"The dishes of America's recent immigrants have become check marks on a cultural scavenger hunt for society's elite."

—Ruth Tam

I watch a lot of competitive cooking shows. And it seems like whenever there is a "bizarre" or "exotic" cooking ingredient, it's associated with foods from my culture and childhood. *100 year old egg. Duck bills. Stinky tofu.*

Mainstream media has made a spectacle out of foods from seemingly exotic places.

I've also observed a lot of White chefs create "Asian-inspired" dishes. When going out to eat, I notice many "Asian-fusion" themed restaurants where chefs combine all the countries and flavors in the vast and diverse continent of Asia and throw them together on both plate and menu.

What is "Asian inspired" or "Asian-fusion?" I have a sinking suspicion it's not like when my mom made me sushi with cucumbers, lunch meat, and eggs growing up. Or toast with mayonnaise and pork sung. People used to make fun of the food I eat, and now suddenly, stuff like spam fried rice is selling at a hip new restaurant for $16.

It's frustrating when my culture gets consumed and appropriated as both trend and tourism.

When it comes to food, what's appropriation and what's not can be tricky to think about.

Cultural appropriation is when members of a dominant culture adopt parts of another culture from people that they've also systematically oppressed. The dominant culture can try the food and love the food without ever having to experience oppression because of their consumption.

With food, it isn't just eating food from someone else's culture. It might not be appropriation if you're White and you love eating dumplings and hand pulled noodles. Enjoying food from another culture is perfectly fine.

But, food is appropriated when people from the dominant culture—in the case of the US, white folks—start to fetishize or commercialize it, and when they hoard access to that particular food.

When a dominant culture reduces another community to its cuisine, subsumes histories and stories into menu items—when people think culture can seemingly be understood with a bite of food, that's where it gets problematic.

It's also harmful when the dominant culture controls the economic and material resources to produce that food for their own consumption and profit.

Here are some dining behaviors that are culturally appropriative when it comes to food.

1. Seeking 'Authentic' and 'Exotic' 'Ethnic' Food

Often, when we talk about "ethnic" food, we're not referring to French, German, or Italian cuisine, and definitely not those Ikea Swedish meatballs.

Usually, we're talking about Thai, Vietnamese, Indian, Ethiopian, and Mexican food—places where food is cooked by the "brownest" people.

While food from Western Europe is still connected to ethnic roots, ethnic food has become reserved only for ethnicities that are perceived as exotic and foreign to White folks.

While food can connect people together and also serve as a way to learn about cultures other than our own, what happens is that food becomes the only identifier for certain places. Japan reduced to ramen and sushi, Mexico reduced to tacos and burritos, India reduced to curry, and so on.

Entire regions become deduced to menu options and ingredients without any thought to the many different communities in these places. There's a loss of complexity and cultures end up getting homogenized.

In seeking "authentic" food, we're hoping for a truly immersive experience into another culture. The food experience, whether in a restaurant in someone's home city or as part of a trip somewhere else, comes to represent a larger experience with that culture and community. Our perceptions of what is "authentic" stem from pre-conceived "exotic narratives" of that culture and communities.

"Oh, during my trip to Asia, I had the most authentic [fill in the blank]."

Food culture has travelled and flowed in messy and complicated ways across the globe.

The impacts of historical and ongoing colonization are devastating to many cultures, and many "authentic" "ethnic" cuisines are connected to histories of colonization.

For example, what is now Vietnam had been occupied by China for a thousand years and then colonized by France. This period of colonization is also what led to things like banh mi (sandwiches) and banh ex (crepes). The use of spam in different parts of Asia and the Pacific Islands, like spam musubi or spam in hot pot, are a direct result of US colonization.

If you love a dish and think it's delicious, great! If you're searching for a place that serves a particular dish, also great!

However, seeking "authenticity" fetishizes the sustenance of another culture. The idea of the "authentic" food experience is separated from reality. It also freezes a culture in a particular place in time.

2. Having Your Friend of Color Be Your Food Expert

Don't get me wrong, I love sharing foods from my culture with friends. I also love helping friends with restaurant recommendations and spending a long time on Yelp! trying to find good options for a group to go.

Where I take issue is when I become someone's food ambassador to all of Asia.

Some friends have expected me to know where to get ramen, "real" Chinese food, "street-style" Thai food, Korean BBQ—and they're disappointed when I don't know. These are also the friends that once made fun of my food.

As someone who straddles different cultural identities, as Taiwanese and American, my knowledge of my culture comes from my parents and my personal experiences growing up.

My experiences of Taiwanese food are mostly from following my parents around, and because my language skills are rudimentary, I can never find the restaurant we went to or order the same things they did again.

There's also a lot I don't know about other Asian cultures, about the complex relationships and power dynamics between Asian countries. There's a lot that I'm still learning, too. I do my own research on places to check out and you can too.

"What is the most authentic way to eat this?" "Where can I go to find authentic [fill in the blank]?"

Context matters. For example, asking if I've found any hand-pulled noodle joints that I like in the area is different than asking if I know authentic hand-pulled noodle joints.

The difference is that what you're seeking is one person and one place to represent an entire culture for you.

There is no one right way to eat something and no one perfect dish to eat. People from different cultures all have their own food preferences, too—the unique ways their families make something or the way they prepare their own meal. It'd be like me asking, "Hey, what's the most authentic way to eat a hamburger?"

Don't constantly treat your friend of color as your food tour guide. We're happy eating our cultural foods with you, but that's not what our entire friendship should be about.

3. Wanting Adventure Points for Eating Food

Like early explorers "discovering" spices on their quests for new trade routes, some diners today are on similar quests to "discover" different ingredients and cuisines.

It's great when people want to try foods they're not used to or when they're open to eating different things, but what ends up being problematic is when people want to be rewarded for their bold, adventurous experimentation with another culture. Where people can now literally check in on an app and receive a badge for their food adventures, but others want bonus real life adventure points.

When people think they're being adventurous for trying food from another culture, it's the same thing as treating that food as bizarre or weird.

The person outside of the culture becomes the person with "insider" knowledge about this exotic, other culture. The theme of "Westerner as cultural connoisseur" is rooted in imperialist ideas about discovering another culture and then making oneself the main character in the exchange. "I was transformed by my trip to [fill in the blank]."

Some folks want to be applauded for trying chicken feet, fermented bean curd, or just for eating with chopsticks. It's disconcerting to eat with folks who are going to giggle about ingredients [and] make comments like, "Oh my god, this is so weird! This is gross!" and run back to tell all their other friends about trying it and how "awesome" that experience was.

One of my favorite foods is a Szechuan dish with pig intestine and congealed pigs blood, and my parents get it as take out for whenever I visit home. The thing is, I'm not an "adventurous" eater. The "bizarre and weird" are foods that I'm familiar and comfortable with, food that I grew up eating.

By making a big deal out of someone's culture and food, it reminds them that they're culture is abnormal and doesn't quite belong in this world.

4. Loving the Food, Not the People

When food gets disconnected from the communities and places its from, people can easily start forgetting and ignoring historical and ongoing oppression faced by those communities.

America has corporatized "Middle Eastern food" like hummus and falafel, and some people might live by halal food carts, but not understand or address the ongoing Islamophobia in the US.

Folks might love Mexican food, but not care about different issues such as labor equity and immigration policy that impact members from that community.

There are also really hurtful stereotypes connected to food where people of color get reduced to the food they eat or are called things like smelly because of their food consumption.

Eating food from another culture in isolation from that culture's history and also current issues mean that we're just borrowing the pieces that are enjoyable—palatable and easily digestible. We might not know how kung pao chicken also reflects a story about Chinese immigration or the complex colonial story behind curry and the homogenization of South Asian cultures.

5. Profiting from Oppression

More and more now, part of chefs' culinary training also involves travel in order to learn about different cooking techniques and ingredients, and they're opening up fancy restaurants that repurpose "cheap" eats from working class and poor communities that rely on affordable, local products and ingredients.

Food culture gets re-colonized by chefs seeking to make that "authentic" street food they tried more elegant. Often, these restaurants are inaccessible to the communities they're appropriating from.

This is different from when members from that community repurpose their own traditional foods.

One of the questions that both chefs and diners should ask themselves is, who is laboring and profiting? Where are these recipes from?

Who is this cuisine profiting off, but not supporting—a group that is historically and currently oppressed?

318 Food and Eating in America

Another problem is when ingredients get reappropriated. Corporations have now repackaged local food from different places in ways that make it no longer accessible to the local communities they're from.

Quinoa, which is native to Bolivia is now too expensive for communities there. Last year, Whole Foods declared collard greens the "new kale." Coconuts have now been packaged as high end, luxury water. Tofu, soy, and tempeh are now staples at organic, healthy food markets.

This is food gentrification, where communities can no longer afford their own cuisines and sustain their traditions.

* * *

Food is an important part of communities and cultures—the relationship between food and culture also means that food can be used as a tool of marginalization and oppression.

It's okay if you love the taco truck outside of your workplace, love eating sushi, or enjoy trying out different recipes at home. I'm not against trying and cooking food outside your own culture—I love it, too.

However, it's critical for us to reflect on how we perceive the cultures that we're consuming and think about the relationships between food, people, and power.

Colonization and gentrification are directly related to the appropriation of food. We also need to begin educating ourselves on issues and event[s] that impact the communities that we're drawing our meals from.

Discussion questions

1. What is Kuo's main argument? Do you agree with her?
2. Do you agree with her assertion that seeking out authentic ethnic food is seeking out food cooked by the "brownest" people?
3. How do people gain "points" through eating? And what kinds of points are we talking about here?
4. Do you think she fairly describes the meaning of food choices in America? Can the choice of a restaurant be a form of colonialism? If so, how? If not, why not?
5. Some have looked at the expansion of American tastes as a form of multiculturalism. Does Kuo see things this way? How do food choices marginalize and oppress people?
6. Is there a way to consume the food of "others" without othering or marginalizing them? Is a taco or an egg roll ever just a taco or an egg roll?

Document: 15.7: Photograph of People Waiting for Korean Tacos from the Kogi Truck, Torrance, CA (2009)

Look at the picture below. It is of a truck selling Korean Tacos. Korean Tacos first became available at the Kogi Korean BBQ Truck in Los Angeles in 2008. The dish consists of two crisply griddled homemade corn tortillas, double-caramelized Korean barbecue, salsa roja, cilantro-onion-lime relish, and a Napa-romaine slaw tossed in a chili-soy vinaigrette. At first, no one knew what to make of the concoction, so Kogi started giving its tacos away to bouncers and doormen at popular Los Angeles-area clubs and bars. Word about the tacos, their unique taste, and the concept of the roving food truck soon spread. Kogi used Twitter, founded in 2006, to let people know where its food truck would be and when. In 2009, Newsweek *called the company, the nation's "first viral eatery."*

Soon, fans lined up on street corners and outside of nightclubs to get the spicy Korean Tacos. Kogi made $2 million—selling tacos at $2 a piece—in its first full year in operation. By 2010, Roy Choi, the chef behind the taco, was named by Food and Wine *as one of the "best new chefs" in the United States, and at that point, he didn't even own a restaurant, just a few trucks.*

Discussion questions

1. Kogi declared that the Korean taco was "an icon of the Los Angeles street." What makes this food iconic? Think about what is served, how it is served, and where it is served? What do all of these things tell us?
2. How did Kogi get the word out? Why is this significant?
3. How about the way it delivered the food? What is the significance of the truck? How does the truck differ from a restaurant? What possibilities does it allow?
4. Can you think of other iconic foods that embody this time or other eras?

Document 15.8: Greg Wright, "French Fries, Mais Non, Congress Calls em 'Freedom Fries'," *USA Today* (March 12, 2003)

The 9/11 (2001) attacks on the World Trade Center and the Pentagon rocked the United Stated and altered its foreign policy. Within days of the strikes, President George W. Bush declared a war on terror. Not long after, he sent United States troops to Afghanistan to punish the Taliban-controlled government for providing a safe haven for Osama Bin Laden and Al Qaeda, the leader and organization behind the 9/11 attacks. By the end of 2001, the Taliban had been run out of power.

With Afghanistan under control—on the surface at least—President Bush turned to another objective in his war on terror–the ousting from power of Saddam Hussein. Through his chief surrogates, the President insisted that the Iraqi leader possessed weapons of mass destruction and threated the long-term security and stability of the vital Middle East region. But Bush didn't want to appear to be engaged in regime change on his own. He wanted to build a coalition of allies to take down Saddam. Yet aside from Great Britain and several smaller nations, few of the US's traditional allies supported Bush's initiative. The most notable hold-out was France. "For us," Jacques Chirac, the French President declared in 2003, "war is always the proof of failure and the worst of solutions, so everything must be done to avoid it."

Aided by what he called, "the coalition of the willing," that is Great Britain and that handful of other smaller nations, Bush went ahead with the military campaign against Saddam Hussein. The United States Congress approved military action in 2002, and the invasion of Iraq started in March of 2003.

Like all wars, this one stirred a fierce and sometimes intolerant patriotism. When Natalie Maines of the chart-topping country act, the Dixie Chicks, told a London audience, "We do not want this war, this violence, and we're ashamed that the president of the United States is from Texas," the band immediately faced a backlash. Radio stations across the US banned their records and fans stayed away from their concerts.

It was in this climate that some in United States Congress began to think about the food on sale in their cafeteria. Read the following article about a proposed renaming of fried potatoes on Capitol Hill. How and why do symbolic acts like this matter?

WASHINGTON—Want french fries on Capitol Hill? Better change that order to "freedom fries."

On Tuesday, Ohio Republican Robert Ney unilaterally ordered the word "french" removed from congressional cafeteria menus to protest Frances refusal to back the United States in war against Iraq.

The directive from Ney, House Administration Committee chairman, affects three Capitol Hill cafeterias that sell french fries and five that offer french toast, which now will be dubbed "freedom toast."

Ironically, Ney is of French descent. He also lives in an Ohio town with the very French-sounding name of St. Clairsville. But Ney said he had no qualms about changing the menu to show support for 250,000 U.S. troops sent to the Middle East preparing to fight Iraq.

"The French government is pure wrong," he said. "It's a wonderful gesture to tell our troops overseas that were behind them."

The move to strike the French from fast-food joints and restaurants might have begun in February in another French-sounding town, Beaufort, N.C. Neal Rowland, owner of Cubbies restaurant in the coastal town of about 4,000, was so angry at Frances refusal to support a U.S. war resolution at the United Nations that he transformed french fries into freedom fries on his menu.

Rep. Walter Jones, R-N.C., circulated a letter among lawmakers asking for a similar action in congressional eateries.

Ney thought that was a good idea. So did several people who stopped for lunch at the Longworth House Office Building cafeteria Tuesday.

Nancy White of New Bern, N.C., whose 21-year-old son, Army Pvt. James White, is in Kuwait, planned to send photos of Ney and Jones to her son's unit via e-mail.

"It shows our country and our House of Representatives care," she said.

Bob Dillinger, a lawyer from Clearwater, Fla., complained that thousands of U.S. soldiers died to defend France in World War I and World War II. The least the French could do is show support for America in the fight against terrorism, he said.

"I think it's a good thing," he said of the renaming. "I won't drink Grey Goose (vodka) because its French."

But French Embassy officials in Washington said the move was more ridiculous than insulting. The embassy gets 200 to 800 phones calls a day from Americans about the Iraq war, spokeswoman Nathalie Loiseau said. Most support the French.

"It's exactly a non-issue," Loiseau said of the menu change in Congress. "We focus on the serious issues."

Fries in France aren't French anyway. They're les pommes frites, which literally translates to fried apples. Potatoes, unfried, are apples of the earth, les pommes de terre. And Loiseau said the crispy potato side dish originated in Belgium, not France.

Ney is not the only lawmaker protesting France, which has been an ally of the United States since the Revolutionary War.

Rep. Jim Saxton, R-N.J., introduced a bill banning the Defense Department from participating in air shows in France for the next four years. House Speaker Dennis Hastert, R-Ill., also is considering legislation against French wine and mineral water.

Some Americans said Ney is overreacting.

"I think its goofy," said Lorraine Kelly of Clearwater, Fla., who was eating lunch with Dillinger. "I love to eat french fries."

Dillinger corrected her: "You mean freedom fries."

Discussion questions

1. Just to go back to the question raised at the end of the introduction to this document, what is the point of the renaming of fries? Is this an important and meaningful act? What can it accomplish? Does it open up conversation or close conversation?

2. How does war politicize food consumption? Can you think of other examples from history, from this book?

3. In the wake of the 9/11 attacks and the invasions of Afghanistan and Iraq some Muslim and Halal restaurants in the U.S. faced boycotts, and some Arab Americans faced new rounds of discrimination. Do you think actions like the renaming of French fries to freedom fries (and the boycotting of the Dixie Chicks) fueled this kind of intolerance, or is this, as the Congresswoman says, "goofy," and by implication harmless, act?

4. Was the renaming successful? Does it mean anything that most people in the United States continued to order "French fries" at their favorite restaurants and fast food outlets?

Document 15.9: Kayleigh Rogers, "When Prison Food is Punishment," from the blog *Motherboard* at motherboard.vice.com (September 23, 2015)

In the 1960s, newspaper reports bemoaned, and perhaps exaggerated, a surge in drug use and in crime across the United States. Some liberal lawmakers talked of the need for economic assistance, blaming the rise in lawbreaking on poverty, inequality, and racism. Conservatives and moderates fired back that the only answer to criminality was a heavy dose of "law and order." The right won this debate, and the United States Congress and state legislatures, beginning in the 1970s, began to introduce a slew of new measures that established harsher penalties for a range of criminal offenses, especially drug offenses. Accompanying this move came mandatory minimum sentence legislation and sharp limits on parole.

The end result was a huge jump in the nation's prison population. In 1968, around 200,000 people in the United States were in jail. By 2015, this number had risen to two million. Today, the United States, which contains around 5 percent of the world's population has 20 percent of its prisoners. The rate of what has come be called "mass incarceration" in the United States is the highest in the world, higher than Russia or Iran or Saudi Arabia. Some commentators have started to call the United States a "jailhouse nation."

The rise of mass incarceration has stirred a number of pressing conversations. What role do, and should, prisons play? Are they supposed to punish people or rehabilitate them? How much should a society spend on prisons? Resolving these questions about the intent of prisons and about budgeting means, of course, thinking about food, about what prisoners will eat while they are behind bars. And food, as you will read in Kayleigh Roger's article, is once again a political question, a matter of policy.

Prison food doesn't exactly call to mind the most appetizing of cuisine. Anyone who's watched an episode of *Oz* or *Orange Is the New Black* can imagine the unappealing dishes served to our country's convicts: a single slice of bologna on two pieces of dry bread, nondescript mystery meats swimming in a gravy-like goop, limp iceberg lettuce with a drizzle of sour salad dressing. But imagine mixing all those meals together, mushing them into a loaf, adding in some raisins, baking it, and then eating it. Sound like torture? Well, that's kind of the point.

Nutraloaf is punishment food served to misbehaving inmates in certain prisons and jails around the US. It's a blend of several different kinds of food mashed together and baked into a flavorless, brick-like loaf that meets all of a person's daily nutritional needs. Nutraloaf has spurred legal action in many jurisdictions from prisoners claiming it violates the Eighth Amendment as a cruel and unusual punishment. Though it's gradually falling out of fashion, it's still fed to prisoners in many parts of the country, from New York state prisons to Arizona county jails, and continues to be a point of contention for prisoners, prisoner rights groups, and correctional departments.

For a nondescript lump of food stuff, nutraloaf has in many ways become a symbol for some of the core issues surrounding the criminal justice system. Convicted criminals are expected to give up certain rights when they're doing time, but should such a basic human need like food be used as a punishment tool? Even if it's not illegal, is it ethical?

"It goes to the heart of the question of what is the purpose of prison: is it meant to be retributive or is it meant to be rehabilitative?" Heather Ann Thompson, a mass incarceration historian at the University of Michigan, said in a phone interview. "We want people to come back healthier, not less healthy. So nutraloaf is a very short-sighted way of dealing with punishment, at the very least."

Thompson explained that there have long been issues around prison food in the US. Historically, prison food was nutritionally insufficient, as well as being bland and low quality, she said. Early battles between prisoners and institutions weren't so much about food being punitive, but about not getting enough food at all. It wasn't until the 1960s that the tide started to turn, Thompson said.

"It had a lot to do with food stamps, when we started to have to actually quantify how much a family of four needs to survive," Thompson said. "We had to start to nail down what a sufficient caloric intake is, for example. There was a lot of pressure then on prison systems to adhere to those standards."

Bread and water, long the quintessential prison punishment food, no longer met these standards. Soon after, other nutritionally-insufficient punishment foods were sussed out as well, such as a nutraloaf-like concoction called "grue" that was at one time given to inmates in Arkansas. Grue was made by smushing together "meat, potatoes, [margarine], syrup, vegetables, eggs, and seasoning into a paste and baking the mixture in a pan" according to the supreme court hearing that deemed the 1,000-calorie-per-day substance illegal in 1978.

But correctional facilities weren't about to give up on the food-as-punishment route, and nutraloaf was quickly concocted to take the place of bread and water, with one key difference: nutraloaf provides all of a prisoner's daily requirements for calories, vitamins, and minerals, packed into one mean little loaf of gunk. Recipes vary by institution, but often include some combination of potatoes, bread, beans, vegetables, tomato paste, and fruit. Prisoners who had been forced to eat it (as well as journalists who have volunteered to do so) have described it as "bland, like cardboard," and "as though someone physically removed all hints of flavor."

Usually, a prisoner is only put on nutraloaf if they've violated specific rules. Attacking a correctional officer or another inmate with utensils is one common catalyst—nutraloaf is served without utensils and eaten by hand. Throwing urine or feces is another offense that's often punished with "the loaf," as it's sometimes called. But because regulations vary widely from state-to-state and county-to-county, prisoners can sometimes be put on nutraloaf for things like tearing down an American flag from a jail cell.

That last one was the work of Sheriff Joe Arpaio, the sheriff for Maricopa County, Arizona. Arpaio is known for being a huge proponent of nutraloaf, among his many claims to fame. (He's also made headlines for questioning President Obama's birth certificate, switching the prison's menu to entirely vegetarian fare [to be healthier and save money], and for his officers being found guilty of racial profiling.)

His use of the loaf was brought to court by inmates, but the sheriff won the challenge. He told me as long as the food prisoners are eating is nutritious and safe, it shouldn't matter how it tastes.

"When they assault our officers or do something wrong, we place them in lockdown and take away their regular meals. We're not going to give them utensils if they've already assaulted an officer," Arpaio told me over the phone. "They won't do it again if they like the regular food."

Maricopa is one of the largest county jail systems in the country with about 8,300 inmates. Arpaio proudly boasts that it also has the lowest per-inmate cost for meals: inmates are fed twice daily, at a cost of between 15 and 40 cents a meal, according to his website.

"They get brunch—which was a bologna sandwich but now it's peanut butter and jelly—and then they get a hot vegetarian meal at night," Arpaio said. "They're getting a free meal. Why would they be concerned about what the food is when they're not even paying for it?"

Our views of the role prisons should play in our society has shifted over the years. Consistently, polls show that Americans believe the corrections system should be rehabilitative, not just punitive. Nobody wants prisons to turn into five-star luxury hotels, but the idea of how bad it ought to be has shifted away from the stark, cruel penitentiaries of the 19th century. There's plenty of evidence the system isn't there yet, and there's a growing public desire to make our correctional facilities a place where convicts can go to better themselves, learn, grow, and then return to society.

Those working to improve the system are striving for this goal, while also facing pressures not to overspend public money, or make prison "too nice." Laurie Maurino is a registered dietician and the food administrator for the California Department of Corrections and Rehabilitation. While California's state prisons don't use nutraloaf, some county jails in the state still do, including those in Los Angeles, though it's becoming less frequent, Maurino told me over the phone.

Maurino plans all the menus for the state prison system (every prison runs on the same menu) and said it's a job that requires balancing the health of inmates with budget restraints—the CDCR spends about $3.25 per day per inmate on meals. Right now, her focus is on creating more heart-healthy, lower sodium options, but still finding meals that the inmates will want to eat.

"We're not serving them steak and lobster or anything," Maurino said. "But food is the one thing that inmates look forward to in a day. Inmates with full stomachs are happy inmates, they're not going to be getting in fights. A lot of times riots have started after a bad meal."

But if you think inmates in California are getting gourmet cuisine, all you have to do is look at the foods those on the inside choose to make for themselves to realize the truth. Maurino told me the number one item sold in the commissary is instant ramen noodles. A concoction called "chi chi," made of hot water, ramen noodles, and Cheetos (with some variation on ingredients) is a well-documented favorite among prisoners. If the meals in prison were really that good, why would inmates be mushing up soggy Cheetos in garbage bags and calling it comfort food?

Maurino told me her colleague at LA county jails said nutraloaf is being used less frequently these days. I wrote to several state corrections departments about their use of punishment food, but only New York State Department of Corrections responded. New York's use of the loaf is dropping off a cliff: in 2010, the state doled out nutraloaf to inmates 991 times, according to spokesperson Taylor Vogt. Last year, they only gave nutraloaf 385 times, with just 198 instances so far in 2015.

Vermont, which briefly used nutraloaf at the state level, all but ended the practice after the state prisoners' rights group successfully argued that it was being used a punishment and therefore required due process before being implemented.

"I was just really offended by the idea that in a civilized society we would do that to people, no matter what they did," Seth Lipschutz, the lawyer who argued the case, told me over the phone. "Since we won, this stuff is hardly ever used in Vermont. It's still technically on the books but they have to give inmates procedural due process now. But they don't use it because they figured out how to get along without needing it."

Whether or not it technically violates the Eighth Amendment, many correctional departments are trying to find less controversial ways of dealing with behavioral problems from inmates and backing away from a practice that feels more medieval than modern. Nutraloaf was a trendy way of dealing with misbehaving prisoners for awhile, but the growing feeling is that there are more civilized, human ways of treating inmates. It was a common refrain from everyone I talked to.

Everyone, that is, but Sheriff Arpaio. He doesn't plan on phasing out the loaf any time soon.

"New York prisons? I'm not surprised they're phasing it out," he said. "I'm surprised they even had it in the first place. Don't they usually feed them steak in New York prisons?"

Discussion questions

1. Rogers' essay brings up a number of enduring question about prisons. What are they good for? As mentioned in the introduction, are they meant to be places of punishment or of rehabilitation? What do you think?
2. How should food fit into the mission of a jail or prison?
3. Do you agree with the use of food as a form of punishment? What food rights should prisoners have? Do they have a right to healthy food? Do they have a right to tasty food? Does grue or nutraloaf, as the award-winning historian Heather Thompson suggests in the above article, make people less healthy when they get out of prison?
4. Is better food a smart policy? Is this the best way to prevent possible prison rebellions and riots? Imagine you are a warden: How would you balance costs to ensure that prisoners get decent food? What would you eliminate from your budget if you want to spend more on food?
5. How does the debate about food fit into the larger question of the US becoming a "jailhouse nation"?

Index

Food and Eating in America: A Documentary Reader, First Edition.
Edited by James C. Giesen and Bryant Simon.
© 2018 John Wiley & Sons, Inc. Published 2018 by John Wiley & Sons, Inc.